Global Corruption Report 2005

Global Corruption Report 2005

Transparency International

Pluto Press

LONDON • ANN ARBOR, MI

TRANSPARENCY
INTERNATIONAL

First published 2005 by Pluto Press
345 Archway Road, London N6 5AA
and 839 Greene Street, Ann Arbor, MI 48106

www.plutobooks.com

in association with
Transparency International
Alt Moabit 96, 10559 Berlin, Germany

www.globalcorruptionreport.org

British Library Cataloguing in Publication Data
A catalogue record for this book is available from the British Library

ISBN 0 7453 2397 9 hardback
ISBN 0 7453 2396 0 paperback

Library of Congress Cataloging in Publication Data applied for.

Edited by Diana Rodriguez, Gerard Waite and Toby Wolfe
Contributing editors: Michael Griffin and Sarah Blair

10 9 8 7 6 5 4 3 2 1

Designed and produced for Pluto Press by
Chase Publishing Services, Fortescue, Sidmouth, EX10 9QG, England
Typeset from disk by Stanford DTP Services, Northampton, England
Printed and bound in Malta by Gutenberg Press Ltd

Contents

Part two: Special feature – Corruption in post-conflict reconstruction

Part three: Country reports

Part four: Research on corruption

Acknowledgements

The editors of the *Global Corruption Report 2005* would like to thank the many individuals who were instrumental in the development of this year's report, above all our authors.

We are particularly grateful to our Editorial Advisory Committee for their ongoing commitment to the *Global Corruption Report* and in particular for their large contribution to the thematic section of this year's report: Zainab Bangura, Merli Baroudi, Peter Bosshard, John Bray, Sarah Burd-Sharps, Laurence Cockcroft, Jorge Díaz Padilla, Dennis de Jong, John Makumbe, Devendra Raj Panday, Anthony Sampson, Emilia Sičáková-Beblavá, Neill Stansbury, Frank Vogl and Michael Wiehen.

Many thanks are due to the countless colleagues across the Transparency International movement, from the Secretariat in Berlin to national chapters around the world, who made our challenging task easier with their ideas and advice. TI national chapters deserve special mention for making a tremendous contribution to the expanded country-reports section.

Outside the TI network, thanks are also due to the many people who generously devoted their time and energy to the report: David Abouem, Susan Rose-Ackerman, Ulrich von Alemann, Mahaman Tidjani Alou, Rosenthal Calmon Alves, Jens Chr. Andvig, Claude Arditi, Hans Herbert von Arnim, Sérgio Gregório Baierle, Sultan Barakat, Boris Begovic, Predrag Bejakovic, Peter Birle, Vesna Bojicic-Dzelilovic, Emil Bolongaita, Jermyn Brooks, Martin Brusis, Justin Burke, Rowan Callick, Florence Chong, Dimitris Christopoulos, Neil Collins, Neil Cooper, Sheila S. Coronel, Marcus Cox, Fiona Darroch, Vera Devine, Phyllis Dininio, Sara Rich Dorman, Gideon Doron, Kirsty Drew, Sophal Ear, Aleksandar Fatic, Mark Findlay, Charles Manga Fombad, Maureen Fordham, Arturo Grigsby, Åse Grødeland, Miren Gutiérrez, Andreas Harsono, Omar Al Hassan, Sue Hawley, Marion Hellman, Clement Henry, Sorin Ionita, Claude Kabemba, John-Mary Kauzya, Gurprit S. Kindra, Robert Lacey, Johann Graf Lambsdorff, Daniel Large, Peter Larmour, Alena Ledeneva, Raphael Lewis, Henrik Lindroth, Tom Lodge, Joan Lofgren, Stephen Ma, John Mukum Mbaku, Colm McCarthy, Roberto de Michele, Philippe Montigny, Ed Mountfield, Pip Nicholson, Larry Noble, Justin O'Brien, Abissama Onana, Gabriel Ortiz de Zevallos, Katarina Ott, Alpaslan Özerdem, Marla Petal, Heiko Pleines, Donatella della Porta, Miroslav Prokopijevic, Michael Pugh, Gabriella Tuason Quimson, Mouin Rabbani, Igor Reichlin, Gerardo Reyes, María Teresa Ronderos, Steven Rood, Kety Rostiashvili, François Roubaud, Roberto Saba, Klavs Sedlenieks, Burhan Senatalar, John Sfakianakis, Rajib Shaw, Gurharpal Singh, Marcelo Soares, Bruno Speck, Petra Stykow, Stefanie Teggemann, Gopakumar K. Thampi, Shyama Venkateswar, Carolyn Warner, Glynne Williams, Ben Wisner, Laurence Whitehead, Simon Wigley.

A special thank you to Rachel Rank for all her help in the early stages of preparing the report, and to interns Justyna Pietralik, Sophia Mahmoud, Dominic Elliott and Valérie Callaghan.

Particular thanks go to the Washington, DC and London offices of Covington & Burling for their excellent legal work and to the London-based Solicitors Pro Bono Group.

Finally, we thank our publisher, Pluto Press, for their ongoing enthusiasm for our publication, and our external editors, Michael Griffin and Sarah Blair, for their good humour, patience and talent.

The *Global Corruption Report* receives financial support from the governments of Germany, the Netherlands and Norway. The translation of the 2005 report into French has been funded by a grant to Transparency International from the Canadian International Development Agency.

Foreword

Francis Fukuyama[1]

One of the major changes in the global intellectual climate over the past decade has been a reawakening of interest in, and appreciation for, the role of the state in development. Since the Reagan–Thatcher revolution of the late 1970s to early 1980s, much of the emphasis in public policy has been on reducing the scope of the state and getting government out of the way of private markets. This emphasis was appropriate for countries like China and India that had reasonably competent but overreaching governments. But for much of the developing world, weak state capacity is responsible for persistent poverty, disease, drug and human trafficking, terrorism, and a host of other social dysfunctions.

Free markets are not self-sustaining: they presume the existence of governments that are capable of enforcing the rule of law, adjudicating disputes, and establishing property rights as the basis of long-term investment and growth. Even the act of reducing the scope of a state through privatisation necessitates government agencies that can value and auction state-owned enterprises in a transparent and non-corrupt fashion.

Weak governance has been a problem throughout the developing world. But in some cases, governance has been missing altogether as a result of war or internal conflict, producing collapsed or failed states that abuse or neglect their own citizens and become acute problems for their neighbours and the rest of the world. While international politics of the twentieth century was characterised by clashes between large, powerful and well-organised states, the twenty-first century has seen instability springing from states that are too weak.

Recognition that 'institutions matter' and that good governance is a key part of any development strategy has become widely accepted within the development policy community in recent years. In countries with weak states and poor governance, cutting back the state through privatisation and deregulation is not enough to trigger growth. Market-friendly reforms need to be accompanied by positive acts of institutional reform and state-building.

And yet, the consensus over the importance of institutions and good governance belies several critical weaknesses with regard to implementation. The so-called first-generation reforms – getting macroeconomic policy under control, reducing tariffs, privatisation, deregulation, and so on – were relatively straightforward, because they concerned policies that were at least nominally under the control of governments. But second-generation reforms that focus on strengthening those very state institutions are much more difficult to implement. While a handful of technocrats might be able to 'fix' monetary policy or a dysfunctional central banking system, there is no comparable group of specialists who can reform a legal system or clean up a corrupt police force. Such institutions, which are critical for the functioning of a market economy, are large, complex, and deeply steeped in the local traditions and culture of the societies in which they operate. They are, moreover, at the core of the country's political system and can potentially threaten the interests of wealthy and powerful elites.

It is in this context that the work of Transparency International has been of critical importance. Transparency International was one of the first organisations to recognise the importance of governance to development, and to develop long-term strategies for combating it. Too often in the past, development agencies and multilateral lenders were willing to overlook corruption, believing either that it did not constitute a serious obstacle to development, or else that outsiders had no choice but to work through corrupt local officials. Transparency International broke the mould by putting the need for open and competent government at centre stage.

The *Global Corruption Report 2005* focuses on the construction sector. We are all painfully aware that corruption in construction contracting is not a problem unique to poor countries; industrialised nations from Japan to the United States have faced continuing problems in this sector. Construction projects are big and complex and, most important, they involve lots of money. This report, like those of previous years, presents strategies to deal with the problems it analyses. Iraq in particular serves as an example of the dilemmas faced by nation-builders when contracting in post-conflict situations. There has been great political pressure to write contracts quickly, which sometimes provides the opportunity to waive the normal acquisition rules. How to balance competing requirements for honesty and efficacy is an ongoing dilemma with, as this report indicates, no easy solutions.

Improving governance by fighting corruption has institutional, normative, and political dimensions. Countries need good institutions that minimise the incentives public officials face to take bribes. But even the most optimally designed institutions will not prevent corruption if a society's norms say it is acceptable to take bribes, or if the country's elites regard politics as an arena for self-enrichment. Finally, it is not possible to reform institutions or change norms unless there is political will to do so. While outside donors and lenders can try to influence behaviour through conditionality and advice, it is ultimately up to local elites to come to grips with the problem of corruption and make the painful choices needed to do something about it.

Transparency International contributes enormously in all of these ways: institutional, normative and political. It has laid the groundwork for concrete reform strategies on a country-by-country basis. It has also helped to change the moral and political climate both in developing and developed countries with regard to the acceptability of corruption. This year's *Global Corruption Report* extends Transparency International's record of service to the international community in laying the groundwork for better governance, and hence long-term development.

Note

1. Francis Fukuyama is professor of international political economy at the School of Advanced International Studies, Johns Hopkins University, United States, and author of *State-Building: Governance and World Order in the 21st Century*.

Introduction

Peter Eigen, Chairman, Transparency International

Corruption doesn't just line the pockets of political and business elites; it leaves ordinary people without essential services, such as life-saving medicines, and deprives them of access to sanitation and housing. In short, corruption costs lives.

Nowhere is corruption more ingrained than in the construction sector, the focus of Transparency International's *Global Corruption Report 2005*. From the Lesotho Highlands Water Project (page 31) to post-conflict reconstruction in Iraq (page 82), transparency in public contracting is arguably the single most important factor in determining the success of donor support in sustainable development. Corrupt contracting processes leave developing countries saddled with sub-standard infrastructure and excessive debt.

Building a world free of bribes

However ingrained corruption seems, it can be beaten. Transparency International (TI) has pioneered the no-bribes Integrity Pact, which includes sanctions such as blacklisting if a bidder for a public contract breaches the no-bribes agreement (page 59). Now used in more than 20 countries around the world, in 2003–04 TI's campaigning bore fruit on a global level. The Integrity Pact is increasingly being used by multilateral development banks, a major breakthrough that will bring tremendous benefits to ordinary people in the developing world.

In September 2004 the World Bank announced a decision to require companies bidding on large Bank-financed projects to certify that they 'have taken steps to ensure that no person acting for [them] or on [their] behalf will engage in bribery'. This breakthrough is evidence of the increasing impact of the anti-corruption movement in shaping the global agenda.

Another initiative of TI (together with Social Accountability International and a group of international companies), the Business Principles for Countering Bribery, offers companies practical guidance on how to prevent corruption throughout their operations. In January 2004 at the World Economic Forum in Davos, 19 leading international companies took a major step towards building a corruption-free construction sector when they signed up to Business Principles customised for the engineering and construction industries (see page 49).

The costs of corruption

These and other initiatives are essential if we are to build a world free of bribes. More than US $4 trillion is spent on government procurement annually worldwide. From the construction of dams and schools to the provision of waste disposal services, public works and construction are singled out by one survey after another as the sector most prone to corruption – in both the developing and the developed world. If we do not stop the corruption, the cost will continue to be devastating.

Most horrifically, the cost will be lives lost. In the past 15 years alone, earthquakes have killed more than 150,000 people. As James Lewis writes, '[e]arthquakes don't kill people; collapsing buildings do' (page 23). Examples from Turkey and Italy demonstrate that buildings often collapse because building and planning regulations are ignored – and regulations are often ignored because bribes have been paid to bypass them.

In economic terms, research gathered by Paul Collier and Anke Hoeffler (page 12) demonstrates how corruption raises the cost and lowers the quality of infrastructure. Corruption also slows down development, reducing long-term growth rates. In short, corruption has the potential to devastate emerging economies.

Corruption in the construction sector not only plunders economies; it shapes them. Corrupt government officials steer social and economic development towards large capital-intensive infrastructure projects that provide fertile ground for corruption, and in doing so neglect health and education programmes. The opportunity costs are tremendous, and they hit the poor hardest. Were it not for corruption in construction, vastly more money could be spent on health and education and more developing countries would have a sustainable future supported by a functioning market economy and the rule of law.

Corruption also steers public spending towards environmentally destructive projects. Peter Bosshard (page 19) points to 'monuments of corruption' the world over – huge construction projects that went ahead only because bribes were paid and environmental standards were not applied. The Yacyretá dam in Argentina, the Bataan nuclear power plant in the Philippines and the Bujagali dam in Uganda have all been subject to allegations of the improper diversion of money. Too frequently, corruption results in redundant infrastructure projects with potentially disastrous environmental consequences.

The bricks and mortar of corruption

The list of construction projects plagued by corruption is a long one. The *Global Corruption Report 2005* presents case studies from Lesotho (page 31) and Germany (page 51), while the country reports on China, Costa Rica, the Czech Republic, Norway and others all cite allegations of corruption in construction during 2003–04.

Neill Stansbury describes (page 36) how the characteristics of the construction sector slant it towards corruption: the fierce competition for 'make or break' contracts; the numerous levels of official approvals and permits; the uniqueness of many projects; the opportunities for delays and overruns; and the simple fact that the quality of much work is rapidly concealed as it is covered over by concrete, plaster and cladding.

Too often, international investors and financial institutions are also culpable in supporting corruption. An over-readiness to lend against a background of weak oversight and accounting safeguards has led the World Bank and regional development banks to invest heavily in projects that have been subject to allegations of corruption. Export credit agencies (ECAs) – semi-governmental agencies that provide guarantees and insurance for domestic companies seeking business abroad – have also been heavily criticised for lack of transparency and their willingness to continue working with construction companies known to be corrupt. As Susan Hawley argues (page 55), multilateral development banks and ECAs have an impact and responsibility far beyond the sums of money they themselves invest, not least because the guarantees they issue help mobilise private sector investment.

Rebuilding after war

Corruption in public contracting seems particularly intractable in post-conflict situations, marred by weak government structures, thriving black markets, a legacy of patronage, the sudden influx of donor funds, and the need to 'buy' the short-term support of former combatants. From Iraq to Afghanistan, from Cambodia to the Democratic Republic of Congo, time and again the lessons of the past are ignored and corruption is allowed to thrive in the wake of conflict.

Recognising how tragically frequent conflicts are around the world, the *Global Corruption Report 2005* contains a special feature on corruption in post-conflict reconstruction. Philippe Le Billon examines the nature of corruption in post-conflict situations (page 73), and points to the particular damage it can do, undermining both peace-building efforts and the rule of law, storing up serious long-term problems.

The need for anti-corruption measures is particularly acute in the first years after conflict. As Reinoud Leenders and Justin Alexander argue in their case study of Iraq (page 82), strong and immediate measures to curb corruption will be essential when the real spending on reconstruction starts. Without a systematic commitment to transparency in the reconstruction process, Iraq is at risk of becoming the biggest corruption scandal in history. The consequences for ordinary people will be immense and long-lasting.

Concrete reforms are needed

To combat corruption within the construction sector, all actors need to be involved. Company shareholders, professional trade bodies and civil society organisations all have a part to play in exposing and combating malpractice (see recommendations on pages 65–70).

First and foremost, however, it is governments that bear the greatest responsibility for ensuring the honest and transparent management of public funds. The *Global Corruption Report 2005* launches TI's Minimum Standards for Public Contracting (see box), a baseline for all governments, both for public works and far beyond. As with all anti-corruption measures, getting the rules right is only a first step. As many of the

Global Corruption Report's country reports show, enforcement rarely matches up to the standards to which governments pay lip-service.

Private sector anti-corruption initiatives have been implemented under the auspices of the World Economic Forum (page 49) and by the International Federation of Consulting Engineers (page 40) in attempts to bolster standards. While laudable, such initiatives need to be implemented wholeheartedly and taken up right across the sector. Otherwise, they will remain merely good intentions and will not succeed in creating a level playing field.

International financial institutions have also taken steps to implement reforms. The World Bank, for example, has started to blacklist companies known to be corrupt (page 59). While this is significant progress, it is essential to ensure the adoption of debarment systems by all the regional development banks as well. ECAs are also in urgent need of reform. While they increasingly acknowledge what good practice requires of them, concrete actions are still required. All international financial institutions have a special responsibility to carry out due diligence on the projects and companies for which they provide backing.

Corruption cannot be overcome without political will and courageous leadership. Politicians and government officials are in a position to show that leadership, but civil society must also be ready to monitor their actions, to check that they keep their promises and hold them to account.

Our vigilance will do more than improve government finances and the quality of investments in construction and infrastructure projects. It will ensure public money is used for the public good, and it will save lives.

The *Global Corruption Report 2005* opens with a tribute to one individual, Satyendra Dubey, who was murdered after he courageously spoke out against corruption in the construction of a massive highway project in India. At the Transparency International Integrity Awards 2004, a special posthumous tribute was paid to Dubey in recognition of his contribution to the fight to rid the world of corruption.

Transparency International's Minimum Standards for Public Contracting

Transparency International's Minimum Standards for Public Contracting provide a framework for preventing and reducing corruption based on clear rules, transparency and effective control and auditing procedures throughout the contracting process.

The standards focus on the public sector and cover the entire project cycle, including needs assessment, design, preparation and budgeting activities prior to the contracting process, the contracting process itself and contract implementation. The standards extend to all types of government contracts, including:

- *procurement of goods and services*
- *supply, construction and service contracts (including engineering, financial, economic, legal and other consultancies)*
- *privatisations, concessions and licensing*
- *subcontracting processes and the involvement of agents and joint-venture partners.*

▶

Public procurement authorities should:

1. Implement a code of conduct that commits the contracting authority and its employees to a strict anti-corruption policy. The policy should take into account possible conflicts of interest, provide mechanisms for reporting corruption and protecting whistleblowers.
2. Allow a company to tender only if it has implemented a code of conduct that commits the company and its employees to a strict anti-corruption policy.[1]
3. Maintain a blacklist of companies for which there is sufficient evidence of their involvement in corrupt activities; alternatively, adopt a blacklist prepared by an appropriate international institution. Debar blacklisted companies from tendering for the authority's projects for a specified period of time.
4. Ensure that all contracts between the authority and its contractors, suppliers and service-providers require the parties to comply with strict anti-corruption policies. This may best be achieved by requiring the use of a project integrity pact during both tender and project execution, committing the authority and bidding companies to refrain from bribery.
5. Ensure that public contracts above a low threshold are subject to open competitive bidding. Exceptions must be limited and clear justification given.
6. Provide all bidders, and preferably also the general public, with easy access to information about:

   - activities carried out prior to initiating the contracting process
   - tender opportunities
   - selection criteria
   - the evaluation process
   - the award decision and its justification
   - the terms and conditions of the contract and any amendments
   - the implementation of the contract
   - the role of intermediaries and agents
   - dispute-settlement mechanisms and procedures.

   Confidentiality should be limited to legally protected information.
   Equivalent information on direct contracting or limited bidding processes should also be made available to the public.
7. Ensure that no bidder is given access to privileged information at any stage of the contracting process, especially information relating to the selection process.
8. Allow bidders sufficient time for bid preparation and for pre-qualification requirements when these apply. Allow a reasonable amount of time between publication of the contract award decision and the signing of the contract, in order to give an aggrieved competitor the opportunity to challenge the award decision.
9. Ensure that contract 'change' orders that alter the price or description of work beyond a cumulative threshold (for example, 15 per cent of contract value) are monitored at a high level, preferably by the decison-making body that awarded the contract.
10. Ensure that internal and external control and auditing bodies are independent and functioning effectively, and that their reports are accessible to the public. Any unreasonable delays in project execution should trigger additional control activities.
11. Separate key functions to ensure that responsibility for demand assessment, preparation, selection, contracting, supervision and control of a project is assigned to separate bodies.

▶

12. Apply standard office safeguards, such as the use of committees at decision-making points and rotation of staff in sensitive positions. Staff responsible for procurement processes should be well trained and adequately remunerated.
13. Promote the participation of civil society organisations as independent monitors of both the tender and execution of projects.

Note

1. The Business Principles for Countering Bribery, developed by Transparency International and Social Accountability International, provide a framework for the development of an effective anti-corruption policy (see www.transparency.org/building_coalitions/private_sector/business_principles.html).

Part one
Corruption in construction

1 The costs of corruption

The photo, taken following the 1999 Izmit earthquake in Turkey, suggests that steel reinforcement in concrete columns and at junctions with floorslabs offered inadequate resistance to earthquake motion and to the load upon them. The collapsed floors remained largely intact. (Mehmet Celebi)

Blowing the whistle on corruption in construction: one man's fatal struggle
Raj Kamal Jha[1]

Satyendra Kumar Dubey came from a family struggling to make ends meet in a village in the impoverished eastern state of Bihar. The 31-year-old, who had trained as a civil engineer at the Indian Institute of Technology (IIT) in Kanpur, worked as a technical manager with the National Highways Authority of India (NHAI). His job was to oversee the construction of the Bihar stretch of the Golden Quadrilateral highway project, the prime minister's initiative to knit the country with a network of four-lane modern roads.

On the night of 27 November 2003, Dubey was murdered. Stepping off a train at Gaya, a town not very far from his workplace at Koderma, he waited for his car. When it failed to show up – for reasons still unexplained, the driver was unable to start the car that night – he boarded a cycle-rickshaw. Dubey never made it home: armed men intercepted the rickshaw and shot him dead.

There was no word on his killers and no sign of the rickshaw-puller who witnessed the murder. The case was already being treated as routine, another cold statistic in a state with a poor record for law and order.

On 30 November 2003, however, the Indian newspaper the *Sunday Express* reported that Dubey had written to the Prime Minister's Office (PMO) complaining about corruption along the 60-kilometre stretch where he worked. His request for confidentiality had apparently not been honoured, making him vulnerable to pressure and threats.

In his letter, Dubey highlighted several instances of what he called 'loot of public money' and 'poor implementation' at the project site. He alleged that procurement had been 'completely manipulated and hijacked' by contractors, and that quality had been compromised by subcontracting work to small contractors.

To many in India's construction industry, this had a familiar ring. Such goings-on are commonplace, especially when it comes to contracts. Bribery of officials and muscle-power to browbeat other contenders are often used to win contracts. Substandard works are churned out and public money drained.

'Works are usually being awarded at high cost and contractors are assuring the best quality in the execution of projects. However, when it comes to the actual execution of works, it is found that most of the works (sometimes even up to 100 per cent) are being sublet or subcontracted to small petty contractors who are not at all capable of executing such big projects ... I would like to mention here that the above phenomena of subletting and subcontracting is known to all from top to bottom but everyone is maintaining a studied silence ... These petty contractors are bringing poor equipment and material, giving a big setback to the progress and quality of work', he wrote.

Dubey requested that his name be kept secret, but at the same time he let his identity be known. He had reason to. 'Since such letters from a common man', he wrote, 'are not usually treated with due seriousness, I wish to clarify ... that this letter is being written after careful thought by a very concerned citizen who is also very closely linked with the project ... [K]indly go through my brief particulars (attached on a separate sheet to ensure secrecy) before proceeding further.'

Just the opposite happened. Dubey's letter was riddled with signatures and scribbles of officials, indicating that it had done the rounds of Delhi's bureaucracy. His request for anonymity was apparently ignored, and the letter was sent to his superiors at the highways authority with a copy to the organisation's chief vigilance officer who, it later transpired, had admonished Dubey for writing directly to the PMO.

Dubey wrote a second letter, this time not to the PMO but to the chairman of his own organisation, the NHAI. He mentioned that he had started receiving threatening calls.

No one took Dubey seriously, and he paid for it with his life. Lodging a first information report with the police in Gaya, his brother stated that people whose corruption he exposed were behind the murder. The report did not name anyone.

Gaya's divisional commissioner, Hem Chand Sirohi, who knew Dubey, admitted: 'no one is safe, the mafia [criminals who grab contract tenders] will have its way'.[2]

The sustained coverage of his case, and the realisation that a man was murdered for speaking up against corruption, outraged the public. One of India's best known faces, Infosys Technologies chief mentor and IIT alumnus Nagavara Ramarao Narayana Murthy, issued a statement in which he urged the prime minister to suspend the contract with the contractor involved, investigate the case as a matter of priority, and swiftly and severely punish the guilty. He called for a good whistleblower policy. 'Let this be the last such tragedy in India', Murthy said.[3] The prime minister at the time, Atal Behari Vajpayee, declared that Dubey's killers would be punished 'wherever they may be'.[4]

Dubey's parent ministry, the department of road transport and highways, came out with a statement two days later to deny any slip-up on its part. It echoed what then minister B. C. Khanduri had said earlier: the leak of the letter and the murder were not linked, and Dubey's murder should be seen in the context of Bihar's abysmal record on law and order.

'It is a matter of record that personnel employed in the implementation of the NHDP (National Highways Development Project) in Bihar have been under constant threat ... This has caused an atmosphere of fear and terror and is coming in the way of progress of the work', the ministry stated, claiming that NHAI itself was 'fully alive to the shortcomings of the existing systems and had already initiated a series of measures to improve the procedures'.[5]

The Dubey case was entrusted to the Central Bureau of Investigation (CBI), the country's premier investigating agency, but its handling of the case saw the rickshaw-puller, the prime witness, disappear after questioning. Two suspects were later found dead shortly after they had been questioned.

The CBI director admitted that the death of the suspects called for a harder look at the possibility of a mafia conspiracy behind Dubey's murder. Some arrests have since been made – of poor residents of a village near Gaya. The CBI claims they have confessed to 'robbing him' but no charge sheet has been filed yet.

In January 2004, the supreme court stepped in. Acting on advocate Rakesh Upadhyay's petition seeking protection for whistleblowers in the wake of Dubey's murder, the court issued notices to both the national and local governments. Upadhyay pointed out that Dubey's request for secrecy would have had legal protection had the government enacted a whistleblower act recommended by the Constitution Review Commission in 2002.

In March 2004, the Dubey case received international attention when the London-based Index on Censorship posthumously honoured him with the Whistleblower of the

Year Award. At home, pressure mounted on the government to act.[6] On 5 April, Justice Ruma Pal of the supreme court proposed that a whistleblower protection mechanism be created through an executive order, pending the enactment of suitable legislation.

This was done in April, when Solicitor General Kirit Raval obtained the court's approval for a scheme authorising the Central Vigilance Commission (CVC) to protect whistleblowers and act on their complaints. Whistleblowers can now approach the CVC, in the public interest, with any evidence concerning alleged corruption or misuse of office by any employee of the central government or of any corporation, company, society or local authority controlled by the central government.

The whistleblower cannot withhold his identity, but the CVC is required to protect his or her identity. The CVC can take action against anyone who leaks the whistleblower's name, intervene in cases of harassment by any authority, and order protection for whistleblowers and witnesses. The commission can also request police assistance to investigate complaints and, following investigations, can recommend: departmental proceedings against the official concerned; steps to redress the loss caused to the government; criminal proceedings; or corrective measures to prevent recurrence.

Days after the mechanism came into place, Central Vigilance Commissioner P. Shankar said he would have been happier if the interim arrangement was not such a watered-down version of the proposed legislation, but called it a good beginning. 'If Satyendra Dubey had come to me earlier, I would not have been able to do what I can do for him today', he said.[7]

Notes

1. Raj Kamal Jha is deputy editor of the *Indian Express*.
2. *Indian Express* (India), 11 December 2003.
3. BBC News, 10 December 2003, http://news.bbc.co.uk/1/hi/world/south_asia/3306075.stm
4. Ibid.
5. Ministry of Road Transport and Highways, 11 December 2003, http://pib.nic.in/archieve/lreleng/lyr2003/rdec2003/11122003/r1112200336.html
6. On 9 October 2004, on the occasion of the Transparency International Integrity Awards 2004 ceremony, special posthumous recognition was given to Satyendra Kumar Dubey on account of the courage he showed in standing up to corruption.
7. *Indian Express* (India), 7 May 2004.

The economic costs of corruption in infrastructure
Paul Collier and Anke Hoeffler[1]

To assess the economic costs of corruption in infrastructure, we first need to understand why the sector consistently ranks as the most corrupt. Infrastructure is distinctive as an economic activity in two respects. First, it is intensive in 'idiosyncratic' capital, meaning that its capital has to be designed specifically for installation. Second, it is a 'network' activity, requiring government regulation. Both of these features make the activity unusually prone to corruption.

How corruption raises the cost of capital

Because capital is to an extent different each time, it is difficult to standardise and so benchmark the cost of installation. For example, new buildings are more difficult to price than new trucks. Unlike with new trucks, the supplier – the builder – has much more information about the true costs than does the purchaser. This difference in information – known as an 'information asymmetry' – translates into an opportunity for corruption. The direct effect of such corruption is to drive up the cost of building infrastructure – that is, the *capital* cost. This direct effect can have various secondary effects that alter the *allocation* of budgets.

Recognising the problem of corruption in the construction sector, budget decision-makers may skew spending away from the sector. For example, a former minister of finance for Eritrea adopted the policy of minimising construction expenditures because he doubted the capacity of his ministry to police such spending. While the evidence below suggests that this is a common response, if budget decision-makers themselves are corrupt, they may decide to skew the budget *towards* infrastructure spending so as to increase opportunities for corruption. If roads are more capital-intensive than primary education, the budget may be skewed towards roads and away from education. And if there is more opportunity for corruption in road construction than in road maintenance, then roads may be built, allowed to fall apart, and then rebuilt: a common scenario in Africa.

Even if decision-makers are indifferent or oblivious to corruption, the raised cost of capital for infrastructure will induce a 'substitution' effect whereby less of it is purchased than if its price were not inflated. So corruption is likely to lead to more being spent but less being delivered.

How corruption raises the cost of running infrastructure services

Infrastructure is not fundamentally a heap of structures; it is a flow of services. Roads are an input into transport services, power stations are an input into electricity provision, and phone lines are an input into telephone services.

Governments usually regulate infrastructure services as their distribution systems often include points of monopoly power, which operators could otherwise exploit. Regulation is difficult when regulators know less than the service provider, as is often the case. Further, the regulators themselves may need to be regulated, as suppliers may bribe them – a phenomenon known as 'regulatory capture'.

A supplier may spread monopoly profits around the organisation in the form of reduced effort, inflated payrolls, and other forms of managerial slack. Employees may exploit the monopoly in their dealings with customers; for example, they may extract bribes for what should be standard performance.

These forms of corruption raise the *recurrent* cost of providing services. Further, as with the capital cost, excess recurrent costs have both direct and indirect effects. The direct effect is simply the waste involved in the services actually provided. The indirect cost is that customers will substitute for the service. For example, across Africa the failure of monopoly provision of electricity has induced self-provision. Some small manufacturing firms spent three-quarters of their investment on power generators.[2] If this behaviour renders manufacturing uncompetitive in global markets, the true costs of corruption in electricity provision in terms of job losses are enormous.

Quantifying the impact on capital costs

For many years proposals for infrastructure construction in Nigeria were approved without serious scrutiny. Oby Esekwesili, the president's senior adviser on fighting corruption, now scrutinises the federal procurement process and has introduced a competitive bidding process. The initial introduction of such scrutiny in effect catches 'red-handed' the degree of cost-inflation that was previously normal. *The new procurement system has resulted in average cost reductions of 40–50 per cent.*[3]

This finding is complemented by econometric studies that take a comparative approach, relating differences in the level of corruption to differences in the cost of infrastructure (whether capital or recurrent). Econometrics has various ways of coping with the fact that many factors other than cost vary between cases. The global study summarised below controls carefully for differences between countries. The first study instead tries to minimise the differences by focusing on a single country (Italy) and studying variations between regions.

Infrastructure investment in 20 regions of Italy

Del Monte and Papagni examined regional-level public investment, which they regard as a good approximation for investment in infrastructure, to quantify the first type of cost identified above – the increased cost of capital.[4] They use an objective regional measure of corruption, namely the official number of crimes committed against the regional administration. Their measure of performance is the rate of economic growth, again region by region. This measure captures both the direct effect of an increased cost of capital – the waste involved – and the indirect effects, the substitution into or out of infrastructure.

Unsurprisingly, Del Monte and Papagni's research shows that infrastructure investment raises the growth rate and that corruption lowers it. Their key finding, however, is that – controlling for these effects – a high level of corruption reduces the contribution that a given level of infrastructure investment makes to growth. The effect is highly significant in the statistical sense, and it is also substantial in the economic sense.[5] Specifically, an increase of one 'standard deviation' in the level of corruption reduces the contribution of infrastructure investment to the growth rate by 0.29 percentage points. In other words, instead of the region growing by 1.4 per cent – Italy's average growth rate during the 1990s – a region one standard deviation below the average would have grown only 1.11 per cent. Over the course of a decade, that region would become 3 per cent poorer relative to the regional average.

If all of Italy's regions could reduce their corruption levels by one standard deviation, the annual savings *just from the increased effectiveness of infrastructure investment* would be double the entire Italian aid budget.

Global infrastructure investment in telephones and electricity

In a global study, Henisz presents a picture of investment in telephone networks and electricity generation over the course of a century, using data on more than 100 countries.[6] The study uses two distinct measures of performance. The first is the length of the lag between the world's first installations of a telephone network and an electricity grid (in the United States), and their installations in each country under review. The second is the level of subsequent investment in telephone networks and electricity generation. Henisz investigates whether a high level of corruption lengthens the lag in initial adoption and whether it lowers the level of subsequent investment.

Henisz measures the level of corruption by the ability of the political environment to impose effective checks and balances on the abuse of power. He begins by counting the number of nominally independent checks and balances in the system of political decision-making. Then he introduces the extent to which each of these nominally independent centres of power is likely to be independent in practice. To do so, he looks at the political heterogeneity of power centres; for example, if all power centres are controlled by the same political party, they are less independent than if they are controlled by different parties. Finally, Henisz allows for the degree of political heterogeneity *within* each power centre. A low-corruption environment involves many checks and balances, each politically independent and each subject to the discipline of internal political contest. At the other extreme, corruption thrives where checks and balances are few in number and ineffective because of a concentration of political power.

Henisz finds that corruption, so defined, has significant and substantial effects. He considers the benefits if political constraints are one standard deviation better than the average. In Africa, such an improvement would have raised the likelihood that a telephone network would be installed within 50 years of the first global installation from 15 to 38 per cent. The study found similar effects in other regions, and for electricity generation. The same improvement of one standard deviation would also have raised the subsequent rate of infrastructure investment. It would have raised the annual rate of investment in the telephone network by 0.8 percentage points, and in electricity generation by 0.5 percentage points. Over decades, such effects amount to major differences in infrastructure provision.

Corruption and infrastructure investment: a summary

Both of these best practice studies have the same message: *corruption has large and adverse effects on infrastructure investment*. The global study finds that, controlling for other features of the environment, a high level of corruption will substantially *delay* the introduction of new types of infrastructure and will substantially *reduce* the pace at which it is subsequently accumulated. The Italian study shows that even this substantially understates the damage done by corruption. It finds that a given level of expenditure on infrastructure investment is much *less productive* in corrupt environments. Hence the distinct effects found in the two studies are cumulative: *corruption lowers expenditure on infrastructure and reduces the productivity of that expenditure.* Yet the costs of corruption do not stop here.

Quantifying the impact on recurrent costs

Turning to the effects of corruption on recurrent costs, the following set of comparative econometric studies again adopt complementary approaches: two focus on a particular region and sector at a particular time, to reduce problems of comparability; the third takes a global approach and looks at a wide range of infrastructure services.

Water in Africa and electricity in Latin America

The regional studies focus on running costs of utilities, taking their capital investment as a given. They are concerned with how efficiently a given amount of capital investment is combined with labour and other inputs to produce a flow of services.

In their study of water utility companies in Africa, Estache and Kouassi compare productivity among 21 companies.[7] Benchmarking on the most efficient company, they measure the extent to which the other companies fall short of this standard and attempt to explain why they are less efficient. The level of corruption prevailing in the country is one among many explanatory variables. Controlling for all other variables, the authors find that the level of corruption is highly significant in the statistical sense, and is substantial in the economic sense.

The level of corruption is measured on a 16-point rising scale with the average level being 10.2. Estache and Kouassi find that a one-point reduction in corruption raises the level of operating efficiency by 6.3 per cent. If these water utilities were operating in non-corrupt environments (1 on the scale), they would have an average increase in efficiency of 64 per cent. The prices the firms charge could thus be 64 per cent lower. In other words, nearly two-thirds of the operating costs were due to corruption. Even a reduction of corruption by one point from the 10.2 average to 9.2 (which is entirely within the range of the data) reduces costs by 6.3 per cent, which is a large effect. Indeed, the authors point out that it exceeds the total gain achieved from privatisation.

A study by Bo and Rossi of 80 electricity utilities in 13 Latin American countries uses two measures of national variations in corruption, TI's Corruption Perceptions Index and the International Country Risk Guide corruption index.[8] It finds both to be significant. This study controls for other effects on the efficiency of electricity generation. It uses two measures of performance, the number of workers employed – and hence labour productivity – and total operational and maintenance costs. With two measures of corruption and two measures of performance, the authors are able to check the robustness of their results. They find that both measures of corruption significantly and substantially affect both measures of performance.

Bo and Rossi consider what would happen if the median country in their sample (Brazil) had the corruption level of the least corrupt country in their sample (Costa Rica). This is approximately equivalent to asking what would happen if all countries reduced their corruption to the level of Costa Rica. The effects on efficiency would be substantial. The labour force needed to produce the same amount of electricity would be reduced by 12 per cent.[9] Electricity would certainly be cheaper; the authors find that operational and maintenance costs would fall by 23 per cent.

Hence both studies find large and significant effects of corruption on the recurrent costs of infrastructure services. Both assess direct costs only, namely the higher prices that must be paid for services actually delivered. These studies do not estimate indirect costs from poor services, such as the loss of jobs and investment in manufacturing.

The global performance of infrastructure services

Kaufmann, Leautier and Mastruzzi take a global view of the performance of infrastructure services.[10] Their basic unit of observation is not a country but a city: they consider 412 cities in 134 countries. Their measure of performance is access to services and the quality of service delivery for water, sewerage, electricity and telephones. The authors' measure of corruption includes information at the level of the city as well as for the country as a whole. They observe the extent of bribery for utilities in cities; at the national level, they measure the extent of 'state capture' of the regulatory process, and the extent to which corruption is controlled. The question is whether, controlling for other characteristics, these measures of corruption affect the delivery of any or all of the infrastructure services considered.

They find that each measure of corruption has significant and substantial effects on both access to services and on the quality of service delivery. The many findings support the conclusion that corruption at the city level is important, over and above other influences, for the quantity and quality of service delivery.

Corruption and infrastructure services: a summary

These 'best practice' studies convey the same broad message – *corruption significantly and substantially worsens infrastructure services*. Yet the detailed problems to which they point are distinct. The focused studies are concerned with the costs of operation. They show that corruption raises the cost of delivering a particular volume of service. The wide-angle study is not concerned with the cost of operation but with the volume and quality of services delivered. It finds that corruption reduces access to services, which may well be a direct consequence of the cost-raising effect: with higher costs of operation, less can be provided. The adverse quality effect is entirely distinct, however. Indeed, higher operating costs caused by corruption may have been expected to be compensated by higher quality. The opposite is the case: *corruption both raises costs and lowers quality*.

Conclusion: costs, costs and more costs

Initial research on the consequences of corruption encountered the technical problem of 'endogeneity' – corruption was clearly *correlated* with a lot of adverse outcomes but may not be their *cause*. Recent research has gone a long way to overcome these problems of interpretation. One approach is to narrow the question. The studies discussed above all focus not on the general consequences of corruption, but on various specific problems related to infrastructure. Further, within infrastructure, some focus on investment in the sector, whereas others focus on the services it provides. Another approach is to narrow the range of observations considered. Some of the studies have concentrated on a single type of infrastructure and a single country or region.

What comes out of this more focused approach is both greater confidence in the results, and a range of distinct costs generated by corruption. Between them the studies reviewed have found four distinct, yet coexisting, costs of corruption to be significant and substantial for infrastructure:

1. Corruption delays and reduces expenditure on infrastructure investment (for example, globally, a modest reduction in corruption would increase investment in telecoms by 0.8 percentage points).
2. Corruption reduces the growth generated by a given expenditure on infrastructure investment (for example, in Italy, the same modest reduction in corruption would increase growth by 0.3 percentage points, even with unchanged investment).
3. Corruption raises the operating cost of providing a given level of infrastructure services (for example, in Latin America, reducing corruption to the level of Costa Rica would reduce operating costs in electricity by 23 per cent).
4. Corruption reduces the quality of infrastructure services and limits access, especially for the poor.

The true total cost of corruption in infrastructure is at least the sum of these costs. It amounts to lower current living standards, with the poorest hit hardest; and slower growth. Indeed, expensive and low-quality infrastructure may inflict costs on society that are far in excess of the money directly wasted in the process of provision.

However, the approach taken in these studies also carries an implicit message of hope. The basis for the studies is *variation* – we can quantify the costs of corruption only because its extent differs so markedly between places that are in other respects rather similar. In other words, *it doesn't have to be this way*.

Notes

1. Paul Collier is professor of economics at Oxford University where he directs the Centre for the Study of African Economies. Anke Hoeffler is a research officer in the economics department.
2. P. Collier and J.W. Gunning, 'Explaining African Economic Performance' in *Journal of Economic Literature* 37 (1999).
3. Personal communication to the authors.
4. Alfredo Del Monte and Erasmo Papagni, 'Public Expenditure, Corruption and Economic Growth: the Case of Italy' in *European Journal of Political Economy* 17 (2001).
5. 'Significance' is a statistical concept, indicating to what extent the result is reliable. A result can be statistically significant and yet of little interest if the effect it identifies is small in economic terms.

6. Wiltold J. Henisz, 'The Institutional Environment for Infrastructure Investment' in *Industrial and Corporate Change* 11 (2002).
7. Antonio Estache and Eugene Kouassi, 'Sector Organization, Governance, and the Inefficiency of African Utilities', mimeo (World Bank Institute, 2002).
8. Ernesto Dal Bo and Martin A. Rossi, 'Corruption and Efficiency: Theory and Evidence from Electric Utilities', mimeo (University of California, Berkeley, and University of Oxford, 2004).
9. This does not imply that in a low-corruption environment 12 per cent of electricity workers would lose their jobs. Because electricity would be cheaper, more of it would be produced.
10. D. Kaufmann, F. Leautier and M. Mastruzzi, 'Governance and the City: An Empirical Investigation into the Global Determinants of Urban Performance', mimeo (World Bank, 2004).

The environment at risk from monuments of corruption
Peter Bosshard[1]

In July 2002 a British subsidiary of the Norwegian construction company, Veidekke, admitted having made a payment of US $10,000 to a senior Ugandan civil servant in 1999. Richard Kaijuka, at the time Uganda's energy minister, acknowledged receiving the payment, but maintained it was not a bribe. After the payment Veidekke became a member of the construction consortium chosen for the Bujagali hydropower project, following a procurement decision that was not based on full international competitive bidding. When allegations of bribery surfaced the World Bank suspended its financial backing, and the project became the subject of anti-corruption investigations by the World Bank and four different governments.[2] At the time of writing, the Bujagali dam project is still stalled. The cumulative environmental impacts of Bujagali and other dams on the Nile have never been assessed.

A case study from Indonesia

The Jatigede dam on the Cimanuk River is supposed to produce power and bring irrigation to the farmers of West Java, Indonesia. It will submerge a land area of 49 km^2, drown 30 villages and displace around 41,000 people. Construction is expected to start in 2005. The US $964 million dam project will increase erosion in the reservoir area and flood a valuable archaeological site.

In September 2003 the Bandung Legal Aid Institute, an Indonesian NGO, claimed that US $700,000 earmarked as compensation for two communities affected by the Jatigede dam were diverted from the project budget. On average, the farmers covered by the institute's survey received only 29 per cent of the official value of their land and houses. The dam project has also been associated with serious human rights abuses.[3]

Environmental experts argue that the Jatigede dam is not needed. Rehabilitating deforested lands and reviving the region's silted rivers would do more to prevent floods and droughts. 'Reforestation should become the first priority for maintaining the water catchment area, without which there would not be enough water to fill up the reservoir', says Usep Setiawan of the Working Group on Conservation for Nature and Natural Resources. Supardiyono Sobirin of the Sunda Forestry and Environment Expert Board agrees. 'The main difficulty of reservoirs in West Java is the water supply because river flow areas have been damaged and cannot provide water to the reservoirs', he said. 'Why would they build more reservoirs if there is no water?'

The plan to build the Jatigede dam rather than promote more sustainable alternatives may be part of a wider pattern of distortion in Indonesia's development planning process. In August 1997 staff members of the World Bank's Jakarta office prepared a confidential report on corruption in development projects in the country. The leaked report found that:

> Most GOI [Government of Indonesia] agencies have sophisticated informal systems for diversion of 10–20 per cent of the development budget under their management, and for utilising the proceeds diverted to supplement their inadequate operations funds and their compensation. These arrangements vary widely among GOI agencies, but almost universally depend on the payment of percentage or lump sum rebates or 'kick-backs' by contractors implementing projects from the agency development budget. Such payments are informal but regarded as an overhead or informal 'tax' by most firms doing business with GOI, and are typically included in the unit prices or bills of quantity for the contract.[4]

'In aggregate', the report estimates that 'at least 20–30 per cent of GOI development funds are diverted through informal payments to GOI staff and politicians'. All payments identified by the report are linked to decisions favouring new investment projects. The document mentions numerous cases in which 50–80 per cent of the funds budgeted for land acquisition and resettlement assistance were diverted. This is hardly an incentive for minimising resettlement.

Communities affected by projects like the Jatigede dam pay the price for the diversion of development funds. Society at large and the environment also suffer indirectly from a decision-making process that is fraudulently skewed towards approving new investment projects even when other options – for example, reforestation or sustainable water management programmes – are more appropriate.

Monuments of corruption

Corruption in the development planning process is not an isolated phenomenon, nor is it confined to Indonesia. The Bataan nuclear power plant is the Philippines' largest investment project and cost more than US $2 billion. Westinghouse was controversially awarded the main contract after the late Filipino dictator, Ferdinand Marcos, personally overturned the initial contract decision.[5] Westinghouse admitted paying US $17 million in commissions to a friend of Marcos, though it maintained that the payments were not a bribe. The reactor sits on an active fault line that is part of the Pacific's 'rim of fire', creating a major risk of nuclear contamination if the power plant ever becomes operational. Completed in the 1980s, the plant has never produced a single unit of electricity.

Yacyretá on the border of Argentina and Paraguay is one of the largest hydropower projects in Latin America. Built with World Bank support, the dam is flooding the Ibera Marshes, a unique ecosystem that has remained almost undisturbed for centuries. Due to cost overruns, the power generated by Yacyretá is not economic and needs to be subsidised by the government. According to the head of Paraguay's General Accounting Office, US $1.87 billion in expenditures for the project 'lack the legal and administrative support documentation to justify the expenditures'.[6]

Enron's Dabhol power plant threatens to destroy a fragile coastal area in India. A representative of Enron admitted that the company paid US $20 million 'on [the] education and project development process alone, not including any project costs'.[7] The multi-billion dollar plant was mothballed in 2001 because its electricity was prohibitively expensive.

The reservoir of the Bakun dam in Sarawak, Malaysia, will submerge 700 km^2 of tropical rain forest. The mandate to develop the project went to a timber contractor and friend of Sarawak's governor. The contractor had never developed a power project before and lost the contract after a few years, but he managed to log the project area during this period. The provincial government of Sarawak is still looking for customers to consume the power to be generated by the project.

The list goes on. None of the projects mentioned above make any economic sense. They had serious environmental and social impacts, and should never have gone forward in the first place.

The political economy of infrastructure development

Corruption and cronyism have environmental and social impacts that go far beyond the individual projects tainted by bribery. They skew the planning and decision-making processes in important sectors of infrastructure development. Large, centralised, capital-intensive greenfield projects offer decision-makers more scope for kickbacks, bureaucratic control and political prestige than decentralised, community-based services. They also offer more scope for private gain than the rehabilitation of existing infrastructure, or non-structural options such as reforestation programmes or demand-side management measures. Because of this bias, decision makers often favour large-scale public works projects even if the alternatives would make better economic sense and would have less harmful social and environmental impacts.

Corruption – the misuse of public or private office for personal gain – extends beyond straightforward bribery. Planning processes in the infrastructure sector touch on important vested interests. Their outcomes affect the prestige of politicians, the budgets and personnel of bureaucrats, and the follow-up contracts of external consultants. Decision-makers are therefore under strong pressure to treat project options on the basis of factors other than their merits.

The special role of the consulting industry

Consultants who are commissioned to assess development options in a particular sector are usually aware that their clients have an interest in promoting new greenfield investments. They are equally aware that environmental impact assessments should not stop projects that enjoy political support. Even if they find that a project has unacceptable environmental impacts, they are under pressure to recommend mitigating measures for it, rather than promote less destructive alternative options. If consultants assess projects solely on their merits, they risk obtaining no future contracts. This causes what a World Bank report on involuntary resettlement in 1994 called 'excessive appraisal optimism'. It is a form of corruption that distorts the planning process to the benefit of projects with large budgets, contracts and prestige – and often with massive social and environmental impacts.

The 'political economy' of infrastructure development was clearly identified by the independent World Commission on Dams (WCD). The WCD's report, published in 2000, says:

> At whatever level, vested interests can distort the decision-making process, undermining development. Decision makers may be inclined to favour large infrastructure as they provide opportunities for personal enrichment not afforded by smaller or more diffuse alternatives. The consequences frequently directly affect the poor and the environment. Allegations of corruption have tainted many large dam projects in the past but have seldom resulted in prosecution in court.[8]

Overcoming corruption in infrastructure development

Transparency International has developed tools such as the Integrity Pact for combating corruption in the field of public procurement. Integrity Pacts are contracts between government offices and companies bidding for particular projects. They prohibit bribery, ensure transparency in the bidding process and foresee sanctions in the case of violations. In infrastructure projects, such pacts can also include private investors and consultants.[9]

'Comprehensive Options Assessment' is one of the strategic priorities proposed by the World Commission on Dams.[10] The principle has been officially endorsed by many governments and financial institutions, but is often not implemented in practice.

The World Bank has adopted a specific guideline to rule out conflicts of interest in dealing with consultants. This guideline states:

> Bank policy requires that consultants provide professional, objective and impartial advice and at all times hold the client's interests paramount, without any consideration for future work, and that in providing advice they avoid conflicts with other assignments and their own corporate interests.[11]

If strictly adhered to, this guideline would go a long way towards avoiding fraudulent practices in assessing and preparing options of infrastructure development. However, like other guidelines, it is not always implemented.

Sunlight is the best disinfectant. Complete transparency is needed to discourage fraudulent practices in the process of assessing the needs and options of infrastructure development. Parliaments and civil society organisations must hold governments and financial institutions accountable for their decisions even during the early planning stages of infrastructure development.

Notes

1. Peter Bosshard is policy director at the International Rivers Network.
2. The Norwegian authorities dismissed the case in 2003 through lack of evidence (see Norway country report). For a summary of the Veidekke/Kaijuka case, see *Development Today*, 5 August 2002.
3. Bandung Legal Aid Institute, *Facts of the Violations of Human Rights and the Law: Corruption in the Jatigede Dam Project in Sumedang, West Java* (Bandung: 2003).
4. 'Summary of RSI Staff Views Regarding the Problem of "Leakage" from World Bank Project Budgets', undated.
5. See A. Timothy Martin, 'International Arbitration and Corruption' in *Transnational Dispute Management* 1 (2004).
6. Francisco Galiano, head of Paraguay's General Accounting Office, as quoted in *Ultima Hora*, 3 September 2004.
7. Testimony by Linda F. Powers before the Committee on Appropriations, Subcommittee on Foreign Operations, US House of Representatives, 31 January 1995.
8. World Commission on Dams, *Dams and Development* (London: WCD, November 2000).
9. For an elaboration of this principle in the context of dam building, see Michael H. Wiehen, 'Transparency and Corruption Prevention on Building Large Dams', paper for the World Commission on Dams (1999).
10. WCD, *Dams and Development*.
11. World Bank, *Guidelines: Selection and Employment of Consultants by World Bank Borrowers* (Washington, DC: World Bank, 2004).

Earthquake destruction: corruption on the fault line
James Lewis[1]

Earthquakes don't kill people; collapsing buildings do. While earthquakes may not be preventable, it is possible to prevent the disasters they cause. In the past 15 years, there have been more than 400 recorded earthquakes in 75 countries rendering almost 9 million people homeless, injuring 584,000 and causing 156,000 deaths.[2] Many of these deaths were the result of buildings that folded in on themselves because concrete was diluted, steel bars were excised, or otherwise substandard building practices were employed. It is difficult to evaluate the extent to which corruption might have played a role. However, the accompanying examples from Italy and Turkey illustrate that the marriage of corrupt contractors and corrupt building inspectors and other public officials resulted in ignored building codes, lax enforcement and the absence of on-site inspection, which is deadly when it occurs in earthquake-prone areas.

The building process

Building construction involves a process of physical covering. Starting in the ground with foundations, it proceeds with the superstructure of walls, columns, floors, staircases and roofing. Each stage is concealed, from foundations under the ground, steel reinforcement before concrete is poured, to the last coat of paint. Mistakes and omissions (accidental or intentional) have to be identified and rectified within each stage. Pressures on builders to complete on time, increased by financial incentives and impeded by late deliveries and weather, create circumstances in which temptations are rife for expediency and shortcuts.

Areas at risk of being hit by an earthquake or other natural disaster present construction firms and engineers with an additional level of complexity. Reinforced concrete is relatively cheap and a convenient, though rigid, construction material, whereas timber is more flexible but requires skills and materials not always locally available and is inappropriate for larger buildings. Flexibility responds to earthquake motion where rigidity does not. Concrete can be used in earthquake-resistant constructions, but needs to be of high quality and applied using a vibration machine to ensure that it penetrates throughout necessarily complex steel reinforcement. Vibrators require on-site generators or mains electric power, which imply additional costs. Controlled concrete is best achieved by specialist and centrally inspected off-site suppliers; less easily inspected on-site mixing is subject to expediency, substitution and omission.

Engineered buildings design in an additional 'earthquake factor' for earthquake resistance, the degree of which is a matter for regulation or professional analysis. But the factor can be exceeded by actual earthquakes of greater magnitude. Even inspected buildings can fail; older and decayed buildings can collapse.

Problems with oversight

Most countries, regardless of their stage of development, have moderate-to-good building and safety codes. Many could be improved: in India, for instance, where an earthquake in Gujarat in 2001 killed 20,000, codes required inspectors to inspect plans but not the buildings themselves during the building process. In most cases, though, the main problem is implementation of codes. A proper enforcement system needs trained engineers, rules and regulations, and periodic inspection. Corruption adds to this problem when building permits are obtained through bribes and political favours, or inspectors are paid to turn a blind eye to design or building practices that deviate from the code specification.

Financial resources and trained personnel are needed to be able to inspect the work of contractors. Public officials employed to inspect building codes and grant permits are rarely well paid in any country, and there is almost always the problem of understaffing. Where the rate of housing growth is rapid, such as in Turkey, 'it is a daunting task to carry out proper building inspections even assuming the necessary political and ethical will', according to Alpaslan Özerdem, an expert in disaster management.[3] He suggests another approach would be to increase public awareness and make potential house buyers become the inspectors: 'if people showed as much interest in earthquake safety ... as they show in the type of tiles, doors and taps ... building contractors would stick to the rules and regulations'.

The state's role in the construction of dangerous buildings is not limited to failure to ensure proper inspections. Acts and omissions by states can actually contribute to the extent of disasters, especially when this occurs in a context where corruption is prevalent throughout government services. Research into the catastrophic 1999 Kocaeli earthquake in Turkey identified 'organisational deviance' in the pursuit of risk-laden policies, corruption tolerated or tacitly encouraged to serve organisational goals, failure to develop regulation in the construction industry, encouraging or forcing land settlements in hazardous zones, post-disaster cover-up and concealment of evidence, and promotion of policies directly contributing to corrupt practice in the construction industry.[4]

Agencies such as UNESCO and UN-Habitat have helped push for codes for earthquake-resistant construction, and international demands for improved construction are repeated after every earthquake. The *UN Chronicle* recently carried a plea by experts working in the field for 'the enforcing of internationally accepted standards of safety for schools and hospitals everywhere in the world'. To mitigate the impact of earthquakes by reducing the risk of corruption:

- legislation and enforcement should be tightened, and adequate, trained and empowered inspections should be made of construction projects both during the design and the building stage

- controls over building construction by local governments should be evaluated and redefined

- participation in earthquake insurance should be encouraged and made to be a vehicle for requiring independent certification of conformity with construction codes

- training, licensing and regulation of engineers and architects should include training in earthquake-resistant construction

- standardised design of government buildings should be re-examined with a view to more stringent applications

- strict restrictions should be placed on overcrowding and upper-storey extension of existing buildings and on maintenance of old, damaged and poorly maintained buildings

- access to controlled provision and supply of (off-site) ready-mixed concrete should be facilitated.[5]

The media and civil society have an important role to play in pushing for an improved construction system in earthquake-prone areas:

- citizens need to be encouraged to hear a second opinion on safety if they have any doubts about the work of contractors

- citizens should be trained to spot the most egregious departures from building codes

- local NGOs should provide second opinions and act as watchdogs, possibly with the help of voluntary pools of engineers from local universities or chambers of engineers.

Box 1.1 The Italian mafia's legacy of high-rise death traps

David Alexander[1]

In Italy there are four mafias, all based in the Mezzogiorno, the southern half of the country: *Cosa Nostra*; the *Camorra*; the *Ndrangheta* and the *Sacra Corona Unita*. Traditionally all four have been active in extortion, racketeering, theft and smuggling. The gradual relaxation of border controls and the increase in the volume of international trade and travel led them to shift their focus to the drugs trade, gambling, people-trafficking and the construction industry, all of which are more lucrative than their traditional activities. Money laundering and illicit investment in the construction trade have been natural consequences of the vast sums accumulated in the conduct of these businesses.

During the period of the so-called 'First Republic' (1948–90), Cosa Nostra and the Camorra developed strong links with leading Italian politicians in the ruling Christian Democrat party. This enabled them to expand their business activities enormously under the cover of parliamentary approval engineered by powerful figures in the political establishment. One of the most visible effects of corruption was the huge investment in unregulated building projects, which not only caused ubiquitous environmental damage but also spread vulnerability to earthquakes.

In Italy, earthquakes are larger and more numerous in the Mezzogiorno. A major seismic event may destroy or significantly damage up to half a million buildings, leading to a massive demand for reconstruction and, obviously, the funds to achieve it. During the second half of the twentieth century the main source of the latter was direct, regressive taxation, particularly through increases in the price of gasoline at the pump. As there was no organised system of insurance of structures against earthquake damage, the government acted as the 'insurer of last resort', directing large amounts of public money to regional, provincial and local authorities, and to state agencies such as the Cassa per il Mezzogiorno (Southern Development Fund). South of Rome, all of them were reportedly corruptible.

In 1968 14 small earthquakes caused significant damage and more than 200 deaths in the Belice Valley of western Sicily. By 1983 very little had been done to reconstruct buildings, and large sums of government money had simply disappeared, the victim of poor accounting, opaqueness in public administration and the business interests of the underlying black economy. Eventually, reconstruction did occur, but under the impetus of concerted attempts to break the power of the mafia, attempts that led to the assassination of an armed forces general and various senior investigative judges.

The largest earthquake of the second half of the twentieth century occurred in 1980 in an area extending from Naples to the boundaries of Apulia. Some 2,735 people were killed, 8,841 were injured and 400,000 were left homeless. Some 637 settlements spread over an area of 23,000 km² reported damage. In terms of mass casualties, the worst effects took place where large, fully occupied buildings collapsed spectacularly. One of the most notorious examples was the complete collapse of the maternity wing of a

▶

six-storey hospital at Sant'Angelo dei Lombardi, in Avellino, east of Naples. Almost all of its occupants were crushed to death. Subsequent investigation showed that the plans for this fairly new, reinforced concrete-framed building were adequate, but it had been built with substantial economies in materials (the foundations were too shallow and several hundred structural members were missing from the frame). While it is not clear that the Camorra were involved, there was certainly a failure to control and inspect the building works and a desire to flout the rules on the part of the builders. Many other such lapses were revealed amid the wreckage of modern buildings that failed to withstand the tremors. An unknown but probably large number of these were related to illicit speculation in construction promoted by the Camorra.

During the aftermath of the 1980 earthquake, clear evidence emerged of attempts by the Camorra to take command of the rebuilding process and to siphon off the funds. There were widespread delays in the reconstruction of basic infrastructure, schools and hospitals at the same time as there was a boom in speculative building of housing. This dual process indicates the success of the Camorra's strategy, as it points to interference in the urban planning and building-contract tendering processes. Many of the new buildings were not built sufficiently well to withstand major earthquakes, either because building codes were ignored or because they were slow to be updated. Prominent local politicians, such as the mayor of Pagani, who opposed the Camorra's involvement in reconstruction, were assassinated.

It was left to Italy's 'Second Republic', shorn of its most notorious corrupt political leaders, to investigate and impose controls on how central government funds were distributed to potentially corrupt local and provincial authorities. This did not happen until 1993–94.

The historical roots of corruption, and the persistence of the social and economic conditions that foster it, mean that it will not disappear overnight. The four mafias have suffered considerable setbacks, including loss of the parliamentary support that was once so unwavering, but they are resourceful and have diversified business enterprises. If nothing else, the huge rash of uncontrolled speculative building that they promoted in the late twentieth century represents a major source of vulnerability to future earthquakes in southern cities such as Reggio Calabria, Messina and Catania. In Italy, neither corruption nor earthquakes is an exclusively southern phenomenon, but they are both decidedly more pronounced and deep-rooted in the Mezzogiorno.

Note

1. David Alexander is professor and head of the disaster management subject group at Coventry University, Britain. His books include *Natural Disasters*, *Confronting Catastrophe*, and *Principles of Emergency Planning and Management*.

Box 1.2   Turkish homeowners demand an end to earthquake devastation

William A. Mitchell and Justin Page[1]

During the twentieth century Turkey experienced about 60 severe earthquakes, which contributed to more than 250,000 casualties and almost 650,000 destroyed buildings.

▶

Most of the buildings were improperly sited, poorly built and inadequately reinforced. The Dinar earthquake in 1995, occurring just over three years after the Erzincan earthquake, generated a crescendo of public awareness and media outcry. This outcry was especially strong in urban Turkey, home to over 70 per cent of the population of about 70 million.

Much of the population shift to the cities results from villagers moving from economically non-viable areas of the east and entering informal squatter communities (*gecekondu*) in the suburbs of large cities. These settlements are greatly at risk from earthquakes, and the problem is increasing. Although earthquakes are not preventable, the material and human damage that often accompany them can be greatly reduced by implementing a combination of social and technological changes. Enforcing, and complying with, statutory construction codes, honesty in granting contracts, and ethically conducted public procurement tenders could prevent thousands of fatalities in Turkey.

Corrupt construction practices place even more financial stress on the existing macroeconomic stabilisation plans to correct the chronic short-term problems of capital flight, loss of foreign exchange reserves, inflation, and large current account deficits. When an earthquake disaster occurs, the extremely difficult but important actions necessary for long-term economic stability are forced to the background and Turkey's longer-term structural adjustment challenges are compounded.

In Turkey, as in other countries, earthquake victims are often described as people simply experiencing an act of fate or God's will. What this masks, however, is inadequate knowledge of the basics of seismic-resistant construction, which has allowed a worsening of corruption within the Turkish construction industry and in the enforcement of building codes. Such a tendency was reinforced by a lack of critical scrutiny from Turkish officials and the media towards faulty construction in most major earthquakes up until the most recent disasters.

Following the 1992 Erzincan disaster, the public began to learn more about reasonable expectations for seismic-resistant construction and started to call for more efficient governmental management of construction. The print media, especially the *Turkish Daily News*, began to directly criticise the government of Erzincan for 'incompetence and inexperience' as well as 'inefficiency'. Other news stories focused on the blatant violation of construction codes in place since 1973, which prohibited the construction of buildings more than three stories tall. Many of the buildings exceeding the three-storey legal limit collapsed or were heavily damaged, presenting clear evidence of faulty construction.[2]

The Erzincan disaster reinforced the voluminous literature demonstrating that poorly built, non-reinforced structures constructed on improper sites with disregard for geology and seismology, particularly near and on the North Anatolian fault zone, collapse in severe or major earthquakes with large numbers of casualties.

The Dinar earthquake was Turkey's sixth significant earthquake in 25 years. There was a relatively low cost in terms of human lives, but major or total damage was suffered by 37 of Dinar's public buildings constructed entirely by government contractors using questionable techniques and standards. Following the Dinar earthquake, the level of awareness of the Turkish public towards disasters was heightened and there were increased demands for more sound construction practices.[3]

While the Dinar earthquake served as a catalyst for more public awareness of faulty construction techniques and corrupt practices, the 1999 Izmit disaster was a full awakening to the problem facing urban populations. More than 15,000 people died with more than

▶

twice this number injured and 200,000 left homeless. The disaster led to a crescendo of opposition towards corrupt and shoddy building practices, spearheaded by a number of outspoken newspapers. Immediately following the earthquake, media outlets launched harsh criticism of the government's slow disaster response which caused more fatalities as victims waited for assistance in the form of sanitation, water, shelters, and search and rescue. Attention soon focused on corruption and its impact on construction as a direct reason for the massive loss of lives.

If the Izmit response represented the worst side of Turkey's public administration, the response to the Bingol earthquake in 2003 embodied the best. Governmental and military response and search and rescue were both quick and efficient and garnered high praise. The issue of past corruption in construction was brought to the forefront and the press was quick to assert that this earthquake was similar to most previous ones concerning quality of construction. Many political leaders and academics complained and accused builders, contractors and the government of disregarding building codes, quality control and geological considerations. President Ahmet Sezer publicly urged punishment for those who were responsible for constructing the government buildings that collapsed. Prime Minister Tayyip Erdogan was quick to assert that 'the ideas of stealing materials, corruption, illegalities and injustice [must be corrected]'.[4]

Corruption remains a major problem in Turkey. A first step in attempting to combat corruption is the admission of its existence, something the government has done under Prime Minister Erdogan, thanks to pressure from the Turkish people whose ambivalence and fatalistic attitudes have changed dramatically. While there has been progress, there is much more to do, however.[5] Putting a transparent national plan into effect, with integrity, is crucial for a sustainable Turkey.[6]

Notes

1. William A. Mitchell is a professor in the political science department, holds the Jo Murphy Chair in International Education, is a Middle East Area specialist, and has lived in Turkey for more than 12 years. Justin Page is a Baylor University graduate student in Middle East international relations and has completed research in Turkey, Iraq and Egypt.
2. William A. Mitchell, *The Republic of Turkey and Earthquake Disaster Management* (New York: Global Humanities Press, 2004), p. 146.
3. Ibid., p. 156.
4. Quoted in Relief Web, 4 May 2003, www.reliefweb.int/5/4/03
5. After the Izmit earthquake, public education campaigns on dangerous practices in reinforced concrete construction and introducing the basic principle of seismic-resistant construction were carried out in Istanbul by the Istanbul Governor's Office and Bogazici University's Disaster Preparedness Education Programme. This latter programme reached 1.5 million school children and hundreds of thousands of parents in four provinces and is now being expanded nationwide with the support of the ministry of education. A network of ombudsmen could also help support the public demand for safe construction.
6. The METU Disaster Management Implementation and Research Center (in conjunction with the government of Turkey – created under the UNDP cost-sharing project 'Improvement of Turkey's Disaster Management System') is an excellent initiative to bring geo-science and social science together to work for a better understanding of social attitudes and citizen participation for disaster preparedness and mitigation in Turkey.

Notes

1. James Lewis is an architect, consultant and writer on environmental hazards, and a visiting fellow in development studies at the University of Bath (Britain).

2. EM-DAT (2004) OFDA/CRED International Disaster Database: Université Catholique de Louvain, Brussels, Belgium, www.em-dat.net

3. Alpaslan Özerdem, 'Tiles, Taps and Earthquake-Proofing: Lessons for Disaster Management in Turkey' in *Environment and Urbanisation*, October 1999.

4. Green, al-Husseini and Curry, 'Disaster Prevention and the 1999 Turkish Earthquakes', http://online.northumbria.ac.uk/geography_research/radix/turkey-bingol5.htm

5. Ben Wisner and James Lewis, 'Exchange: Why do Schools and Hospitals Collapse in Earthquakes?', UN Chronicle Volume XL No. 3, 2003, www.un.org/Pubs/chronicle/2003/issue3/0303p49.asp

2   Corruption in practice

A worker at the world's largest liquefied natural gas plant in Dabhol, India. Embroiled in controversy since the mid-1990s over allegations of corruption, high costs and disputes between Enron and the local state utility over debts, the plant stopped generating power in May 1999. Now maintained by a workforce of 250, over 5,000 workers were laid off following the closure of the plant. (AP Photo)

Case study: Lesotho puts international business in the dock
Fiona Darroch[1]

Even while the court trials are still continuing, enough has already been established to make the Lesotho Highlands Water Project (LHWP) one of the most prominent cases of international bribery ever. In a small and very poor country, several major international construction companies have been taken to court and dealt with resolutely. The case sets many important precedents, not only for the legal pursuit of such cases, and for how international financial institutions (such as the World Bank) respond, but also in the wider message that it sends out: companies that bribe to win international business risk punishment and blacklisting, irrespective of where they commit the crime.

In 1986 the governments of Lesotho and South Africa signed a treaty that gave rise to the LHWP. With five major dams, 200 kilometres of tunnels and a powerful hydroelectricity station to be completed by 2020, the US $8 billion infrastructure scheme was to control and exploit the flow of the Senqu River (known as the Orange River in South Africa). In doing so, the project was also expected to provide water for Gauteng province in South Africa, and to generate electricity and money for the people of Lesotho.

After a civilian government replaced the military regime in Lesotho in 1993, the government commissioned an audit of the project's two oversight bodies, the Lesotho Highlands Development Authority (LHDA), a semi-autonomous state corporation, and the Trans-Caledon Tunnel Authority (TCTA), the implementing agency for the relatively small part of the project in South Africa. The audit revealed substantial administrative irregularities within the LHDA and gave rise to an inquiry into the conduct of its chief executive officer, Masupha Ephraim Sole. By 1996 Sole had been dismissed from the LHDA, a decision that was upheld in subsequent appeals.

During the investigations, classic 'red flags' revealed that Sole was living far beyond his means: extravagant housing, cars and holiday arrangements, and instances of nepotism were the obvious indicators. Recognising that certain contracts negotiated under Sole's watch had caused the LHDA to suffer substantial losses, and in view of the fact that Sole refused to disclose his bank accounts, the development authority initiated civil proceedings for the recovery of the losses. The company also aimed to secure compensation for damages that arose from the unjustified awarding of a contract to one of the many consortia working on the LHWP.

Sole in court

Given Sole's refusal to produce bank records and his persistent denial that any accounts remained to be divulged, the court subpoenaed Sole's bank manager. This move finally produced evidence of bank accounts in Ladybrand and Bloemfontein in South Africa as well as with the Union Bank of Switzerland.

In August 1997, the Lesotho government requested that a Swiss court order the disclosure of a number of Swiss bank accounts, including those belonging to Sole. Although a number of the contractors and consultants working on the LHWP, who also held bank accounts in Switzerland, attempted to block the effort, the presiding magistrate granted the request. The federal appeal court upheld her decision and in early 1999 bank records were delivered to the Lesotho government. Sole's records indicated that he had received large sums, for which he offered no explanation. Civil proceedings concluded in October 1999, with a judgment against Sole for damages of US $1.4 million. Sole appealed in April 2001, to no avail.

The Swiss bank records showed that, as CEO, Sole had consistently received large sums of money through middlemen or intermediaries from companies and consortia that had been awarded contracts in the LHWP. The pattern, size and timing of the payments indicated bribery. The Lesotho government proceeded to prosecute not only Sole, but also many of the corporations and intermediaries. In December 1999, Sole and 18 other defendants were charged with bribery. Sole also faced charges of fraud and perjury. Seven of the defendants failed to attend the initial hearing.

Sole's trial began in June 2001. Charged with 16 counts of bribery and two of fraud, Sole still chose not to furnish evidence. Judge Brendon Cullinan, a former chief justice of Lesotho, found Sole guilty as charged and sentenced him to 18 years in prison. In his judgment, Cullinan observed that the transactions in question 'inextricably bound together' the defendant consultants and contractors, the intermediaries, and Sole himself. Sole appealed, but succeeded only in reducing the sentence to 15 years.

The preliminary rulings and the final judgment of Sole's case provide highly cogent benchmarks for use in the prosecution of corruption in a common law jurisdiction. In particular, the judge addressed questions of jurisdiction (could the matters be tried in Lesotho?), citation (did a company have a legal personality?), bribery (what were the constituent elements of the offence?) and whether circumstantial evidence was sufficient to support a conviction for bribery.

The Acres trial

The Canadian engineering giant Acres International had been involved in two contracts within the LHWP, one of them financed by the World Bank, and was the first company to be tried in connection with the payments to Sole. Prosecutors alleged that Acres had made payments to Sole through Zaliswonga Bam, one of the intermediaries, who died of a heart attack in 1999. Evidence showed a clear pattern of payments made by Acres to Bam, using numbered Swiss bank accounts. Bam took a percentage and then moved the remainder of the money into Sole's accounts.

Acres agreed that it had made such payments to Bam; however, the company argued that such payments were made pursuant to a 'representation agreement' it had made with Bam, for services rendered by him to the company in his capacity as its agent or representative. Acres argued that Bam had indeed performed such services, that payment of such sums of money was commonplace in such circumstances, that nothing adverse should be inferred from the fact that the payments were made in such secrecy, and that in any event the company had had no idea whatsoever that Bam made payments to Sole.

The company failed to convince Judge Mahapela Lehohla of the virtue of these arguments. Lehohla concluded that the relationship between Acres and the LHDA was so well established that Acres had no need for a 'representative'. Furthermore, there was no tangible evidence of Bam's alleged company, 'ACPM', which was named on the Swiss bank account. The judge could see no evidence to show what services Bam performed, nor why he would have performed them, given his role in charge of a Housing Association in Botswana. Applying the law as it had been set out by Cullinan in Sole's trial, Lehohla concluded that the representation agreement was a sham, that Acres had benefited from bribing Sole – to the detriment of its competitors – and that the company was therefore guilty as charged. On being convicted and sentenced to a fine of US $2.5 million, Acres refused to accept the ruling of the court, suggesting that the judge had been incompetent and the trial unfair. Acres' appeal failed.

After the Acres conviction

Before the criminal trial began, the World Bank had initiated debarment proceedings against two of the LHWP companies that had benefited from its financing. The Bank had initially concluded that there was insufficient evidence to debar Acres. However, the World Bank found that 'new evidence' had emerged during the Acres trial, and thus resumed debarment proceedings against Acres. In July 2004, the World Bank's sanctions committee debarred Acres for a period of three years.[2] The period of debarment was shorter than it might have been, largely because the sanctions committee took into account the fine which had already been imposed by the Lesotho courts, and the fact that those who had been responsible for the bribery no longer worked for the company.[3]

Following the trial of Acres, the German company Lahmeyer found itself in court. Although the facts of the case were different, the arguments were almost identical. Bam had once again played the intermediary, and the evidence to justify the representation agreements between Bam and Lahmeyer was insubstantial. The trial followed the same pattern as the Acres' proceedings, as did the appeal, and the World Bank may also respond with similar debarment proceedings.

Another intermediary charged with bribery, the South African Jacobus du Plooy, pleaded guilty. It was clear at his sentencing that he was in a position to assist the prosecution, although it remains to be seen whether such assistance will facilitate further successful prosecutions.

A French company, Spie Batignolles, was the next defendant, and proceedings have also begun against Impregilo, an Italian company, with the first hearing scheduled for October 2004. At the time of writing, evidence was also being gathered against other companies.

Lessons learned

These trials provide a number of crucial lessons. First and foremost, from the perspective of Lesotho, no other small and impoverished country has taken such a comprehensive approach to the excision of corruption from its economy by prosecuting international companies that engage in bribery. Many have expressed their admiration for the determination and tenacity of the attorney general and the prosecutors. The trials went ahead without external financial support, in spite of promises that it would be given, although more recently Lesotho has at least benefited from some mutual legal assistance.

Since many of the legal aspects of corruption have now been thoroughly tested in the Lesotho courts, judges and lawyers can refer to clear, developed common law jurisprudence on the questions of jurisdiction and citation. In addition, the definition of bribery has been further refined to ensure that both sides are equally held to account: the bribe taker as much as the briber.

It should be noted that the World Bank's proceedings may be seen as incongruent with criminal litigation, in terms of both evidence and procedure. 'New evidence' that emerged from an adversarial criminal trial was used in a debarment process that was essentially inquisitorial, where evidence was gathered but not tested in cross-examination. Different methods of evaluating the same pieces of evidence could give rise to different rulings. Furthermore, the World Bank lies outside the jurisdiction of judicial review. It has conducted its own inquiry into corporate corruption in Lesotho, and its procedures are not subject to judicial scrutiny. In contrast, the trials in Lesotho have been subject to such scrutiny at every turn; they have effectively provided the World Bank with the materials used in its debarment proceedings.

Nevertheless, there has been close cooperation between the Bank and the prosecuting team in Lesotho, and the work done by the Bank's investigative team has been exhaustive, resulting in the first debarment of a major international company.

Looking ahead

Other international financial institutions (IFIs) would be well advised to follow the World Bank's lead. Debarment is arguably feared more than a criminal conviction in a far-flung country, since it is likely to have a sharper impact upon the company's business than a fine. IFIs whose money was used to finance contracts negotiated and fulfilled by a company that is subsequently convicted of bribery should examine their own procedures, and give proper consideration to the imposition of similar sanctions. Failure to do so will give rise to the perception that Acres and Lahmeyer have been treated with disproportionate discrimination.

The international response to the prosecutions was initially very supportive, but this response did not automatically translate into any tangible form of assistance – save for the full cooperation of the Swiss authorities, and the exchange of information between the World Bank and the Lesotho prosecuting team – until relatively recently, after a group of non-governmental organisations exerted pressure within the European Parliament for such assistance to be increased. Further mutual legal assistance has now been forthcoming, although there is no financial support other than loans offered to the Lesotho authorities.

The World Bank's decision to debar Acres has been heralded as a clear indication from the Bank that its policies do have teeth when it comes to eliminating corruption from its lending practices, although there is a need to reconsider the relationship between Bank procedures and the due process of criminal litigation elsewhere. Responses to the debarment of Acres have yet to emerge from other IFIs. Ideally, anti-corruption strategies among IFIs should be coordinated so that the debarment of a company by one IFI automatically results in debarment by *all* IFIs. Debarment could thus become a much more effective deterrent to a company considering the bribery of a foreign public official.

Notes

1. Fiona Darroch is a barrister at law at Hailsham Chambers, London.
2. Shortly before the sanctions committee gave its ruling, Acres was bought by a larger corporation, Hatch.
3. Acres has subsequently put in place a Business Integrity Management System in line with the proposals of FIDIC (the International Federation of Consulting Engineers).

Exposing the foundations of corruption in construction
Neill Stansbury[1]

Surveys reveal corruption to be higher in construction than in any other sector of the economy.[2] The scale of corruption in construction is magnified by the size and scope of the sector, which ranges from transport infrastructure and power stations at the larger end to domestic housing at the smaller. It is a sector that includes projects initiated by both governments (often termed 'public works') and the private sector. Estimates of the total size of the global construction market are around US $3,200 billion per year. Its share of the economy varies from 5–7 per cent of GDP in developed and advanced developing countries, and around 2–3 per cent of GDP in lower-income developing countries.[3]

There is significant variation across the industry as to the nature and extent of corruption. Some sectors and territories are relatively free from corruption, and a significant number of organisations and individuals try to avoid corruption at all costs. The majority of contractors who do engage in corrupt practices tend to do so not because they want to, but because they feel they are forced to by the way the industry and the political environment operate.

Why is construction so prone to corruption?

Construction projects usually involve a large number of participants in a complex contractual structure. Figure 2.1 illustrates one possible (simplified) contractual structure for building a power station. Each line represents a contract between two actors (companies, governments, banks and so on).

In the construction of a power station, the 'client' (or owner) will normally be a government or a public corporation. At the project planning stage, the client contracts consultants and engineers (see top right of the figure) to carry out feasibility studies, environmental impact assessments and other planning exercises. The client will also raise project funds by negotiating agreements with commercial banks, development banks and international financial institutions (see top left of the figure). The client then awards the main construction contract to a single company (the 'main contractor') after carrying out a public tender according to the relevant regulations on public contracting.

The 'main contractor' is likely to be a private sector construction or engineering company, which may then subcontract key parts of the project according to its own guidelines for awarding contracts. Subcontractors may in turn sub-subcontract parts

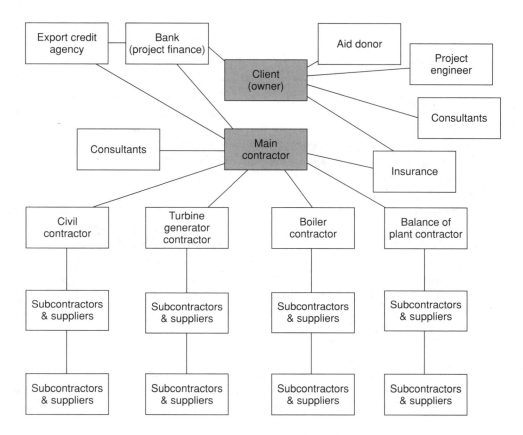

Figure 2.1: A simplified contractual structure for the construction of a power station

of their work, and sub-subcontractors may purchase equipment and materials from suppliers, or award further subcontracts.

The following features of construction projects make them particularly prone to corruption:

1. **Size of projects.** While construction projects vary in scale, infrastructure projects in particular are often huge. The costs of dams, power stations, industrial plants and highways can run into billions of dollars. It is easier to hide large bribes and inflated claims in large projects than it is in small projects.
2. **Uniqueness of projects.** The fact that many major construction projects are one-off makes costs difficult to compare, which in turn makes it easier to inflate costs or hide bribes.
3. **Government involvement.** Most infrastructure projects are government-owned. Even privatised projects require government approvals for planning or agreements to pay for end-product use. The industry tends to be heavily regulated at both national and local government level. Numerous permits are often required. Where there are insufficient controls on how government officials behave, their power

– combined with the structural and financial complexity of the projects – makes it relatively easy for officials to extract bribes.

4. **The number of contractual links.** While there are numerous variations to the project structure outlined above, the contractual cascade could easily have more than 1,000 links, each depending on other contractual links in the chain. Every single link provides an opportunity for someone to pay a bribe in exchange for the award of a contract. In addition, work and services are exchanged for payment in relation to every contractual link. Every item of work and every payment provide further opportunities for bribes to be paid in return either for certifying too much work, certifying defective work, certifying extensions of time or paying more expeditiously.

5. **The number of phases makes project oversight difficult.** Projects normally have several different phases, each involving different management teams and requiring handovers of the completed phase to the contractors undertaking the next phase. For example, a power station project may have the following phases: demand determination, choice of type (hydroelectric, coal, oil, gas), design, excavation, foundations, civil works, building works, equipment manufacture, equipment erection, commissioning and operation. Even if a single contractor undertakes all the project's phases, it will normally subcontract different elements of the task to individual subcontractors, which creates difficulties in control and oversight.

6. **The complexity of projects.** Because of project complexity, the interrelationship between contractors and events is often uncertain. People working together on a project frequently appear not to know, or to disagree upon, the reasons why something has gone wrong, or why costs overrun. This makes it easier to blame others and to claim payment, even when such claims are unjustified. Bribes and inflated claims can easily be hidden and blamed on other factors, such as poor design or mismanagement. Complexity also generates reasons to pay bribes since decisions on cause and effect and their cost consequences can have an enormous impact.

7. **Lack of frequency of projects.** Major projects come at irregular intervals. Winning these projects may be critical to the survival or profitability of contractors, which provides an incentive to contractors to bribe.

8. **Work is concealed.** Most components in construction end up being concealed by other components. Structural steel may be concealed by concrete, brickwork by plaster, engineering components in casings, and roof structures by cladding. The industry places an enormous dependence on the individuals who certify the correctness of the work done before it is concealed; once an item is concealed, it can be very costly or difficult to check if it was completed to the required standard. This cost and difficulty creates an incentive for contractors to do defective work or use inferior materials, and to bribe the relevant official to certify that the work was done according to specification.

9. **A culture of secrecy.** There is no culture of transparency in the construction industry. Costs are kept secret even when it is public money that is being spent. Commercial

confidentiality takes precedence over public interest. The routine inspection of books and records that might uncover malpractice does not normally occur.

10. **Entrenched national interests.** Local and national companies often have entrenched positions in their own market. These positions have often been cemented by bribery. International companies seeking to enter these markets may find it impossible to win work unless they pay a bribe.

11. **No single organisation governs the industry.** Construction brings together a wide range of professions, trades and specialist contractors, leading to varying standards of skill, integrity and oversight. The professions include architects, engineers, surveyors, accountants and lawyers; and the trades include machine operators, scaffolders, bricklayers, electricians and plumbers. Contractors' skills range from excavation to insulation, and from generators to cooling systems. Each profession or trade may have a different professional association, with different codes of conduct and levels of enforcement of these codes. No single organisation has overall responsibility.

12. **Lack of 'due diligence'.** The scale of funds involved in major infrastructure projects places great influence in the financing bodies that determine whether a project goes ahead, and which companies win the contracts. Commercial banks and global or regional development banks provide most of the funds, while government-sponsored export credit agencies may underwrite risky international projects. Their frequent lack of due diligence on participants in construction projects allows corruption to continue.

13. **The cost of integrity.** It is striking how many people working in the construction sector either accept the status quo, or make no attempt to change it. Bribery and deceptive practices are so engrained that they are often accepted as the norm. Bribery is frequently a routine business cost that many companies expect to include in the contract price. The fact that so many businesses in construction routinely pay bribes or engage in deception makes it very costly for any one company to act with integrity since that company would risk losing out to its less scrupulous competitors. As a result, many companies find themselves in a vicious circle in which they engage in corruption, often reluctantly, as a defensive measure against the corrupt practices of other companies. Fortunately, some businesses and industry associations are taking steps to change the status quo (see Box 2.1).

The mechanisms of corruption in construction[4]

Corrupt practices are found at every phase in construction projects: during planning and design, in the award of contracts, during the construction process, and during the operation and maintenance of projects after construction is finished.

Corruption in planning and design

During the planning and design stage, corruption can result in the initiation of projects that are overdesigned or overpriced. Corruption may result in the approval of projects that are unnecessary. In certain cases, projects are conceived solely as vehicles for

Box 2.1   A business perspective: promoting integrity in consulting engineering

Jorge Diaz Padilla[1]

Consulting engineering has evolved to become a major industry worldwide. The International Federation of Consulting Engineers (FIDIC)[2] estimates that this market represents almost US $500 billion in annual consulting fees, of which more than half is delivered by independent, private consulting companies. Clients are increasingly requiring assurance that consulting firms operate in a corruption-free environment, especially when it comes to government procurement.

Most consulting firms are doing their best to define and implement anti-corruption policies. Such approaches tend to be piecemeal, however. What is missing is an integrity baseline that can connect and transform isolated acts of integrity assurance into what FIDIC calls a complete Business Integrity Management System (BIMS), with formal procedures to identify potential risks, prevent and combat corruption, and implement business integrity policies for every project throughout the organisation. The 'Guidelines for Business Integrity Management in the Consulting Industry' and a FIDIC policy statement on integrity were issued in 2001, and the 'Business Integrity Management Training Manual' was published in 2002. Many companies have since developed and implemented a BIMS following the FIDIC guidelines, and some have obtained certification based on the ISO 9000 Standard.

The main steps for designing and implementing a BIMS are:

1. **Formulation of a code of conduct.** In order to ensure commitment, it is essential that the board of directors and senior management develop a code of conduct, which should be clear, simple, and easy to communicate and apply.
2. **Formulation of a business integrity policy.** The guideline requirements for an integrity policy are based mainly on the OECD Anti-Bribery Convention and FIDIC's code of ethics. The integrity policy hinges upon the fact that corruption is eliminated only by across-the-board honesty and integrity. Honesty is interpreted as freedom from fraud or deception, and integrity as the firm refusing to obtain or keep what does not fairly belong to it. The policy should be in keeping with all local rules and regulations as well as the company's code of conduct. The integrity policy must be documented, implemented, communicated internally and externally, and made publicly available.
3. **Appointment of a representative.** A senior member of the firm's management staff should be appointed as a representative to ensure that all the BIMS' requirements are met. A member of staff could also be selected to communicate between management and consultants.
4. **Identification of requirements for the BIMS.** The requirements should focus on the processes in a given firm that are vulnerable to corruption. The requirements might depend on: size and structure of the firm; the nature of its consulting services; local and national regulation and market forces; and the expectations and requirements of all the stakeholders.
5. **Analysis and evaluation of current practices.** An assessment should be made of how the firm currently deals with anti-corruption issues. The gap between current practices and the BIMS' requirements should be identified.
6. **Implementation tools for the BIMS.** A consulting firm should use the following tools to support the planning and implementation of its BIMS: a code of conduct; an

▶

integrity policy; definition of roles, responsibilities and authority; business integrity procedures for the main processes (proposal bidding and negotiation; project execution and delivery; project collection); accounting structure; enforcement measures; and a declaration of business integrity in the annual report. The firm must also establish a procedure to evaluate its sub-consultants and external advisers based on their own integrity policies, and keep records of their commitment to business integrity management.

7. **Documentation.** A BIMS must be well documented in order to provide evidence that all processes that may affect the business integrity of the services offered by the firm have been thoroughly anticipated. The extent of documentation is critical – over-documentation may reduce staff and management interest in using the procedure. The BIMS should be documented in a general Business Integrity Manual and, if required for significant projects, in a Project Integrity Records File.

8. **Analysis of current practices.** The BIMS must establish actions to be taken in case of failure to comply with the Business Integrity Policy. Appropriate actions in cases where corrupt practices are proven range from admonition to suspension or dismissal from the firm.

Once the BIMS is operating properly, and the consulting firm is confident that the guidelines are met, the firm should initiate an evaluation process to ensure continuous compliance. This process can involve: first-party evaluation, where the management and the staff representative evaluate the BIMS; second-party evaluation based on client feedback; or third-party evaluation, by an outside body. If an external evaluation is undertaken, it may be performed as part of an ISO 9001:2000 quality certification process.

In future, a new ISO standard could be developed to certify that a company has a functioning Business Integrity System. Such a standard need not be industry-specific; FIDIC's experience with integrity management could lead to an integrity standard for the construction industry as a whole, or even for other business sectors.

Notes
1. This article is based on the work developed by the FIDIC Integrity Management Task Force, chaired by Felipe Ochoa, and the Joint Working Group on Integrity, created under the auspices of FIDIC, with participation of the World Bank, the Inter-American Development Bank and the Pan American Federation of Consultants (FEPAC). Jorge Diaz Padilla is president-elect of FIDIC.
2. FIDIC, Fédération Internationale des Ingénieurs-Conseils, is the world's leading organisation representing the international consulting engineering industry. Founded in 1913, and with its headquarters in Geneva, it represents more than 30,000 firms in 70 countries.

corruption and would not have even passed the planning stage without that motivation. In others, a project might have been abandoned in the planning phase because of a critical environmental impact assessment, for example, had a bribe not been paid.

Most projects require approval, which is usually controlled by one or more public officials. Developers or contractors may pay bribes to obtain planning approval. The approval of public construction projects may also depend on the support of elected politicians at a national or local level. In such cases, opportunities exist for developers and contractors to buy support for their project by providing funds for politicians, their parties or the charitable causes that they favour.

Sometimes contractors may bribe the client's consulting engineer rather than the client's representative. A consulting engineer (which could be a major international firm) that undertakes the design for a client is in a powerful position since the engineer can design the project to favour a specific contractor's technology. In some instances, designing a contract in this way may be done in good faith in the belief that the relevant technology is best. In other cases, it may have been done in exchange for a bribe or the promise of future work.

Corruption in the award of contracts

Bribery

Bribery in relation to the award of contracts is the most visible form of corruption, particularly when contracts are for major works. This type of corruption normally involves the contractor paying a representative of the client a fee to secure the award of the contract. In some cases, the contractor bribes the consulting engineer who will advise the client that the briber's bid is the best. The payment, whether to client or consulting engineer, may be direct, though it is often made through intermediaries to obscure its identity and purpose.

- **Agents.** The most common form of intermediary is the agent. The contractor appoints an agent who has contacts with a representative of the client or with the government of the country concerned. The contractor pays the agent a percentage of the contract price on being awarded the contract. The agent passes part of the payment to the representative of the client or government in return for the contractor winning the contract. The payment is usually made in foreign currency into an offshore account. Contractors hide the bribes in formal agreements that state the scope of the agent's work. The scope of work will often be false or exaggerated, however, and the size of the payment significantly in excess of the value of any legitimate services the agent carries out.

- **Joint ventures and subsidiaries.** The level of due diligence by export credit agencies, banks and auditors is lower in some countries than others. When a contractor bids as part of an international joint venture from several countries, the joint venture may arrange for the agency agreement to be executed – and the commission paid – from the country least likely to discover the commission. Similarly, where the contractor is part of a multinational group, the commission may be paid by a subsidiary in a country where the commission is less likely to be detected. The subsidiary will then be repaid by the contractor through intercompany charges for false services or services of inflated value.

- **Subcontractors.** A contractor may also channel a bribe through a disguised subcontract arrangement. For example, a subcontractor might agree to provide equipment and materials to a contractor in return for a certain payment, but in reality it will not provide the services, or will provide services of a vastly lower value than the price agreed. The balance of the payment can then be passed on to the relevant party as a bribe.

In many cases, the contractor would prefer not to pay a bribe at all, but is informed by the client's representative or an agent that no contract will be awarded without one. This is sometimes referred to as extortion. On other occasions, the contractor initiates the payment. A contractor may approach the representative of the client or government and request the right to negotiate a contract on a non-competitive basis in return for a bribe. The absence of a competitive tender is likely both to raise the price and expand the scope of work.

A contractor may also initiate a bribe because it knows that its competitors in the bidding process are likely to offer bribes, so that it concludes that it has to pay the bribe to 'level the playing field'. However, one innovative tool developed by Transparency International – the Integrity Pact – overturns this logic by committing all bidders to refrain from bribery (see Box 2.2).

Box 2.2 Integrity Pact sheds light on Mexican electricity tender
Transparencia Mexicana

Developed by Transparency International, the Integrity Pact (IP) is aimed at preventing corruption in public procurement. It consists of an agreement between a government or government department and all bidders for a public sector contract. Under an IP, both sides agree not to pay, offer, demand or accept bribes, or collude with competitors to obtain the contract, or engage in such abuses while carrying it out. Bidders are asked to disclose all commissions and similar expenses paid by them to anybody connected to the contract. Sanctions apply when violations occur, ranging from loss or denial of contract, forfeiture of the bid or performance bond and liability for damages, to blacklisting. Criminal, civil or disciplinary action may also be taken against employees of the government. The IP allows companies to refrain from bribing in the knowledge that their competitors are bound by the same rules. It allows governments to reduce the high cost of corruption in procurement, privatisation and licensing.

Transparencia Mexicana, TI's chapter in Mexico, had completed 15 IPs between 2001 and the time of writing, and had another 12 ongoing. The Mexican IP follows the same principles as the broader TI Integrity Pact, but has built in extra features that are intended to increase citizen participation in the contracting process. The main difference is that the Mexican IP introduces a so-called 'social witness' to oversee the process. The social witness is designated by Transparencia Mexicana and must be technically expert, independent, and enjoy a good reputation in the field. He or she must produce a final report that includes observations and recommendations about the process, a review of qualifying criteria for bidders, an assessment of the field of bidders and an evaluation of the rationale behind decisions taken by the contracting authority.

An example of the IP in practice is the 2002 bidding for a 1,228 GWh hydroelectricity plant, known as 'El Cajón', which was billed as Mexico's most important infrastructure project of the decade. This was the first time the federal government, via the Federal Electricity Commission (CFE), had accepted independent monitoring by a civil society organisation of a bidding process in the energy sector, which in Mexico has historically been perceived by the public to be tainted by high levels of corruption.

The IP lasted from August 2002 to June 2003. The first step in introducing the IP was to designate a social witness to monitor the process. The bidders were then required to

▶

submit Unilateral Integrity Declarations to Transparencia Mexicana as a condition for competing for the contract. These were signed by the highest-level officials of the bidding consortia. Declarations were also submitted by CFE officials and by all government officials involved directly in the contracting process. As part of the IP, Transparencia Mexicana met each of the bidders to ask them which parts of the process they considered might be most at risk of irregularities. Respondents said they were most worried about the fair evaluation of their proposals.

Thirty-one companies bought the guidelines for the contracting process. Of these, 21 did not submit proposals, and the remaining 10 split into three consortia that submitted proposals. These were evaluated on technical and economic grounds. The technical test was whether they complied with the qualifying criteria; the economic test was simply to determine the lowest bid. On the basis of the evaluation, the contract was offered to the consortium comprising Constructora Internacional de Infraestructura, Promotora e Inversora Adisa, Ingenieros Civiles Asociados, La Peninsular Compañía Constructora and Energomachexport-Power Machine. An offer of US $748 million was made for the contract, below the government's allocated budget for the project of US $812 million.

The complaints process
During the bidding process Transparencia Mexicana received one complaint by email about an alleged irregularity – that the CFE had provided confidential information to one of the bidders five months before the public tendering. Transparencia Mexicana requested a meeting with the complainant but did not receive a reply. Transparencia Mexicana also asked the CFE for an explanation. The CFE replied that it had posted information on the Internet about the 'El Cajón' project months ahead of the tender, requesting feedback about the project from interested parties.

None of the bidders filed complaints about the qualification criteria, nor the legal framework for the contracting process. At the time of writing, Transparencia Mexicana was not aware of any complaints that had not been resolved.

Next steps
Transparencia Mexicana's involvement in the 'El Cajón' contracting process represents a small opening of a door to a sector that has hitherto been closed to civil society and has been damaged by allegations of corruption.

The experience also serves to demonstrate some of the limitations of the IP, however. While an IP can help safeguard the contracting process against corruption, there is no guarantee that once underway the project will not be plagued by irregularities or unethical decision taking, potentially leading to massive cost overruns. The federal government should allow for civil society to go beyond the contracting process and oversee the execution of a public works project for compliance with the contract.

The tender process may be corrupted by international pressure. For example, the government of a developed country may influence the government of a developing country to make sure that a company from the developed country is awarded a project, even if it is not the cheapest or best option. Such pressure can take many forms, including the offer of aid, arms deals or agreements to support a government's application to join an international organisation. Great lengths are taken to conceal this pressure in some cases. In others, it is remarkably overt.

Although these examples relate mainly to major contract awards, the same principles apply all the way down the contractual chain. At the bottom end, a supplier may make a payment of US $100 to the procurement manager of a company in exchange for a minor supply contract. At the top end, the main contractor may pay US $50 million to the representative of a government in return for the award of a major infrastructure project.

Deception and collusion
Deception and collusion in the award of contracts takes many forms, typically involving a cartel:

- A group of contractors ostensibly in competition may secretly collude, agreeing to share future projects between them so as to keep prices high. They choose the winning bidder for a specific project and note the price to be submitted by the bidder they have agreed to pre-select. They all tender, but at prices higher than their favoured contractor, who the client then chooses as the cheapest option. The client is deceived into believing there was genuine competition in the bidding process.

- A group of contractors bidding for a project may secretly agree that each will include a pre-agreed sum in their tender that reflects the estimated aggregate bidding costs of all the tenderers. They do not pre-select the winning bidder, but tender in open competition. Whichever bidder is awarded the project then divides the pre-agreed sum between all the other tenderers as a 'loser's fee'.

- A group of suppliers of materials may collude to fix the minimum price of the materials they supply. Even when there is competitive tendering, prices will be kept higher than would be the case with genuine competition.

This form of collusion is often accompanied by bribery. For example, a bribe may be paid to a client's representative in order to obtain internal information on the expected budget, or to limit the number of bidders allowed.

Corruption during construction

Bribery
Bribery does not stop on the award of the contract. There are many actions after the award of a contract that can have a significant financial impact on the participants and which are therefore prone to bribery:

1. **Agreeing 'variations' to the contract.** It is rare for a contract to be completed in precisely the same form as originally agreed. Changes to the design or construction method may be required due to error in the original design, the intervening circumstances (such as unknown ground conditions), or the client's decision to change the requirements after the project is started. Changes to design or method are normally reflected in 'variations' (or 'change orders') to the contract. Variations

normally have cost consequences, as parts of the agreed work may be wasted, new items may have to be ordered, or additional labour and materials may be required. Variations therefore create opportunities for bribery between the contractor and the representative of the client, or the architect or engineer responsible for authorising the variation and approving its cost consequences. Major infrastructure projects can contain thousands of variations, ranging in cost from a few hundred to several million dollars. The cost effect is not only felt at the level of the main contract. Because of the complexity of the contractual structure in large construction projects, the effects and costs of variations need to be agreed between all affected participants, offering multiple opportunities for bribery.

2. **Concealing deferred bribes.** Variations provide a mechanism to conceal deferred bribes. A contractor may win a contract tender as the lowest-priced bidder without including a bribe in the contract price, but with a clandestine arrangement with the client's representative that a large variation including a bribe will be agreed at a later stage. Deferring a bribe until after the appointment of the contractor can be an effective means of concealment since there is no competitive tender for variations, and post-contract variations attract much less publicity than competitive tenders. The price of any variation (and of the bribe concealed within it) can therefore be extremely significant.

3. **Project delays.** It is very common for a project to finish later than scheduled whether due to adverse weather, variations, subcontractor failure or defective materials. The cost effect of delay can be significant. If the delay is the contractor's fault, the client may be entitled to claim liquidated damages from the contractor. If the delay is the client's fault, the contractor may be entitled to claim additional costs for delay and disruption from the client. As a result, the person responsible for agreeing the time and cost effect of delays is vulnerable to bribery. These ramifications may be felt all the way down the contractual structure, offering multiple opportunities for bribery.

4. **Concealing substandard work.** The quality of construction is central to a project. Since a large proportion of the work and materials is concealed as the project progresses, it can be difficult or costly to verify bad workmanship or inferior materials after the work has been covered. Therefore, checkers need to certify work as it progresses. These checkers are vulnerable to bribes to certify that defective or non-existent work is acceptable. The defects may not be discovered until many years later.

While some of the above examples depict the contractor bribing the architect or the client's representative, the converse is equally possible. The client may bribe the architect to certify falsely that the contractor delayed the project, with the result that the client is entitled to deduct liquidated damages from payments due to the contractor. The client may bribe the project engineer to certify falsely that the contractor's works are defective, entitling the client to withhold the contractor's retention payment.

The dispute resolution process is also not immune. Witnesses can be paid to give false evidence; experts can be paid for false 'independent' reports; and judges or arbitrators can be bribed to hand down favourable judgments. Construction disputes can be very complex: it may be difficult to prove that the opinions of witnesses, experts and judges have been unfairly influenced. Bribes to witnesses or experts may be cash, but they could equally involve the promise of future or continued employment.

Deception

Deceptive practices during project execution do not receive the same level of attention as bribes paid to win contracts, but deception is extremely common during this phase and may exceed the costs of bribery in terms of financial wastage. Deception involves actions that many people in construction regard not as corrupt, but as 'part of the game'. Deception can have an enormous impact on the overall contract price. It can occur at every contractual link and the cost of overcharges at the bottom end of the contractual ladder may be passed all the way up with a charge added at every rung, magnifying the cost of the initial deception. This is known as claims fraud or claims inflation.

- As noted earlier, variations can be made to the scope of contracts during execution and projects can be delayed. The cost consequences of variations and delays are sometimes resolved to the advantage of one contractual party through bribery, but a more common response is deceptive conduct. If the client issues a contractor with a variation order to change the scope of work, the contractor may take the opportunity to exaggerate the cost of the variation or the delay it causes. The contractor may also blame a delay that is the contractor's own fault on the client or the architect in a bid to avoid liquidated damages for delay, and to entitle the contractor to claim additional costs from the client.

- The client may also create artificial claims against the contractor. For example, a client may falsely allege that the contractor has delayed the project, or used inferior work or materials, in order to lay the foundations for an exaggerated or false claim to set off against sums due to the contractor. In doing so, the client knows the contractor can only receive payment by going to court or arbitration, which is expensive and time-consuming. The client may hope that the contractor will either give up the claim, or settle for a lesser payment than the amount actually due.

- An architect appointed by the client to work in the dual and conflicting roles of designer and certifier may avoid issuing a certificate entitling the contractor to additional cost or an extension of time, if the cause of that cost or time was a design error by the architect. This is deceptive conduct by the architect, who should exercise the function of certifier impartially.

- Deceptive practices by subcontractors and suppliers can also inflate project costs. A scaffolding firm may exaggerate the amount of scaffolding on site, or the number of men used to put it in place. An earth-works subcontractor may falsify the amount of earth removed.

- Lawyers and other professional advisers, whose livelihood depends on claims, can materially exacerbate the situation. They may allocate too many staff to work on a claim, charge for too many hours of work or give the client over-optimistic advice as to the likelihood of a claim's success.

- A contractor or client may enhance the deception by appointing an 'independent' expert to give testimony to support their case. An independent expert is meant to be impartial so as to help the dispute resolution tribunal come to a decision. If the expert gives an opinion which is not independent but slanted to one party's case, it may have a significant impact on the outcome of the hearing. Similarly, employees may give evidence that they know to be false in order to help their employer win a case.

- In many claims, a significant amount of false extra cost is added as a 'negotiation margin'. The claimant's logic in including this margin is that the opponent will automatically seek to reduce the claim and so a sufficient margin must be added to enable negotiations to arrive at the 'correct' figure.

Corruption during operation and maintenance

Once the project is completed, it will need to be operated and maintained. The operation of the project may require the supply of consumables such as fuel and raw materials. Roads need to be repaired and industrial plants need routine maintenance, repair and refurbishment.

As many opportunities for bribery and deception exist in this phase as during the contract award and construction phases. Bribes can be paid to win operation and maintenance contracts, and deceptive practices can lead to inflated costs. In many projects, the cost of operation and maintenance will exceed the actual capital cost of constructing the project. As a result, the opportunities for bribery may be greater.

Sometimes the same contractors that build the plant will also operate and maintain it, and so the bribe paid to win the main contract may also cover operation and maintenance. In some public/private projects, where a private consortium builds, owns and operates a project and then supplies the government or local utility with the end product, substantial opportunities exist for bribery in relation to agreeing the price that will be paid for the end product.

In high-technology projects, the contractor that built the project may be the only company capable of maintaining it. This gives it a monopoly of supply during the maintenance period, making cost comparisons difficult, and increasing the opportunities for concealing bribes and inflating claims.

In addition, high operating and maintenance costs may be a direct result of corruption during the contract award or construction phase. Corruption in the bidding process may be linked to the over-specification of a project, which may increase the costs of operation and maintenance. Corruption in the construction process may lower the standard of construction, increasing the subsequent need for expensive repair and maintenance.

Countering bribery

The construction sector is complex, diverse and fragmented, all of which contribute to a lack of effective control and the absence of uniform integrity standards. When combined with the complexity of the contractual structure, enormous opportunities are provided for corruption to flourish. The lack of transparency surrounding projects and the contentious environment both tend toward bribery and deception. The fact that bribery and deception are such common parts of industry practice leads many participants to accept them as the status quo, rather than attempt to change the way business is done. However, there are things that can be done – this report's recommendations (see page 65) set out concrete proposals for reform – and positive steps are being taken by some businesses to counter bribery in the sector (see Box 2.3).

Box 2.3   WEF task force adopts the Business Principles for Countering Bribery

Transparency International

At the World Economic Forum's (WEF) Annual Meeting at Davos, Switzerland, in January 2003, some leading engineering and construction companies formed the WEF Governors' Engineering and Construction Task Force in order to tackle corruption in the sector. The Task Force, working in close collaboration with Transparency International and the Basel Institute on Governance, met several times during 2003. As a result of agreements achieved at these meetings, 19 leading international companies from 15 countries with aggregate annual revenues in excess of US $70 billion signed the 'Business Principles for Countering Bribery in the Engineering and Construction Industry' at the WEF meeting at Davos in January 2004. This document was closely modelled on the 'Business Principles for Countering Bribery' developed in 2002 by Transparency International, in conjunction with Social Accountability International and several leading multinationals. An organisation which adopts the Business Principles commits:

- to adopt a policy that bribery in any form is prohibited;
- to implement a management programme which puts into effect its anti-bribery policy.

The Business Principles also provide practical guidance in relation to the scope and implementation of the anti-bribery programme.

Engineering and construction companies have traditionally been unwilling to take a public stand against corruption. The public announcement of the adoption of the Business Principles by these 19 companies broke with this tradition, and proves that key companies in the international industry believe that something can and must be done to deal with corruption. As Alan Boeckmann, chair and CEO of Fluor Corporation and head of the WEF Governors describes, 'nothing has been more frustrating than losing a great opportunity to a competitor who is willing to pay bribes'.

The Task Force continued to meet during 2004. These meetings focused on the following key issues:

- How to increase the number of international construction companies which adopt the Business Principles. In order to have any real effect on corruption, a significant

▶

majority of companies in the sector must commit to effective anti-corruption policies. Each member of the Task Force agreed to try to bring in additional signatories from its own territory or sector.

- How to ensure that companies that announce they have adopted the Business Principles are actually implementing a genuine anti-corruption programme. One of the ways of achieving this would be to obtain external accreditation of a company's anti-corruption programme. This idea is actively being pursued by the Task Force.
- How to ensure that companies that implement an effective anti-corruption programme are rewarded, and not penalised, for doing so. If some companies adopt an anti-corruption programme, and others do not, those that do not may continue to win work though bribery, therefore disadvantaging those that refuse to bribe. One way of ensuring that ethical companies are rewarded, is to request international financing institutions such as the World Bank, and public sector clients, to permit bids for projects only from companies that have adopted the Business Principles. In due course, once a system of external accreditation of the Business Principles has been established, only companies that have achieved the accreditation should be placed on bidders' lists. The Task Force has commenced discussions with the World Bank on this proposal and is greatly encouraged that the World Bank will in future require borrowers on large projects to certify that they will neither directly nor indirectly engage in bribery.

The next issue requiring urgent consideration by the Task Force is what inspection mechanisms should be put in place within projects to ensure that companies do not bribe. As with all voluntary codes, sceptics will question the credibility of subscribing companies' intentions. If bidders' lists require anti-bribery policies as a condition precedent, some companies may adopt them so as to reach the bidders' list, but will in practice continue to bribe. This could prejudice the companies that do adhere to the anti-bribery policy, and it is therefore in those companies' interests that proper inspection and enforcement mechanisms are put in place. TI has proposed to the Task Force the inspection and enforcement mechanisms referred to on pages 65–70.

Notes

1. Neill Stansbury is project director for construction & engineering at TI(UK). He is a lawyer specialising in the construction and engineering industry.
2. Transparency International's 2002 Bribe Payers Index (summarised in the *Global Corruption Report 2003*) reported that construction/public works are perceived to have the highest level of bribery of any sector, higher than both the arms industry and the oil and gas sector. Control Risks Group carried out a survey of business leaders in six developed countries (Britain, Germany, Hong Kong, Netherlands, Singapore and the United States), which also found construction/public works to be the most corrupt sector of all. See *Facing Up to Corruption* (London: Control Risks, 2002), summarised in the *Global Corruption Report 2004*.
3. UNCTAD, Regulation and Liberalization in the Construction Services Sector and its Contribution to the Development of Developing Countries (UNCTAD, 2000), available at www.unctad.org/en/docs/c1em12d2.en.pdf
4. TI defines 'corruption' as 'the abuse of entrusted power for private gain'. The expression 'corruption' in this article includes both bribery and deception.

Case study: Oversized incinerator burns up Cologne's cash

Hans Leyendecker[1]

A trial in Germany, which concluded in 2004, revealed the scale of bribery in the construction of waste processing facilities. The scale of abuse is due, among other reasons, to the low number of contractors sharing the market for lucrative large-scale projects. In the country's waste-disposal sector, bribery has come to be known as 'artificial respiration'. In the case of a waste incinerator being built in Cologne, among the last projects of its kind, competition for the contract was especially fierce.

Cologne, Germany's fourth largest city, has always been known for a somewhat fluid approach to rules and ethical standards. The saying 'live and let live' is a local favourite, capturing a laissez-faire attitude known as 'Kölner Klüngel', the Cologne clique system – a misleadingly harmless name.

The dominant political parties, the Christian Democratic Union and the Social Democratic party (SPD), are part of this clique system. Their representatives often assist each other, passing along official posts and contracts. The assistance is even non-partisan: winners prop up losers, because one never knows who will be on top tomorrow.

In 2002 the city was rocked by one scandal in particular. Investigations exposed the flow of approximately DM 21.6 million (US $13.3 million) in bribes into local pockets during the construction of a half-billion dollar waste incineration plant in a Cologne suburb. Politicians, managers and lobbyists were all involved in the affair. What emerged was an endlessly corrupt and distasteful web that ensnared the city's political caste.

A web unravels

The discovery began with an anonymous tip-off. In June 2000 an informant told local tax authorities that millions of deutschmarks in kickbacks had changed hands during the construction of a waste incinerator in the 1990s. Investigators were initially sceptical. A similar investigation in 1996 had got nowhere.

This time around, federal and regional officials were investigating bribe payments in conjunction with large-scale construction projects elsewhere. So as Cologne officials rummaged through federal archives, they found interesting data on the construction sector in their backyard and across the country. It seemed the entire waste-processing landscape had been fertilised with cash.

Dishonest designs

Investigators then took a series of suspects into custody, including a former construction manager, a civil servant, industry lobbyists and an SPD official. It appeared that stacks of tainted cash had changed hands at every stage of the venture. Even years later, though, just who had initiated the scheme remained unclear.

An engineer who has designed half of all garbage incinerators in Germany, Hans Reimer, alleged that he met with a civil servant named Ulrich Eisermann in the early 1990s to talk about an engineering contract for the planned incineration facility. Eisermann allegedly remarked at the time that DM 20 million (US $12 million) in kickbacks should be built into the price. The engineer, who maintains that bribes are paid on many large-scale projects, turned down the offer. Eisermann denies the conversation ever took place.

A clique comes together

In 1993 the manager of construction firm LCS Steinmüller met with Eisermann, the official in charge of the project. In a delicate conversation, the manager allegedly indicated how badly his company needed the contract, so badly in fact that they were ready to bribe.

Although willing, neither knew how to go about it. That was when garbage entrepreneur Hellmut Trienekens entered the game. With his extensive experience, Trienekens was able to recommend conducting bribe payments via Switzerland. He had been playing the political field for years and knew all the right channels. He had shown great interest in being involved in the waste incinerator project and he was, with his network of influence, an essential partner.

A crooked scheme

Eisermann was to ensure that LCS Steinmüller got the contract for constructing the plant. There were four bidders for the project, which had a number of phases. Eisermann had been instructed by his superiors to choose as general contractor the firm that came in as cheapest on the greatest number of project phases.

According to evidence revealed in the trial, Eisermann took the proposals home, opened the sealed envelopes with steam and carefully removed the offer letters. He had agreed with LCS Steinmüller boss Sigfrid Michelfelder to write up the competing offers to the last detail. That same night he gave the note to Michelfelder, who revised his firm's offer. Some components were cheaper, others now more expensive. The cost of the gas flue cleaning system, for example, had increased by over DM 10 million (US $6 million). Eisermann accepted the new offer, slipped it into the original envelope and resealed it. The scheme worked. LCS Steinmüller won the contract with Trienekens as the waste facility's co-partner.

The political parties were active from the beginning, with certain politicians lobbying vociferously for the garbage plant. They used their influence with Eisermann to strategically place major construction firms as subcontractors in the project. The parties knew that they could count on quasi-legal contributions, known as 'thank you' donations, from firms that won public contracts through the parties' lobbying efforts.

Later, at trial, the local SPD was particularly implicated. Under-secretary Norbert Rüther allegedly collected 30 such dubious donations[2] – some with, some without, a receipt. A party treasurer had accepted a total of DM 510,000 (US $320,000) in major contributions originating from LCS Steinmüller and other contractors. He allegedly wove the funds into the party's account by writing receipts to party supporters for donations they never made. In a further blow, Eisermann claimed to have paid Rüther a DM 2 million (US $1.2 million) bribe for initially advocating for the incinerator project in the city council. Rüther consistently repudiated the charge.

Once the project was underway, general contractor LCS Steinmüller regularly transferred millions of deutschmarks into the account of a shell company with a Zurich address by the name of Stenna Umwelttechnik AG (Stenna Environmental Engineering). Although an offshore entity, Stenna was responsible for monitoring the Cologne project's engineering services. A manager from LCS Steinmüller later went on record as saying that the Swiss staff of Stenna had 'randomly added official stamps and legal provisions' to documents and had 'only pretended to verify anything'.

The arrangement was a profitable one for Stenna. The shell company billed more than DM 4 million (US $2.5 million) for taxes, banking fees and operation costs. But then, because the illicit cash flow no longer seemed safe, the connection to Stenna was dissolved in 1996 and a new shell firm was activated.

The bitter end

In May 2004 the Cologne corruption trial came to an end. Trial judges accused public prosecutors of having withheld relevant documentary evidence until it was too late for the defence to make use of it. Consequently, the accused came away with mild sentences.

Eisermann, who was alleged to have received the lion's share of bribe payments, was given a prison sentence of three years and nine months. Michelfelder, director of LCS Steinmüller, came away with a suspended sentence but had to pay a €1 million fine (US $1.2 million). There is broad speculation in the media that Trienekens collected a portion of the kickbacks – a fact he vehemently denies. He was initially sentenced to two years' imprisonment, but the sentence was reduced to two years' probation on the condition that he post €10 million bail, the highest amount ever imposed for a tax-related crime. Social Democrat Rüther was cleared of all charges.

The crux of the matter was not individual shortcomings. The presiding judge explained that not only 'in developing nations, but also in Germany, it is customary for people to help themselves when it comes to major construction projects'. Council members had 'allowed themselves to be drawn in on all sides'. Garbage entrepreneur Trienekens had seen to it that that an 'unending list of donations' flowed to local politicians. Damage of 'immense proportions' had been incurred.

The story illustrates that corruption always has its victims. In this case they were, once again, ordinary citizens: after all the crooked dealings, their municipal garbage collection fees had tripled, and the city had landed a facility larger than it could possibly use. The project had initially been designed to process around 400,000 tonnes per year. Behind the scenes, the influential garbage lobby manipulated figures and was able to push through a far larger facility. Trienekens even imported refuse from Naples in specially chartered trains to be incinerated in oversized plants, scattered throughout the Rhine-Ruhr region. There was money to be earned in garbage.

Notes

1. Hans Leyendecker is one of Germany's most renowned investigative journalists. Since 1997 he has been senior political editor at the *Süddeutsche Zeitung*, a major German daily.
2. *Süddeutsche Zeitung* (Germany), 11 November 2003.

3 International finance and corruption

A migrant carries a desk salvaged from her home as she moves across the Yangtze River to Fengdu town, upriver from the giant Three Gorges dam project. Citing the potential for environmental damage, the World Bank and the US Export-Import Bank declined to back the project and China turned to competing Export Credit Agencies with lower standards. Amid accusations of widespread corruption, including the diverting of relocation funds, more than a million people are being forced to move due to the dam. (GOH CHAI HIN/AFP/Getty Images)

Financing corruption? The role of Multilateral Development Banks and Export Credit Agencies

Susan Hawley[1]

Infrastructure projects – where the vast majority of construction contracts are won – have had a bad name. Grandiose, unnecessary, 'white elephant' projects have diverted precious resources away from vital services and saddled developing countries with bad debts. The economic and social benefits of necessary and much-needed infrastructure projects meanwhile have been whittled away, if not eliminated completely, by corruption.

Many of the large infrastructure projects around the world that have been plagued by corruption allegations were backed in part by either a multilateral development bank (MDB) or an export credit agency (ECA). Many of the projects in developing countries mentioned in this report, such as the Lesotho Highlands Water Project, have been backed by one or both types of body. Given their major role in financing, and facilitating finance for, infrastructure projects, MDBs and ECAs have a critical role to play in preventing corruption in the construction sector. While they have taken significant steps in recent years, serious vulnerabilities remain.

The scale of international finance for infrastructure

According to the World Bank, 'the greatest source of finance [for infrastructure in developing countries] traditionally has been commercial banks, often in connection with officially backed export credit agencies and multilateral organizations'.[2] Without support from either an ECA or an MDB, projects in poorer, unstable or high-risk developing countries would often not go ahead.

In 2002, the MDBs, consisting of the World Bank and the regional development banks, together spent US $16.6 billion on infrastructure, which represented 39 per cent of their overall spending.[3] Since 2003 the World Bank has started to re-prioritise infrastructure, and is set to increase its infrastructure lending from US $5.4 billion to US $7 billion by 2005.

Despite the fact that their direct funding for infrastructure is small compared with the total estimated global spending of US $250 billion annually on infrastructure,[4] the MDBs are highly influential in this field, for three reasons:

- *MDBs act as a catalyst for further financial support from the private sector.* MDBs' private sector arms, particularly the World Bank's International Finance Corporation and Multilateral Investment Guarantees Agency, are influential in mobilising private sector support for infrastructure projects.

- *MDB projects are a major source of contracts for companies.* World Bank-financed projects result in 40,000 contracts being awarded annually and account for one-third of total international contracts in developing countries.[5]

- *MDBs help set developing countries' policy on infrastructure.* Privatisation of infrastructure has featured as a condition in many structural adjustment loans to developing countries, and has been a significant factor behind the 58 per cent increase in foreign construction contracts between 1986 and 1998.

ECAs are, for the most part, governmental or semi-governmental agencies that help their domestic companies and banks win investment and export business overseas, through a mixture of government-backed loans, guarantees and insurance. ECAs tend to provide cover for larger sums, longer periods and higher-risk countries than the private sector is willing to do.

Despite their relative anonymity, ECAs are the largest source of publicly backed finance for private sector projects, and particularly of large-scale infrastructure projects in the developing world. During the 1990s, export credit backing of project finance for infrastructure projects grew dramatically. In 2002, long-term credits (of over five years) from the ECAs of OECD countries to the construction and engineering sectors stood at around US $2 billion, up from around US $900 million in 1998.[6] This figure does not take into account, however, the involvement of construction and engineering companies in other sectors, particularly energy generation and supply (which received US $1.8 billion of long-term credits in 2002) and transport (which received nearly US $7.5 billion of such credits in 2002).[7] Nor does it take into account short-term credits and investment insurance, which would make the total value of ECA backing for infrastructure much higher.

How public international financial institutions aggravate corruption

Until recently, the impact of MDBs and ECAs in facilitating corruption in the construction and other sectors, primarily through negligence, was largely overlooked by these institutions and the governments that support them. As the damage caused by corruption has moved up the policy agenda, however, their role has increasingly come under scrutiny. According to one recent estimate, between US $26 billion and US $130 billion (5–25 per cent) of the US $525 billion lent by the World Bank since 1946 may have been misused or lost to corruption.[8] The World Bank contests this estimate.

High levels of corruption in MDB-backed projects have been blamed on several factors, which include weaknesses in the MDBs themselves. First, the institutional 'pressure to lend' leads to an emphasis on, and staff incentives for, the quantity rather than quality of projects supported.

Second, and equally important, are weak internal controls at the banks, particularly in the supervision and auditing of projects. In the mid to late 1990s, the US General Accounting Office found that audit reports on projects were poor quality, financial management supervision often unsatisfactory, and intensive procurement reviews rare. In 1998–99, only 54 out of 1,500 projects had such a review.[9] At other development banks, observers have reported poor project evaluation, including a 'no fail' culture of internal evaluations.[10] Accounting for how funds disbursed through structural adjustment loans have been spent remains, in the words of one expert, 'the weakest link in the system'.[11]

A third factor exacerbating corruption in MDB-backed projects has been inadequate due diligence and risk assessment. Assessing the risks of corruption to the economic viability of a project, and to its potential environmental and social impacts, whether posed by the country and sector in which the project is taking place or the track record of a company awarded a contract, has not been, until recent years, fully mainstreamed in project assessments.

Two final factors are the banks' lack of accountability and transparency. The legal immunity enjoyed by the banks, and the lack of active oversight by most member countries, undermines the incentive for banks to practise optimal financial management and root out corruption. At the same time, while some banks, particularly the World Bank, have gone a long way to becoming more transparent in recent years, the full and timely disclosure of many documents is still lacking.

Because ECAs have no development or social remit, and exist solely to support domestic exports and foreign investment, preventing corruption has never been high on their agenda.

Almost all ECAs have the potential to underwrite bribes directly, whether knowingly or not, because the cost of commission payments made by companies to win a contract – long recognised as a route through which bribes may be paid – is included in the overall sum that they underwrite. Former Director-General for Development at the European Union, Dieter Frisch, has described this as 'an indirect encouragement to bribe'.[12] Despite the risks involved in underwriting commission payments, the practice of requiring full details on what such payments were for, and to whom they were paid, is only a very recent development, and not universally observed.

ECA negligence towards corruption takes other forms. ECAs have had poor due diligence procedures with regard to risks posed by corruption in the countries and sectors where they operate. For example, many ECAs do not check, let alone require, that contracts they back are won through competitive tender or transparent procurement methods. ECAs have given support for projects, in some instances, despite publicised allegations of corruption and concerns raised by other donor agencies, and have failed to investigate bribery allegations when they have arisen. Companies embroiled in corruption scandals have meanwhile continued to receive ECA support, and faced little sanction. Unlike the MDBs, few ECAs say they will use debarment as a sanction for bribery, and none has ever done so in practice.[13] Finally, ECAs have historically lacked transparency. Until recently, few ECAs disclosed publicly the projects that they supported and, even today, disclosure is patchy.

Recent anti-corruption reforms

In recent years, major strides in recognising the problem of corruption have been taken – partly as a result of external pressure from NGOs – at both MDBs and ECAs. There is considerable room for improvement, however, if corruption in the infrastructure sector is to be rooted out.

The World Bank has led the way on fighting corruption among MDBs. Since 1995, when James Wolfensohn took over as president, the World Bank has introduced various new measures to improve its anti-corruption procedures and has placed corruption firmly on the policy agenda. The other regional development banks have been slower in adopting anti-corruption procedures. All MDBs, however, have now taken a range of steps, including the debarment of companies found guilty of fraud and corruption (see Box 3.1), and have, or are in the process of creating, some form of unit that investigates and penalises fraud and corruption.

Box 3.1 Blacklisting corrupt companies

Juanita Olaya[1]

'Blacklisting' or 'debarment' in the realm of public contracting is a process whereby, on the basis of pre-established grounds, a company or individual is prevented from engaging in further contracts for a specified period of time. Debarment may be preceded by a warning of future exclusion should the conduct persist, be repeated, or occur under aggravated circumstances. An investigation that could lead to debarment may be promoted by an existing judicial decision, or when there is strong evidence of unethical or unlawful professional or business behaviour. Many debarment systems today allow the latter form as judicial decisions are often slow to obtain.

The key function of debarment in public contracting is prevention and deterrence. For companies debarment means a damaged reputation, lost business prospects and even bankruptcy. It therefore increases the opportunity cost of engaging in corrupt practices.

Debarment systems have been around for some time, both at the national and the international level. The US debarment system is among the oldest, and its grounds for debarment include anti-trust violations, tax evasion and false statements, in addition to bribery in procurement-related activities. The World Bank has taken the lead internationally: its debarment system was made publicly available in 1998. Since 2003, the European Commission's financial regulations have included a debarment system that is currently being developed. Almost all development banks now have debarment systems of some kind and, at the national level, many countries have, or are seriously considering, blacklisting systems.[2]

Many of the current debarment systems have been criticised for being closed, poorly publicised or unfair, and for failing to include big companies with proven involvement in corrupt deals.[3] The debarment of Acres International Ltd by the World Bank (see page 33) signals an emboldening of institutions that wish to demonstrate intolerance of corruption. The decision to debar Acres also helps dispel the fear that debarment agencies might face reprisals, such as allegations of slander or misjudgement.

The two main problems Transparency International has encountered with blacklisting are: an unwillingness to debar on the basis of 'strong evidence' (without a court order); and resistance to giving the public access to blacklists.

In order to be effective and to stand up to scrutiny and possible legal challenges, certain steps need to be taken when designing and implementing a debarment system. Effective debarment systems must be fair and accountable, transparent, well publicised, timely and unbiased.

1. **Fairness and accountability.** Clear rules and procedures need to be established and made known to all the parties involved in a contracting process, ahead of time. The process needs to give firms and individuals an adequate opportunity to defend themselves.
2. **Transparency.** Sanctions and the rules regarding the process must be made public in order to minimise the risk of the debarment system being subjected to manipulation or pressure. The outcomes must also be publicised. Contracting authorities and export credit agencies need to be given access to detailed information from the debarment list so that they can carry out due diligence on potential contractors (for overseas tenders this might mean accessing the debarment system in the home country).

▶

This process is especially complicated because owners of debarred companies may simply start up a new company operating under a new name. Up-to-date public debarment lists can help procurement officers and due diligence analysts keep track of such cases. Publicity also has an important impact on the legitimacy, credibility and accountability of debarment agencies, and facilitates monitoring by independent parties. The information made public in debarment lists needs to include the company or individual's name, the grounds for investigation, the name of the project, the country of origin of sanctioned firms or individuals, as well as the rules governing the process.

3. **Functionality.** Publicly available debarment lists facilitate electronic matching and other information-sharing features that organisations such as the World Bank's International Finance Corporation already have in place. Systems could be interconnected internationally, for example, among development banks, or between countries. Such networking may even reduce operating costs, and make systems more effective.

4. **Timeliness.** Debarment systems should be timely. The Lesotho case (see page 31) shows that delays in beginning the debarment process increase costs and erode credibility.

5. **Proportionality.** For some companies, being barred from a particular market might mean bankruptcy, so in certain cases a debarment of five years could be too much. The system should allow for a sliding scale of penalties, and should provide entry and exit rules. If a company has shown that, after the offence, it implemented substantial changes, for example, by enforcing codes of conduct, or changing policies and practices, it should be possible to lift the debarment.

Notes
1. Juanita Olaya is the programme manager for public contracting at Transparency International.
2. These countries include: Bangladesh, Brazil, China, the Czech Republic, France, Germany, India, Kenya, Nepal, Pakistan, the Philippines, Romania, Senegal, Singapore, South Africa, South Korea, Sweden, Tanzania, Turkey, Uganda, the United States and Zimbabwe.
3. See, for example, Steven Schooner, 'The Paper Tiger Stirs: Rethinking Suspension and Debarment', *Public Procurement Law Review*, forthcoming in 2004, and related articles in the same issue.

In addition to imposing sanctions, the World Bank has developed stricter procurement guidelines, and improved financial management and oversight. Anti-corruption efforts are now a key focus of the bank's analysis and lending decisions. Diagnostic work on governance and corruption risks has been expanded, and transparency has been improved. The other regional development banks have in some instances followed suit, though many fall well behind the World Bank in their procedures.[14]

Despite these improvements, many commentators believe that there is considerable scope for enhancing anti-corruption procedures at the World Bank, and even more so at the other regional development banks.

Areas of ongoing weakness in MDB anti-corruption procedures include:

- Staff time for supervision has been reduced and resources for supervision remain low.[15] Resources at the units that safeguard institutional integrity, particularly at the regional development banks, are insufficient.

- MDBs do not require anti-bribery compliance or corporate governance programmes by companies as a prerequisite for receiving contracts. The World Bank's recent requirement for companies bidding on large civil works projects to certify that they have 'taken steps to ensure that no person acting for us or on our behalf will engage in bribery'[16] is a small step in the right direction. However, it will be meaningless unless the World Bank employs active due diligence with regard to companies and their use of agents, and fully inspects and enforces company certification.

- A report in July 2004 from the Government Accountability Project found that 'none of the banks have reliably safe channels for whistleblowers to make a difference against corruption'.[17]

- Mainstreaming anti-corruption has yet to be fully achieved. For example, the World Bank's 2003 Infrastructure Action Plan makes no mention of corruption, despite the fact that support for 'high-risk' projects is to be increased, and despite the known risks of corruption in infrastructure projects. Mainstreaming anti-corruption could include: staff incentives that reward corruption-free projects; rigorous corruption risk assessment throughout project cycles, such as in the calculation of the economic rate of return, and environmental and social impact assessments; and extending the commitment made by the World Bank with regard to the extractive industries sector (to operate governance indicators and refuse support to new investment 'where the risks are deemed too great and cannot be mitigated'[18]) to all sectors, including infrastructure.

- Disclosure and transparency could be improved further and public participation increased. Oversight would be enhanced by the publication of documents throughout a project's lifecycle, including audit reports, all contracts between the government and contractors and subcontractors, and full details of the bidding process on Bank-backed projects, including initial budget and final budget, as well as of more general MDB documents such as board minutes and correspondence, and performance evaluations. Citizen participation in project design and in oversight committees would help reduce opportunities for corruption – a fact the World Bank recognises and in some instances has taken on board.

Over the last four years, the OECD's Working Party on Export Credits and Credit Guarantees (ECG) has undertaken considerable work on the issue of bribery in export credits. This includes:

- In December 2000, the ECG issued an Action Statement on Bribery and Officially Supported Export Credits, under which ECAs agreed to: inform applicants about the legal consequences of bribery; 'invite' applicants to sign a no-bribery warranty; refuse support where there was 'sufficient evidence' of bribery; and take appropriate action against any company where bribery was proven after support had been given.

- Since 2002 the ECG has periodically published a survey of member country procedures to combat bribery in officially supported export credits.

- In November 2003, the ECG issued 'Best Practices to Deter and Combat Bribery in Officially Supported Export Credits' – a document still under negotiation during 2004 that suggested several best practices that should be made official ECA practice. The 11 best practices include: requiring details on commission payments over 5 per cent; requiring companies to declare whether they have been blacklisted by a multilateral organisation or convicted of bribery by a court; automatic referral of suspicions of bribery to national investigative authorities; application of enhanced due diligence where suspicion of bribery arises; suspension of payments and support to companies where sufficient evidence of bribery emerges until an official investigation is concluded; and application of all possible sanctions, including debarment, where a company is convicted.

- During 2004, there were ongoing negotiations about revising and enhancing the OECD's original Action Statement to reflect emerging best practices, and bribery was one of the important priorities for discussion at the ECG.

Despite these important steps, there remain considerable weaknesses in ECA anti-corruption procedures. The best practices outlined by the OECD have by no means been universally adopted, and few of them appear to have been put to the test in practice. Between November 2002 and May 2004, only five countries took any action with regards to suspicions and evidence of bribery.

The main areas of ongoing weakness are:

- *Agents.* Despite the OECD Best Practices paper and the obvious risks of backing agents' commissions without strong safeguards, nine ECAs, including those of Canada, Germany, Italy, and Sweden, still do not require companies to provide any details of the commission payments they underwrite.[19] High standards for due diligence on agents' commissions are essential, and some ECAs, particularly Britain's Export Credits Guarantee Department, are leading the way in this regard.

- *Debarment.* Both the commentaries on the OECD Anti-Bribery Convention and the OECD's 1997 Revised Recommendations on Combating Bribery specifically recommend exclusion from publicly supported commercial activities as a sanction. Only the Swiss, New Zealand, Danish and Canadian ECAs, however, say they would debar companies convicted of corruption, and Canada would not do so if the company puts in place anti-corruption management procedures. Debarment for a specific period of time is a powerful tool for changing company behaviour, and would have a strong deterrent effect.

- *Due diligence.* ECAs by their very nature operate in high-risk environments. Ensuring that the projects they provide support for are free of corruption, and that the companies they back are operating good corporate governance standards, is key both for the integrity of the project and of the ECA itself. Requiring companies to have an externally monitored anti-corruption compliance programme or ethical code, and that contracts to be backed are won through competitive tender or transparent procurement processes, would be major steps forward.

- *Transparency.* Proper disclosure of both ECA policies and project information is essential for fostering accountability. Recent international developments with regard to ECA disclosure of details on high-risk projects prior to approval need to be extended to all projects. Most importantly, mechanisms to make communities aware of projects under consideration, and to allow for stakeholder consultation for such projects, need to be developed. The involvement of stakeholders and communities could be an important way of helping ECAs become aware of problems and risks posed by possible corruption at an early stage in the project cycle.

Conclusion

Investment in good infrastructure projects in developing countries is fundamental to reducing poverty and meeting the international community's Millennium Development Goals. By some estimates, developing countries need US $300 billion of annual investment in infrastructure.[20] If future investment in infrastructure in developing countries is to be effective, making certain that infrastructure projects are free of corruption and built on the principles of accountability and transparency is fundamental. Those bodies responsible for providing public international finance for infrastructure need to play a lead role, not least by stepping up their anti-corruption reform efforts.

Notes

1. Susan Hawley is a researcher and policy adviser on corruption issues at the Corner House, a UK-based research and advocacy group focusing on human rights, the environment and development.
2. World Bank, *Global Development Finance 2004* (Washington, DC).
3. Ibid. The World Bank group consists of its two lending arms (IBRD and IDA), its private sector development arm (IFC) and its political risk guarantees provider (MIGA). The regional banks are: the Asian Development Bank, the African Development Bank, the Inter-American Development Bank and the European Bank for Reconstruction and Development. The banks are involved in varying degrees; infrastructure accounts for 25 per cent of World Bank spending, while 42 per cent of the Asian Development Bank's portfolio in 2003 was for roads and transport.
4. United Kingdom Department for International Development, 'Making Connections: Infrastructure for Poverty Reduction' (2002).
5. United Nations Conference on Trade and Development, 'Regulation and Liberalization in the Construction Services Sector and its Contribution to the Development of Developing Countries', 12 September 2000, para. 27.
6. www.oecd.org/dataoecd/13/44/7084900.pdf
7. Ibid.
8. Senator Richard Lugar, 'Opening Statement', Combating Corruption in the Multilateral Development Banks, Senate Foreign Relations Committee, US Senate, 13 May 2004.

9. United States General Accounting Office, 'World Bank: Management Controls Stronger, but Challenges in Fighting Corruption Remain' (2000).
10. Martin Erwin Andersen, 'Corruption Corrodes Development Banks', *Insight on the News*, 1 October 2002; www.interaction.org/files.cgi/3086_IDB_Transparency_Accountability_Corruption_Fact_Sheet.pdf; Steve Herz, 'Zero Tolerance? Assessing the Asian Development Bank's Efforts to Limit Corruption in its Lending Operations' (Washington, DC: Bank Information Center and TERRA, March 2004).
11. Professor Jerome Levinson, Washington College of Law (former General Counsel for the Inter-American Development Bank). 'Statement before the committee on Foreign Relations of the United States Senate: Corruption and Multilateral Development Banks', US Senate, 13 May 2004.
12. Dieter Frisch, 'Export Credit Insurance and the Fight Against International Corruption', TI Working Paper, 26 February 1999.
13. OECD Working Party on Export Credits and Credit Guarantees (ECG), 'Responses to the 2002 Survey on Measures Taken to Combat Bribery in Officially Support Export Credits – as of 14 May 2004'.
14. See John B. Taylor, US Under-Secretary for the Treasury on International Affairs, 'The Multilateral Development Banks and the Fight against Corruption', Testimony before the Senate Foreign Relations Committee, US Senate, 21 July 2004.
15. Nancy Zucker Boswell, Managing Director, TI USA, 'Testimony', Combating Corruption in the Multilateral Development Banks, Senate Foreign Relations Committee, US Senate, 13 May 2004; Manish Bapna, Executive Director, Bank Information Center, 'Testimony', Combating Corruption in the Multilateral Development Banks, Senate Foreign Relations Committee, US Senate, 13 May 2004.
16. Transparency International press release, 'World Bank Move to Reduce Private Sector Bribery Welcomed by Transparency International', 23 September 2004.
17. Government Accountability Project, *Challenging the Culture of Secrecy* (Washington, DC: GAP, 2004).
18. World Bank, 'Striking a Better Balance – The World Bank Group and Extractive Industries: the Final Report of the Extractive Industries Review', Draft World Bank Group Management Response, 4 June 2004.
19. OECD, 'Responses to the 2002 survey'.
20. Berne Union, *Berne Union Yearbook 2004* (London: Berne Union, 2004).

4 Recommendations

Transparency International[1]

A sign stands at the construction site of Sydney's new office and retail centre, the World Square. An annual report released in March 2004 by a government-commissioned taskforce set up to prosecute unions and employers alleged widespread corruption in the construction industry, prompting federal Workplace Relations Minister Kevin Andrews to say 'the culture of unlawfulness and thuggery and intimidation still exists in the building industry'. (GREG WOOD/AFP/Getty Images)

Governments bear the greatest responsibility for ensuring the honest and transparent management of public funds. Governments must put in place rules on public contracting that meet minimum international standards. Transparency International's Minimum Standards for Public Contracting (see page 4) provide a global baseline.

Putting in place the right rules is not enough, however, given the widespread tolerance of corruption within the construction sector and given the frequent failure to enforce laws. Fortunately, actions to curb corruption within the sector are already being taken, by companies themselves, by the banks and export credit agencies (ECAs) that fund infrastructure projects, by civil society and by governments. A few of these initiatives, such as Transparency International's Integrity Pact and the effort by leaders of some of the world's largest construction companies to agree on corporate anti-corruption principles, were outlined in Chapter 1 (see pages 9–27).

None of these actions by itself will change the situation. Both public and private actors, and the banks and ECAs that finance projects, need to work together to eliminate corruption. This chapter addresses recommendations to the different actors involved in the sector which, if followed with rigour, could materially reduce corruption.

The recommendations distinguish between private and public clients because when it is public money that is being used to fund a project the standard of probity must be absolute. However, they acknowledge an overlap between the two spheres: a public contract is unlikely to be executed by the winning company exclusively, but rather by a web of subcontractors with potential for corruption at each private-to-private subcontracting level.

Many of the recommendations are not exclusive to the construction sector, but there are features of the sector, such as its size, complexity and importance to broader service provision, that render them all the more urgent.

1. **Actions for clients (public and private sector)**
   (The term 'client' means the developer or owner of a project, and includes government departments and agencies in the case of public works).

   1.1 Implement a code of conduct which commits the client and its employees to a strict anti-corruption policy.
   1.2 Allow a company to tender for the client's projects only if the company has implemented a code of conduct that commits the company and its employees to a strict anti-corruption policy.
   1.3 Maintain a blacklist of companies that have been found guilty of corruption. Alternatively, adopt a blacklist prepared by an appropriate international institution. Do not allow a blacklisted company to tender for the client's projects for a specified period of time after the offence (see page 59).
   1.4 Require the use of a project integrity pact during both tender and project execution phases (see page 22).
   1.5 Where not covered by integrity pacts, ensure that all contracts between the client and its contractors and suppliers require the parties to comply with strict anti-corruption policies.

2. **Additional actions for public sector clients**
   (The following recommendations summarise Transparency International's Minimum Standards for Public Contracting, see page 4).

2.1 Public contracts above a relatively low threshold should be subject to open competitive bidding. Exceptions must be limited, and clear justification must be given for selecting any other method.

2.2 The contracting authority must provide all bidders, and preferably also the general public, with easy access to information about tender opportunities, selection criteria, the evaluation process, the terms and conditions of the contract and its amendments, and the implementation of the contract and the role of intermediaries and agents. Confidentiality should be limited to legally protected information.

2.3 In order to give a potentially aggrieved competitor the opportunity to challenge the award decision, a reasonable amount of time must be allowed between publication of the contract award decision and the signing of the contract.

2.4 Internal and external control and auditing bodies must be independent and functioning, and their reports should be accessible to the public. Any unreasonable delays in project execution should trigger control activities.

2.5 Contract 'change' orders altering the price or description of work must be monitored at a high level.

2.6 The contracting authority should separate functions, and ensure that responsibility for demand stipulation, preparation, selection, contracting, supervision and control of a project is vested in separate offices.

2.7 The contracting authority should apply the standard office safeguards, such as the four-eyes principle and rotation of staff in sensitive positions. Staff responsible for procurement processes should be well-trained and adequately remunerated.

3. Actions for construction and engineering companies

3.1 Implement a code of conduct that commits the company and its employees to a strict anti-corruption policy (see page 49 on the WEF initiative and page 40 on the FIDIC initiative). The code should contain management, training, reporting and disciplinary procedures.

3.2 Employ effective due diligence on agents, joint venture and consortium partners, subcontractors and suppliers, so as to be reasonably certain that they will not engage in corrupt practices in connection with the company's business.

3.3 Ensure that all contracts between the company and its agents, joint venture and consortium partners, subcontractors and suppliers, require the parties to comply with strict anti-corruption policies.

3.4 Where possible, enter into sector-wide and project-specific integrity pacts (see page 43 on Integrity Pacts). The pacts should be independently monitored, and should contain enforceable sanctions. In appropriate cases, relevant government departments and financing institutions should also join in the pact.

(a) A sector integrity pact is an agreement between companies working in the same sector to act with integrity when they compete against each other in tendering for projects.

(b) A project integrity pact is an agreement between the participants in a specific project to act with integrity in relation to that project. A project integrity pact can have the following two components:

  (i) The pre-qualification and tender integrity pact is between the client, designer and all bidding companies.

  (ii) The project execution integrity pact is between the client, designer, certifier and the appointed company.

4. **Actions for international financial institutions, banks and export credit agencies**

4.1 Agree to provide finance or guarantees in relation to a project only if all key participants have implemented codes of conduct that commit them to a strict anti-corruption policy.

4.2 Agree to provide finance or guarantees only in relation to projects that are to be placed through competitive tender or a transparent procurement process.

4.3 Undertake greater due diligence to try to ensure that there is no corruption in relation to the project. Increase staff time and resources for supervision. Require full disclosure in relation to payments to agents and other intermediaries.

4.4 Maintain a blacklist of companies that have been found guilty of corruption (see page 59). Alternatively, adopt a blacklist prepared by another international institution. Deny project finance or credit support to blacklisted companies for a specified period of time after the offence.

4.5 Require the use of a project integrity pact (see page 49) during both tender and project execution phases.

4.6 Introduce reliable whistleblower protection.

4.7 Make all documentation relevant to the planning, approval and implementation of a project available to the public in a timely manner.

5. **Actions for trade and professional associations**

5.1 Publicly speak out against corruption.

5.2 Increase awareness amongst the association's members of corruption and its consequences through publicity and training.

5.3 Implement a code of conduct that commits the association's members to a strict anti-corruption policy. The code should provide a disciplinary mechanism under which members who breach the code are sanctioned.

5.4 Support the development and implementation of industry-wide anti-corruption mechanisms.

6. **Actions for auditors**

Undertake greater due diligence during audits to try to ensure that companies and clients are not engaging in corrupt practices.

7. **Actions for shareholders**

7.1 Question the boards of companies and clients to ascertain whether the companies are at risk from the consequences of corrupt practices.
7.2 Refuse to invest in companies and clients that do not operate effective anti-corruption policies.

8. **Actions for government**

8.1 Support the development and implementation of the above actions.
8.2 Support the undertaking of the following actions by an independent international body or bodies:

(a) The development and management of an international externally audited ethical standard that construction companies and clients can achieve if they adopt effective anti-corruption policies. Companies that breach the standard would lose their accreditation for a fixed period. Tender lists for public works would eventually include only companies that have the accreditation in place.

(b) The development and management of an accreditation procedure for independent assessors. Independent assessors would be skilled individuals who monitor the pre-qualification, tender and execution of projects to ensure as far as possible that they operate in an environment free from corruption. Independent assessors could be appointed under the contract, under integrity pacts, or by alternative appointment mechanisms.

(c) The provision of a corruption reporting service which would:

(i) receive reports on corrupt activities
(ii) pass these reports on to the appropriate authorities in the relevant jurisdiction
(iii) follow up reports with the relevant jurisdictions to ensure that they are being dealt with
(iv) publicise reports of corrupt activities on their website.

(d) The operation of a public, transparent and effective blacklist of companies that have participated in corrupt activities.

8.3 Ensure that a specialist corruption investigation and prosecution unit for the construction industry is operational and effective. If no such unit exists, establish one that:

   (a) is staffed by personnel with experience of the construction sector
   (b) is multidisciplined, containing engineers, forensic auditors, quantity surveyors, programmers and lawyers
   (c) has jurisdiction throughout the country
   (d) has powers to search premises, seize documents and interview witnesses
   (e) cooperates with the law enforcement agencies of other countries
   (f) cooperates with anti-money-laundering authorities
   (g) investigates all cases upon receipt of compelling evidence from companies, individuals, NGOs and dispute resolution tribunals
   (h) prosecutes cases where the investigation results in sufficient evidence
   (i) publicises prosecutions and convictions.

8.4 Improve the effectiveness of anti-money-laundering mechanisms so as to make it more likely that bribes paid in relation to construction projects are identified in the international banking system.

8.5 Sign, ratify and enforce the United Nations Convention against Corruption, and actively comply with the OECD Anti-Bribery Convention.

9. Actions for civil society organisations

9.1 Monitor the tendering and execution phases of public sector projects to try to ensure they are free from corruption. To do so, demand access to information relating to projects.

9.2 Work with the media to publicise concerns about corruption in the construction sector.

10. Actions for all participants

10.1 Work to increase transparency in the construction sector. The greater the transparency, the more difficult it will be to conceal corruption.

10.2 Report corrupt practices to the authorities, and to any applicable trade or professional association.

Note

1. Transparency International (UK) has since September 2003 been leading an anti-corruption initiative in the construction sector, which involves working with the industry to eliminate corruption, and developing and promoting the anti-corruption tools and actions presented here.

Part two

Special feature – Corruption in post-conflict reconstruction

Some 2,000 Iraqis work on one of the largest landfill sites in Iraq in a project to create a waste treatment plant and sewage facility to serve Baghdad. The project is bankrolled by a small part of the US $18.4 billion reconstruction package approved by the United States in 2003. (ROSLAN RAHMAN/AFP/Getty Images)

5 Overcoming corruption in the wake of conflict

Philippe Le Billon[1]

Many post-conflict countries figure among the most corrupt in the world, and corruption is one of the key concerns of local populations.[2] Corruption often predates hostilities, and, in many cases, it features among the factors that triggered political unrest or facilitated conflict escalation.[3] Wartime generally sees an entrenchment and diffusion of corrupt practices as governmental structures break down. Armed factions use corruption as a tool for sustaining power structures, justifying it in the context of war. For lack of an alternative, ordinary people resort to corruption in order to deal with the hardships of war. Corruption is thus frequently entangled in the political economy of many contemporary conflicts, whereby economically motivated abuse of power by public authorities, and informal survival practices by ordinary people, prolong war. In Cambodia, for example, the corruption of local and regional authorities as well as the participation of ordinary people in the (official) illegal logging sector benefited the Khmer Rouge, helping to sustain the conflict for several years.

War generally strengthens corruption, but not always. Ideals and strict discipline have restrained corrupt practices in many rebel movements, such as the Eritrean People's Liberation Front and, in its early days at least, FRELIMO in Mozambique. In Afghanistan, the Taliban regime was initially well received by the population for putting an end to the corruption of mujahedin warlords.[4] Years of discrimination, repression, and fraud can also strengthen the political will of local politicians and civilians to resist and combat corruption, as in the case of Kosovo.

Many authorities become more corrupt in peacetime, suggesting that the transition to democracy, and in many instances to a market economy, is also to blame. Immediate private gain is undeniably attractive when facing the uncertainties and opportunities of the transition from war to peace. For war veterans and exiles freshly in power, reconstruction can become a 'pay-back' scheme, with wartime 'sacrifices' being used to justify the misuse of newly controlled public offices and positions.

Post-conflict 'national reconciliation' often results in politically driven distribution of state assets, sometimes with a tacit agreement on corruption built into peace accords. Power-sharing arrangements can undermine institution building and reduce accountability as each faction asserts 'sovereignty' over its territorial or institutional turf. For example, the failure of the UN to secure the result of the 1992 elections in Cambodia led to a 'coalition' government led by the newly elected prime minister and the outgoing prime minister who refused to cede power. This government was characterised by widespread corruption before ending in a bloody *coup d'état* in 1997.

Post-conflict political transition may reinforce the importance of party financing. A shift from overtly coercive modes of political control to a regime of patronage and vote buying may aggravate political corruption in the form of illegal (or dubious) political donations and economic activities, misappropriation of public funds, or abuse of state resources. There is therefore a high risk that the transition to democracy increases political corruption in the absence of formal instruments of party financing. The biased control and wholesale disposal of public assets by political factions has characterised many transitions to peace.

The transition to a market economy that has accompanied many post-conflict reconstruction processes in the 1990s offers major corruption opportunities that post-conflict institutions may be unwilling or unable to address. Corrupt practices were particularly widespread in many former communist countries, such as Mozambique, where inadequate institutional safeguards were in place to curb abuses by politicians and their cronies. The prioritisation of private over public ownership by international agencies may unintentionally play into the hands of local corrupt elites.

Economic and political transition often takes place in a weak or highly politicised institutional framework. Recurrent problems affecting the level of corruption include poor fiscal leverage, judicial backlogs and bias, low-wage-related corruption and shadow economic control. Anti-corruption institutions frequently remain weak or instrumentalised, and critics are often silenced or co-opted.

The post-conflict context is often dominated by informal and sometimes criminal activities. The presence of aid agencies, as well as large numbers of foreign troops, often leads to highly inflated local prices and salaries, thereby contributing to an economic context favourable to corruption. Greater 'market' access to land and other assets, and a 'booming' private sector will favour local actors with access to seed capital, often the proceeds of wartime criminal activities and corruption. Aid agencies are sometimes obliged to work with local firms under the control of these new 'entrepreneurs', and there is a high risk of fraud or politicisation. In some cases, international Western donors and financial institutions were aware (if not tacitly accepting) of this evolution and remained largely inactive, instead portraying this process as a 'normal route to capitalist development'.[5]

Box 5.1   Reconstruction and the construction sector

The importance of the construction sector in reconstruction efforts varies widely according to the economies and priorities of the particular country and the concerns of donors. For example, industrialised countries in the Balkans tend to receive a greater proportion of aid for construction than developing countries in sub-Saharan Africa. The bulk of large-scale capital expenditure projects are allocated to infrastructure projects.

Given the risks of corruption in the construction industry in general, special attention is warranted for this sector. However, available information suggests that most of the

▶

---

corruption within post-conflict countries resides outside the donor-funded construction sector. Rather, most corruption occurs through the mismanagement of public utilities, privatisation of public assets, tax evasion and petty corruption in public services. The strict monitoring standards imposed by many international donors and implementing agencies largely explains this.

Many risks remain, however, and one of the foremost dangers is that infrastructure projects may be designed according to the needs of empowered officials and institutions, rather than of needy populations. This risk is particularly high with bilateral assistance, when major projects are sought to maximise capital return to the donor country through the use of construction companies from the donor country. In such cases, reconstruction aid acts as a subsidy for the contractor. Major construction projects also enable high-level corruption and influence peddling between a donor country, local politicians and local interests. Concentrating reconstruction in a particular geographic area, or infrastructure promoting powerful private interests, can easily take on a political bias.

A second risk factor is that post-conflict reconstruction is particularly prone to changes in land-use and urban planning. Access to land previously denied by hostilities, and rising prices in urban centres, lend themselves to speculation and fraud. Displaced populations are particularly vulnerable. Reconstruction presents an opportunity for officials colluding with developers to take control of 'squatter' settlements, some of which constitute prime real estate areas, such as the Boa Vista in the Angolan capital. The award of construction contracts and licences offers fertile ground for corruption and interference in allocation procedures. Similarly, construction projects may accompany new economic sectors that have opened up with the onset of peace, including through privatisation.

A third set of factors relates to the implementation of projects. The continued risk of violence often involves security measures and delays, which can provide opportunities for corruption. Contractors may need to pay protection money or build a 'special project' to get the protection of former warlords turned local politicians. Auditors may not be able to visit construction sites when the project has been completed – for 'security reasons'. Widespread subcontracting on large projects with multiple sites may also undermine donor and governmental supervision. The attempt by donors to accelerate the pace of reconstruction, as in the case of Iraq, results in major risks of wastage and fraud.

High standards of supervision by donors and implementing agencies are not sufficient. Broad consultation and multilayered monitoring that involve local communities are necessary to reduce the risks of corruption. The case of the National Commission for Social Action Sierra Leone provides an interesting example where a chain constituted by consultative forums, technical committees and local community-based appraisal committees provides greater guarantees that a construction project will be locally relevant, cleanly funded and of good quality.[1]

Note

1. See Zainab Hawa Bangura, 'Addressing Corruption and Implementing Reconstruction in Post-War Sierra Leone: Institutional and Procedural Dimensions', paper presented at 11th Anti-Corruption Conference, Seoul (South Korea), 25 May 2003.

Consequences of corruption

Corruption may occasionally have short-term positive effects, for example, in helping secure some degree of political, economic and social stability. It is also often very difficult to address local sources of grievances and conflict rapidly and effectively. In these respects, some of the political and social effects of corruption may provide short-term solutions – such as buying out 'peace spoilers' or authorising informal economic activities.

Many examples, however, suggest that such 'quick fixes', tempting though they may be, may have long-lasting negative effects. Buying out spoilers is a risky venture, as impunity and economic rewards can sustain rebel movements, as demonstrated in Angola with UNITA or Sierra Leone with the RUF. Informal economic activities strengthen the grip of quasi-criminal groups in the economic and government spheres, and negatively affect future economic development.

The most immediate consequence of corruption is a negative effect on the volume, quality and targeting of reconstruction assistance provided by international donors and local authorities. But the harmful effects of corruption reach much further.

Corruption can act as a deterrent to attracting donor support when it appears in local public finances, particularly when combined with a lack of commitment towards reconstruction goals and where local authorities appear to have the resources to finance some of the reconstruction. Despite massive reconstruction needs in Angola, donors have expressed reluctance to assist the government due to sustained allegations of large-scale corruption in this oil and mineral-rich country.

To the extent that economic variables are key determinants of the risk of renewed conflicts, corruption can also undermine peace building. Aid targeted solely at political constituencies, and biased bidding processes favouring companies serving the interests of politicians, can impair the security of the most vulnerable populations and overall economic growth. Poor beneficiary targeting, incompetent or wasteful contractors, inappropriate infrastructure and economic assistance projects can all contribute to major setbacks.

A political consequence of corruption may be the entrenchment of an imbalanced power or political status quo inherited from the conflict. As the groups empowered by the outcome of the war sustain dominant political and economic positions through corruption, they may prevent the redistribution of power, and stifle adequate checks and balances. In extreme cases, donors may end up dealing with war criminals as official interlocutors – a situation that has been avoided in some cases only through granting executive powers to international agencies through trusteeships and transitional authority mandates, as in the case of the Office of the High Representative in Bosnia.

Finally, post-conflict mismanagement and embezzlement of reconstruction assistance can also delegitimise the local government and lead to social unrest. Corruption facilitates criminality and persisting violence in post-conflict societies by compromising the conduct and independence of the police and judiciary, and through the recycling of former combatants into the private militias of corrupt politicians or organised crime.

What can be done to reduce corruption in post-conflict reconstruction?

For the effective reduction of corruption, three main areas need to be jointly considered, with relevant measures tailored to individual situations.[6]

- *Ensuring public support* aims at ending apathy, defeatism, and complicity on the issue of corruption, and associating the transition to peace with new values. Such a process can start with a survey of corruption perception, followed by public awareness campaigns and feedback on instances of corruption and enforcement.

- *Providing an appropriate economic and regulatory context* can help eliminate incentives and opportunities for corruption. Such a process can start with the regular payment of adequate salaries for public employees and the regulation of political party financing, reconstruction contracts and corporate practices.

- *Securing a legal framework for transparency and accountability* can start with rules of disclosure for politicians and high-ranking civil servants, as well as the criminalisation of corruption in the legislation. Attention must be directed not only at local authorities, but also at aid agencies and contractors.

Measures within these three areas need to be built into the reconstruction process from the outset, as prevention measures are more effective than an often-elusive search for accountability. A comprehensive plan is crucial, but hard to design and to implement fully given the diversity of organisations involved in reconstruction and local politicians' room for manoeuvre. Ongoing coordination and cooperation efforts should ensure that local authorities remain on board, and that donors and implementing agencies mutually reinforce one another rather than undermining each other's activities. Both companies and civil society also play a major role and should be involved from the outset.

Good governance

Good governance is the key element for reducing corruption in post-conflict countries for the long term. The main measures include establishing adequate reconstruction management procedures, passing anti-corruption legislation, creating implementing agencies, and reforming political party financing, bureaucracies and the judiciary. Local authorities should make a public commitment to the priorities and principles guiding reconstruction, and demonstrate that clear and transparent fund allocation procedures and accountability mechanisms are in place to manage reconstruction efforts. The allocation of reconstruction funds, like all public budget expenditures, should be approved by the legislative branch of government and subject to the scrutiny of an inspector general's office. Contracting should be submitted to proper tendering procedures.

Post-conflict transition often involves extensive transformation of legal instruments, including the constitution. Careful attention should be devoted to addressing the causes and mechanisms of corruption when revising legislation. A new constitution, for example, should include a commitment to fight corruption, and an effective separation of powers and government structures. It should also address immunity issues for high officials and due judicial process to protect political opponents against politically motivated accusations of corruption.[7] The key role of the judiciary frequently necessitates a high degree of involvement of the international community to assist with reforms, including the nomination of more independent judges, if necessary from foreign countries.

Party financing is a major cause of political corruption, but is particularly hard to tackle in a post-conflict environment. The incumbent party generally plunders the state in advance of elections and international donors are understandably reluctant to finance political parties directly. These issues need to be addressed at the stage of the peace agreement through preventative measures prohibiting the sale of state assets for an interim period, creating a framework for the international supervision of public accounts and laying out the rules for party financing.

Civil service reforms to depoliticise and professionalise the bureaucracy are key, with Bosnia and Herzegovina and Rwanda providing examples of relative success.[8] In Cambodia, in contrast, coalition parties jockeyed to reinforce their position within a system of patronage that resulted in a bloated administration of underpaid staff, with corruption being orchestrated by ministers or heads of department.

A culture of integrity can be promoted through codes of conduct for civil servants and companies, mass education, or media programmes protecting and improving the standards of journalism.

International assistance

During the height of the cold war, foreign sponsors supported corrupt leaders as long as they remained allies. The past 15 years have seen a sharp evolution in the statements and policies of donors and international agencies in this regard. Most have emphasised good governance and condemned corruption, yet aid has continued to be allocated to corrupt governments. The record of the US administration in this regard is particularly poor: it has allocated the most aid to the most corrupt governments.[9] On the grounds that a corrupt government is more likely to assist or tolerate terrorist organisations, there has been an increased call for public integrity and good governance since the terrorist attacks of September 11, 2001. However, practices continue to reflect ad hoc vested interests. On the frontline of the 'war on terror', it has been argued that the US has largely abetted, and continues to tolerate, the corruption of allied warlords in Afghanistan.[10]

Donors and implementing agencies are generally not keen on denouncing corruption. They often fear a possible backlash in domestic public opinion that could undermine future support, the risk of local political instability or retribution from local authorities which may lead to the end of programmes benefiting vulnerable populations. Exposing corruption may also lead to a loss of credibility and reputation when direct mismanagement is involved. Donors' preferences for long-term macroeconomic reforms may mean that governments that support trade liberalisation, tight fiscal discipline and political pluralism are less likely to face public criticism and pressure on the part of Western donors and International Financial Institutions (IFIs) – whatever their actual practices.

After a careful analysis of potential political and humanitarian consequences, donors and international agencies should be ready to suspend non-humanitarian aid to avoid consolidating the power of corrupt politicians. An example of this was when the EU suspended its aid to the Republika Srpska in 1997, acknowledging a political impasse and widespread corruption.

Particular attention should be given to the risk of embezzlement of reconstruction funds. The monitoring of bids for reconstruction contracts should include background checks on bidding companies for political ties. Reconstruction programmes should be designed to ensure maximum transparency and hold officials, both local and foreign, accountable at both planning and implementation stage. Preventive measures should include maximum participation and supervision by local communities over projects and implementing companies, as well as built-in mechanisms of transparency and accountability.

Donors and agencies need to be exemplary in applying standards of transparency and accountability, beginning with the oversight of their own programmes. The example of Iraq is particularly dismal in this respect.[11] The Coalition Provisional Authority (CPA) and Department of Defence initially had only 80 people examining the largest reconstruction programme in history, half the number needed according to the Association of Inspectors General, and eventually outsourced oversight to private companies giving rise to potential conflicts of interest. International supervision has been even worse: the work of the International Advisory and Monitoring Board for Iraq, set up to monitor the Development Fund for Iraq independently, has been substantially delayed.

Agencies representing the international community have increasingly been assigned executive powers in post-conflict countries since the mid-1990s, as in Bosnia and Herzegovina, East Timor and Kosovo. This allows for new anti-corruption standards and task forces to be put in place, such as the Anti-Fraud Unit and Legal Reform Unit of the Office of the High Representative in Bosnia and Herzegovina. It also allows for greater direct control of public works and services. This does not guarantee probity, however, as demonstrated by the case of Joseph Trutschler, convicted of financial fraud while in charge of the rehabilitation of the electricity sector for the UN Interim Administration Mission in Kosovo.[12] Critics of UN interventions have pointed to the corrupting effect of the authority and money made available to international workers.[13] Many seek to protect their jobs by sidelining capable 'locals' and prolonging their mandate and projects.

International actors must avoid providing examples of institutionalised corruption. Restraint rather than lavish spending and salaries can help to reassert the values of public service. Donors should also think twice before contracting vastly more expensive foreign companies and NGOs simply for the sake of avoiding the risk of petty corruption by local entrepreneurs and officials.

Donors also need to keep their side of the reconstruction bargain and help prevent corruption in the first place rather than assign blame when it occurs. Timely disbursement of pledged funds can address one of the sources of corruption, whereby ministers, heads of department, and companies can rely on promised revenue flows rather than having to cut corners and engage in corrupt practices to ensure the payment of wages or avoid bankruptcy.

Box 5.2   Aid and corruption

Donors and aid agencies face a number of dilemmas in post-conflict political and economic transition.

Matching rapid and efficient assistance delivery with adequate control to ensure probity. Rapid disbursement runs the risk of poor oversight if adequate monitoring institutions are not yet in place. It is therefore crucial to budget for, and establish, such institutions properly from the outset. It is common for pledged money to reach communities even a year or two after donors have taken a decision. Not only can such delays affect the security and well-being of targeted communities, they can also induce local authorities and businesses to find inappropriate 'quick fixes' and turn to corruption or the informal or criminal economy. Assistance is also often sharply reduced after a few years – as new crises attract the attention of donors – while the absorptive capacity and needs of the recipient country are higher.

Balancing local ownership and safeguards. Local representatives and communities should be engaged to ensure local ownership, while avoiding strengthening peace-spoilers thereby risking higher levels of corruption or reinforcing social fault lines. Bypassing local authorities through funding local and international NGOs in order to accelerate disbursement and implementation, or to preserve the integrity of the project for fear of local government corruption, may prove counterproductive.

Addressing the challenges of the informal economy. A sense of urgency in the reconstruction sector is often used to justify the creation of parastatal organisations that can access off-budget funding, evade controls by public agencies, and be easily controlled by a few high-level officials. Such parastatal organisations are often used to channel resources for private political or economic interests.

Although aid can foster better governance, a huge influx of aid money can also prove counterproductive. As foreign aid comes to substitute for taxes, the local population loses a degree of leverage over local authorities, thereby undermining the so-called taxation-representation nexus, as aid donors (rather than citizens) become the main constituency of local authorities. Aid can also damage the economy through inflation. Higher wages in the NGO sector can cause competent civil servants to leave government to work for foreign agencies or cause others to seek to achieve similar standards of living through corruption.

Private sector

Private consultancies and construction companies play a major role in reconstruction, often being allocated the bulk of reconstruction funds. Auditing of contractors is imperative. Audits should be conducted both externally and internally, with a reinforcing system of incentives and sanctions. The level of corruption in these cases can be significant.

Civil society and the media

Raising public expectations is key to the long-term success of reconstruction so that corruption becomes unacceptable rather than unavoidable. Local civil society organisations and media constitute a key element of corruption prevention and accountability. In many instances, however, such organisations are weak or non-existent.

Many have close ties to political parties, and end up channelling aid or opinions in the interests of their political patrons.

Although independent organisations can often flourish under favourable circumstances, they are often ill equipped to detect and report corruption and are vulnerable to pressure and coercion from powerful corrupt groups, as testified by the imprisonment or killing of numerous journalists and activists. Reconstruction assistance can help raise awareness and build capacity towards an effective, national, anti-corruption consensus.[14] Early intervention in the reconstruction process is key, encouraging new media, civil society leaders and public institutions to emerge.

Corruption, reconstruction and peace-building

The challenges faced by conflict-affected countries are formidable, and rebuilding infrastructure is only one, albeit important, facet of the reconstruction and recovery process. Less corruption in post-conflict reconstruction means not only better-targeted, higher quality, and more efficient assistance, but also a greater contribution to the transformation of the local political economy, as well as the consolidation of more effective state institutions and legitimate political parties. In short, less corruption can help build a stronger peace.

Tackling corruption, however, should not take precedence over peace building, but rather complement it. The first priority in this regard is to maintain security for the population. An assessment of the capacity of corrupt 'peace spoilers' is needed before moving against them. The international community may wisely let corruption buy a temporary peace when the risk of renewed conflict is too high. The legacy of such an approach is risky, however, and a better tactic than complacency or complicity is to drive a wedge between peace spoilers and their main power base: combatants and economic interests. Amnesties and enticing demobilisation and reintegration packages can ensure the cooperation of middle and low-ranking combatants, while war crime indictments can isolate their leaders. International supervision can help to protect public finances and key economic sectors from embezzlement, and secure a smoother transition towards accountable and transparent economic management.

The second priority is to restore the confidence of the population, most notably in its government and the political process. A corrupt government rarely has the support of its population, but in many cases patronage is the legitimating link between individual rulers and the ruled. To move beyond corruptly financed modes of redistribution and power holding, both institutional arrangements and political culture have to change. Better detection and accountability mechanisms should ensure the validity of accusations of corruption, a prominent political dimension in the reconstruction period.

Confidence in foreign interveners is also necessary to ensure an optimum partnership. Institutional reforms are key in building transparency and accountability, but their implementation is slow and difficult. A short-term priority is to keep the public informed about what is happening and how it affects the general citizen. Broad-reaching and high quality information is crucial to ensure that the goals of transparency and accountability are more rapidly achieved.

Notes

1. Philippe Le Billon is assistant professor at the Liu Institute for Global Issues and the Department of Geography at the University of British Columbia.
2. Opinion poll for the Balkan region: 'South East Europe Public Agenda Survey' by the South East Europe Democracy Support, 2002; for Nicaragua: 'National Integrity Survey', CIET International, 1998; for Sierra Leone, see 'Governance and Anti-Corruption Report' (Washington, DC: World Bank, 2003).
3. Philippe Le Billon, 'Buying Peace or Fuelling War: The Role of Corruption in Armed Conflicts', *Journal of International Development* 15 (2003).
4. Christopher Cramer and Jonathan Goodhand, 'Try Again, Fail Again, Fail Better? War, the State, and the "Post-Conflict" Challenge in Afghanistan', *Development and Change* 33(5) (2002).
5. Joseph Hanlon, *Are Donors to Mozambique Promoting Corruption?*, paper presented at 'Towards a New Political Economy of Development', Sheffield (Britain), 3–4 July 2002.
6. For examples of detailed strategies, see 'A Comprehensive Anti-Corruption Strategy for Bosnia and Herzegovina', Office of the High Representative, 15 February 1999; 'Governance and Anti-Corruption Report' and 'Governance and Anti-Corruption (GAC) Strategy' for Sierra Leone (Washington, DC: World Bank, 2003).
7. On the case of the Afghan constitution, see Susan Rose-Ackerman, 'Corruption', www.cic.nyu.edu/conflict/conflict_translations.html
8. Vera Devine, 'Corruption in Post-War Reconstruction: The Experience of Bosnia and Herzegovina', Transparency International workshop on Corruption in Reconstruction After War, 25 May 2003.
9. Alberto Alesina and Beatrice Weder, 'Do Corrupt Governments Receive Less Foreign Aid?' *American Economic Review* 92 (2002).
10. *Washington Times*, 7 February 2002.
11. 'Iraq: The Missing Billions: Transition and Transparency in Post-War Iraq', Briefing Paper for the Madrid conference on Iraq, 23–24 October 2003, London, Christian Aid, www.christian-aid.org.uk/indepth/310iraqoil/iraqoil.pdf; Adam Davidson and Mark Schapiro, 'Spoils of War' in *Marketplace* (San Francisco: Center for Investigative Reporting, 21 April 2004); Barbara Crossette, 'No Simple Place to Pin Blame for Iraq Oil-For-Food Problems', *UN Wire*, 10 May 2004; Press releases from www.iamb.info/pressrel.htm (downloaded 29 April 2004).
12. *UN Wire*, 17 June 2003.
13. Jayati Ghosh, 'Donors and Dependency in the Expatriate's Paradise', *Macroeconomic Policy* (New Delhi: International Development Economics Associates, 2003); Jarat Chopra, 'Building State Failure in East Timor', *Development and Change* 33 (2002).
14. See 'Building Capacity in Post-Conflict Countries', *Social and Development Notes: Conflict Prevention and Reconstruction* 14 (2003).

Case study: Corrupting the new Iraq

Reinoud Leenders and Justin Alexander[1]

Wednesday 9 April 2003 was not only the day that most Iraqis rejoiced at the fall of Saddam Hussein's regime. In the eyes of many Iraqis, it was also the day that marked the beginning of a new era of intensified theft of state property, corruption and conflicts of interest. When asked to give their views on the birth of the new Iraq, the probability is high that Iraqis will refer not only to the widespread looting by 'Ali Babas'[2] but also to the looting by Iraq's new democratic leaders.

Taking advantage of the power vacuum, scores of political factions took possession overnight of numerous public buildings and settled in opulent villas vacated by Saddam's henchmen. The old regime's car park became the scene of the new political elite's gluttony, with hundreds of SUVs that once served as the status symbol of Saddam's secret agents now being driven to the headquarters of the new political parties. Iraq's new politicians found numerous justifications for this usurpation of state property; some of which could indeed be cited as mitigating circumstances. But in the eyes of dismayed Iraqis, the political parties had managed to ruin their reputation before the business of governance had begun. 'The political parties took everything they could get hold of', said one Iraqi businessman.[3] 'State property went up for grabs. If they could get away with this, how do they expect ordinary people to behave?'

Perceptions, misperceptions and evidence

One year into Iraq's reconstruction programme, opinions are divided over what the Coalition Provisional Authority (CPA) and the now dissolved Interim Governing Council (IGC) have achieved in repairing the damage caused by decades of mismanagement, sanctions and wars. Yet across the board, corruption has been identified as one of the main obstacles to getting Iraq back on its feet. A survey held in early May 2004 revealed that 58 per cent of Iraqi respondents had heard of corruption in the reconstruction process, and 32 per cent believed that such malpractices involved CPA officials.[4]

Almost unanimously, Iraqi businessmen complain about bribery affecting virtually all government operations. Contractors alleged that inspectors checking up on the refurbishment of schools by Iraqi companies in September 2003 were bribed to turn a blind eye to shoddy or unfinished work.[5] Iraqi protestors amassing in front of the gates of the 'green zone', the CPA headquarters in Baghdad, routinely mentioned corruption on their banners. In Nasariyya, Sunni Muslim clerics expressed their anger over what they believed was widespread corruption in the CPA and local authorities.[6] Foreign company workers said they witnessed corruption 'everywhere and on all sides'.[7]

None of these allegations should be taken at face value. Accusations of corruption are often made for reasons other than actually having witnessed it. Iraq is no exception. That the presence of public works in Basra is much lower than anticipated is cited as 'proof' that the local contracting process is rigged and that the funds have been pocketed. The fact that the governorate had not initiated any works because of a genuine lack of funds did not prevent local businessmen describing in graphic detail the crookedness of tenders that were never held.

Iraqis have felt largely excluded from the political process going on in Baghdad, and the impression that something dishonest is going on behind the scenes understandably makes Iraqis reach out for the c-word to make sense of developments. The weakness of Iraq's political parties also encourages corruption, and allegations directed against opponents can serve as substitutes for party programmes or meaningful political debate. In this context, accusations of malpractice are designed to smear rather than to contribute to a culture of accountability.

Yet there are plenty of reasons to believe that high levels of corruption have indeed taken hold in the new Iraq. At the Ghazil market in central Baghdad and the *suq* of old Basra, salesmen and consumers engage in a booming trade in stolen medicines and medical equipment supplied by corrupt public servants. CPA officials, contractors and high-ranking ministry employees have admitted to corruption in their midst. According to a senior official at the ministry for trade, corruption between ministry officials and traders permeates the distribution of rationed food and other consumer items at all levels of procurement, storage and allocation.[8] A former trade minister, Ali Allawi, accused officials at his own ministry and the CPA of embezzling US $40 million in the procurement of wooden doors with funds of the 'Oil-for-Food' (OFF) programme, adding that the case represented 'the tip of the iceberg'.[9]

A context in which corruption can thrive

Corruption thrives in a context of confusion and change. In Iraq, public institutions are even struggling to find out how many employees they have on their payrolls. Obvious institutional safeguards are yet to be put in place and ministries and state companies lack proper inventory systems. As one Iraqi director-general pointed out, '[i]t's very easy to turn a three into a 30 for example, since the Arabic zero is a dot'.[10] It is within this climate that the Iraqi state and US funding organisations are expected to spend nearly US $14 billion in 2004.

Under Saddam, loyalty to the regime was systematically bought by distributing favours, effectively creating a 'shadow state' in which bureaucratic procedures applied only to the unfortunate and underprivileged.[11] However, it was not until the UN sanctions in the 1990s that corruption and facilitation payments became endemic at every level of society. The OFF programme exacerbated corrupt behaviour among senior Iraqi officials who enriched themselves by striking corrupt deals with foreign companies and politicians at the expense of ordinary Iraqis.[12] For some public servants, corruption was the only way for them to feed their families on salaries as low as US $5 a month.

The former regime's control of the economy also left a legacy of corruption. Heavy state procurement and subsidies still distort market prices increasing the temptation to sell low-priced goods on the black market or to smuggle goods to neighbouring countries. Reforming these state policies is not only going to hit the poor hardest, it will also generate new opportunities for corruption. There is a danger that rapid privatisation is soon to be enforced by the IMF and the Paris Club of official creditors as a condition for reducing and rescheduling some US $120 billion foreign debt accrued under Saddam.[13] Experiences in the former Soviet Union, and other indebted countries that have been forced into rapid privatisation, suggest that the selling off of state-owned enterprises under conditions of opaque governance, combined with the lack of a free market, is almost certain to result in widespread corruption.

Another major factor that risks fuelling corruption is Iraq's dependence on oil. Very few oil-producing countries have established effective mechanisms to prevent the plunder of oil revenue. The transition period in Iraq has focused on power sharing along sectarian and regional lines and very little thought has been given to how the new Iraq can be more effective in managing oil revenues. As one senior Iraqi official put it, 'governance takes place on a day-by-day basis. We will repeat the same mistakes of the past if we don't think this through.'[14]

Ideas have been floated about establishing a transparent oil fund insulated from the daily bickering at cabinet and parliamentary levels, but serious debate on this issue is yet to begin and, as Iraq's own experience in the 1950s established, an oil fund provides no guarantees of freedom from greedy politicians.[15] In the meantime, Iraq's oil revenues have been channelled into the UN-authorised Development Fund for Iraq (DFI) and managed by the CPA's Programme Review Board (PRB).[16] A UN body to audit the Fund, the International Advisory and Monitoring Board (IAMB), found gross irregularities by CPA officials in their management of the DFI, and condemned the United States for 'lack of transparency' and providing the opportunity for 'fraudulent acts'.[17]

US contracting

The lack of transparency and accountability in the CPA's management of Iraqi oil revenues touches on a wider problem characterising the US's handling of the reconstruction process. In its procurement strategies, the US has been a poor role model in how to keep corrupt practices at bay. Even before the invasion was launched, questions were being asked about the extensive contracts secretly awarded to Bechtel, Halliburton and others.

Critics of the Bush administration have argued that the reconstruction contracts have resulted in three levels of corruption.[18] First, concerns have been expressed over the selection of companies that are close to the Republican Party – either as donors or through high-ranking members of the party serving on the boards of the private companies that were awarded contracts (for example, Vice President Dick Cheney, who was CEO of Halliburton prior to taking office in 2000). These concerns were reinforced by the highly secretive nature of the contracting process, especially during the war preparations, and the type of contracts awarded. For instance, according to the US Project on Government Oversight, 'the Orwellian-sounding Indefinite Delivery Indefinite Quantity [contracts] allows the government to award an unspecified amount of future work to approved contractors'.[19] This system restricts the ability of poorly connected and smaller companies from bidding for contracts. In addition, the phenomenon of 'contract bundling', which joins together two or more separate procurement requirements into a super-sized contract, effectively disqualifies smaller companies because only the very largest contractors are able to compete.

Second, many US contractors in Iraq have been wasteful and have taken what many would see as excessive profits, both of which can be attributed to 'cost-plus' contracts in which companies are reimbursed for all costs with an additional percentage added as guaranteed profit. Serious questions also arose about the subcontracting practices of the companies working in Iraq. Ed Kubba, a member of the American-Iraqi Chamber of

Commerce, mused, 'If you take US $10 million from the US government and sub the job out to Iraqi businesses for US $250,000, is that business, or is it corruption?'[20]

Finally, individual employees of prime US contractors have been accused of being directly involved in bribe taking in the form of kickbacks from other companies seeking subcontracts.[21] Translators, who are seen as holding particular leverage, are alleged to have demanded 10–50 per cent of the value of a subcontract in return for facilitating access to the main contractor.[22]

Tackling corruption

In the past year, some modest initiatives have been taken to tackle corruption in Iraq. Most importantly, the CPA helped establish an independent office of general inspectors, with an inspector attached to each ministry. The office is backed by two other institutions – the Commission on Public Integrity and the revived Supreme Audit Board. Yet both these institutions have yet to do any significant work and a chair of the Public Integrity Commission had to be imposed by the CPA after the now dissolved Iraqi Interim Governing Council failed to agree on an appointment.[23]

Another important development has been the adoption of a National Integrity Law which forces state officials and politicians to declare their wealth prior to assuming office. In addition, in June 2004 the CPA promulgated a law protecting anti-corruption whistleblowers. Contracting partners for USAID, including Bechtel, have announced that they have introduced business ethics into management courses for their subcontractors and Iraqi government officials, although the topic of corruption was lumped together with other issues such as job safety and sexual harassment in courses taking little more than a few hours.[24]

When participating in tenders to US contracting organisations, Iraqi companies have been instructed in conducting transparent bidding processes and business accounting. A common complaint among Iraqis, however, has been that the CPA, among others, has failed to explain why some bidding companies had lost and others won, thereby undermining trust in the process. Nor did the CPA consistently resort to tendering in awarding contracts.[25]

Despite an awareness among some Iraqis about the importance of stringent anti-corruption measures, many Iraqi officials and businessmen have demonstrated a poor understanding of how to deal with the problem. For example, when asked how the governorate of Basra is preparing itself for its procurement tasks to be fair and transparent, one of its officials summed up this city's 'anti-corruption policy' by saying that contracts will be granted by 'religious men who are by nature more honest'.[26]

Another misconception is that the elections that are to be held by January 2005 will eradicate corruption for once and for all 'because the electorate will simply vote any corrupt politician out of office'.[27] Elections may be a necessary condition for effectively countering corruption but they are far from a sufficient one. Relatively free elections in Kurdish Iraq in 1992 failed to root out corruption and there have been widespread complaints that collusion between Kurdish political parties and business has been the rule rather than the exception.

The new inclusive style of politics has progressed unevenly, which has tended to cause institutional gridlocks. Politicians have been able to treat ministries and other state bodies as their private fiefdoms. As happened in post-conflict Lebanon, power concentrated in this way, combined with intensive demands from the Iraqi public for government jobs,[28] may lead Iraq to the situation where sectarian leaders distribute public resources and jobs among their constituencies, a phenomenon known as *muhasassa* (apportionment).[29]

Moving on

It is likely that we have not yet seen the full scale of corruption in Iraq for the simple reason that much of the anticipated expenditure on building contracts and procurement has yet to begin.[30] But with so many factors fostering, and threatening to foster, corruption, the reconstruction process demands a much more aggressive approach to corruption than is currently being taken by the new Iraqi government, the coalition forces and foreign donors.

If reconstruction is to generate actual processes of accountability and ownership of the process by local stakeholders, it is essential that these institutions place much greater emphasis on the decentralisation of both governance and aid projects. Supporting local media to serve as an independent and reliable watchdog is another essential step to promote accountability.[31] Foreign governments should apply anti-corruption legislation to companies operating in Iraq and any pressures on Iraq to meet the requirements of a free market system should take into account that markets need strong institutions to avoid giving way to a form of capitalism dependent on personal connections rather than the forces of the open market.

Most importantly, the effective management of Iraq's oil revenue must be put high on the agenda and must learn from the lessons of other oil-producing countries and Iraq's own past.[32] A good start would be to grant the Iraqi Supreme Audit Board a seat on the International Monitoring and Advisory Board, to familiarise it with international auditing standards and improve Iraq's local expertise.

Concerns over corruption in Iraq should not be a reason for delaying the transfer of funds already committed to reconstruction in Iraq, as many donors now appear to be considering. In the absence of an economic revival the demands on a fragile Iraqi government will be too great to initiate a process of building sound institutions. Nevertheless, strong and immediate measures must be taken to address corruption before the real spending on reconstruction starts. If urgent steps are not taken, Iraq will not become the shining beacon of democracy envisioned by the Bush administration, it will become the biggest corruption scandal in history.

Notes

1. Reinoud Leenders is a Middle East analyst based in Beirut. Justin Alexander heads the Jubilee Iraq campaign. The views expressed in this article are the authors' own.
2. A term coined by US soldiers that many Iraqis consider a denigration of a heroic figure in Iraqi literature. In the story it is the 40 foreign interlopers who are the thieves.

3. Authors' interview in Baghdad, 10 March 2004.
4. *Al-Mashriq* (Iraq), 4 May 2004.
5. Authors' interviews with Iraqi contractors in Baghdad, April 2004.
6. See *Az-zaman* (Iraq), 11 March 2004.
7. Authors' interviews with foreign contractors and private security company officials in Baghdad and Basra, March–April 2004.
8. Authors' interview in Baghdad, 9 March 2004.
9. Cited in the *Los Angeles Times*, 2 February 2004.
10. Ibid., quote from Ahmed al-Talibi, DG of Kimadia, the state company for drugs.
11. For details see Charles Tripp, *A History of Iraq* (Cambridge: Cambridge University Press, 2002).
12. The US General Accounting Office estimated that Saddam made US $4.4 billion from kickbacks during the seven years of the OFF programme. The Iraqi newspaper *Al-Mada* revealed on 25 January 2004 a controversial list of 270 firms and individuals who were alleged to have received bribes.
13. See www.jubileeiraq.org/resources.htm
14. Authors' interview with Fa'iq Abdul-Rasul, deputy minister of planning, Baghdad, 10 April 2004.
15. For the origins of the 1950s Development Board see Fahim Issa Qubain, *The Reconstruction of Iraq: 1950–1957* (New York: Praeger, 1958).
16. Following the formal handover of sovereignty in June 2004, the PRB has been dissolved and the Development Fund is now managed by the Iraqi Ministry of Finance and audited by the IAMB.
17. See www.iamb.info/dfiaudit.htm
18. See www.southernstudies.org/campaignpage.asp; www.house.gov/reform/min/inves_admin/admin_contracts.htm; www.publicintegrity.org/wow/
19. www.pogo.org
20. Cited by Naomi Klein, *The Nation* (United States), 5 January 2004.
21. Authors' interviews with Iraqi and foreign contractors, Baghdad March 2004; Marketplace, *Minnesota Public Radio*, 23 April 2004 at http://marketplace.publicradio.org/features/iraq/
22. Ibid.
23. Earlier attempts to impose financial discipline were shaken by the arrest of the ministry of finance's chief anti-corruption watchman, Sabah Nuri, on charges of embezzling US $22 million in the country's otherwise successful currency exchange for new dinars.
24. Authors' interview with Bechtel official in Baghdad, 5 March 2004.
25. One-third of total contract value in 2003 was awarded without any competition. See Office of the Inspector General, CPA, *First Quarterly Report to Congress*, 30 March 2004.
26. Authors' interview with municipal official in Basra, 30 March 2004.
27. Authors' interview with a Kurdish human rights activist in Sulaymaniyya, 4 June 2004.
28. When asked in a poll about their expectations vis-à-vis political parties, 49 per cent of Iraqi respondents answered 'more government jobs'. Opinion survey cited in Christopher Foote, William Block, Keith Crane and Simon Gray, *Economic Policy and Prospects in Iraq*, Public Policy Discussion Paper Federal Reserve Bank of Boston (2004). www.bos.frb.org/economic/ppdp/index.htm
29. See Reinoud Leenders, 'Public Means to Private Ends: State Building and Power in Post-War Lebanon', in Eberhard Kienle (ed), *Politics from Above, Politics from Below: The Middle East in the Age of Economic Reform* (London: Saqi Books, 2003).

30. Of the US $18.4 billion in US Congress funds allocated for Iraq's infrastructure, at the time of writing the PMO had spent only US $1.93 billion (or 10.5 per cent) on actual projects under construction. See PMO, *Pentagon Backgrounder*, 24 May 2004, www.rebuilding-iraq.net/pdf/pmo_update_brief_24_may_04.pdf

31. Iraqis do not read many newspapers and those who do say they do not trust them. See Iraq Center for Research and Strategic Studies, *The Results of the Third Public Opinion Poll in Iraq*, 23 October 2003. Some initiatives have been taken to bolster Iraqi media in holding politicians more accountable. For example, the Institute for War and Peace Reporting supports a dynamic training programme for Iraqi journalists to report, among other issues, on corruption. See www.iwpr.net/iraq_index1.html

32. Some general principles designed for oil revenue management could directly feed into such a debate. See www.publishwhatyoupay.org

Part three
Country reports

6 Key developments in corruption across countries

Cobus de Swardt[1]

Corruption poses a threat to the development and internal stability of countries the world over. Although each country faces its unique combination of challenges, corruption is observed across the globe wherever there is a lack of transparency. The country reports in the *Global Corruption Report 2005* illustrate the wide scope of recent corruption scandals: electoral irregularities in Panama; police corruption in Cameroon; allegations of bribes to build a German soccer stadium; the Yukos affair in Russia; and allegations against the judiciary in Sri Lanka. There are examples of corruption from numerous sectors of the economy, including public works and construction, health care, banking, and oil and gas. Public contracting remains particularly vulnerable to corruption, as seen in examples from Burkina Faso, Canada, the Czech Republic and Poland.

Anti-corruption strategies, whilst underpinned by universal principles, have to be tailored to the specific requirements of each country. The anti-corruption challenges facing governments are diverse and the issues addressed in different country reports reflect this diversity. What the country reports have in common, however, is that they all tell the story of a quest for higher standards of governance, accountability and transparency.

International commitments

By focusing on country-level developments, there is a risk of understating the importance of international commitments, whether made by governments or businesses. There has been a proliferation of international anti-corruption conventions in recent years, illustrating both the transnational nature of large-scale corruption and the pressure for reform that countries can bring to bear on each other. However, the ratification, implementation and enforcement of anti-corruption conventions remains a major challenge.

On 9 December 2003 the UN Convention against Corruption was signed in Mérida, Mexico. Agreeing on a global standard was a tremendous achievement, but it may take some years before the convention is widely ratified and implemented. The UN convention requires the ratification of 30 countries before it can enter into force, but only nine had ratified it at the time of writing (including only Kenya and Sri Lanka of the 40 countries profiled in the *Global Corruption Report 2005*). Nevertheless, the convention has already paved the way for the UN Global Compact to adopt a 10th principle, which clearly states that '[b]usinesses should work against all forms of corruption, including extortion and bribery'.

Overall, a broad and comprehensive global legal framework is starting to take shape, and the OECD Anti-Bribery Convention (which makes bribery overseas a criminal offence at home) has already been ratified by all OECD countries and some others. However, passing this – and other conventions – into domestic laws has not yet been done satisfactorily, and there have still been very few prosecutions under the OECD convention. Monitoring the ratification, implementation and enforcement of conventions is a key global priority for Transparency International (TI).

Legislative change

Pushed in part by international commitments, a positive trend in many countries is the number of anti-corruption laws that have been proposed, passed or implemented. Frequent areas for reform include TI's global priorities:

- improving public procurement (such as the implementation guidelines drafted for a new government procurement law in China)
- providing access to information (such as new legislation in Turkey)
- tackling political corruption (such as new campaign contribution limits in Canada)
- measures to prevent money laundering (in Indonesia and Ireland)
- regulating conflicts of interest (in Croatia and the Czech Republic)
- whistleblower protection (in Japan).

The need for political will and stability

While legal change is important, a major challenge facing all countries is the implementation and enforcement of anti-corruption legislation at all levels of government. Above all, this process requires political will. Some leaders have shown a determined commitment to curb corruption, whilst political will seems to be lacking in other countries, such as Zimbabwe. Kenya exemplifies the importance of political will at a time of political transition – while the first post-Moi government came into office with a series of anti-corruption laws and major investigations, after 18 months observers were questioning whether the new government was willing to root out corruption in its own ranks.

The current upsurge in transnational terrorist attacks and global insecurity has provided the impetus for change in many countries. Global terrorism and international crime often rely on corrupt activities such as money laundering. Official anti-corruption initiatives are frequently linked to new security measures, as in Britain and Japan. While such measures can have a positive impact on corruption, it is important to ensure that they do not infringe human rights, as we cautioned in the *Global Corruption Report 2003*.

Many of the country reports show that anti-corruption initiatives cannot prosper without political stability (for example, in Palestine and Peru). Political stability is in turn threatened if electoral procedures are corrupt or if human rights abuses are tolerated or even sanctioned by the state (for example, in Sri Lanka and Zimbabwe). A highly volatile and unstable political environment often characterises post-conflict countries in particular (for example, the Democratic Republic of Congo and Cambodia).

In those countries where civil society is mobilised and coalitions of civil society organisations have been created (see the recent examples in Cameroon, Croatia and Latvia), it has been possible to press governments to address corruption as a matter of priority. A striking example is Georgia, where the previous government was overthrown because of broad-based social mobilisation against rigged parliamentary elections. The transition resulted in the formation of a new government with a strong anti-corruption programme, committed to transforming a previously corrupt system.

Introducing the country reports

The country reports are mostly written by TI's national chapters. There has been an expansion in the number of country reports in the *Global Corruption Report* from 34 in 2004 to 40 this year. Care has been taken to ensure a mix of regions and countries in order to reflect anti-corruption activities in large and small, as well as developed and developing countries, including both politically stable countries and others where there are high levels of political unrest. The inclusion or absence of a specific country does not, however, imply anything about its level of corruption.

Each country report begins with the country's score and rank in TI's Corruption Perceptions Index as well as a list of which anti-corruption conventions the country has signed or ratified (or failed to sign or ratify). The reports then briefly present relevant legal and institutional changes of the year July 2003–June 2004. The main part of each country report is an analysis of key corruption-related issues arising during the year under review. The reports do not attempt to be comprehensive in their coverage of issues.

The country reports in the *Global Corruption Report 2005* demonstrate the successes and failures of anti-corruption approaches at all levels of a country's state, private sector and civil society. They illustrate the progress that anti-corruption coalitions have made, but also the setbacks and the challenges ahead.

Note

1. Cobus de Swardt is the director of global programmes at Transparency International.

7 Country reports

Argentina

Corruption Perceptions Index 2004 score: 2.5 (108th out of 146 countries)

Conventions:
OAS Inter-American Convention against Corruption (ratified October 1997)
OECD Anti-Bribery Convention (ratified February 2001)
UN Convention against Corruption (signed December 2003; not yet ratified)
UN Convention against Transnational Organized Crime (ratified November 2002)

Legal and institutional changes

- In December 2003 the government issued decree 1172/03, which aims to increase **transparency in government** (see below).

- A presidential decree issued in June 2003 that establishes more rigorous and transparent procedures for improving the **selection of supreme court judges** has been put into practice. Previously the president nominated supreme court judges and the senate ratified the appointments (see *Global Corruption Report 2004*). Under the new regulations, the general public and the legal community are invited to make observations or present objections about nominees. The decree failed, however, to open up senate hearings to discuss the president's shortlist of candidates, as requested by civil society organisations.

- Decree 588/03, signed in August 2003, extended the above procedures to the **selection of the attorney general, national ombudsman, public prosecutors and circuit court judges.**[1]

- The anti-corruption office has drafted a bill to **reform the public ethics law** of 1999. A public debate was held on the bill, which looks at the functioning of the national public ethics commission, at conflicts of interest, at sanctions and at the use of sworn declarations. At the time of writing the proposal was being examined by the ministry of justice, security and human rights.

- A new **chief prosecutor for administrative enquiries**, Manuel Garrido, was appointed in November 2003. The position carries the rank of head of the anti-corruption office and responsibility for investigating improper behaviour by public officials. The attorney general selected Garrido from a shortlist drawn up through a public competition. Garrido is well known for his anti-corruption work.

Improving the quality of democracy and its institutions

Decree 1172/03 on 'Improving the Quality of Democracy and its Institutions' represents an advance in terms of transparency of government contacts with powerful interest groups in Argentina. It goes part way to answering the public demand for radical change that faced President Néstor Kirchner when he took office in May 2003. But its application is patchy and it leaves important government sectors untouched. The decree was proposed by the sub-secretariat for institutional reform and strengthening democracy and by the anti-corruption office, and incorporates the recommendations of civil society organisations.[2]

The decree establishes the following mechanisms within the executive: high-ranking members of the national executive must record every meeting with lobbyists or special interest groups, providing the names of all participants at the meeting, its purpose and results; all agencies of the national executive, private organisations that receive state subsidies and privatised utilities must provide information within 10 days to any party who requests it; the official gazette must be made available in its entirety and free for posting on the Internet; an institutional space will be created to allow the public to make proposals and recommendations on all administrative rulings and draft laws submitted by the executive to congress; and the executive and bodies that regulate public services must hold public hearings and open meetings on policy changes, though the opinions that emerge are not legally binding.

In terms of access to information, the decree represents a clear advance since citizens will henceforth have the right to request and receive information from organisations under the jurisdiction of the executive. The decree does not overturn previous laws restricting access to public information, however. Moreover, the NGO Poder Ciudadano has monitored compliance with the conflict of interest aspect of the decree and found it to be variable from institution to institution.

The decree has a number of other shortcomings, too. First, its jurisdiction is limited to the executive; it generates no obligations for the legislature, the judiciary or sub-national bodies. These are aspects of government that face harsh questioning for their lack of openness and poor access to information.[3]

Second, the regulation of a constitutional right,[4] such as citizens' access to public information, should not be limited or granted by presidential decree, but rather should be the subject of a law adopted by the legislature. A bill on access to information, currently before congress, has received initial approval by the lower house, but is likely to falter if the senate fails to pass it before the end of the 2004 parliamentary year.

It is vital that the mechanisms included in the decree be applied to other areas and levels of government, such as the legislature, the judiciary and state governments, and that it be guaranteed by more robust laws – at present the decree could be modified or repealed by another presidential decree. Special attention should be paid to the problems that may arise from its implementation. It is too early to draw conclusions, but what is clear is that further steps are required if a gap is not to open between the new norms and their full implementation.

Plea bargaining: a path to truth?

In December 2003, two civil servants confessed to acts of corruption and offered to help law enforcement agencies with investigations that eventually threatened to envelop government officials of the highest rank. Confessions such as theirs are rare in Argentina, though they would be more common if proper witness-protection legislation were adopted.

Mario Pontaquarto, a former senate clerk, reportedly admitted to having been dispatched in April 2000 by the government of Fernando de la Rúa (December 1999–December 2001) to bribe a number of senators into voting for a law that effectively reduced workers' employment rights and which passed in May 2000. The total amount of the bribe was apparently 5 million pesos (the equivalent of US $5 million before Argentina's financial collapse), which was allegedly siphoned from the state intelligence service's secret funds. The scandal came to light when Hugo Moyano, a leader of the General Labour Confederation, said former labour and social security minister Alberto Flamarique had told him that he 'had the Banelco' (a local debit card) for those senators who opposed the reform. The case lay forgotten, however, until December 2003 when Pontaquarto came forward.

The judge in charge of the investigation, Rodolfo Canicoba, took testimony from Pontaquarto, former intelligence secretary Fernando de Santibáñez and senators José Genoud and Emilio Cantarero. The information they gave was solid, the judge said, and there was ample evidence that bribery had taken place.

In July 2004 the first Buenos Aires criminal appeals court revoked the trial court decision on the grounds that the investigation had been 'defective' and that the details provided by Pontaquarto had not been rigorously checked. Further investigations were ordered that ultimately confirmed his story.

Meanwhile Roberto Martínez, a secretary to former justice minister Raúl Granillo, alleged that all the ministers and a number of secretaries apparently received an additional secret salary of 50,000 pesos (US $50,000) per month during the administration of Carlos Menem (1989–99). The money, he said, had been paid through the office of former cabinet chief Jorge Rodríguez. No receipts were issued or signed. Martínez confessed he had withdrawn an envelope with 50,000 pesos from the cabinet chief's building every month from July 1997 to November 1999.

Others like Pontaquarto or Martínez might step forward if Argentina were to adopt laws to comply with article 37 of the UN Convention against Corruption, which urges signatories to encourage persons who have participated in proscribed offences to confess in exchange for relative clemency. The law at present guarantees neither protection to informants, nor reduced sentences for penitent criminals who come forward with information.

Mixed success for new campaign finance in the 2003 presidential campaign

Law No. 25.600 regulating electoral campaign financing was applied for the first time during the presidential election campaign of 2003. The legislation provides for limits on permitted spending, disclosure of individual and corporate donors, and declaration of expenditure. Parties must also present a preliminary estimate of income and expenditure 10 days before voting and a final report one month later, and district judges must publish the financial statements of political parties on the Internet. This allows for campaign expenditures to be monitored by civil society organisations. The results of the first efforts to monitor the new law signal a gap between the regulations and their application.

The majority of the 21 parties or coalitions that contested the April 2003 elections complied with reporting requirements in a timely fashion. The final reports of the three most popular presidential candidates indicated that total spending was in the region of US $2.6 million, compared to nearly US $48 million in 1999.[5]

There was a big difference between the estimated spending projected in the preliminary report and the final reports, however. According to a report issued by the CNE (the national electoral commission) auditors, the discrepancies, of up to several hundred per cent, 'can distort the decision of the elector since they take into account a preliminary report when deciding their vote, which will be significantly different from the final version'.

There was also an enormous discrepancy between what the candidates said they spent and the traceable spending evidently invested in media campaigns. In the preliminary report supplied by his financial managers, Kirchner declared he had spent only US $1 in the 10 days before the election and that his sole donors were the two men responsible for his campaign, who allegedly contributed US $89 each. The final report included contributions in kind – mostly advertising – worth just over US $527,000, which was supposedly spent after the election. The auditors' report tells a different story, concluding that more than US $1.2 million in expenditure was left out of Kirchner's final report. Poder Ciudadano has estimated that Kirchner's television campaign cost at least US $2.6 million.

Menem's alliance disclosed income and expenditure of slightly over US $400,000, of which US $329,000 was spent on printing ballot papers.[6] Menem spent nothing on advertising, by official accounts, but media and NGO enquiries revealed that as much as US $5 million was allocated to this purpose. Two foundations from Salta[7] allegedly made a combined donation of US $714,000 to the Menem campaign, although this was not declared to the electoral authority.

In conclusion, parties now have to provide detailed reports on their financing, which is an improvement, but these reports too often remain in the realm of fiction. To close the gap, the supervisory body responsible for enforcing the law needs to be strengthened. One concrete recommendation is that the enforcement body be given the resources necessary to carry out a nationwide media audit, as the Mexican Federal Electoral Institute does.

Laura Alonso, Pilar Arcidiácono, María Julia Pérez Tort and Pablo Secchi
(Poder Ciudadano, Argentina)

Further reading

The International Budget Project, *Latin-American Index of Budgetary Transparency: The Experience of 10 Countries, 2003* (Mexico, 2003)

Poder Ciudadano Foundation, 'Banco de datos de Políticos Argentinos' (Data bank on Argentine Politicians), www.poderciudadano.org/elecciones2003/index.asp

Poder Ciudadano Foundation, *Manual para el monitoreo del Consejo de la Magistratura* (Manual on the monitoring of the Judicial Council) (Buenos Aires: Manchita, 2003) and *Manual de monitoreo de medios en períodos electorales* (Manual on monitoring the media in election campaigns) (La Crujia: Buenos Aires, forthcoming)

Organization of American States, 'Report of the Experts Committee on the Mechanism for Monitoring Implementation of the Inter-American Convention against Corruption', Washington, DC, 2003, www.oas.org/juridico/english/mec_rep_arg.pdf

Daniel Santoro, *Venta de armas – Hombres de Menem* (Arms Sales – Menem's Men), (Buenos Aires: Planeta, 2003)

Fundación Poder Ciudadano (TI Argentina): www.poderciudadano.org

Notes

1. At a sub-national level, the autonomous government of Buenos Aires and the province of Santa Fe introduced in September 2003 and January 2004, respectively, new criteria for the selection of magistrates, public prosecutors and other legal appointees, making them subject to the approval of the local legislatures.
2. In its wording the decree acknowledges the input of the Political Reform Board and the NGOs Argentine Dialogue and the Social Forum for Transparency.

3. Organization of American States, 'Report of the Experts Committee on the Mechanism for Monitoring Implementation of the Inter-American Convention against Corruption' (Washington, DC, 2003).
4. The right of access to public information is guaranteed in the Constitution because article 75, section 22 gives constitutional status to international treaties that include respect for this right.
5. Based on information given by candidates to Foundation Poder Ciudadano.
6. Both the central government and political parties print ballot papers. Political parties receive public funding for this purpose.
7. Research by Daniel Santoro of the daily newspaper *Clarín* revealed that the Foundation Argentina Solidaria and the Salta Foundation, both formed by friends of Juan Carlos Romero, the governor of Salta who was also Menem's candidate for vice-president, made these donations.

Azerbaijan

Corruption Perceptions Index 2004 score: 1.9 (140th out of 146 countries)

Conventions:
Council of Europe Civil Law Convention on Corruption (ratified February 2004)
Council of Europe Criminal Law Convention on Corruption (ratified February 2004)
UN Convention against Corruption (signed February 2004; not yet ratified)
UN Convention against Transnational Organized Crime (ratified October 2003)

Legal and institutional changes

- The Azerbaijan parliament adopted **a new anti-corruption law** in January 2004. The law provides definitions of corruption and its perpetrators, and outlines the responsibilities of public officials. Though widely welcomed, the law fails to secure public disclosure of the income and property of public officials, and is overly permissive in its obligations to disclose close relatives as third parties in official transactions (see below).

- The March 2004 presidential decree on the application of the new anti-corruption law stipulates that the law will come into force in January 2005. The **deferred implementation** of the law is seen by many as a means of providing corrupt officials the opportunity to conceal their misdeeds prior to implementation. The decree establishes an anti-corruption agency under the prosecutor-general (see below).

- In April 2004 the **Commission for the Fight against Corruption** was constituted at the first meeting of the Civil Service Executive Board. A major weakness of the commission is its exclusion of civil society and the media. The commission is made up of a mix of presidential, parliamentary and constitutional court appointees. Both the executive board and the commission are headed by Ramiz Mehdiyev, the head of the presidential administration (see below).

Accusations of corruption

Following the ill health (and subsequent death) of former communist leader Heidar Aliev, the presidential elections of October 2003 saw Heidar Aliyev's son, Ilham, elected to the presidency of Azerbaijan. The change of administration triggered an unravelling of the relative cohesion between territorial-ethnic and economic interest groups, largely held in abeyance under the former leader, and unleashed mutual, wide-scale accusations of corruption.

The principal division which opened up during the elections on the issue of corruption focused on the disposal of state assets in the transition from a centralised economy to a form of market economy. Conservatives, mainly opposition groups, had supported retention of state assets and tight state control over the private sector. Reformers, led by the presidential office, had supported moderate liberalisation. For both groups, corruption, or accusations of corruption, became a key issue in attacking the legitimacy of the opposing camp.

During the elections the conservative camp sought to attack the poor corruption record of the incumbent government, dominated by the Yeni Azerbaijan Party (YAP), and to demonstrate how dispersal of state monopolies had provided a cover for racketeering and widespread corruption. The main opposition parties in particular attempted to make 'the Kozeny scandal' one of the key issues of the election campaign.

Dating from early 2000, accusations of large scale corruption had surrounded the Czech-Irish national Viktor Kozeny, following his failure to secure the privatisation of the State Oil Company of the Azerbaijan Republic (SOCAR) for a US-based investment group (Omega Advisers Inc.).[1] Kozeny had admitted to the *Wall Street Journal* in September 2001 that he had spent US $83 million on bribes to high-ranking Azeri officials. He further claimed this was done with approval of his client and filed a complaint in a US district court against his US investors, naming several high-ranking Azerbaijan government officials as recipients of bribes.[2]

This scandal resurfaced again on the eve of the 2003 Azerbaijan presidential elections when, in October 2003, a charge of fraud was filed, again in the US, against Kozeny. Charges included appropriation of Omega Advisers Inc.'s clients' money to the tune of $182 million, funds intended for the purchase of SOCAR.[3]

For their part, the reformist camp has portrayed retention of state control of assets as serving the interests of a small elite of high-ranking public officials seeking to protect its control of Azerbaijan's limited markets and resources. The conservative agenda, they argue, is an attempt to sustain a system of patronage, preventing independent players from the private sector from emerging. In his public speech in February 2003, President Ilham Aliyev openly criticised monopolies supported by high-ranking government officials in basic commodities, such as trade in flour and bread products.[4]

In the main, however, the reformist retort to allegations of corruption within its own ranks appears to have been to level allegations of corruption at opposition figures. Such smear campaigns first appeared in spring 2004 with the publication of articles in the official state newspaper *Azerbaycan*, which severely criticised a group of high-ranking government officials reputed to belong to the conservative wing. The article portrayed them as incompetent and corrupt.[5]

The smear campaigns continued in June 2004. Opposition MP Sabir Rustamkhanli complained in parliament about corruption among chairpersons of the parliamentary commissions. Sirus Tabrizli, deputy chairman of the ruling Yeni Azerbaijan Party, demanded concrete facts.[6] These allegations were downplayed by the chairman of parliament on the grounds that Rustamkhanli had provided no names. Nevertheless, allegations were picked up again by Gohar Bakhchalieva, parliamentary vice-speaker, who also forwarded anonymous accusations against unnamed governmental figures opposed to the reformist agenda.[7]

Both locally and internationally there has been widespread criticism that the allegations of corruption against public officials are politically motivated. Locally, figures such as Presidential Chief of Staff Ramiz Mehtiyev have been publicly accused of orchestrating such campaigns.[8] There has been no response to the allegations of corruption from law enforcement bodies.

A new anti-corruption law

In his March 2004 decree, President Ilham Aliyev endorsed the law 'On the Fight against Corruption' and thus satisfied a precondition of Azerbaijan's admission to the Council of Europe. The law will come into effect in January 2005.

Though the delay for implementing the law has attracted criticism from observers who see this as a 'probationary period' in which to rectify previous misdeeds,[9] there are indications that such moves have improved public confidence in the ruling party's commitment to tackle corruption. A nationwide household survey conducted by Transparency Azerbaijan in May 2004 revealed that nearly all respondents believed that the implementation of a national anti-corruption programme and the establishment of a special anti-corruption agency would curb corruption. Only one quarter of all respondents did not believe that any serious anti-corruption efforts would result.

Despite such public optimism, it is not clear that the legislation that has been introduced represents a genuine commitment to fight corruption. On the positive side, the law stipulates the creation of a commission for the fight against corruption. However, the fact that both the board and the commission are chaired by a single high-ranking government official, the head of the presidential administration, calls into question the ability of this body to carry out its work impartially. The exclusion of civil society and the media from the commission can do little but accentuate this anxiety.

The track record of the Azerbaijani government in its ability to smother legislation is further cause for concern. Both the law on unfair competition and the law on anti-trust policy worked well in appeasing an international audience, but they failed to prevent the emergence of monopolies.

In the absence of a well-defined national anti-corruption programme to complement the anti-corruption legislation, there is every reason to suppose that this legislation will similarly fail when it comes to implementation. Given the legislation's deferment until after the parliamentary elections of November 2004, there is a very real danger that the legislation will be effectively shelved after the election. The failure to address these issues prior to the elections should ensure the issue of corruption will again dissolve into a political football between interest groups, as it did during the presidential elections.

Moreover, the presidential decree makes provisions for the establishment of an anti-corruption agency under the Azerbaijani prosecutor-general an office which, like the anti-corruption commission, is dependent on executive power. The law does not contain any special provisions envisioning conditions for the release of the chief prosecutor from his duties at a later date. Prosecutors have no legal right to refuse 'orders' coming from the executive authorities.

The drive within the ruling party to develop corruption-related legislation in 2003–04 should be seen as both aimed at appeasing domestic disquiet over corruption in the approach to parliamentary elections, and an attempt to bolster Azerbaijan's poor reputation for corruption at an international, particularly European, level. The likelihood of new waves of clashes between competing groups within the government and between government and opposition parties is very real.

Rena Safaralieva (TI Azerbaijan)

Further reading

Caspian Revenue Watch project, www.eurasianet.org

Elizabeth Lash, *Azerbaijan and Corruption* (Sommerville: Tufts University, 2002), www.transparency-az.org

R. Safaralieva, ed., *Corruption: A Business Ethics Manual for Azerbaijani Companies* (Baku: TI Azerbaijan, 2003)

TI Azerbaijan: www.transparency-az.org

Notes

1. *Fortune* magazine (United States), 6 March 2000.
2. Turan News Agency (Azerbaijan), 4 April 2000.
3. *Echo* (Azerbaijan), 11 October 2003.
4. *Echo* (Azerbaijan), 2 February 2003.
5. *Azerbaycan* (Azerbaijan), 20 April 2004.
6. *Adalet* (Azerbaijan), 5 June 2004.
7. *Zerkalo* (Azerbaijan), 12 June 2004.
8. *Eurasia Insight* (Azerbaijan), 5 May 2004, www.eurasianet.org
9. *Nedelya* (Azerbaijan), 9 January 2004.

Bangladesh

Corruption Perceptions Index 2004 score: 1.5 (145th out of 146 countries)

Conventions:
UN Convention against Corruption (not yet signed)
UN Convention against Transnational Organized Crime (not yet signed)

Legal and institutional changes

- In February 2004 parliament passed the **Anti-Corruption Commission Act**, paving the way for the establishment of an independent body to fight corruption in the country. The act provides the legal framework to set up a commission to promote good governance and ensure transparency in public administration. The commission is to consist of three commissioners with a chairman to be appointed from among them by the country's president. Whether the commission will truly be independent, however, is doubtful (see below).

- The planning ministry introduced new **public procurement regulations** in October 2003, in an attempt to promote transparency and accountability in the public procurement system. The regulations aim to ensure value for money in public procurement and that procurement is conducted in a fair, transparent and non-discriminatory manner. A major limitation of the regulations, however, is that exceptions are allowed on matters of state security, including military procurement. The rules also fail to mention price-quality considerations in procurement and delays in delivery. Most importantly, the regulations do not have the full force of a law. The government can, therefore, prevent their implementation at its own discretion.

Government efforts at reform: the creation of an independent anti-corruption commission

The Anti-Corruption Commission Act 2004 was passed by parliament in February 2004. The commission replaces the Bureau of Anti-Corruption, which had failed to address the endemic corruption in Bangladesh and which was itself widely believed to be riddled with corruption.

The impetus to create a new commission was the result of increasing pressure from civil society groups. From 2001 onwards, the regular appearance of Bangladesh at, or near, the bottom of Transparency International's Corruption Perceptions Index was particularly influential in keeping corruption on the political agenda. In 2004, all the major political parties included the creation of an independent anti-corruption commission in their election manifestos.

The objective of the commission is to prevent corruption and conduct investigations into corruption-related offences. Under the law, the commission is to consist of three commissioners with a chairman to be appointed from among them by the country's president. The commissioners are to be nominated by a five-member selection panel, which will include two judges, the comptroller and auditor general, the chairman of the public service commission and the most recently-retired cabinet secretary. Commissioners are appointed for a four-year term.

The commission's mandate includes several functions: to conduct inquiries and investigations, file and conduct cases, review the legally accepted measures for preventing corruption, promote honesty and integrity in public life and make recommendations to the president. It will also have the powers of arrest, to take testimony from those involved in allegations, to demand individuals to submit a statement of assets and liabilities, and to take possession of property in excess of known sources of income. A new court is also to be established.

While the decision to abolish the Bureau of Anti-Corruption and establish a new agency is welcome, the new law has serious shortcomings that call into question the potential effectiveness of the commission. First and foremost, the commission's autonomy appears seriously limited. Aside from the obvious weakness that the head of the commission is appointed by the president, the commission will also be dependent on the government for decisions about its organisational structure and, notably, its budget. The absence of civil society representation on the selection committee further jeopardises the neutrality of commissioners. There are no civil society oversight mechanisms and no provisions in the law for civil society to play a role in raising public awareness and preventing corruption.

Several amendments to the current law would strengthen the commission. The power of arrest should be made more specific; left as it is, such power is open to abuse. In addition, it is crucial that the commission be provided with adequate resources and personnel as soon as it is established. In order to avoid the fate of the Bureau of Anti-Corruption, the commission must achieve quick results to gain public respect. The credibility of the institution could be enhanced by introducing an asset-declaration requirement for the commissioners.

Bringing about institutional change in Bangladesh is no simple task; it will inevitably meet strong resistance. In the case of the new anti-corruption commission, it is the international donor agencies that have taken the most interest, though domestic civil society groups have done their best to back up demands for more public accountability.

Speeding up justice

The call for judicial reform in Bangladesh revolves around two themes, the abuse of judicial office for political ends and the chronic inefficiency of the judiciary leading to a poor quality of justice and the presence of widespread 'low level' bribery. The April 2004 act that extends the 2002 'Speedy Trial Act' for two years is set to impact both these phenomena in complex and even opposing ways. While increasing the speed of trials may prevent certain types of 'low level' bribery, it may exacerbate the use of the judiciary for political ends.

The main objective of the act is to speed up the settlement of cases that have direct bearing on social violence and on the poor state of law and order in the country, both of which are popularly perceived to be on the rise in Bangladesh. In this regard, the notorious reputation of the Bangladeshi judiciary for slowness is richly deserved. Delays of several years have been reported in respect to child and sexual abuse cases for which the law requires a verdict within 90 days. The crimes covered by the act include extortion, destruction of public and private goods, public assault, intimidation causing anarchy, and violation of tender procedures. Under the law, investigations of these crimes should be completed within seven days of filing a case; the accused should be brought into the court within 24 hours; and a case should be settled within 30 days (60 days if the accused has absconded).

While the act does not specifically address the topic of corruption, the settling of such cases within a specific time frame could have a substantial impact on a major source of graft in Bangladesh. One particularly widespread technique of corruption has been for judicial officers to slow down judicial processes in order to compel the parties to pay bribes to achieve a judicial verdict. Indeed, the popular term for a bribe in Bangladesh is 'speed money'.

Gains in the area of 'low level' bribery for speedier trials may, however, come at the cost of exacerbating other forms of corruption. Critics of the act have argued that the law can be easily misused by the government to intimidate its opponents. Opinion polls conducted by TI Bangladesh have suggested that about one quarter of the cases heard under the Speedy Trial Act have been politically motivated. The country's opposition parties have all expressed objections to the law.

Reporters without Borders and the Bangladesh Centre for Development, Journalism and Communication have also protested against the misuse of the law to arrest journalists, including Abdul Mahbud Mahu of the local daily *Ajker Desh Bidesh* and Hiramon Mondol, a reporter for the daily *Prabartan*, saying that the journalists had no time to prepare a defence.[1]

A further worrying effect of speedy trials is that an increasing number of the accused are not present during their trials. There also seems to have been a lack of thought about the implications of accelerated trails for other areas of the judicial system. No additional resources were allotted to cope with increased activities of the courts or to deal with the knock-on effects in higher courts of appeal.

Md. Abdul Alim (TI Bangladesh)

Further reading

Centre for Policy Dialogue (CPD), *Developing a Policy Agenda for Bangladesh: Civil Society's Task Force Reports 2001* (Dhaka: 2003)
Federation of Bangladesh Chamber and Commerce Industry (FBCCI), *The Cost of Doing Business Study* (Dhaka: 2004)
Transparency International Bangladesh (TIB), Corruption Database (Dhaka, 2003)

TI Bangladesh: www.ti-bangladesh.org

Note

1. See www.rsf.org/article.php3?id_article=7778 and www.rsf.org/article.php3?id_article=9282

Bolivia

Corruption Perceptions Index 2004 score: 2.2 (122nd out of 146 countries)

Conventions:
OAS Inter-American Convention against Corruption (ratified February 1997)
UN Convention against Corruption (signed December 2003; not yet ratified)
UN Convention against Transnational Organized Crime (signed December 2000; not yet ratified)

Legal and institutional changes

- A **presidential anti-corruption delegation** (DPA) was created in October 2003, replacing the secretariat for the fight against corruption and for special policies, which was created in August 2002 under the auspices of the vice-president's office. The DPA's main task is ensuring compliance with the Inter-American Convention against Corruption, and coordinating anti-corruption efforts of the judiciary, the auditor general, the public prosecutor and the bank regulator. The delegation has drafted a wide-ranging action plan for 2004–07 focused on promoting public ethics; establishing monitoring mechanisms for corruption-prone bodies and processes; and supporting and strengthening authorities with powers to investigate and penalise corruption. Since starting, it has released a number of bulletins and reports, including analyses of specific corruption cases, and has established mobile anti-corruption brigades for rural municipalities as well as civic anti-corruption networks. The delegation also receives complaints related to corruption. Its effectiveness is limited, however, by its lack of investigative and prosecutorial powers. Another problem is that it was created by presidential decree and therefore has weak legal status, and as part of the executive has no legal authority over the judiciary or the legislature. It has also been criticised for its lack of independence, since it is part of the central government. Its success at a regional level has been mixed: in the state of Cochabamba, for example, in April 2004 the DPA delegate was allegedly given no support or office space by the head of the department, and eventually resigned.

- In the absence of a law on **access to information**, new rules were issued by presidential decree in February 2004 requiring public officials to give public access to information that is not of a confidential nature. The DPA is studying ways to implement the decree across government departments. A more extensive access to information bill has been drafted, but is unlikely to be discussed by the legislature in 2004.

- Congress agreed in March 2004 on the order in which a bicameral constitutional commission would investigate a series of **high-profile cases** involving corruption. They include allegations against former president Gonzalo Sánchez de Lozada as well as the Kieffer case (see below). Each legislative chamber has a separate ethics commission that can also look into corruption allegations, but political in-fighting has limited the effectiveness of these commissions. One advance was the modification in March 2004 of procedures for dealing with cases; the ethics commissions of both chambers can now take on cases directly, without the prior approval of the president of the respective chamber.

- At the time of writing, congressional commissions were drafting bills on the **criminalisation of illegal enrichment, whistleblower protection and the creation of a general anti-corruption prosecutor**. Fighting between political parties was likely to delay these legislative processes beyond 2004.

Kukoc scandal prompts legislature to deal with misuse of discretionary funds

The level of discretionary funds granted to government ministries has increased in recent years, reaching between US $120 million and US $140 million in 2003, in a country with a government budget for the same year of only US $1 billion. The general public can do little more than speculate about how this money is spent. The high-profile case of Yerko Kukoc, government minister under the second administration of Gonzalo Sánchez de Lozada (August 2002–October 2003), included allegations of the abuse of discretionary funds, and galvanised the legislature into debating a bill that would increase oversight as to how such money is spent.

The official justification for the discretionary funds is that they are spent on national security projects, such as countering drugs trafficking or quelling disturbances, which would be compromised if the spending were made public. Unofficially, however, they have allegedly been used to top up the salaries of senior government officials, including former presidents.

The auditor general's office is charged with supervising the discretionary funds, in line with an executive decree issued in May 2003, which was a first attempt to exercise control over how the funds are spent. In October 2003, mass protests against planned energy and gas sales, in which more than 100 people were killed, forced President Sánchez de Lozada to resign. Just before he did so, he issued a decree stating that accounts pertaining to reserved funds should be presented to the president only, and not to the auditor general.

Kukoc was appointed minister in March 2003 and was, along with the president, one of the most prominent figures during the October clashes. He too was forced to resign as a result, and fled the country. Three weeks later Kukoc returned and stated his readiness to talk about how the discretionary funds had been spent.

The public prosecutor initiated investigations in December 2003, after US $277,000 in cash was reportedly discovered in the house of Kukoc's alleged childhood friend, Milder Rubén Arzadum Monzón, who testified that Kukoc had asked him to hide the money. According to the public prosecutor, the money was from the ministry's discretionary funds.

Kukoc argued that he could account for most of his ministry's funds, except for those used to quell the October uprisings, which were covered by the presidential decree overturning the requirement to present accounts to anyone other than the president.

His position was further complicated when one of Bolivia's main trade unions, Central Obrera Boliviana, a key player in the uprising, accused Kukoc of ordering the withdrawal of 13.6 million bolivianos (US $1.8 million) from the central bank around the time of the presidential decree exempting officials from presenting discretionary fund accounts to the auditor general. The president of the central bank, Juan Antonio Morales, confirmed this. Kukoc reportedly admitted that he had transferred money to other ministers and officials, and that he had deposited part of the money he withdrew from the central bank in a private account.[1]

Kukoc was put under house arrest in January 2004, and posted bail later that month. He eventually pleaded guilty to stealing from the state, and received a two-year suspended sentence on condition that he would provide information about money embezzled by other public officials. He is the first person to be convicted in Bolivia for misusing discretionary funds.

Sánchez de Lozada's successor, President Carlos Mesa, revived the original decree requiring accounts to be presented to the auditor general, and in January 2004 issued new rules for spending, and accounting for, discretionary funds. In April 2004, a draft bill was submitted to congress to regulate discretionary funds, stipulating explicit prohibitions on certain uses of the funds, and requiring accounts to be presented not only to the auditor general's office, but also to a legislative commission. The law, if approved by the legislature, will be less easily amended or repealed than a decree.

Power, immunity and the reach of justice: the case of Fernando Kieffer

Bolivia's judiciary, which appears weak relative to the executive and legislature, has time and time again proved unable to convict members of the political and economic elite for corruption. Political interference and the broad immunity from prosecution enjoyed by legislators are further stumbling blocks in the fight against official corruption. The case of Fernando Kieffer, a former defence minister and former congressman who allegedly misused money donated by the international community to help earthquake victims, illustrates how difficult it is to hold Bolivia's powerful and privileged to account.

Kieffer was first accused before the legislature in August 2000, but has yet to go on trial. There are three charges: that he diverted international donations for the people of Aiquile and Mizque who suffered an earthquake in 1998; that some of the money was used to buy an overpriced executive jet; and that he was behind the irregular purchase of Galil weapons for the army.

As a congressman, Kieffer claimed immunity from prosecution until the end of his term in 2002. The case stalled for another six months until Vice-President Jorge Quiroga ordered the case file to be transferred to the congressional commission responsible for examining high-level corruption cases. At the time of writing, it is now third in a list to be examined by the commission.

In the case of the aeroplane, the auditor general reportedly concluded that Kieffer had paid extravagantly more than the market value, and in late 2001 Kieffer and the head of the company that brokered the deal were ordered to pay the state just over US $1.1 million, which was the sum by which they had overpaid.[2] Kieffer unsuccessfully challenged the order. A second court again ordered him to pay in July 2003, and finally the defence ministry froze Kieffer's assets and gave him 10 days to pay the fine. Kieffer filed for an injunction, and has reportedly still not paid. He also allegedly accused anti-corruption delegate Lupe Cajías of obstructing his defence.[3] Faced with public pressure, the government found alternative sources of funds to transfer US $780,000 to each of the two provinces affected by the earthquake. The investigation into the unlawful weapons deal is ongoing in the legislature.

However slowly the courts appear to be moving in this case, things could have been worse. It looked as though the case might be shelved in May 2004, along with many others that ran into the four-year statute of limitations that applied under the old criminal code. The case falls under the jurisdiction of a new code of criminal procedure, however, first introduced in May 2001, which has helped transform the justice system from a closed, written system to a system of transparent oral trials.

Kieffer apparently continues to move freely within the highest echelons of Bolivia's political class, a tier of politicians apparently immune from, or inured to, the scorn normally poured on corrupt political leaders. Though the government has made some attempt to bolster the justice system, the level of impunity for officials is generally high. Political parties reportedly tend to protect their own, causing cases to stall in the legislative commissions charged with investigating them and, in the case of parliamentarians, with lifting immunity.

Jorge González Roda (Fundación Etica y Democracia, Bolivia)

Further reading

H. C. F. Mansilla, *La Policía Boliviana, entre los códigos informales y los intentos de modernización* (The Bolivian police, between informal codes and attempts to modernise) (La Paz: ILDIS – Plural, 2003)

Marco Antonio Gonzales and Fernando Fernández Orozco, *Basta ya de impunidad* (Enough impunity) (La Paz: Fondo Editorial de los Diputados, 2002)

Martín Sivack, *El dictador elegido* (The elected dictator) (La Paz: Plural, 2001)

Rafael Archondo, *Incestos y blindages, radiografía del campo político periodístico* (Incest and armour-plating, a radiography of political journalism) (La Paz: Plural, 2003)

Notes

1. *La Razón* (Bolivia), 17 January 2004.
2. *La Razón* (Bolivia), 17 July 2003.
3. *La Razón* (Bolivia), 29 July 2003.

Brazil

Corruption Perceptions Index 2004 score: 3.9 (59th out of 146 countries)

Conventions:
OAS Inter-American Convention against Corruption (ratified July 2002)
OECD Anti-Bribery Convention (ratified August 2000)
UN Convention against Corruption (signed December 2003; not yet ratified)
UN Convention against Transnational Organized Crime (ratified January 2004)

Legal and institutional changes

- The ruling issued by the superior electoral court in 2002 requiring candidates who participated in the national elections to present their **campaign expenditure** statements electronically was extended to candidates participating in the forthcoming 2004 municipal elections. The superior electoral court is expected to approve new procedures regulating the presentation of political parties' annual expenditure statements. Among other requirements, all statements must be presented electronically, in conformity with the system generated by the electoral court. Although parties have had to render accounts since 1993, the new regulation will provide a broad picture of party finance for the first time.

- The **Council for Public Transparency and the Fight against Corruption**, established within the inspector general's office in May 2003, had its structure approved and its functions regulated in December 2003. It is difficult to foresee what impact the council is likely to have, however, as it is an advisory body with no executive or enforcement power. It does have civil society representatives, but contrary to the government pledge to set up a centralised anti-corruption organisation with wide-ranging powers, it cannot impose reform programmes on other ministries. The result is that important anti-corruption initiatives are spread out across a number of uncoordinated offices.

- The law on the **budget guidelines** for 2005 was submitted to congress in April 2004. President Lula da Silva was first advised to refuse full access to budget expenditure on the grounds that strategic information should be protected, but apparently under pressure by the media and opposition forces in congress, he relented. The law was approved in August 2004 and gives members of congress access to computer data on the budget.

The not so beautiful game

Over the past few years, Brazilian football has been dogged by numerous problems allegedly largely attributable to dishonest and unaccountable management. Repeated corruption and embezzlement scandals have had a negative impact on football development. Although Brazil has an unmatched record on the field at international level, the country's domestic football shows severe financial difficulties. The exodus of top players seeking lucrative contracts abroad has resulted in a sharp decline in revenues coming from supporters at home.

A series of media reports on scandals involving team administrators, managers and player agents, following Brazil's defeat by France at the 1998 World Cup and its elimination by Cameroon at the 2000 Olympics, led to two congressional inquiries to investigate the 'dark secrets' of the sport. Included in the list of scandals was Ricardo Teixeira, the president of the Brazilian Football Confederation (CBF), accused of fraud and misappropriation of funds, and Wanderley Luxemburgo, the former coach of the Brazilian national team, involved in a case of alleged unreported income stashed in undeclared foreign bank accounts.

The investigation conducted by the lower house of parliament focused on alleged irregularities in a US $400 million sponsorship agreement between Nike and the CBF, but the investigation was shelved, reportedly after interference by Eurico Miranda, president of the Vasco da Gama club and member of the investigating commission.

However, a senate inquiry referred to irregularities including income tax evasion, non-payment of social security tax, money laundering, evasion of foreign exchange controls, skimming of gate revenues and paying off referees to help fix match results. The final report called on the prosecutor general to indict 17 officials on allegations of mismanagement and other crimes, but, so far, many of them remain in office, thanks either to their political connections or to the public prosecutors' inefficiency.

Besides the investigation of crimes and misconduct of football officials, the senate inquiry proposed new legislation in order to enforce transparency and accountability in the administration of clubs and federations. After two years of negotiations, President da Silva sanctioned, in mid-2003, the so-called 'Law of Moralisation in Sport', together with a more ambitious law, the 'Supporters' Statute', a bill of rights for football supporters.

The new legislation obliges football clubs and federations to publish their accounts annually and submit them to independent auditors, allows for the preventive removal of directors accused of misconduct, and encourages clubs to become companies and to abide by standard business regulations.

Not surprisingly, less than a week after Lula da Silva sanctioned the laws, the directors of some of Brazil's leading clubs threatened to suspend the national championship indefinitely in protest against the new legislation. Under a barrage of criticism from government officials, supporters and the media, and faced by the president's firm personal stand in favour of the laws, the football bosses backed down. Given the long history of widespread corruption associated with Brazilian football, it seems too early to foresee whether the new legislation will have the hoped-for impact on combating unethical and illicit conduct, and enforcing transparency in the administration of clubs and federations.

Politics, gambling and organised crime

The 52 million Brazilians who backed Lula da Silva's Workers' Party in the 2002 presidential election could have taken a major gamble, unwittingly. Early in 2004 President da Silva, having announced in his annual address to congress the government's intention to enact specific legislation to regulate gambling in bingo halls, decided to outlaw the activity, as the government considered it to be a front for money laundering and organised crime.

The government's move to ban gambling followed the disclosure of a videotape showing Waldomiro Diniz, an adviser to Jose Dirceu, the presidential chief of staff and one of the most influential men in the government, allegedly asking for bribes and campaign contributions from a major industrialist. Although the scandal does not directly involve Jose Dirceu, the episode dented his authority and credibility, and the opposition in congress began calling for a full-scale investigation and his removal from office.

This scandal, and the exposure in June 2004 of a ring of health ministry officials, lobbyists and businessmen who had allegedly conspired to inflate the price of government purchases of blood and blood derivatives, damaged the government's authority and the Workers' Party's clean image. In both cases President da Silva reacted immediately, firing the presidential assistant, banning bingo halls throughout the country, and calling for an in-depth investigation of the health ministry.

Analysts see the bingo ban as an almost naive effort to distance the government from involvement in dishonest behaviour. For many, the government is looking in the wrong direction, failing to assess correctly the magnitude of the problem. A number of analysts argue that the scandal represents more than an isolated case of corruption inside the government, but rather unveils dangerous connections between organised crime and political campaign financing in Brazil.

Nevertheless, it appears that the government bingo crusade is going to continue. After the approval of the presidential decree in the chamber of deputies, in a surprising result the senate rejected the measure as unconstitutional and allowed bingo halls to reopen. At the time of writing, the government was to introduce a bill in congress, in the same terms as the earlier decree, to try once more to outlaw gambling throughout the country. No inquiry to investigate the connections between political financing and organised crime had been proposed.

Ana Luiza Fleck Saibro (Transparência Brasil)

Further reading

Claudio Weber Abramo, 'Corruption in Brazil: The Perspective from the Private Sector, 2003', survey by Transparência Brasil in association with Kroll Brasil, April 2004, www.transparencia.org.br

Bruno Wilhelm Speck and Claudio Weber Abramo, eds, Primeira pesquisa sobre o mercado de compra de votos na cidade de Campinas: demandas e ofertas (Survey on the vote buying market in the city of Campinas: supply and demand), survey by Transparência Brasil and Ponto-de-Vista, September 2003, www.transparencia.org.br

Bruno Wilhelm Speck and Claudio Weber Abramo, eds, *Corrupção na municipalidade de São Paulo* (Corruption in the city of São Paulo), 2003, www.transparencia.org.br

Transparência Brasil (TI Brazil): www.transparencia.org.br

Britain

Corruption Perceptions Index 2004 score: 8.6 (11th out of 146 countries)

Conventions:
Council of Europe Civil Law Convention on Corruption (signed June 2000; not yet ratified)
Council of Europe Criminal Law Convention on Corruption (ratified December 2003)
OECD Anti-Bribery Convention (ratified December 1998)
UN Convention against Corruption (signed December 2003; not yet ratified)
UN Convention against Transnational Organized Crime (signed December 2000; not yet ratified)

Legal and institutional changes

* In July 2003 the Joint Parliamentary Committee published its report on the draft corruption bill, which had been published by the government in March 2003. The report was highly critical of the draft bill, particularly in relation to the government's definition of corruption. The government published its official response to the report in December 2003, accepting some of the recommendations, but defending itself strongly against others, particularly in respect of the definition of corruption (see below).

* In November 2003 the Crime (International Cooperation) Act 2003 was passed, which provides new powers for cross-border information sharing between the Serious Fraud Office and overseas police bodies.

* In March 2004 the government published a white paper entitled *One Step Ahead: A 21st Century Strategy to Defeat Organised Crime*, which proposed that a new national police organisation, the Serious Organised Crime Agency (SOCA), should be established. SOCA would be responsible to the home secretary and would investigate organised immigration crime, drugs trafficking, and the recovery of criminal assets (see below).

* In May 2004 the Export Credits Guarantee Department announced new policies specifically designed to combat bribery and corruption (see below).

Corruption at the crossroads?

In March 2003 the government published its draft corruption bill, which aimed to codify existing corruption legislation, but its future remains uncertain.

The draft bill originated from a report by the Law Commission in 1998, following which a working group was established comprising, among others, the Law Commission, the Crown Prosecution Service, the treasury, the Serious Fraud Office (SFO), and the home office. The group published a White Paper in June 2000, *Raising Standards*

and Upholding Integrity: The Prevention of Corruption, which was subsequently sent out for public consultation.

The White Paper's proposals, which set out to codify existing laws into a single piece of legislation, attracted only limited though focused criticism, including from Transparency International (UK). Consequently the draft bill contained nearly all the recommendations that were first made public in 1998.

In July 2003 the Joint Parliamentary Committee considering the bill published its report, which was drawn from oral and written evidence made by a number of organisations, including Transparency International, the SFO, the OECD Expert Group on Bribery and the attorney general. The evidence presented by these and other witnesses was highly critical of the bill, which led the committee to suggest a number of fundamental changes to the proposed legislation.

The committee argued that the bill would not be 'readily understood by the police, by prosecutors, by jurors and by the public, including – especially – the business and public sector communities, and their advisors, both here and abroad'.[1] The report also criticised the definitions of 'corruption' and 'corruptly' contained within the bill as 'opaque', and argued that they fail 'to cover some corrupt conduct such as when the head of one firm bribes the head of another or when an employer consents to the bribery of his agent'.[2] The report made further suggestions regarding corruption in the private sector and parliamentary privilege.

In December 2003, the government published its official response to the report, which accepted several recommendations, but defended the bill against criticisms over its definition of corruption.[3] The government argued that the proposed legislation remained consistent from 1998 to 2003, in which time it underwent three periods of consultation, a fact attested to by the committee's report.[4]

Why, then, had these previous consultations not provided more substantive criticisms that could have been addressed in either the 2000 White Paper, or the 2003 bill itself?

One possible reason is simply the complexity of the area, in which few can agree on a definition of corruption. A second reason could be that there is a lack of political will within the government, and that legislative reform is simply not high enough on the government's agenda. Defenders of the government may point to its signing of the UN Convention against Corruption in December 2003. In order to ratify the convention, however, the government admitted that it needs to put in place primary and secondary legislation and there is no timetable for this process as yet. Indeed, it seems the government more heavily favours legislation on the fight against fraud and organised crime rather than corruption per se, as evidenced for example by its recent white paper *One Step Ahead: A 21st Century Strategy to Defeat Organised Crime* (see next section). The apparent lack of will may have resulted in public indifference.

As things stand, the future of reform is uncertain – although the redrafting process is ongoing, there is now no definite date for its completion. Reform of existing legislation, therefore, still appears to be some distance off.

A fragmented fight?

Although anti-corruption organisations appear to be successful in Britain, the relationship between them is complex and somewhat confusing. Any coordination that does occur takes place in three major ways: joint investigations; information sharing; and developing common standards.

In February 2004 David Blunkett, the home secretary, announced the creation of a new joint investigation body, accountable directly to him. The role of the Serious Organised Crime Agency (SOCA) was fleshed out in the White Paper, *One Step Ahead*. It is proposed that SOCA will be charged with combating drug trafficking and organised immigration crime, as well as the recovery of criminal assets. It was hoped that the creation of the new agency would 'reduce the number of organisations with which the police and others have to deal, improving efficiency and reducing bureaucracy'.[5]

The Department for Work and Pensions (DWP) contains another example of a joint investigation agency. To promote co-operation between the various units within the DWP, other government departments and local authorities, a joint working unit was established, whose aim is to improve the number and quality of anti-fraud operations across organisational boundaries. In addition, the DWP has also worked in conjunction with the Inland Revenue and HM Customs and Excise, using intelligence and shared information jointly to investigate traders suspected of operating in the shadow economy with the aim of detecting and penalising benefit or tax fraud.

One example of information sharing is the Financial Fraud Information Network (FFIN) that covers regulators, government departments, professional bodies, law enforcement and the markets. Founded in 1992 to facilitate cooperation between the wide range of public bodies concerned with financial fraud, in 2003 the FFIN secretariat became part of the Financial Services Authority.

An example of developing common standards is the Public Audit Forum, a consultative and advisory body that provides a forum for developing professional standards. The forum is made up of the four national audit agencies and, in addition, has a consultative forum with representatives from central and local government, the national health service, and the accountancy and audit profession.

How effective these agencies will be is, of course, open to debate. What does seem to be important is that the examples of inter-organisational cooperation outlined above appear to reinforce the view that the government is currently focused on fraud and organised crime rather than corruption. Anti-corruption commentators have argued, for example, that SOCA will have little impact on cases of overseas bribery or corruption carried out by white collar criminals, which has recently been backed by a government announcement that the SFO would be the first agency to consider cases of overseas bribery and would take a lead in any subsequent investigations.[6]

Inter-agency cooperation seems intuitively to be a good thing, especially in an area as complex as corruption, but this very much depends on what type of cooperation is promoted. Information sharing, too, is an inherently sensible activity, but this must be considered in light of some agencies playing a key role in investigations: to what extent will they be willing to share information with others?

Perhaps most importantly, coordination is needed for common standards on corruption, particularly in terms of overseas bribery and corruption. Transparency International's recent National Integrity Systems study on Britain has argued that there is 'a certain hypocrisy at the heart of government commitment to integrity. On the one hand it is developing ethical frameworks to regulate the behaviour of public bodies in the UK. At the same time, it appears to condone the activities of government and business when operating overseas.'[7] This problem is highlighted in the case of the Export Credits Guarantee Department (ECGD).

Export Credits Guarantee Department

The ECGD is a separate government department, answerable to the minister for trade and industry, whose main role is to provide insurance to British exporters and British companies investing overseas. It also provides guarantees to British-based banks to make loans to overseas investors. In 2000, the ECGD underwent a major review of its mission, but in 2004 further anti-corruption measures were unveiled.

The ECGD is in a particularly strong position to detect and prevent corruption, and is also able to influence corporate behaviour in the rejection of bribery in the conduct of foreign business. Its application procedure includes a non-bribery declaration, and a request for information that the applicant has exercised all caution that no bribe has been paid during the course of the proposed transaction. The ECGD announced new policies and procedures specifically designed to combat bribery and corruption, which came into effect in May 2004. They include provisions to increase the ECGD's powers to inspect exporters' contractual documents; requirements that applicants demonstrate that they have procedures in place to prevent corrupt activity; and an extension of declaration requirements to include affiliates as well as the directors and employees of companies.

These measures have only been introduced, however, after stringent public criticism. Recent media coverage has argued that the ECGD 'has been pervaded by an institutional culture of negligence when it comes to corruption',[8] which is particularly worrying in light of the ECGD's own claim that there has not been a single occasion since the 2000 review where ECGD cover has been refused due to any evidence or suspicion of corrupt practices.[9] The question arises, then, as to why cover has not been refused under what appear to have been less than transparent circumstances, particularly as it has been alleged that:

Throughout the 1990's and into the early 2000's, the ECGD consistently supported projects, which were over-priced and plagued by corruption allegations, from dams such as the Lesotho Highlands Water Project to power plants such as the Dabhol Power Plant in India. In some instances it gave or continued backing despite knowing about these allegations.

In most instances, it revealed a deep reluctance to investigate such allegations or pass them on to the relevant UK or local authorities.[10]

Such concerns are exacerbated by the scale of the ECGD's business: 95 per cent of all debt owed to Britain by developing countries is actually owed to the ECGD. It is crucial, then, that the new regulations prove to be effective rather than merely rhetorical. Until then, suspicion will remain that Britain has a very different approach to corruption abroad than it does at home.

The case of the ECGD therefore unites the themes of this report. A coordinated approach to common standards would seem to be the most logical way to combat bribery and corruption, particularly in overseas cases. Such an approach would best be tackled through legislation, which lays down clear rules to underpin Britain's anti-corruption strategy. Yet such legislation is being held up due to a variety of factors, which in turn has a knock-on effect on Britain's commitments to international anti-corruption measures such as the UN Convention. Despite Britain's relatively good standing in the Corruption Perceptions Index, then, there is still a need for the government to provide a clear foundation upon which to build an improved, consistent anti-corruption strategy.

Michael James Macauley (Teesside Business School, Britain)

Further reading

S. Hawley, *Turning a Blind Eye: Corruption and the UK Export Credits Guarantee Department* (Dorset: The Corner House, 2003)

S. Hawley, *Underwriting Bribery: Export Credit Agencies and Corruption* (Dorset: The Corner House, 2003)

TI (UK): www.transparency.org.uk

Notes

1. 'Draft Corruption Bill – Report and Evidence' (HL Paper 157 HC 705).
2. The committee suggested that the definition in the draft bill should be replaced by the following definitions: 'A person acts corruptly if he gives, offers or agrees to give an improper

advantage with the intention of influencing the recipient in the performance of his duties or functions'; 'A person acts corruptly if he receives, asks for or agrees to receive an improper advantage with the intention that it will influence him in the performance of his duties or functions.'

3. 'The Government Reply to the Report from the Joint Committee on the Draft Corruption Bill', CM 6086 (2003).
4. According to the bill, 'The draft Bill is the product of a long policy-making process ... The Law Commission published a Draft Bill on corruption in essentially similar terms five years ago.'
5. Home Office, *One Step Ahead: A 21st Century Strategy to Defeat Organised Crime*, Cm 6167 (London: HMSO, 2004).
6. *Financial Times* (Britain), 25 June 2004.
7. Transparency International, *National Integrity Systems, Transparency International Country Study Report, United Kingdom 2003* (London, 2004).
8. *Observer* (Britain), 2 February 2003.
9. 'New Procedures on Bribery and Corruption in Export Deals Announced by ECGD', 11 April 2004, www.ecgd.gov.uk/news_home.htm?id=6095
10. *Observer* (Britain), 2 February 2003.

Burkina Faso

Corruption Perceptions Index 2004 score: not surveyed

Conventions:
AU Convention on the Prevention and Combating of Corruption (signed February 2004; not yet ratified)
UN Convention against Corruption (signed December 2003; not yet ratified)
UN Convention against Transnational Organized Crime (ratified May 2002)

Legal and institutional changes

- The Public Accounts Court, established in 2002, delivered its first reports to the National Assembly in September 2003 for the period 1995–2000 and on 2001. The court's mandate is to monitor the **execution of budgetary legislation** and the management of the state's funding of political parties. The need for scrutiny in this area was underlined by the court's findings. In addition to delays in payments and the transmission of documents, the reports identified accounting errors and the non-reimbursement of loans made to government officials and parliamentarians.

- In January 2004 an **all-party group of parliamentarians** established a coalition to fight corruption that may serve as a link between them and anti-corruption activists as well as international networks, such as the African Parliamentarians' Network against Corruption. The year also saw the submission of a bill on parliamentarians' salaries to the parliamentary office, intended to tighten rules on gifts and contributions.

- In January 2004 REN-LAC, a nationwide anti-corruption network of more than 30 civil society organisations, submitted a memorandum to President Blaise Compaoré calling for more effective controls on corruption. Amongst a range of measures, REN-LAC recommended the introduction of **comprehensive anti-corruption legislation** governing all relevant institutions. The memorandum also called for greater independence and powers for the existing control structures, including the Public Accounts Court, the General State Inspectorate and the High Commission for the Coordination of Anti-Corruption Activities. These offices currently have few enforcement powers, their reports are not made public and the government has final say over their membership. The government has not responded to REN-LAC's recommendations at the time of writing. The umbrella group intends to issue a new memorandum each year that includes an assessment of which of its recommendations the government has acted on during the preceding year.

- A workshop on good governance in the private sector was held in January 2004 at the initiative of Shell-Burkina and involving around 100 companies. The workshop called for a **private sector code of good conduct** that is expected to be adopted by multinational and national firms in the oil industry and other sectors during the course of 2004. The code will require them to comply with national legislation; to introduce specific anti-corruption rules and ensure compliance by their employees; and to monitor the practice of giving gifts, and forbid benefits in kind or abnormally high payments that might amount to bribery. The main challenges will be to mobilise other companies behind the code, and also to make it effective in the context of the close relationships that exist between political parties and the country's largest economic players.

- In April 2004 the majority of civil society organisations adopted a **code of conduct** including principles of good governance relating to financial management, human resources management, democratic management and the rejection of corruption. A national review committee comprising several important civil society figures was established to publish each year a register of those organisations that have adhered to the code. Questions are already being raised about the criteria that should be used for establishing the list.

Anti-corruption commission struggles to assert credibility

The High Commission for the Coordination of Anti-Corruption Activities (HACLCC) delivered its first annual report to Prime Minister Paramanga Ernest Yonli in January 2004. The report was not made public, nor were the reports from the Technical Inspectorate of Public Services, the General State Inspectorate and the General Inspectorate of Finances, all of which provided evidence for the HACLCC submission. In an unexpected move, however, the HACLCC organised a press conference after submitting its report, which had the effect of bringing back into the public eye well-known cases that had been gathering dust on the inspectors' shelves.

President Compaoré established the HACLCC, which officially began work in April 2003, as a way of demonstrating

the government's commitment to fighting corruption at a time when, to use the prime minister's words, 'corruption [was] becoming a professional practice for some'. The commission's stated mission is to 'coordinate the fight against corruption and assist the government in the prevention, detection and fight against fraud and corruption within government'.

The press conference opened up a public debate as to whether the HACLCC reports should be publicly available. Against the backdrop of a nascent national anti-corruption strategy, the principle of publication was accepted – a victory for the advocates of transparency. Under pressure from lobby groups, international financial partners and the private sector, the prime minister responded by accelerating the formulation of a national anti-corruption policy under the auspices of the HACLCC. The resulting policy, made public in April

2004, has several strands: strengthening regulatory and legal measures; making existing monitoring systems and law enforcement more effective; improving the efficiency and transparency of public services; strengthening international cooperation; and improving civic participation in the fight against corruption.

The HACLCC has an immense task ahead in implementing the new anti-corruption policy. It must first deliver by establishing its own credibility. The commission began its work discreetly and is perceived in some quarters to be surplus to requirements, given the existence of similar bodies. To win the confidence of the public, it will need to send out a strong signal by bringing criminals to justice, particularly in large-scale corruption cases. The HACLCC's good faith will be put to the test by the way it deals with the cases brought to light by the General State Inspectorate.

To satisfy expectations it is essential that the HACLCC's work is visible to the public. The good work done to date by the General State Inspectorate has not been apparent due to the scope for government interference (including political blackmail and the invoking of secrecy rules) in following up its findings, and because of its lack of decision-making power.

The commission will therefore be judged by its success in making its work publicly visible and in bringing those responsible for corruption to justice. Otherwise, Burkina Faso will be no better than other countries in which anti-corruption agencies have become pawns in a political game of posturing to please development partners, or to scare off the opposition.

Success in the fight against corruption also depends on other official institutions, and the HACLCC report contained several recommendations directed at them. These included extending the scope of the Technical Inspectorate of Public Services to the fight against corruption and allocating extra staff and resources to it; the creation of a review committee for inspectorates; and strengthening the authority of the disciplinary committees within each government department by enforcing the clauses of the decree relating to civil service reforms.

The report also called for the HACLCC to establish a blacklist of individuals who have mishandled public funds, which would be held by the council of ministers and the government's general secretariat.

Scandal of government contract for verification of imported goods

There was considerable media interest during 2003–04 in the award of a government contract for the verification of imported goods, with allegations of bribes worth hundreds of thousands of dollars. The allegations were made against ministers, members of the commission that awards public sector contracts, journalists and customs officials.

Four companies proposed bids in response to an international tender in October 2003. The proposals were evaluated on technical merit, but the award committee's findings were not accepted and it was asked to repeat its assessment twice – with a new set of members on the committee the third time round. With the new set of members in place, the committee's initial findings were reversed in December 2003.

A combination of leaks to the press and an inquiry by REN-LAC led to public indignation about the apparent reversal of the committee's assessment and allegations of corruption in its decisions. Media and civil society pressure resulted in the government publishing the results of the tender in April 2004. The losing bidders then lodged an official complaint with the finance ministry's Commission for Out-of-Court Settlement of Litigation (CRAL).

To further complicate the allegations, a number of claims were made that some of the media coverage of the case had itself resulted from bribes. According to one of the losing bidders' complaints to the CRAL: 'It should be recorded that numerous articles have appeared in the local press, which, aside from their polemical and libellous nature … disclosed a great deal of confidential information about the bidders to which only the contract award committee should have been privy.' The publisher of a trade periodical alleged he had received a bribe for an article he wrote based on documents hand-delivered by a director of one of the companies that lost the bid.

In June 2004, the CRAL completed its investigation into the import verification contract case. Its report concluded:

'Regarding the irregularities noted, the CRAL believes that the results of the bidding process … should be declared null and void in accordance with legal and regulatory rules relating to the tendering process.' The case is far from closed. At the time of writing, the decision lay in the hands of the finance minister. If the minister rules against the CRAL's conclusions, the complainants can appeal to an administrative tribunal. While the case is ongoing and allegations of corruption remain unproven, it continues to provoke public concern.

Luc Damiba (REN-LAC)

Further reading

Conseil économique et social (CES), *Rapport 2003 d'activités* (2003 report of activities) (CES, 2003)
Comité national d'éthique (CNE), *Rapport 2002* (2002 report) (Ouagadougou: IP, 2002)
REN-LAC, *Rapport 2003 sur l'état de la corruption au Burkina Faso* (2003 report on the state of corruption in Burkina Faso) (Ouagadougou: Editions REN-LAC, 2004)
UNDP, *Rapport sur le développement humain 2003: Corruption et développement humain* (Human development report 2003: corruption and human development) (Ouagadougou, 2004), www.pnud.bf/RAPDH2003.htm

REN-LAC: www.renlac.org

Cambodia

Corruption Perceptions Index 2004 score: not surveyed

Conventions:
UN Convention against Corruption (not yet signed)
UN Convention against Transnational Organized Crime (signed November 2001; not yet ratified)

Legal and institutional changes

- In September 2003 Cambodia was admitted to the **World Trade Organisation** (WTO), although the new National Assembly still needs to ratify the measure. WTO membership requires the creation of a commercial court to bring transparency in dispute adjudication in line with international standards. There are doubts, however, that the political will exists to create such a court that is both separate from the existing judicial system and free from political intervention.

- In what is widely viewed as a substantial step towards reforming the corrupt legal system, Cambodia's first school to train judges and prosecutors, the **Royal School of Judges and**

Prosecutors, opened in November 2003. The new graduates will eventually replace the 190 judges who currently preside. Critics, however, are concerned about the selection of students: one candidate who failed the entrance exam was reportedly offered admission in exchange for US $15,000.[1]

New government compromised by claims of illegitimacy

Following the country's second national election in 1998, the political situation in Cambodia has been highly unstable and corruption has flourished amid intense power struggles. In the run-up to the third national election in July 2003, Cambodian civil society groups and donors widely anticipated widespread corrupt activity. The international community threatened withdrawal of donor support if the election was not declared 'free and fair', and the National Election Committee (NEC) promptly declared them to be so. The civil society election monitor, the Committee for Free and Fair Elections in Cambodia (Comfrel), dispute this.[2]

Despite the three main parties signing a voluntary code of conduct for political parties (drafted by the NEC, the National Democratic Institute and the political parties themselves) in June 2003, there were reports of widespread vote buying, violence and intimidation by all contesting parties, particularly in rural areas. The ruling Cambodian Peoples' Party (CPP) bore the brunt of most of these allegations, and election monitors and opposition parties both accused the CPP of doling out money, rice and sarongs in exchange for votes. Other parties were accused of distributing gifts to participants at their rallies in an attempt to influence results.[3]

Civil society played an important role up to, and during, the election by distributing voter guides, arranging public discussion forums and participating as election observers at polling stations. Their presence created a relaxed atmosphere and assured voters that the process was fair. The presence of international and national election monitors was limited.

The CPP, which has been in power since 1979, won without an outright majority causing a political deadlock that lasted for 11 months. A fudged, and some argue unconstitutional, agreement between the CPP and the National United Front for an Independent, Neutral, Peaceful, and Cooperative Cambodia (FUNCINPEC) eventually resolved the deadlock and allowed a coalition government to be formed. Despite the questionable legitimacy of the current administration, however, there was very little criticism of the incoming government from academics, civil society groups or international observers. Instead, there was widespread agreement that the 2003 election was, at least, an improvement over that of 1998, with more open and issue-driven debates, and an overall reduction in the number of reported electoral irregularities.

While the CPP's continuing majority cannot be solely attributed to vote buying and intimidation, the voting demographics in Cambodia may keep such practices a prominent feature of the electoral landscape. The increasing loss of CPP's powerbase in the expanding, better educated urban areas creates an incentive to make up for this shortfall in the rural areas where the majority of corrupt practices already occur.

Corruption in rural areas is encouraged by two primary factors. First, in spite of the code of conduct for political parties, those buying the votes and doing the intimidating are local party leaders who were neither involved in the design of the code, nor the formulation of party election strategy. Their position reflects Cambodia's patron–client social structure in which a small elite determine overall political direction and only their local deputies actually have contact with voters. Since many local functionaries identify passionately with their party, and enhance their stature according to the number of votes they can 'farm' in their commune or district, they are frequently indifferent to the means they have to use to get those votes.

The second explanation for high levels of corruption in rural areas is that Cambodians have come to expect gifts at election time and can easily fall victim to intimidation because of their poverty, illiteracy and lack of awareness both of legal procedure and even the political differences between the parties for which they have been pressured to vote.[4]

National anti-corruption law

There is a widespread belief that it is only through legislation that the so-called 'culture of corruption' will change in Cambodia. There has therefore been a great deal of civil society pressure to pass the Law on Anti-Corruption (LAC). Progress, however, has been painfully slow. The national assembly, a parliamentary committee and civil society groups combined to create a first draft in 1994. At a June 2002 donor conference, Prime Minister Hun Sen pledged to pass the LAC within 12 months. After more delays, and threats by the international donor community to withdraw funding unless the LAC was passed, it began its passage through parliament only to have its ratification interrupted by the June 2003 elections.

While the drawn-out process of attempting to pass this legislation has continued, civil society groups have been playing an active role in attempts to strengthen the draft of the LAC. In forming its recommendations reformers have drawn on similar laws in other countries and, most particularly, the UN Convention against Corruption (UNCAC), which Cambodia has not yet signed.

The LAC fails to meet the requirements of the UNCAC in a number of respects. The LAC is weaker in its definition of corruption and does not acknowledge the importance of international cooperation in reducing it. The LAC outlines five forms of corruption: bribery, the accepting of bribes, the offer or acceptance of any kind of favour, illegal use of influence or power, and 'any secret conspiracy with a lack of transparency'. In contrast the UNCAC contains separate and specific offences relating to bribery, embezzlement, the abuse of influence and illicit enrichment. In addition, the UNCAC contains definitions of 'illicit enrichment' – a lifestyle beyond the reach of a civil servant's official remuneration – that are absent from the LAC.

Another weakness that needs to be addressed is the implementation of the LAC, which in the present draft is the responsibility of the Supreme National Council against Corruption (SNCC). At present the LAC stipulates that the SNCC should be composed of seven members drawn from the royal court, the senate, the national assembly, the constitutional council, the government, the supreme council of magistracy and the national audit authority. Critics claim, however, that such a composition guarantees the SNCC's lack of independence.

If the LAC is passed, coalition trade-offs mean that it is unlikely to have a significant impact on the behaviour of high-ranking officials and is much more likely to function as an agency for snaring low-profile, middle-ranking officials. This is not, however, necessarily an argument against its adoption. The prosecution of lower-level officials may create a public demand to investigate higher up the professional ladder.

Christine J. Nissen (Centre for Social Development/TI Cambodia)

Further reading

Zim Chea and Bruce McKenney, Trading Forest Products in Cambodia: Challenges, Threats, and Opportunities for Resin, Working Paper No. 28 (Cambodia Development Resource Institute, 2003)

World Bank, *Cambodia Governance and Corruption Diagnostic: Evidence from Citizen, Enterprise and Public Official Surveys* (World Bank, 2001)

Toshiyasu Kato, Jeffrey Kaplan and Chan Sophaland Real Sopheap, *Enhancing Governance for Sustainable Development* (Cambodia Development Resource Institute and the Asian Development Bank, 2000)

Centre for Social Development (TI Cambodia): www.online.com.kh/users/csd

Notes

1. *Phnom Penh Post* (Cambodia), 21 November–4 December 2003.
2. Comfrel, *Final Statement and Report on the National Assembly Elections 2003* (Cambodia, 2003).
3. Ibid.
4. The Asia Foundation, *Democracy in Cambodia 2003: A Survey of the Cambodian Electorate* (2003).

Cameroon

Corruption Perceptions Index 2004 score: 2.1 (129th out of 146 countries)

Conventions:
AU Convention on the Prevention and Combating of Corruption (not yet signed)
UN Convention against Corruption (signed December 2003; not yet ratified)
UN Convention against Transnational Organized Crime (signed December 2000; not yet ratified)

Legal and institutional changes

- A law was passed in April 2004 regarding the organisation and operation of a **Constitutional Council**, and is due to come into effect some months after the presidential election in October 2004 (see below).

- In December 2003 parliament approved final provisions on the **National Electoral Observatory**, first established by legislation in 2000. The observatory's purpose is to achieve transparency and eliminate corruption from the electoral process. In its report on the June 2002 elections, it identified numerous malfunctions in the electoral system and made proposals to overcome them.

Forestry and corruption in Cameroon

In July 2003 the government of Cameroon created a ministerial unit to combat corruption in the ministry of the environment and forests. Like similar units in other departments, its objectives include proposing, implementing and monitoring measures to combat corruption within the ministry, and promoting ethical conduct.[1] However, as the units are headed by officials who answer to their superiors at the ministries, and therefore lack independence, there is a strong risk that they will be ineffective. The lack of means of coercion, and of material and financial resources, will further limit their actions. At the time of writing the anti-corruption unit within the ministry of forests had yet to take actions, in spite of widespread corruption in the sector.

Two related studies in 2003 by Greenpeace and Forests Monitor and by the British Department for International Development and the IMF indicate the scale of corruption in forestry in Cameroon, as well as extensive tax losses for the state as a consequence. The studies highlight two major groups of offence: illegal exploitation of the forest, in cases where there is no authorisation; and anarchic exploitation, which refers to operations that are authorised, but where there are serious violations, such as uncontrolled logging, the exploitation of trees outside concessions, or inaccurate tax returns. The studies indicated that 41 out of 92 concessions are exploited illegally. One of the studies, which looked at 21 concessions, found that a tax loss of FCFA 59.7 billion (US $115 million) plus FCFA 432 billion (US $834 million) in damages over five years, amounting to around one-quarter of the government's budget for 2004.

Corruption is surely at the root of the persisting illegality. Corrupt foresters use their influence on all those involved in the allocation, exploitation and management of the forests. In consequence, their activities, even when illegal, are legitimised year on year by the small size of penalties, whose payment is negotiable and always open to downwards revision.

In April 2004 the ministry of the environment and forests published its annual list of the 'top ten' companies in breach of forestry regulations. The publication of the list, which gives a partial view of the financial impact and tax loss suffered by the state through the anarchic exploitation of forests, was part of a package of measures required by the World Bank and IMF to accompany the current structural adjustment programme. Some companies appear on the 'top ten' list year after year.

Can the Constitutional Council guarantee electoral transparency?

The creation of a Constitutional Council, for which legislation was passed in April 2004 (in accordance with the 1996 constitution), will fill what some observers consider to be a legal vacuum, even though its powers are currently exercised by the supreme court. The council will rule on the constitutionality of laws and on conflicts of powers between state institutions and between central and regional governments. It will also monitor the lawfulness of elections and referenda, and will announce election results.

There are doubts, however, as to whether the provisions of the legislation will provide a satisfactory guarantee of the council's independence. The law provides that the 11 members of the Council (in addition to former presidents) shall be appointed as follows: three by the president, three by the president of the national assembly, three by the president of the senate and two by the judicial service commission. At times when Cameroon's president is also the president of the judicial service commission and leader of the party in power, and when that party has the majority in parliament, the choice of nearly all council members may be determined by the executive. The potential lack of independence may undermine the council's credibility.

Another factor that might further diminish its credibility is the fact that its offices will be run by a secretary general appointed by the president. The secretary general will play an important role in the council's functioning. Any lack of neutrality on his part would be bound to have an impact on the effectiveness and independence of the institution as a whole. Even if the council members make a concerted effort to remain independent, the secretary general may become the executive's Trojan horse within the organisation. If the Constitutional Council's independence is to be ensured, its enabling legislation needs to be amended.

Mounchipou: transparency trial or smokescreen?

Since the appearance of Cameroon at the bottom of TI's Corruption Perceptions Index in 1999, the courts have increasingly taken centre-stage in the fight against corruption in Cameroon. But a series of so-called 'transparency trials' has raised questions as to whether the courts are demonstrating a real determination to combat corruption and the embezzlement of public funds or whether they are merely creating a smokescreen to improve public and international perceptions.

The most sensational of the trials is known as 'the Mounchipou case' after the former minister for post and telecommunications, Mounchipou Seidou. The singularity of the trial lies in both the prominence of the main defendant, Mounchipou Seidou, and in the large number of defendants and the nature of the offences with which they were charged.

More than 20 defendants, including Seidou, numerous senior officials from the ministry of post and telecommunications and five company directors, were charged with embezzling public funds, forgery and using forged documents, fraud, and deriving a personal interest from a public act. The charges related to the award of contracts for building works and the purchase of equipment for the ministry. Although the proceedings were opened in 1999, the defendants were only tried in 2003 because of delays in the judicial system. After a trial lasting more than seven months, the verdict was handed down in November 2003. The court sentenced seven of the accused to 20 years' imprisonment combined with the confiscation of their assets, acquitting other defendants.[2]

However, despite the heavy penalties, the significance of the case remains unclear. Many observers point to the fact that, since the trial began in 1999, there have been no other prosecutions, in spite of numerous allegations of corruption in other government departments.

The police: a body riddled with corruption?

In TI's 2003 Global Corruption Barometer survey,[3] in response to the question 'If you ... could eliminate corruption from one of the following institutions what would your first choice be?', 14 per cent of Cameroonian respondents chose the police, second only to the courts at 31 per cent. There are serious public concerns about police conduct, and even Pierre Minlo Medjo, the director of national security, admitted in December 2003 that 'From time to time we are informed of cases involving the illegal subcontracting of public service, of brazen swindling, of deliberate violence against individuals, of foreigners being cheated almost systematically, of abuses of all kinds, particularly of large scale corruption on the part of corrupt officials who see their office as an unlimited opportunity for personal enrichment.'[4]

These observations reflect the daily reality. To take one example, taxi drivers are routinely forced to bribe police officers FCFA 1,000 (US $2) or more for imaginary offences such as 'refusal to carry passengers', 'blocking the public highway', or having a 'double windscreen' in the case of taxi drivers who wear glasses.

This situation became so extreme that taxi drivers went on strike in March 2004, denouncing police harassment and demanding, among other things, that the rate set for fines should be respected. At the end of negotiations between the government and the taxi drivers' unions, the authorities published a list of official documents and other ancillary items to be produced when police checks are carried out, and a classification of fines. The taxi drivers resumed work, but corruption in the police is only likely to be stamped out by exemplary penalties for corrupt officers and the imposition of effective discipline.

Talla Jean-Bosco (TI Cameroon)

Further reading

Lucien Ayissi, *Corruption et gouvernance* (Corruption and governance) (Yaoundé: PUA, 2003)

Friedrich Ebert Stiftung, *Lutte contre la corruption: Impossible n'est pas Camerounais?* (The fight against corruption: nothing is impossible in Cameroon) (Yaoundé: PUA, 2002)

Pierre Titi Nwel, ed., *De la corruption au Cameroun* (On corruption in Cameroon) (Yaoundé: Gerddes-Cameroun and Friedrich Ebert Stiftung, 2001)

Babissakana and Abissama Onana, *Les débats économiques du Cameroun et d'Afriques* (The economic debates in Cameroon and Africa) (Yaoundé: Prescriptor, 2003)

Notes

1. 'Mise en oeuvre du programme national de gouvernance' (Implementation of the national governance programme) (Yaoundé, December 2003).
2. *Cameroon Tribune* (Cameroon), 1 December 2003.
3. Available at www.transparency.org/surveys/index.html#barometer
4. *Cameroon Tribune* (Cameroon), 26 December 2003.

Canada

Corruption Perceptions Index 2004 score: 8.5 (12th out of 146 countries)

Conventions:
OAS Inter-American Convention against Corruption (ratified June 2000)
OECD Anti-Bribery Convention (ratified December 1998)
UN Convention against Corruption (signed May 2004; not yet ratified)
UN Convention against Transnational Organized Crime (ratified May 2002)

Legal and institutional changes

- A law adopted in March 2004 (Bill C-4) restructured the office of the **Ethics Commissioner** so that it is now a body of parliament. Established in 1993 to provide advice to members of the lower house of parliament and investigate allegations of ethical violations, the commissioner previously reported to, and served at, the discretion of the prime minister. The same bill created a parallel post of Senate Ethics Officer for the upper house, which had long resisted such regulation despite its much-maligned reputation. The bill finally passed the senate when an informal compromise was reached by which the prime minister would appoint the ethics officer from a shortlist prepared by the chamber itself.

- New **campaign contribution limits** passed in 2003 as part of Bill C-24 came into effect in January 2004. In addition to a C $5,000 (US $3,870) per party cap on individual contributions, the most notable restriction is a ban on corporate or union contributions to parties, except for a C $1,000 allowance for donations to constituency associations or individual candidates. As partial recompense, a scheme of increased public financing was implemented. The bill also closed a loophole in the elections law that allowed parties to pay workers, claim them as an expense for tax purposes and then have the workers donate the funds back to the party. The June 2004 federal election was the first to be governed by the new rules.

- In response to an ongoing sponsorship scandal (see below), a number of institutional reforms have been proposed or implemented. Bill C-25 proposes improved **whistleblower protection** for public sector employees, establishing a procedure for the disclosure of wrongdoing and protection from reprisal for exposing government corruption. Critics have argued that the bill contains significant weaknesses and fails to cover important subsectors of the public service such as political staff, the Royal Canadian Mounted Police and national security staff. The bill would establish a public service integrity commissioner, but would repeat the mistake of the original ethics commissioner legislation by making the office report to a minister rather than to parliament. It would also oblige potential whistleblowers to report allegations to their superiors before contacting the commissioner, which could subject them to intimidation, and it would allow the government to specify penalties for allegations deemed 'frivolous' or 'in bad faith'.

- The March 2004 federal budget outlined plans to reintroduce the office of **Comptroller-General**, also in response to the scandal, and to establish new accredited comptroller positions within government departments to vet new spending. Enhanced auditing requirements and governance regulations for public corporations were also revealed.

- The Treasury Board[1] announced new appointment procedures for executives of public corporations in March 2004 as a scandal-elicited 'preview' of a more comprehensive **review of public corporation governance**, scheduled for release in September 2004. The Treasury Board also announced a detailed **review of the financial administration law**,[2] to consider enhanced enforcement and recovery provisions as well as the application of sanctions to public servants, public corporation employees and office-holders.

The sponsorship scandal

2003–04 will be remembered primarily for the shockwaves sent out by the most damning auditor general's report ever, which detailed massive misappropriation and misuse of public funds in the department of public works.[3] Prime Minister Paul Martin, newly installed in December 2003, was immediately put on the defensive, acknowledging and sharing public outrage over the lack of accountability in the programme's administration, while claiming no direct knowledge of the abuses. The subsequent scandal was a major campaign issue in the June 2004 federal election, which saw Martin's Liberal Party, which had previously seemed assured of a fourth straight majority, entangled in a bitter contest and ultimately reduced to an unstable minority government.

In the years following the narrow defeat of the 1995 sovereignty referendum in Quebec, C $250 million (US $193.5 million) was spent on a sponsorship programme that was run under the department of public works and was intended to create a more positive perception of the federal government in Quebec. The then prime minister Jean Chrétien had fought Quebec nationalism throughout his political career and was determined to press the federalist cause. But zeal for funding the project combined with lack of adequate financial controls to produce disaster. Auditor general Sheila Fraser found little evidence to justify most of the expenditures and concluded that as much as C $100 million (US $77.4 million) was siphoned off to advertising firms – some with political connections to the government – through schemes involving over-billing, artificial invoices, fictitious contracts and other forms of abuse and mismanagement. Further, the audit concluded that 'parliament was not informed of the programme's objectives or the results it achieved and was misinformed as to how the programme was being managed'.[4]

The first indications of misuse of funds emerged in 2000 with anecdotal reports of high and poorly documented expenditures. In 2002, spurred by additional revelations, the auditor general conducted a narrower audit of contracts within the sponsorship programme and declared that 'senior public servants broke just about every rule in the book' in awarding C $1.6 million in contracts to Montréal's advertising agency, Groupaction Marketing – a key player, as it turned out, in the wider scandal.[5] By late 2003, with Fraser's investigation yielding ever-more-alarming details, the government recognised the magnitude of the situation; on Martin's first day as prime minister he terminated the programme and its administering agency, Communications Canada.

Fraser's report was thunderous in its denunciation: 'The pattern we saw of non-compliance with the rules was not the result of isolated errors. It was consistent and pervasive. This was how the government ran the programme.'[6] Furthermore, the payments 'appear designed to provide commissions to communications agencies, while hiding the source of funds and the true nature of the transactions'.[7]

The government's response to the report was swift and, in addition to attempts at damage control and blame avoidance, contained a number of parallel investigations and the institutional reforms noted above. Alfonso Gagliano, who as minister of public works had overseen the programme, was recalled from a diplomatic posting to face inquiries into his role and that of his department. A special counsel for recovery was appointed, with a mandate to pursue reclamation of improperly received funds. Most visibly, the parliament's public accounts committee began immediate hearings into the matter.

In his testimony to the parliamentary committee, Gagliano claimed ignorance of the misappropriations and argued that, despite the principle of ministerial responsibility, he could not be held accountable for the actions of his department because he did not have hiring and firing authority over the agency involved. He instead blamed Communications Canada's administrator Charles Guité. Others involved, however, described weekly meetings supervised by Gagliano and generally contradicted his testimony. Guité also claimed innocence, pointing the finger of blame at his superiors, especially Gagliano.

Daily developments, charges and counter charges, firings and suits for wrongful dismissal or loss of reputation continued from February to May 2004.[8] With the calling of a federal election in May, the investigation was suspended by the dissolution of parliament. The inquiry was replaced by campaign rhetoric as opposition parties took advantage of the scandal to attack the Liberal Party. The police are pursuing a number of criminal investigations at the time of writing, however, and an independent judicial inquiry was scheduled to begin in September 2004. Overall responsibility for the affair remains in dispute and the auditor general pointedly warned that the incidents uncovered so far might only be the tip of the iceberg: her office's resources only allow direct audit oversight of a fraction of government spending, chosen on the basis of risk. The question is whether the sponsorship abuses are the product of an exceptionally overheated, undermanaged (and overfunded) but isolated programme, or whether they represent a more widespread erosion of responsibility in the government and public corporations.

Ultimately, detailed rules and regulations exist that should have been applied to the activities of Communications Canada, and if applied, would have prevented the abuses from going so far. The problem appears to be that lack of accountability allowed administrators to exploit enthusiasm for the implicit anti-separatist goals of the programme and engage in practices that invited corruption by abrogating 'two fundamental principles of internal control: segregation of duties and appropriate oversight'.[9] With a small group of individuals effectively exercising control over all disbursements, there was no resistance to 'temptation', and no exposure until the excesses drew the attention of the auditor general.

Police corruption in Toronto

In January 2004 six police officers were charged with offences including conspiracy, extortion, assault, perjury and obstruction of justice at the end of a two-and-a-half-year internal investigation into corruption in the Toronto Police Central Field drug squad.[10] Affidavits released by the investigating task force alleged a wide range of illegal acts, including the theft of hundreds of thousands of dollars from safe deposit boxes during the execution of search warrants, and the sale of weapons and narcotics to drug dealers.[11] The head of the task force hinted at wider corruption, indicating that prosecutors had chosen to charge only those individuals whose cases were so egregious as to result in certain conviction.

The drug squad had previously been disbanded after a number of complaints against its members. Since 1999 as many as 200 drug prosecutions in Toronto had been stayed due to problems with the credibility of officers, and cash payments were made to settle at least three civil suits brought against them.[12] Meanwhile, a separate investigation resulted in charges against several more officers – including two sons of a former chief of police and the president of the police union – for allegedly running a protection racket for downtown bars and restaurants.[13] As of June 2004 more than 20 officers and detectives had been charged or notified of potential charges.

Police Chief Julian Fantino announced a number of measures in response to the charges and enlisted retired Superior Court Judge George Ferguson to craft specific recommendations. Ferguson suggested a variety of measures including improved hiring, training and promotions procedures; mandatory drug and psychological testing; time limits for assignments to 'high-risk' elite units such as the drug squad; new methods for handling informants; spot checks by senior inspectors; an enhanced internal affairs unit with separate facilities; an internal 'snitch line' for allegations of police misconduct; and better protection for whistleblowers.[14]

But Fantino had already publicly alienated a number of key members of the civilian Police Services Board, as well as the newly elected mayor of Toronto (by actively campaigning for a rival) and civil liberties activists. Although he was not personally implicated, his detractors criticised him as slow to react to the problems in the drug squad. The board approved all Ferguson's proposals, but then announced plans for its own, civilian-led inquiry into police management practices. The board did not extend Fantino's contract as chief when it came up for renewal in June 2004.[15]

As with the sponsorship scandal, both civil and criminal investigations are continuing, with the final disposition of the individuals involved – and the institutional after-effects – likely to be subjects of debate for an extended period. There is no shortage of reform proposals in the wake of Canada's largest law enforcement corruption scandal, but with municipal politics affecting high-level decisions on how to conduct and even conceptualise the daily work of the police, real structural improvement may be difficult to accomplish.

Maureen Mancuso (University of Guelph, Canada)

Further reading

Report of the Auditor General of Canada (Ottawa: November 2003) www.oag-bvg.gc.ca/domino/reports.nsf/html/03menu_e.html

O.P. Dwivedi and Maureen Mancuso, 'Corruption as a Threat to Good Governance: Lessons from Canada', in Gerald Caiden, O.P. Dwivedi and Joseph Jabbra, eds, *Where Corruption Lives* (Bloomfield: Kumarian Press, 2001)

Ian Greene and Eleanor D. Glor, 'The Government of Canada Approach to Ethics: The Evolution of Ethical Government', in *Public Integrity* 5 (Winter 2002–03)

Kenneth Kernaghan, 'Corruption and Public Service in Canada: Conceptual and Practical Dimensions', in Seppo Tiihonen, ed., *The History of Corruption in Central Government*, International Institute of Administrative Sciences (Amsterdam: IOS Press, 2003)

Denis Saint-Martin, 'L'Affaire Groupaction: un cas de politisation de la fonction publique fédérale?' in *Canadian Public Administration* 46 (2003)

TI Canada: www.transparency.ca

Notes

1. The Treasury Board is a powerful cabinet committee, with overall responsibility for the financial, personnel and administrative duties of the executive. It is considered the general manager and employer of the public service.
2. The law governs public service procedures, responsibilities, offences and sanctions. It is essentially a rulebook for how the government and public service handle money.
3. The author acknowledges the research assistance of Josh Alcock, Nick Erdody, Jordan Hatton and David Hornsby in tracking and digesting this evolving scandal.
4. Government of Canada, *Report of the Auditor General of Canada* (Ottawa: November 2003), section 3.1.
5. Auditor General of Canada, press conference, 8 May 2002, www.oag-bvg.gc.ca/domino/other. nsf/html/02ossp_e.html
6. *Report of the Auditor General*, section 3.122.
7. Ibid., section 3.44.
8. In addition to Gagliano, Guité and Pelletier, Crown Corporation presidents Marc LeFrançois (VIA Rail) and Michel Vennat (Business Development Bank of Canada) were fired, and André Ouellet (Canada Post) was suspended without pay pending investigation of his corporation's role in the scandal. Numerous executives at the various ad agencies and public relations firms involved were also dismissed or charged with offences.
9. *Report of the Auditor General*, section 3.21.
10. Canadian Broadcasting Corporation, www.cbc.ca/stories/2004/01/07/police040107
11. *Ottawa Citizen* (Canada), 20 January 2004.
12. Ibid.
13. *Ottawa Citizen* (Canada), 27 April 2004.
14. Many of Ferguson's proposals arose from his report, *Review and Recommendations Concerning Various Aspects of Police Misconduct* (Toronto: 2004), which Fantino commissioned in November 2001 in parallel with the early stages of the task force probe.
15. *Toronto Sun* (Canada), 26 June 2004.

China

Corruption Perceptions Index 2004 score: 3.4 (71st out of 146 countries)

Conventions:
UN Convention against Corruption (signed December 2003; not yet ratified)
UN Convention against Transnational Organized Crime (ratified September 2003)

Legal and institutional changes

- The regulations on the **procedures for the handling of administrative cases** were published in August 2003 by the ministry of public security to control the use of coercive measures by police officers. The regulations responded to concern that police officers used unlawful detentions to exact fines or used force to obtain confessions from innocent people.

- The central disciplinary committee in January 2004 issued 'Document No. 1', which called for reform of the much-abused system of **confiscating land for building** purposes, with the aim of strengthening the rights and interests of peasants (see below).

- In February 2004 the Chinese Communist Party (CCP) enacted new regulations on **party supervision and disciplinary policy**. These had yet to be fully implemented at the time of writing. The new regulations emphasise the independence and supervisory powers of the Disciplinary Inspection Committee (DIC), which is responsible to the central committee of the CCP, and introduce monitoring mechanisms for provincial-level officials and central government ministries.

- A Guideline to Build Law-Based Government was introduced by the central government in April 2004 and addresses the **separation of government functions** from the management of state-owned enterprises, and the separation of powers and functions between levels of government and government departments. It also calls for a system to monitor government officials.

- The CCP in April 2004 implemented temporary regulations on the resignation of officials in an attempt to call senior party leaders and civil servants **to account for their actions**. The regulations stipulate circumstances under which resignation is mandatory, including for certain specified severe mistakes, severe misconduct or serious under-performance, even though such misdeeds may not be criminal offences.

- A **real estate register** has been drawn up in Beijing for the first time. Published in May 2004, the regulations provide for a complete map of land ownership in the capital, which is made available for public scrutiny at the national land and building bureau. Visitors are allowed to copy the register. Previously, information on real estate ownership was kept secret.

- The Supreme People's Procuratorate and the ministries of construction, communications and water resources decided in May 2004 to introduce a **blacklisting** system to combat corruption in the **construction** sector in five pilot areas (see below).

- The municipalities of Guangzhou and Shanghai are implementing plans to widen **public access to information** in 15 government departments. Guangzhou passed the necessary legislation in 2003, followed by Shanghai in May 2004. In Shanghai, all information related to economic management and social public services, except that kept confidential by law, will be made totally or partially available to the public. Among the departments concerned are education, personnel, real estate, water supply, quality inspection, programming, commercial business, police, foreign business and trade, sanitation, labour protection, finance and city administration. Government branches have to compile and publicise guidelines for opening up access to government information, and provide the names and telephone numbers of those responsible for providing information to the public. The Shanghai government has launched a training programme to help ensure effective implementation of the scheme.

- Implementation guidelines for the **Government Procurement Law**, which came into effect in January 2003, have been drafted and are under review. Related measures including guidelines on procurement procedures, registration of bidding agents and evaluation mechanisms for central procurement bodies have also been drafted and several of them were expected to be approved in late 2004.

Corruption in China's booming construction sector

As the Chinese economy gallops ahead, the huge investment in new infrastructure projects combined with weak enforcement of contracting regulations has created numerous opportunities for corruption. Local officials play a decisive role in the tendering process and in many cases have ignored the relevant regulations. From 1997 to the present, 14 directors of transport in nine provinces have been investigated for corruption. Three successive heads of transportation in Henan province were caught taking bribes and convicted for complicity in other crimes.[1]

Similar malpractice exists in land development and real estate. China is feverishly modernising its cities. Large numbers of old houses are being swept aside to make way for new high-rise offices and dwellings. This process not only offers opportunities for officials to misappropriate the property in their charge, it provides tangible evidence of their 'professional achievement' and improves their career prospects. With such a skewed motivation, it is little wonder that officials become spellbound by 'image projects' that can have serious consequences on the long-term development of the local economy. Investors have been induced to tie up their savings in projects that fail to materialise, while householders have been forced by corrupt municipal councils and provincial governments to move out of their homes, which are then demolished and the sites developed. This phenomenon has sparked popular protests around the country, especially on the fast-growing coast and in the capital, Beijing.

At the presentation of his 'Work Report' in March 2004, Prime Minister Wen Jiabao reiterated his demand that confiscation of land be strictly controlled and carried out with due consideration for the law and for planning priorities. Flooded with complaints, the country's chief prosecutor announced in December 2003 that the fight against corruption in the real estate sector and in construction project tenders would be a high priority for his offices in 2004.

There have been some improvements to the legal framework in recent years. In January 2000 the Tendering and Bidding Law entered into force, and the construction ministry subsequently issued a series of regulations on the tendering process for urban infrastructure and civil construction projects specifically. As early as 1994, the construction and supervision ministries helped promote the Tangible Construction Market (TCM), a market for open tendering and bidding for civil or urban infrastructure construction projects involving investment from the government or majority state-held companies. Currently 325 of China's 336 cities have established similar procurement centres. Although the TCM has had some impact on reducing corruption in procurement, it remains under-resourced and under-utilised.

In May this year the government introduced blacklisting for building contractors convicted of bribery in five areas – the provinces of Jiangsu, Zhejiang and Sichuan, Chongqing municipality and Guangxi Zhuang Autonomous Region. Under this pilot scheme, the blacklist will be made available to local governments and those responsible for construction projects in these areas. Debarment can be either temporary or permanent. The scheme is modelled on a blacklisting system introduced in Wuxi, in Jiangsu province, in 2002.

The period 2004–08 will be the key period for the construction of venues and transport facilities for the 2008 Olympic Games in Beijing. Construction and service projects related to the Games will provide as much as US $16 billion in business opportunities for domestic and foreign investors. To counter the risk of corruption, the Beijing municipal government and the organising committee for the Games have set up an Auditing and Supervision Department (ASD), comprising 23 members from the ministries of supervision, finance and construction and the state commission for development and reform of the National Sports Bureau. The ASD will supervise the bidding and facilities-development processes and is developing a code of conduct for relevant staff. Protests at the forcible requisition of land and the forcible demolition of homes to make way for the sports centres, hotels and restaurants needed for the Games have already cast a shadow over the process, however.

High-level corruption captures the public imagination

Cases of senior government officials travelling abroad to spend the proceeds of bribery and other corrupt acts have pushed the issue of corruption high up the public agenda. In tandem, China has increased its cooperation with international bodies in its fight against corruption and has entered into international agreements – for instance by ratifying international anti-graft instruments – that commit the government to tackling the problem with seriousness.

In April 2004, the US authorities handed Yu Zhendong to the Chinese police at Beijing's Capital International Airport. Yu is former president of the Kaiping city branch of the Bank of China in Guangdong and is suspected of embezzling bank money between 1993

and 2001, of which US $485 million has since been restored to China. Cases such as this one may well be just the tip of the iceberg: research indicates there may be as many as 4,000 others suspected of corruption or bribery who are still abroad. The total sum of money stolen may amount to five billion yuan (US $600 million), according to official sources.[2] There is a growing trend for Chinese officials to send their children abroad to study or live, a luxury many would be unable to achieve through the legal use of their authority or income.

The decision to focus the anti-corruption drive of recent years on corruption by high-ranking officials has won popular support. According to a series of household surveys conducted by the Central Commission for Discipline Inspection of the Communist Party of China, people's satisfaction with the anti-corruption drive has increased from 33 per cent in 1996 to 52 per cent in 2003.

A concern, however, is the capacity of China's judicial system to prosecute and sanction wrongdoers impartially. In 2003, 13 provincial or ministerial officials were convicted of corruption. One of them was sentenced to death and another two were given death sentences that were later suspended for two years. A separate case, that of Liu Yong, a former chairman of Kiyang Group in Shenyang, who was sentenced to death for 27 separate crimes including bribe paying, involvement in criminal gangs and illegal ownership of weapons, illustrates the closed nature of the judicial process. His sentence, handed down by an intermediate court in Tieling District, Liaoning province in April 2002, was subsequently suspended for two years, from August 2003, on the grounds that his confession had been extracted under torture. This decision was overturned again by the supreme court, and his immediate execution was ordered. The general public was not informed about what motivated the vacillations over his sentence.

Guo Yong (Tsinghua University, China) and Liao Ran (Transparency International)

Further reading

Li Yongzhong, 'China will Launch a Decisive Anti-Corruption Battle', Beijing, *Liaowang Dongfang Journal*, 2004

Guo Yong, 'Study on Character and Trends of Corruption Cases Involving China's Senior Public Officials', in *Comparative Economic and Social Systems*, 2004

Xie Ping and Lu Lei, 'Study on China's Financial Corruption: from Quality to Quantity', *Comparative Studies*, Vol. 8, 2003

Notes

1. *People's Daily* (China), 7 April 2004.
2. China News Agency, 29 September 2003.

Colombia

Corruption Perceptions Index 2004 score: 3.8 (60th out of 146 countries)

Conventions:
OAS Inter-American Convention against Corruption (ratified November 1998)
UN Convention against Corruption (signed December 2003; not yet ratified)
UN Convention against Transnational Organized Crime (ratified August 2004)

Legal and institutional changes

- President Álvaro Uribe's **national development plan** 2002–06, called 'Towards a Communitarian State' and approved by congress in June 2003, contains the stated intention to increase the transparency and efficiency of state functions by involving civil society in decisions about how the public administration should operate. The two components of the plan with the greatest potential to reduce corruption are: reforms to the public contracting process, in particular making more information public about contracts and the budget; and a tightening of sanctions for public officials whose actions by design or default led to the loss of public funds.

- In November 2003 a law regulating **citizen watchdog groups** entered into force. The groups monitor public authorities, be they administrative, political, judicial, electoral, legislative, fiscal or disciplinary. The groups may also monitor private sector entities and national or international NGOs that execute projects that use public resources. These groups have existed without being regulated since the late 1980s. The law prohibits organisations from monitoring public entities with which they have service-provision or similar contracts.

Public prosecutions office faces its worst crisis yet

The public prosecutions office was created in 1991 with the hope that it would help bring down the high levels of impunity that existed in Colombia. The reality has not met these expectations and 2004 saw the body mired in its worst ever crisis, facing allegations of corruption and of infiltration by paramilitary soldiers and drug traffickers.

In Cali, in the west of the country, 16 officials were suspended for alleged links to drugs traffickers in February 2004. That same month, the public prosecutions delegate to the supreme court, Justo Pastor, was forced to resign when he could not explain why one of the people involved in a criminal process had given him an expensive watch. Shortly afterwards, in March 2004, Carlos Arias was forced to resign from his position as national director of public prosecutions offices, for allegedly putting pressure on the judiciary to alter rulings and for sexual harassment.

Party politics may have motivated some of the allegations directed at the public prosecutions office. The public prosecutions office is currently headed by Luis Camilo Osorio, a member of the Partido Conservador who was appointed during the administration of former president Andrés Pastrana; a number of the allegations come from supporters of opposition parties.[1] In February 2004, for example, a parliamentarian from the opposition Polo Democrático Party claimed that members of paramilitary groups had infiltrated the public prosecutor's office in the northern city of Cúcuta.

According to an analysis of the cases by the weekly magazine *Revista Semana*,[2] a number of the dismissals at the prosecutor's office may have been aimed at avoiding criminal investigations that would have affected individuals higher up the political strata. In one case the prosecutor responsible for preparing charges against the security chief under former president Pastrana, Royne Chávez, saw the arrest warrant he had prepared withheld by Osorio. Osorio's decision was finally overturned, however, and Chávez was arrested.

There are institutional reasons that make the public prosecutions office vulnerable to corruption, in addition to the fact that the office is operating in the context of a countrywide conflict between paramilitary and guerrilla groups, and a powerful illegal

drugs industry. First, the chief public prosecutor has the power to appoint, transfer or dismiss the 16,000 officials that work for the office. Second, he or she has discretionary power to assign and reassign cases to prosecutors, who themselves enjoy little autonomy since they must provide detailed updates on every case to the chief prosecutor's office at regular intervals. This situation may be remedied with the entry into force of a new code on criminal procedures in 2005. This code will strip the public prosecutions office of its judicial power, restricting its functions to investigation and accusation, giving judicial authority back to criminal judges. The reform establishes an accusatorial system, with oral hearings, which should speed up processes. Analysts have expressed concerns about one aspect of the reform, however, which is that it increases the public prosecutor's scope to decide whether or not to open investigations into certain types of crime.

Electoral corruption

The electoral process continues to be one of the aspects of Colombian life that is most affected by corruption. Corrupt practices include: vote buying with small quantities of cash, tiles or cement, food, promises of medical or other help; false registration of voters, including the registration of dead people as voters; moving voting poll booths without prior notification; throwing away votes; falsifying or fixing the official vote tallies; fabricating or withholding voter identification cards; and registering individuals who are not allowed to vote.

The high level of irregularities has meant that a number of elections have had to be annulled in recent years. In August 2003, the attorney general's office asked the state council to annul the March 2002 election for the present congress and carry out a recount, excluding the votes cast at 20,503 ballot boxes where irregularities had been observed. This would have amounted to 30 per cent of the total voting stations and would have changed the composition of congress. In Barranquilla, the capital of one of the most seriously affected departments, Atlántico, the national electoral council calculated that 30,000 of the 215,000 registered voters were fabricated or corresponded to people who lived outside of the district.[3] The national electoral council eventually annulled 180,000 of the 400,000 votes that the attorney general requested be annulled.

These cases have reopened the debate about the need for electoral reform and for a reorganisation of the political party system. A number of analysts argue that the large number of political parties and movements that compete in elections, about 70 in all, weakens their ability to monitor each other. A criticism made by the national planning council – a formal platform for citizen input into the national development plan – is that the national electoral council needs to be more independent and more professional. The national planning council also proposed changes to the financing of politics beyond the duration of election campaigns.

Transparency pacts for mayors and governors

One of the pillars of the fight against corruption launched by President Álvaro Uribe in his national plan 'Towards a communitarian state', is the so-called transparency pacts between mayors and governors, and civil society organisations. Officials from the office of the vice-president act as witnesses to the signing of the pacts.

The pacts commit mayors and governors to be accountable to their constituents and to increase citizen participation and transparency in their administrations. Civil society organisations are supposed to follow up and evaluate compliance with these commitments through monitoring committees. The presidency proposed that the pacts should be signed in all 32 departments and in 30 per cent of the country's municipalities.

The impact of the scheme has been limited, not least because of reluctance by sectors of civil society to support the scheme. Many people have criticised the strategy for its failure to define goals and clear measures of compliance. This makes it difficult for civil society organisations to measure advances or setbacks. Another criticism is that the monitoring committees have not been given the resources needed to carry out their work. The programme could fail if it depends on the political will of the signatories and the existing capacity of civil society organisations.

This is not to say that the intention to curb corruption at regional and municipal level is ill conceived. Several cases of corruption in public contracting and in the use of public money have emerged in 2003–04 within departments and mayoralties. In some cases there have been signs of influence by paramilitary groups and drugs traffickers in local government, in particular in several municipalities along the Caribbean coast. According to the Fundación para la Libertad de Prensa, four journalists were murdered in 2003 as a result of their investigations into local corruption in Neiva, Barrancabermeja, Maicao and Buenaventura.

Rosa Inés Ospina (Transparencia por Colombia)

Further reading

Corporación Transparencia por Colombia, *Índice de integridad de las entidades públicas nacionales* (Integrity index of national public bodies) (Bogotá: Transparencia por Colombia, 2002 and 2003)

Organization of American States, Report of the Committee of Experts of the Mechanism for Follow-up of Implementation of the Inter-American Convention against Corruption: Report on its Implementation in Colombia (Washington, DC, 2004), www.oas.org/juridico/english/mec_rep_col.pdf

Eduardo Wills, 'La relación entre la corrupción y el proceso de descentralización en Colombia' (The relation between corruption and the process of decentralisation in Colombia) in *Evaluación de la descentralización municipal en Colombia: Balance de una década* (Evaluation of a decade of municipal decentralisation in Colombia) (Bogotá: Departamento Nacional de Planeación, 2002)

World Bank and Colombian vice-presidency, *Estudio sobre corrupción, desempeño institucional y gobernabilidad: desarrollando una estrategia anti-corrupción para Colombia* (Study of corruption, institutional performance and governance: developing an anti-corruption strategy for Colombia) (Bogotá, 2002)

Transparencia por Colombia: www.transparenciacolombia.org.co

Notes

1. The president nominates a shortlist of three candidates for the post of chief public prosecutor and the supreme court makes the final selection.
2. *Revista Semana* (Colombia), 19 April 2004.
3. *Revista Semana* (Colombia), 18 October 2003.

Democratic Republic of the Congo

Corruption Perceptions Index 2004 score: 2.0 (133rd out of 146 countries)

Conventions:
AU Convention on the Prevention and Combating of Corruption (signed December 2003; not yet ratified)
UN Convention against Corruption (not yet signed)
UN Convention against Transnational Organized Crime (not yet signed)

Legal and institutional changes

- In June 2004 the national assembly, followed by the senate, passed a law determining the organisation, powers and functioning of the **Commission for Ethics and the Fight against Corruption** (CELC). The purpose of the commission is to: make people more aware of ethical questions and the fight against corruption; influence political, public and religious authorities; increase the capacity of national institutions to promote integrity; and ensure the operating capacity of all national institutions involved in the fight against corruption. Although it is chaired by a representative of civil society with the rank and powers of a minister, the CELC is in practice controlled by the government, which may limit its ability to take effective action against public corruption. It is also important that the CELC's existence be confirmed in the forthcoming constitution.

- In May 2004 parliament began examining a bill to amend the **criminal code**. The bill is concerned with the fight against money laundering and the financing of terrorism, and if passed will amend the law relating to corruption, illegal payments, the trading of favours and culpable failures to act on the part of officials.

- The General Directorate of Taxes (DGI) promulgated a **tax code** in March 2004. Both a large companies directorate and a tax centre directorate were created within the DGI, in order to simplify procedures with a view to reducing the opportunities for corruption.

Fighting corruption in transition

In June 2004, in a letter to the vice presidents of the current transition regime, published in the press, President Joseph Kabila acknowledged the anxiety felt by civil society and the international community on account of the level of corruption in the country: 'The reports of international organisations, editorials in the newspapers, complaints from the churches, reports from all sectors of the population, show the persistence, if not the resurgence, of corruption and the misappropriation and embezzlement of public funds in all sectors of national life. The leaders of the people cannot be indifferent to this state of affairs.' If the number of speeches were a measure of change, there would be real hope for the fight against corruption in the Democratic Republic of the Congo (DRC). Some observers believe that the government's statements on corruption have been given force by exposures in 2003–04 of financial scandals perpetrated by leaders of state-owned companies and even members of the government.[1]

However, many observers are questioning the significance of the government's stated good intentions. One of the distinguishing features of the DRC as a country undergoing reconstruction after years of war, is that the people who in the past played a part in the embezzlement and plundering of resources are now in power, thanks to the inter-Congolese negotiations which gave rise to the transition regime. The fear of seeing the precarious political equilibrium collapse inhibits initiatives that might be taken to eliminate corruption and related offences.[2] Furthermore, the plundering of natural resources, which was condemned by

a UN inquiry, is still ongoing according to many reports. The loss of resources provides the income that keeps the troubles and the war alive.

To respond to the critics, President Kabila has invited parliamentary commissions to take on the role of monitoring the government and in particular state-owned companies. Following the invitation, the CELC organised a seminar for the managers of state-owned companies in June 2004. It also drew up a strategic plan to fight corruption in the DRC and initiated radio and television programmes intended to increase public awareness of the problem.

If change is to take place, both legal and institutional reforms are required. Initial steps towards public administration reform are being taken, following recommendations made during a World Bank seminar on good governance and the fight against corruption in September 2002. Full reform of the public administration will involve requiring certain officials to retire, carrying out a census of the workforce and eliminating fictitious employees, training officials, creating a civil service college, creating a school for judges and law officers, making the public servants' code of conduct more understandable to the general public, and increasing government officials' salaries.

Judicial reform is also needed. From October 2003 to March 2004, a multidisciplinary team of consultants carried out an audit of the judicial system in order to identify specific support needs. Since 2003 the NGO Justice and Democracy has been organising training for police officers from the national police force in partnership with the ministry of the interior. The trained officers are monitored on a regular basis. It is also organising educational work with law officers, judges and prosecuting authorities.

Public procurement contracts in the DRC

The DRC does not have a credible or efficient public procurement system. Public officials lack technical skills and the provisions governing public contracting are out of date. Temporary changes to regulations have been made to meet immediate needs, but they have not formed part of an overall modernisation of the legal framework. As a result many legal and regulatory provisions, far from clarifying the regulations, simply add to the difficulty of applying them.

Projects financed by international donors include procedures that aim to ensure transparency and prevent corruption and that seem to work well, in compliance with international contractual standards. In contrast, only 3 per cent of contracts entered into by the Congolese authorities involve a tendering process.[3] The others are awarded either by restricted allocation or by private contract. There is currently no planning and no programming of procurement contracts. Many public contracts, particularly those awarded by private contract, do not comply with legal requirements.

Furthermore, the weakness of internal and external oversight mechanisms makes it very difficult to identify breaches and apply sanctions. The appeal body, the Conseil Supérieur des Adjudications, has never functioned effectively, and there is no mechanism for independent appeals. Indeed, no corruption case involving a public procurement contract has ever been referred to the courts, because of the difficulty of gathering evidence and a shortage of the necessary skills.

Following the arrival in office of a transition government in June 2003, the government and the World Bank together launched an examination of the system for awarding and executing public contracts. Initially, the government set up a national working group, consisting of a group of government experts. On the basis of their report in May 2004, an action plan was drawn up, which aims to incorporate the concepts of transparency, competition, economy and effectiveness into public contracting in order to combat corruption, among other problems.

Reducing corruption in public contracting will require clarifying the legal framework, strengthening the relevant institutions, but also changing mentalities. Given the practices over many years, a real shift in attitudes is unlikely to happen overnight.

Anne-Marie Mukwayanzo Mpundu (Réseau d'Education Civique au Congo) and Gaston Tona Lutete (Observatoire Anti-Corruption, DRC)[4]

Further reading

UN, Report of the Panel of Experts on the Illegal Exploitation of Natural Resources and Other Forms of Wealth of the Democratic Republic of the Congo (2001), www.un.org/News/dh/latest/drcongo.htm

World Bank, *Rapport analytique du système de passation des marchés publics* (Country Procurement Assessment Report) (2004)

UNDP, *Governance for Human Development in DRC* (UNDP, 2000)

S. J. Leon de Saint Moulin, J. M. Kinkela, N. Paluku and E. Tshimanga, *La perception de la démocratie et de l'Etat de droit en RDC* (Kinshasa: Konrad Adenauer Stiftung and Cepas, 2003)

Notes

1. See Observatoire Anti-Corruption (OAC), 'Corruption et spoliation du patrimoine de l'état dans la liquidation de la BCCE, dans l'ONPT et dans la GECAMINES', Doc. 2 (Kinshasa: OAC, 2003).
2. At the time of writing an amnesty for these crimes was due to be examined by parliament in July and August 2004.
3. World Bank, 'Rapport analytique du système de passation des marchés publics en RDC', volume 1 (2004).
4. With the assistance of Julien Attakla-Ayinon, former programme coordinator at Transparency International on the DRC.

Costa Rica

Corruption Perceptions Index 2004 score: 4.9 (41st out of 146 countries)

Conventions:
OAS Inter-American Convention against Corruption (ratified June 1997)
UN Convention against Corruption (signed December 2003; not yet ratified)
UN Convention against Transnational Organized Crime (ratified July 2003)

Legal and institutional changes

- In April 2004 the legislative assembly gave its initial approval to the **Law against Corruption and Illegal Enrichment in Public Office**. The draft law had been submitted five years before and had yet to be fully approved at the time of writing. The aim of the law is to bring the Costa Rican legal framework into line with the provisions of the Inter-American Convention against Corruption. The law defines corruption crimes and allows asset declarations made by public officials to be invoked in prosecutions.

- The supreme court called in April 2004 for the revocation of a provision of a law creating special courts for cases of **mismanagement of public resources and tax crimes** because the resources necessary to properly implement the law were not allocated. The provision was part of a law adopted in May 2002, that had been criticised for making it more difficult and expensive to tackle corruption cases because they have to be dealt with in a centralised court in the capital, San José.

Trafficking in influence sullies Costa Rica's social security system

Despite a fairly sound legal framework and operational enforcement mechanisms, influence peddling continues to dog public procurement in Costa Rica, with lucrative contracts sometimes going to those companies that are prepared to grease the palms of government officials. One recent case that illustrates the problem, and has sparked anger among the general public,

involved the Costa Rican Social Security Administration (CCSS), the country's biggest buyer of medical equipment, and a pharmaceutical distributor, the Fischel Corporation.[1]

The case came to light after government investigators' suspicions were aroused by a massive increase in the value of medications sold by Fischel Corporation to the CCSS, from US $530,000 in 2002 to US $990,000 in 2003. It was soon discovered that the head of the CCSS, Eliseo Vargas, was renting a luxury house at a cut-price rate from the Fischel Corporation. The company had used a series of firms registered in Panama to buy the property. Vargas resigned in April 2004, after the scandal erupted.

A further investigation was also opened into alleged irregularities in medical equipment purchases using money from foreign loans, from Finland and Spain. Medical equipment worth US $39.5 million had been bought using a Finnish loan that was conditional on the CCSS using at least half of the money on Finnish medical equipment, even though much of the equipment listed in the terms of the loan did not correspond to the priority needs of CCSS hospitals. The company that was eventually given the supply contracts was Instrumentarium-Medko Medical, a Finnish consortium that was represented by Fischel Corporation.

The president created a special commission of four well-respected individuals from the government, judicial, medical and business communities to investigate both allegations. The commission's three-month investigation ran parallel to a legislative inquiry and investigations by the public prosecutor's office, which began in December 2003. This has caused problems: when called to testify before congress, the accused have tended to refuse on the grounds that their statements could be used against them in the parallel criminal process. A second problem is that, according to the chief prosecutor, a number of CCSS officials have been threatened with dismissal or other sanctions if they denounce acts of corruption in the sections where they are employed.

The case has been widely publicised and public pressure generated by the scandal contributed to the decision by the legislature to begin the process of adopting the law against corruption and illegal enrichment, which had been languishing in the legislative assembly for nearly six years. The case also highlights the important role of investigative journalists, who uncovered the links between the Fischel Corporation and CCSS directors who were involved in the scandal.

Technical oversight promises to help uncover corruption

Kilometres of pot-holed highways and bridges that remain incomplete years after they were started beg questions about the administration of public resources and the effectiveness of the contracting and construction processes in Costa Rica. In 2002 the legislature appointed a technical institute to oversee CONAVI, the state body responsible for building and maintaining the country's roads, and to investigate the shoddy construction practices that shortened the useful life of the road network.

The oversight body is the National Laboratory for Structural Materials and Models (LANAMME) of the University of Costa Rica. Since being assigned with the monitoring role, LANAMME has produced a number of reports criticising the quality of roadworks – both their construction and maintenance – which have served as the basis for allegations of conflicts of interest and political interference. The response from CONAVI to the new monitoring body has been lukewarm at best. By law, CONAVI should transfer 3 per cent of its annual budget to LANAMME, but in 2004 it was projecting a total transfer of only 2.1 per cent for the year. With each critical report from LANAMME, payments have tended to be delayed or cancelled, making it difficult for the oversight body to carry out its work.

LANAMME looks at the technical aspects of projects. Its reports show clearly where substandard, cheaper materials have been used and where feasibility studies have not been carried out. One case worth mentioning is the Barranca-Peñas Blancas highway. In this case, the technical specifications of the contract were modified by government officials who wanted the job finished quickly, even though this would mean cutting corners that would create potential problems in the future.

In the case of Barranca-Peñas Blancas, a 200-kilometre and US $16.8 million stretch of the main highway in the north of the country is defective. The investigation showed poor project planning and administration. The decision by CONAVI to waive the preliminary studies required under the terms of the contract is expected to spark an investigation into the reasons behind the irregularities. The money was paid to the contractor even though the work was delayed by 50 days, 80 kilometres of the road have yet to be repaired, and the private company that was subcontracted to monitor the quality of the cement failed in its task. The work went US $4 million over budget.

LANAMME's work ends with technical evaluation, but this may well, as in the above cases, produce enough evidence to trigger investigations into the reasons behind poor decision-taking and poor quality work, and in particular whether corruption was involved. The question now is whether the agencies responsible for looking into the political and criminal dimensions of the many cases LANAMME has investigated have the political will to build on the technical work. A related need is for LANAMME to gain financial independence from CONAVI, which currently has the authority to reduce LANAMME's budget unilaterally. Statistics for the sector demonstrate the urgency of LANAMME's work: only 23 per cent of the country's roads are in a good state of repair, while 38 per cent are in bad condition.

Roxana Salazar and Mario Carazo (Transparencia Costa Rica)

Further reading

Villasuso Estomba and Juan Manuel, *Corrupción en Costa Rica: análisis, discusión y propuesta de acción* (Corruption in Costa Rica: analysis, discussion and proposed actions) (San José: Fundación Ebert, 2003)

Rodolfo Saborío Valverde, 'Rendición de cuentas en Costa Rica: diagnóstico y ensayo de sistematización' (Accountability in Costa Rica: diagnosis and systematisation) in *Colección de documentos del Instituto Internacional de Gobernabilidad*, October 2003

Roxana Salazar y Mario Carazo, *Guía sobre rendición de cuentas. Un compendio* (Guide to accountability) (San José: Transparencia Internacional Costa Rica, 2004)

Roxana Salazar y Mario Carazo, *Principios empresariales antisoborno* (Anti-bribery business principles) (San José: Transparencia Costa Rica, 2004)

Transparencia Costa Rica (TI Costa Rica): www.transparenciacr.org

Note

1. The story was reported in the national newspapers *La Nación*, *Diario Extra*, *Diario Al Día* and *La Prensa Libre* in May 2004.

Croatia

Corruption Perceptions Index 2004 score: 3.5 (67th out of 146 countries)

Conventions:
Council of Europe Civil Law Convention on Corruption (ratified June 2003)
Council of Europe Criminal Law Convention on Corruption (ratified November 2000)
UN Convention against Corruption (signed December 2003; not yet ratified)
UN Convention against Transnational Organized Crime (ratified January 2003)

Legal and institutional changes

- Parliament passed the Prevention of **Conflicts of Interest** in the Exercise of Public Office Act (PCIA) in October 2003, which entered into force later that month. The law extends the obligations and restrictions placed on public officials. Primarily, the PCIA attempts to combat conflicts of interest through preventative measures (see below).

- An **access to information law** was passed in October 2003 and came into force the following month. Shortfalls in the substance of the law are exacerbated by a politically undermined and under-resourced implementing body (see below).

- The **criminal law** was amended in July 2003 to expand the possibility of prosecuting journalists for defamation, removing an earlier provision that protected journalists from prosecution if the intent to defame was not proven. In November 2003 the supreme court overturned the amendment because the proper procedures had not been observed when it was adopted.

- After more than two years in operation, the **Office for Prevention of Corruption and Organised Crime** (USKOK) set up a working party on the creation and implementation of amendments to its charter in March 2004. Changes are being sought to ensure that USKOK has the power to work more effectively with the police and other state bodies, and to take a leading role in the investigation of criminal matters. According to information from the state attorney's office, USKOK received 410 reports accusing 261 people during 2003, of whom 57 were sent for trial.[1]

- A July 2003 amendment to labour legislation includes a provision **protecting whistleblowers** against dismissal where they have filed a report about corruption to the authorities in good faith.

Is the right of access to information law dead in the water?

Following intense lobbying from civil society groups in Croatia, the Right of Access to Information Act (RAIA) was passed in October 2003. Important omissions from the final legislation and its weak implementation procedures, however, call into question whether this legislation complies with internationally accepted standards.

Following recommendations from the Council of Europe to improve access to information in Croatia, civil society groups submitted various drafts of laws for consideration by the Croatian legislature. Although they clearly had an impact on the final draft, crucial elements from the suggested drafts were omitted, including standards relating to the timeliness and extent of the information provided. The act also does not recognise that the information

seeker may need further information to set his or her enquiry in context.

The act also lacks key public interest and proportionality tests. These tests would stipulate that a denial of a request for access to information should not be used to cover up a violation of the law by a public authority, and that a public body cannot deny access to information simply by giving reasons for its decision.

The law's provisions have already been widely ignored. For example, all public authorities are obliged to submit an annual report on the implementation of the law to the central state administrative office for public administration, which, in turn, must submit a cumulative report to the government for submission to parliament. However, at the time of writing, no such reports had been submitted. Similarly, every public body is obligated to appoint an official information officer, in order to ensure that citizens can exercise their right to access information. At the time of writing only one such person had been appointed.

Crucial, planned amendments to the legislation have failed to appear. Subordinate legislation obligating public authorities to keep an official logbook of requests, procedures and decisions regarding the exercise of the right to access information was posited, however, the body responsible for drafting the amendment, the Central State Administrative Office for Public Administration, has so far failed to produce any such instrument.

Although the legislation is a step in the right direction, it is important to acknowledge its limitations. The substance of the legislation is weak and there seems to be little will to improve access to information in Croatia. In a public debate in May 2004, the 'Club of Journalists' described the law as 'dead', in that the government did not respect it and citizens and journalists did not use it.[2] Amendments strengthening the law and implementation mechanisms are urgently required. It is also necessary that resources be made available to allow public offices to comply with the legislation.

What went wrong with the conflicts of interest law?

Following lengthy debate, the Prevention of Conflicts of Interest in the Exercise of Public Office Act (PCIA) was passed in October 2003. Its stated objective is to define the rules of conduct for public officials.

While there are concerns over the substance of the law (e.g. gifts to officials are not fully covered, and a last minute amendment permitted public officials with less than a 2 per cent stake in a company to avoid declaring their involvement with that company), its main weakness relates to its implementation. The control mechanisms demonstrate a clear lack of political will to prevent conflicts of interest in Croatia.

The body charged with overseeing the implementation of the act is the Commission for the Resolution of Conflicts of Interest. The commission consists of seven members who choose a president from among their number. Four of the commission members are members of parliament and the remainder are to be respected public officials. Although the law came into force in October 2003, participating members of the commission were finally announced in February 2004. Only six members were named, reducing the chances of attaining the four member agreement needed for the commission to make a decision, and the first five sessions of the commission were inquorate.[3]

Neither the 2003 nor 2004 budgets guaranteed any money for the work of the commission. Legally the commission does not even exist as it is not yet registered at the National Statistics Department, has not received a unique national registry number, nor does it have a bank account.[4] There are also serious restrictions on the commission's ability to take any action against corrupt members of parliament.

The lack of public outcry about the new law suggests a lack of understanding among the general public about conflicts of interest. There is also an insufficient understanding among public officials of the principles contained in the law. Much work remains to be done in educating public officials and the general public about the legislation and its importance.

Ana First (TI Croatia)

Further reading

Josip Kregar and Gordana Vučinič Palašek, *Korupcija, Sukob Interesa, Dostupnost Informacija; Stavovi i Iskustva* (Corruption, Conflict of Interest and Public Access to Information: Attitudes and Experiences) (Zagreb: TI Croatia, 2003), www.transparency.hr

GFK – Centre for Market Research, *Citizens on Corruption and Bribing* (Zagreb: GFK, June 2001, December 2003 and January 2004), www.gfk.hr/default.htm

TI Croatia: www.transparency.hr

Notes

1. *Slobodna Dalmacija* (Croatia), 7 April 2004.
2. Round Table discussion organised by TI Croatia and the NGO, 'Club of Journalists' on 20 May 2004.
3. *Novi list* (Croatia), 31 March 2004.
4. Statement of Mr Petar Marija Radelj, a member of the Commission for Resolution of Conflicts of Interest in *Slobodna Dalmacija* (Croatia), 8 April 2004.

Czech Republic

Corruption Perceptions Index 2004 score: 4.2 (51st out of 146 countries)

Conventions:
Council of Europe Civil Law Convention on Corruption (ratified September 2003)
Council of Europe Criminal Law Convention on Corruption (ratified September 2000)
OECD Anti-Bribery Convention (ratified January 2000)
UN Convention against Corruption (not yet signed)
UN Convention against Transnational Organized Crime (signed December 2000; not yet ratified)

Legal and institutional changes

- At the end of 2003, parliament adopted **a new law on public procurement** to harmonise existing rules with the European Union, which the Czech Republic joined in May 2004. The law provides for significant changes in the legal framework governing public procurement, but is a missed opportunity in terms of anti-corruption measures. It establishes additional exceptions to procurement rules and limits the filing of appeals against decisions by requiring the payment of relatively high administrative fees and an additional fee that a complainant must pay to submit an appeal. This fee is retained by the control body if it adjudicates there are no grounds for the complaint.

- A 19-member **subcommittee on corruption** was established in the lower house of parliament in October 2003. The new panel will focus on initiating anti-corruption legislation and assessing foreign experiences of anti-corruption strategies.

- A new **conflict of interests bill** was prepared by TI Czech Republic and sponsored by the government in early 2004. The proposal addresses many shortcomings of the current law by requiring officials to regularly update registers of interests and asset declarations. It covers members of parliament and government officials, regional and local politicians and their close family members. Following governmental intervention proposed post-employment limitations were removed. Opposition to this bill is strong. Some mayors, for example, see it as an attack on local government independence. Hot debate over this proposal is expected in late 2004.

- Throughout 2003 Czech **anti-corruption police forces** underwent a major institutional change when two units specialised in investigating corruption and economic crimes were merged into Corruption and Financial Criminality Investigation Unit. Recent investigations of local government officials and sports officials suggest the merger may yield positive results.

- In January 2004 the justice ministry introduced an **anti-corruption hotline** to be used by the public to report misconduct or suspicion of corruption in the judiciary. By establishing the service, the ministry followed other government bodies that had launched similar services shortly before, to no great effect.

New bankruptcy legislation urgently needed

There is little evidence of systemic corruption in the Czech judiciary, with one exception: bankruptcy proceedings. Current bankruptcy legislation lacks transparent criteria for the appointment and removal of bankruptcy administrators by judges. This had provided opportunities for corruption when bankruptcy judges and bankruptcy administrators collude. Specifically, a limited number of bankruptcy administrators may be given access to lucrative bankruptcy cases and collusion between the judge and the administrator may lead to the siphoning off of post-bankruptcy assets.

One illustrative case of the potential for corruption due to such collusion is the ongoing police investigation of Jiří Berka, a bankruptcy judge in the Ústí nad Labem regional court. Police enquiries from 2003–04 revealed that several bankruptcy cases against Zbrojovka Brno, ZKL Klášterec nad Ohří, Stavební podnik Ralsko, Báňské stavby Most and Krušnohorské strojírny Komořany demonstrated a pattern of corrupt practice.[1] First, an indebted company with its head office in Judge Berka's jurisdiction was identified. Berka's accomplices then bought out the company's debts in order to accumulate the claims necessary to file a bankruptcy petition. Immediately after the petition was delivered to the court, Judge Berka declared the company bankrupt and appointed a colluding administrator. The administrator's task was to satisfy claims of those who had bought out the debts and allegedly, in cooperation with the court-appointed appraiser, to siphon off bankruptcy assets.

Although the case is still under investigation, the unfolding details of this and other cases demonstrate clear institutional shortcomings in bankruptcy proceedings in the Czech Republic, the topic of long-time criticism by some private sector investors. At the time of writing, legislation is being prepared to entrust agents other than bankruptcy judges (such as a creditor's committee) with the power of assigning bankruptcy administrators to individual cases so as to induce arms-length relations between bankruptcy judges and administrators. The same proposed legislation aims to impose stricter requirements for entering into bankruptcy administration and, at the same time, establish a body to monitor their conduct.

Suspicious procurements

One of the largest recent corruption cases originated in the ministry of foreign affairs. The secretary of the ministry, Karel Srba, had allegedly been manipulating the bidding process for the reconstruction of embassies abroad and the leasing of other official buildings.[2] As the media picked up on the story, Srba and his accomplices took out a murder contract on Sabina Slonková, a leading investigative journalist with the daily *Mlada Fronta Dnes*, who had managed to trace some of the embezzled money. The police thwarted the attempt and, in June

2003, a court sentenced Srba to eight years' imprisonment for attempted murder.[3]

Meanwhile, the investigation of corruption in ministerial procurement continues. The court hearing will take place in late 2004, but there are already suggestions that the degree of abuse of power at the highest political sphere is far greater than had been previously suspected.

The Srba affair demonstrates clientelism in the award of public contracts that prevails at many levels of public administration. An external audit of public procurements conducted at Prague city hall in 2003 reported that all of the 133 contracts audited were unlawful.[4] Following this first external audit, Prague city hall is considering repeating the exercise on a regular basis. However, as public officials are able to influence the selection of the cases to be examined, substantial concerns about conflicts of interest remain.

In December 2003 parliament adopted a new public procurement law that was intended to bring the Czech Republic into line with EU regulations, and the government widely presented it as an 'anti-corruption law'. It introduced some positive changes, but loopholes remain. The external regulatory framework is still ineffective. The anti-monopoly office that conducts external controls focuses on formal aspects of the contracting process only, and often fails to distinguish between corruption and administrative error. The law also lowered penalties.

The law does not specify the selection criteria to be used in the evaluation of bids, so there is still a possibility to set subjective criteria that favour individual bidders. The selection of bids is also subject to discretionary oversight by procurement officials, and the decision to publish contracts and amendments is made by the contractor, making public control difficult, if not impossible.

In addition, there is no legal limit on subsequent price increases and the content of contracts remains an issue of agreement between contractor and bidder. The opportunities to 'motivate' persons to increase the cost and content of a contract appear considerable. There have been examples of contracts being increased by 1,000 per cent of the bidding offer – notably in the case of the Fata Morgana greenhouse in Prague, the cost of which now amounts to hundreds of millions of crowns (more than US $8 million).

The new law does little to bring transparency to the public procurement process in the Czech Republic and the authorities seem to lack the political will to ensure a fair and effective distribution of public funds. Public procurement issues remain the area most vulnerable to corruption as EU funds come on stream.

Corruption in Czech football

In November 2003, Radek Váňa, the captain of a minor-league football team, approached an investigative journalist with Czech TV and offered to demonstrate that corruption in football was pervasive. Together, they approached three referees with a small bribe of CZK 500 (US $19). All referees accepted without hesitation.[5]

Demonstrating the vulnerability of whistleblowers in Czech society, the football union suspended Váňa from playing from March to December 2004 and his team lost 12 points.[6] Váňa did, however, receive a great deal of moral support from the Czech public and was awarded the Czech Olympic Committee's Fair Play Prize.

Coverage of Váňa's story on Czech TV generated great interest from the public and the authorities and the police instigated an eight month investigation into corruption in Czech football, resulting in bribery charges against five referees and one manager.[7] At the time of writing others were expected to be charged following allegations that 14 of the Czech Republic's 16 premier league teams had bribed referees.[8]

David Ondráčka and Michal Štička (TI Czech Republic)

Further reading

Inna Čábelková, *Entry Restrictions, Corruption and Extortion in the Context of Transition* (Prague: CERGE-EI, 2001)

Chmelík, J. (ed), *Pozornost, úplatek a Korupce* (Favour, Bribe and Corruption) (Prague: Linde, 2003)

TI Czech Republic: www.transparency.cz

Notes

1. ČTK Press Agency (Czech Republic), 16 February 2004.
2. See www.transparency.cz/index.php?id=727
3. Radio Praha online, 30 June 2003, see www.radio.cz/en/news/42476#1
4. Bez Korupce online, 15 January 2003, see www.bezkorupce.cz/vypis_zpravy.php?id=71
5. ČTK Press Agency (Czech Republic), 24 November 2003.
6. See www.transparency.cz/index.php?id=1971
7. See www.transparency.cz/index.php?id=2346
8. BBC Czech Online, 14 May 2004, see www.bbc.co.uk/czech/domesticnews/story/2004/05/040514_football_1830.shtml

Georgia

Corruption Perceptions Index 2004 score: 2.0 (133rd out of 146 countries)

Conventions:
Council of Europe Civil Law Convention on Corruption (ratified May 2003)
Council of Europe Criminal Law Convention on Corruption (signed January 1999; not yet ratified)
UN Convention against Corruption (not yet signed)
UN Convention against Transnational Organized Crime (signed December 2000; not yet ratified)

Legal and institutional changes

- In January 2004, two days after being sworn in, President Mikheil Saakashvili sent a **package of bills** to parliament that aimed to amend 12 laws, including provisions making it easier to arrest those suspected of bribery and to facilitate the confiscation of illegal assets (see below). The bills were subsequently approved by parliament. In an effort to reduce parliament's potential as a safe haven for criminals, a constitutional amendment was passed in February 2004 limiting immunity for members.

- Changes to a **law on corruption and conflicts of interests** within public services in early 2004 made the prosecution of criminal cases possible regardless of whether the defendant is present or not. The amendment plugs a loophole in the legislation that was widely abused by absconding defendants, or ones who claimed ill health, to evade prosecution. The law applies to public officials and the heads of state-run enterprises (see below).

- The judiciary added another tool in the fight against corruption by approving the inclusion of **plea-bargaining in the criminal code** in February 2004. A judge is to oversee the process to ensure suspects do in fact turn over critical information about those more deeply involved in criminal activity.

Saakashvili gets tough

The Rose Revolution that blossomed in reaction to the rigging of the parliamentary elections in November 2003 led to the resignation of former president Eduard Shevardnadze and the rise to power of Mikheil Saakashvili in January 2004. Both as candidate and president, Saakashvili consistently asserted that corruption was his main priority. Indeed, such is the zeal with which Saakashvili has pursued his anti-corruption campaign that concerns have been raised over the respect being paid to civil and human rights in Georgia.

In early 2004, the government made conspicuous efforts to detain Shevardnadze-era officials, including Shevardnadze's son-in-law, Gia Jokhtaberidze who was detained on charges of tax evasion. During this period five high-ranking officials were detained on charges including tax evasion, embezzlement and misappropriation of state property. Besides Jokhtaberidze, these included the former head of Georgia's railway department, a former energy minister,[1] and a former minister of transport and communications.[2] The detentions all made front-page news and bolstered the government's image for being tough on corruption.

Such government actions have won international confidence. The IMF resumed the operations it suspended in summer 2003 and in June it announced a US $144 million three-year loan. The June 2004 Brussels donor conference secured pledges of US $1 billion for 2004–06, of which Georgia had earmarked US $78 million for governance and anti-corruption reform. Later that month, the World Bank announced a further US $24 million for anti-corruption activities. Georgia was one of 16 countries eligible to apply for the United States' Millennium Challenge Account, which is conditional on the level of corruption (see *Global Corruption Report 2004*).

The government's new anti-corruption strategy includes mandatory asset declaration. A draft law states that if the general prosecutor's office has reason to believe a suspect has acquired property or other assets through illegal means, the administrative court can convene a separate investigation and court hearing. Importantly, the provision allows for relatives or close associates of a suspect to come under investigation. If a suspect fails to appear in court, a decision can still be handed down, overcoming the popular escape route of claiming ill health to avoid prosecution. The justice ministry also elaborated legislation modelled on the US Racketeer Influenced and Corrupt Organizations (RICO) laws. Parliament was due to discuss the first draft in September 2004.

A further pillar of the government's anti-corruption policy is the easing of the tax burden on small business in an attempt to reduce Georgia's shadow economy, estimated to amount to 70 per cent of GDP.[3] There is widespread agreement that the cumbersome tax code is at the core of the stifled economy and primarily responsible for driving legitimate business underground. The president announced an amnesty for businesses who had evaded their taxes up to a threshold of US $500,000 and who signed up to a long-term repayment plan. A 15-member team, led by the prime minister and including foreign tax specialists, was at the time of writing drafting a new tax code for parliamentary review in September 2004.

However, while international expectations rose that Georgia was starting to put its appalling corruption record behind it, a rather more muted discourse questioned the price at which this turnaround was being achieved. Some, for example, have questioned the transparency of anti-corruption activities. Many of the high-ranking officials arrested have subsequently paid money to be released and it remains unclear whether the charges have been dropped in response.[4] Allegations of improper treatment of prisoners, including torture, have also spread. Sulkhan Molashvili, the former chairman of the state audit agency, claimed that he was burned with cigarettes and subjected to electric shocks while in official custody on corruption charges.[5] Human Rights Watch warned that high-level official statements praising harsh methods of fighting corruption may encourage human rights violations.

Disappointingly, parliament has scarcely debated these events and few civil society groups or public figures have spoken out on the need for the government to be more accountable for its actions. This muted response can be attributed to several factors, not least of which is Saakashvili's overwhelming popularity, having received 97 per cent of the presidential vote. The breakneck speed of political developments in Georgia and the ongoing crises in Adjaria and South Ossetia[6] have absorbed public attention. The timely payment of pension and salary arrears from funds the state claims it recovered from 19 corrupt officials since January 2004 (US $23.4 million) has also boosted public support for government policy in fighting corruption.[7]

Early assessments of Saakashvili's anti-corruption policy thus suggest there may be reason for both optimism and concern. The current hard-line approach and proposals to increase jobs and economic growth look set to go some way towards reducing incentives for corruption, but care is also needed to protect Georgian civil liberties.

Georgia's smuggling crisis

Research by the Petroleum Advisory Group revealed that the government loses an estimated US $300 million in revenue each year from the smuggling of petroleum products, tobacco and alcohol into Georgia. Contraband, including basic products such as flour and citrus products, streams across the border.

The ministry of the interior and the state border protection service both came under scrutiny in early 2004. The former deputy interior minister resigned in March after he was charged with violations of customs regulations on imported vehicles that left a 9 million laris (US $4.4 million) shortfall in the budget for 2000–03.[8] The border protection service director, Valeri Chkheidze, was accused of corruption and the head of the personnel department was arrested on charges of fraud and counterfeiting after a military investigation.[9]

The president has demanded an end to corruption in customs and, at the time of writing, work is currently underway, with the help of European experts, to rewrite the customs code with special attention to delineating the responsibilities of customs officials. It was also expected that legislation would be passed to ensure that in future goods will be cleared at the border rather than inside the country's breakaway regions, the source of most of Georgia's contraband. Major infrastructural changes will be required to ensure this happens. The head of customs also declared that he is to cut his department's staff by nearly 400 after skills testing of current employees.

However, many of those engaged in smuggling are economically and socially deprived, making any crackdown both a political and social litmus test. Until their livelihood can be enhanced by other means, it might be unwise and even dangerous to pursue a strategy that punishes the offenders without attacking the large-scale smugglers, law enforcement bodies, and corrupt officials who facilitate smuggling and permit it to continue unhindered.

So far the government has not taken this risk. While it has taken some short-term anti-smuggling measures (for example, the destruction of 'smuggler roads'), it appears more interested in an effective, long-term strategy of reform than in prosecuting smugglers who are already in desperate economic conditions.

Johanna Dadiani (TI Georgia)

Further reading

Alexandre Kukhianidze, Aleko Kupatadze and Roman Gotsiridze, *Research Report for American University's Transnational Crime and Corruption Center* (Tbilisi: Georgia Office, 2003)
Georgian Opinion Research Business International (GORBI), *Corruption Survey* (Tbilisi, 2003), www.gorbi.com

TI Georgia: www.transparency.ge

Notes

1. *Georgia Online Magazine* (Georgia), 3 April 2004, at www.civil.ge
2. *The Messenger* (Georgia), 5 February 2004.
3. Alexandre Kukhianidze, Aleko Kupatadze and Roman Gotsiridze, *Research Report for the American University's Transnational Crime and Corruption Center* (Tbilisi: Georgia Office, 2003).
4. *The Messenger* (Georgia), 2 April 2004.
5. See eurasianet.org/departments/insight/articles/eav091104.shtml
6. Abkhazia and South Ossetia are breakaway regions not under central government control. Adjaria was a third breakaway province that came under central control in May.
7. *The Government's Strategic Vision and Urgent Financing Priorities in 2004–2006* (Brussels: 2004), www.civil.ge
8. RFE/RL Newsline, 3 March 2004.
9. RFE/RL Newsline, 19 February 2004.

Germany

Corruption Perceptions Index 2004 score: 8.2 (15th out of 146 countries)

Conventions:
Council of Europe Civil Law Convention on Corruption (signed November 1999; not yet ratified)
Council of Europe Criminal Law Convention on Corruption (signed January 1999; not yet ratified)
OECD Anti-Bribery Convention (ratified November 1998)
UN Convention against Corruption (signed December 2003; not yet ratified)
UN Convention against Transnational Organized Crime (signed December 2000; not yet ratified)

Legal and institutional changes

- In February 2004 Germany's largest association of pharmaceutical companies (Verband der Forschenden Arzneimittelhersteller) presented a **code of conduct** to its members that rules out offers of improper advantage and regulates corporate gifts and entertainment for doctors. Although this was a long overdue development, the code has serious shortcomings in precision that may render it ineffective. Compliance will be monitored by a self-regulatory association that can apply sanctions in case of infringement.

- The states of Saxony and North Rhine-Westphalia and Saxony established **special task forces to combat corruption** in April and March 2004, respectively. In the task forces prosecutors, police officers and accountants cooperate to tackle the increasingly complex networks of corruption. Scandals in both states provided the impetus to strengthen efforts in this direction.

- In March 2004 Hamburg became the first German state to establish by way of law a **blacklist for companies** found guilty of corruption. Other states, including North Rhine-Westphalia, Hessen, Lower Saxony and Baden Württemberg, have introduced blacklists, but their legal foundation is not as strong as in Hamburg because they have been established by administrative order (*Verordnung*), rather than by law. In April, North Rhine-Westphalia announced it wanted to update its provisions in this regard. Its current blacklist is mandatory only for tenders at state level, not at the communal level.

- Germany finally ended its resistance to provisions in the UN Convention against Corruption concerning the **bribery of members of parliament**. The German stance delayed negotiations in 2003. Members of parliament argued that creating such an offence would carry no advantage since nobody would try to bribe them and that, in addition, the rules of appropriate conduct could not easily be specified. In December Germany signed the convention, though it still needed ratifying at the time of writing.

Bribery scandal in Munich

In March 2004 – to considerable public surprise – police raided the offices of Karl-Heinz Wildmoser, the popular and colourful president of Munich's second biggest football club, TSV 1860 München. Wildmoser and his son, Karl-Heinz Wildmoser Jnr, were arrested and accused with two others of receiving kickbacks worth €2.8 million (US $3.4 million) in connection with a contract to build the new football stadium that will stage the opening match of the 2006 World Cup.[1]

Munich's two major football clubs, Bayern München and TSV 1860, currently share the stadium built for the 1972 Olympic Games. In 1997 Bayern München decided to build a new stadium specifically to host football games, although the project only began in autumn 2001. The two clubs formed a joint holding company to manage the project, Münchener Stadion GmbH, with Karl-Heinz Wildmoser Jnr as its senior manager.

From then on the course of events became less clear. Stefan Dung, a school friend of Wildmoser Jnr active in the real estate business, allegedly contacted the Austrian construction company Alpine and received money in return. The actual amount and why it was paid have not been revealed.

It was reported that Alpine claimed Dung had informed them of the tender for the stadium and recommended they work together on it. Alpine officials apparently said they paid him an 'arrangement fee' of €1.4 million (US $1.7 million) for this information, following standard business practice.[2] The Munich public prosecutor Christian Schmidt-Sommerfeld, however, claimed that Alpine paid €2.8 million not as an arrangement fee but as a kickback for classified information about the tender that the company ultimately won. Wildmoser Jnr allegedly admitted he had received more than €2 million, but maintained that his father was not involved in the affair.[3] The father was cleared of the allegations, but the trial of Wildmoser Jnr was due to open in late 2004.

At one level the Wildmoser affair was hardly exceptional – because corruption is perceived to be common in the construction sector and not unusual elsewhere in the economy. But, at another level, it had a profound effect. The alleged involvement of a celebrity and the link to the 2006 World Cup, due to be held in Germany, lent it symbolic importance. Politicians voiced fears that Germany's 'clean' reputation could be seriously damaged and called for a national blacklist of companies convicted of corruption. Just such a bill failed two years ago because of resistance in the Bundesrat (the upper house of parliament), and the ministry of economic and labour affairs has not given it high priority. However, there are chances that the proposal will be revived in connection with a procurement reform. While some states, such as Hamburg, have introduced blacklisting mechanisms on their own, the Bavarian parliament recently rejected a similar motion introduced by the opposition. The Bavarian government argued that action was primarily needed at the federal level.

The Mannesmann case

In January 2004 the controversial trial began of several prominent members of Germany's business elite on charges of breach of fiduciary duty (*Untreue*) after the hostile takeover of Mannesmann AG by Vodafone in February 2000.

At the heart of the allegations lay severance payments totalling €57 million (US $70.4 million) to Mannesmann's former CEO, Klaus Esser, and two other top representatives of the company. Prosecutors originally claimed Esser was bribed into accepting the takeover, a charge that the court refused to accept due to lack of evidence. Instead, the trial centred on whether the defendants – who, in addition to Esser, included Josef Ackermann, CEO of Deutsche Bank, Klaus Zwickel, former head of the powerful trade union IG Metall, and Joachim Funk, Mannesmann's former chairman – had been acting in the interest of the company when they voted for the severance package. While Judge Brigitte Koppenhöfer indicated in April 2004 she thought the prosecution would be unable to prove the defendants did anything criminal,[4] there remained the possibility that the board members contravened the law on listed companies, which would have constituted a civil offence. In July 2004 the court acquitted all the defendants, though state prosecutors lodged an appeal against

the acquittal.[5] Irrespective of the final decision, the trial nevertheless laid bare several important issues.

First, the proceedings were instituted in the face of opposition from the international business press and domestic politicians, who both argued that a trial would be a mistake that could damage Germany's reputation as a place to conduct business. The capacity of the judicial system to act independently of such powerful interests was undoubtedly reassuring.

Second, in spite of reported indications that not all the rules were followed during the takeover,[6] the prosecution was unable to prove its case and had to rely on circumstantial evidence. Many observers highlighted flaws in the prosecution strategy, but this also reflected the highly opaque nature of a case in which important witnesses claimed to have forgotten basic facts[7] and the relevant parties apparently had little interest in uncovering the true story. Though the trial proved significant shortcomings in Germany's corporate governance system, it also illustrated the difficulty of addressing issues such as this through judicial proceedings.

Finally, the public trust that was already strained by corruption scandals and economic decline was further eroded by public exposure of the arrogance of some of Germany's business elite. The payments were considered by many to be an indication of unbridled greed.

NGOs and parliamentarians push for freedom of information

Though a powerful tool for combating corruption, transparency is not a word that springs to mind in connection with Germany's public services. Indeed, access to information is the exception: if there is no explicit provision saying a document is accessible, it is confidential. In this respect, Germany is increasingly isolated in the developed world and, together with Luxembourg, it is the only EU member that has not enacted freedom of information legislation. Though four states have made their administration's documents accessible – Brandenburg (1998), Berlin (1999), Schleswig-Holstein (2000) and North Rhine-Westphalia (2002) – action is needed at federal level, if only to send out a strong signal.

Prospects looked promising after the change of government in 1998 when the ruling, two-party coalition documented its intent to introduce freedom of information legislation, but the project did not get off the ground. A working group of civil servants in the ministry of the interior began drafting a bill in 1999 but, after five years of resistance from the business sector and ministries – notably defence, economic affairs and foreign affairs, which all demanded far-reaching exceptions – it finally gave up the effort in March 2004.

At this crucial moment a coalition of five professional associations and NGOs –

Deutscher Journalisten-Verband, Deutsche Journalistinnen- und Journalisten-Union in ver.di, Netzwerk Recherche, TI Germany and Humanistische Union – stepped in. Frustrated by inaction at the federal level and wishing to revive the public debate, the alliance began to draft a freedom of information bill in mid-2003. The finished document was handed to the president of the Bundestag in April 2004.[8] The draft gained widespread publicity and, more important, lent momentum to an initiative by several parliamentarians who in parallel were drafting a bill, intended to be introduced on behalf of the ruling coalition. The proposed legislation would only cover federal agencies, which could speed up the procedure since the upper house of parliament would not need to vote in favour. Its disadvantage is that it would not affect information at the communal level, since the states enact their own legislation in this area.

Carsten Kremer (TI Germany)

Further reading

Hans von Arnim, ed., *Korruption – Netzwerke in Politik, Ämtern und Wirtschaft* (Corruption – Networks in Politics, Public Agencies and the Business Sector) (München: Knaur, 2003)

Britta Bannenberg and Wolfgang Schaupensteiner, *Korruption in Deutschland* (Corruption in Germany) (München: Beck, 2004)

Hans Leyendecker, *Die Korruptionsfalle* (The Corruption Trap) (Hamburg: Rowohlt, 2003)

Michael Wiehen, *OECD Convention: Overcoming Obstacles to Enforcement. Summary Report on Germany* (October 2003), www.transparency.de/Stellungnahme_Pruefbericht.113.0.html

TI Germany: www.transparency.de

Notes

1. *Financial Times* (Britain), 11 March 2004.
2. Associated Press (US), 18 March 2004.
3. *Der Spiegel* (Germany), 15 March 2004.
4. *FAZ* (Germany), 1 April 2004.
5. *Financial Times* (Britain), 24 July 2004.
6. See for example *Der Spiegel* (Germany), 2 February 2004.
7. *FAZ* (Germany), 2 April 2004.
8. www.transparency.de/uploads/media/DOK406_IFGNeufassung_040402.pdf

Greece

Corruption Perceptions Index 2004 score: 4.3 (49th out of 146 countries)

Conventions:
Council of Europe Civil Law Convention on Corruption (ratified February 2002)
Council of Europe Criminal Law Convention on Corruption (signed January 1999; not yet ratified)
OECD Anti-Bribery Convention (ratified February 1999)
UN Convention against Corruption (signed December 2003; not yet ratified)
UN Convention against Transnational Organized Crime (signed December 2000; not yet ratified)

Legal and institutional changes

- The powers of the **General Inspector for the Public Administration** (GIPA), established in November 2002, were amended in 2003 to allow it to call for disciplinary measures against employees found violating the law. Another legislative amendment empowers GIPA's 'special inspectors' to control, inspect and investigate; to act as prosecutors; and to carry out administrative interrogations. In its first year of operations, GIPA investigated 386 cases, of which 49 referred to corruption and transparency. GIPA's 2003 report included a number of proposals for combating corruption and increasing transparency in the public administration.

- During 2003 the first supreme court decisions were issued on cases involving the newly reformulated offence of bribery, which had been modified in response to the EU's anti-corruption convention. Unlike the previous wording of the law, the supreme court ruled that it is not illegal to give bribes *after* the action they are supposed to influence has taken place. As a result **gratitude gifts** are now allowed despite the obvious risk that they may create an obligation from the employee to the gift giver.

- The new government elected in March 2004 made a number of **legislative proposals** for public administration reform, including: reform of the law on influence peddling between the media and public works contractors (see below); a proposal to eliminate the so-called 'mathematic formula' which was seen to be an inadequate and non-transparent means of selecting contractors; and the creation of ministerial committees with the participation of NGOs for drafting the new legislation.

Mass media and public contracts

In 2003 public bodies for the first time included in bids for public contracts the provisions of a new law on mass media and public contracts. The law, based on a constitutional amendment in 2001, is intended to promote transparency and limit the trade in influence by prohibiting owners or shareholders of mass media organisations from participating in companies that implement public contracts. Violators of the law face serious penalties, with the possibility of recall of a broadcaster's licence, and cancellation of the public contract.

The law follows several occasions in the last few years in which the Greek press published reports alleging that the award of public construction contracts had resulted from the influence of media owners who were also shareholders – or their relatives were – in the companies that won the contracts. With the massive increase of public building required for the 2004 Olympic Games, such cases naturally generated considerable publicity.

The new law refers to the broad public sector, including: contracts with the state and municipalities; private companies whose board is selected by the state or which receive substantial public funding; and companies founded by the state. The law applies to all public contracts worth more than €250,000 (US $302,000), many of which are for public works and construction projects.

Under the new law for companies to participate in a bid above the threshold, all board members, directors and shareholders with more than a 5 per cent participation; the shareholders of the shareholding companies; and their relatives all have to sign a declaration that they are neither an owner nor shareholder in a media company. Even a small firm with three shareholders, a board of five members and two directors, all from small families, might have to send a list of 150 names, while figures of up to 500 names are not unusual.

However, in the event that one of the persons listed is indeed connected with a media company, he or she merely has to prove financial independence from the relative participating in the company's bid. Since a mass media organisation and a construction company, even if owned by the same group of individuals, may easily be financially independent of one another, this provision makes it easy to avoid application of the law, in spite of its apparent severity. The law can also be by-passed by off-shore companies, which cannot be obliged to publish the names of their shareholders.

Initial hopes that the new law would prevent misuse of influence receded in 2003, just months after it was implemented.

Although such cases were broadly discussed in the media, only one reached the courts, and not as a criminal procedure. The case in question, which concerned annulling the award of a construction project to a company owned by the sons of a media owner, was heard in the supreme administrative court.

The requirements that the law introduced were clearly impractical and bureaucratic, while providing ample scope for evasion. The New Democracy government, elected in March 2004, proposed to amend the law later in the year, but any amendment will come long after the Olympics and Greece's largest publicly funded construction boom in recent years.

A specialised police agency

In 2003 the Greek government responded to calls for a specialised agency to tackle corrupt public employees. The need for such an office had been obvious for years, judging from the number of public complaints about corruption and the lack of prosecutions.

Instead of building a new agency, an existing institution, the Directorate of Internal Affairs of the Greek police had its competence broadened. This move followed the recommendations of the GRECO inspection team, which visited the directorate in 2001, evaluated positively its anti-corruption work in the police force and proposed expanding its activities to other areas of public administration.[1]

Choosing an already well-functioning, experienced and broadly independent institution has already proved effective. During its first year, in 2003, 396 complaints against police officers and 65 complaints against public officers – all for corruption – were filed. Twelve cases against public officers were prosecuted and will be brought to trial. Bribery already constitutes the second largest group of violations (after violation of duty) investigated by the Directorate.

The Directorate of Internal Affairs was established in 1999. It has functional independence, reports directly to the chief of police and is supervised by a high-ranking prosecutor from the court of appeals. The directorate is responsible for all crimes committed by police personnel, including corruption, and following the broadening of its powers, it is now empowered to investigate acts of bribery and extortion by any public officer. These include employees of the ministries, public agencies, municipalities, prefectures, tax inspectors, and so on. Only port authority employees are excluded, since the relevant ministry has its own internal affairs directorate. Unlike other anti-corruption authorities in Greece, including the GIPA, the directorate primarily has a penal function, while the others are mainly administrative.

The directorate investigates complaints, which can be anonymous, but may also act independently (for example, on inside information). The investigations are conducted secretly but with caution so as not to harm the reputation of wrongly accused public officers.

Several of the 2003 cases were brought against tax inspectors who had been specifically assigned to combat corruption in the field of taxation. Several scandals relating to them had led to frequent public questioning of 'Who will control the controllers?' Their investigation by the Directorate of Internal Affairs is of major importance, not only in answering this question, but in preventing future corruption.

Markella Samara (TI Greece)

Further reading

TI Greece: www.transparency.gr

Note

1. Council of Europe Group of States against Corruption (GRECO), 'Evaluation Report for Greece' (2002).

India

Corruption Perceptions Index 2004 score: 2.8 (90th out of 146 countries)

Conventions:
UN Convention against Corruption (not yet signed)
UN Convention against Transnational Organized Crime (signed December 2002; not yet ratified)

Legal and institutional changes

* The **Central Vigilance Commission (CVC) bill** became law in September 2003. The law permits inquiries into corruption offences alleged to have been committed by certain categories of public servants. The legislation came in response to a 1997 recommendation by the supreme court to increase the independence of the Central Bureau of Investigation (CBI) and other investigative bodies that probe high-level corruption by transferring supervision of the CBI from the government to the CVC. The CVC law, however, fails to give the CVC a strong mandate. The law restricts the CVC's supervision of the CBI and

fails to address other key problems highlighted in 1997 such as the need to establish a special agency to oversee cases of high-level corruption.

- Several laws on **election finance** were amended in September 2003. The amendments aim to counter the purchase of political favours through increased transparency and accountability of party financing. The changes should also help parties mobilise more campaign funds. They grant corporations tax exemption for political party contributions and require political parties to report all private or corporate donations above 20,000 rupees (US $435) to the election commission. Failure to do so forfeits the tax deduction on the contribution. The bill also provides indirect public funding in the form of allocation of time on the cable television network and electronic media.

- An **anti-defection law** received presidential assent in January 2004. This legislation aims to curb corruption in the electoral process by limiting the number of ministers in central and state government. One of the methods of destabilising governments has been to lure members of parliament to change party with promises of a cabinet position. Under the new law, some of the states with excessively large cabinets had to reduce them by June 2004. The law also bars 'defectors' from becoming ministers until the following election. While the law reduces incentives for corruption, it also sanctions parliamentarians who vote against their party line and may therefore stifle internal party debate. In addition, the law provides that the parliamentary speaker is the final authority in determining disqualification for defection, leaving the door open for political manipulation.

- Following a directive of the supreme court and pending enactment of suitable legislation, the government issued a **resolution on whistleblowers** in April 2004. The resolution assigns the CVC as the agency to receive complaints by whistleblowers of allegations of corruption or misuse of office by public servants. While a welcome step, the resolution is weak in relation to the draft whistleblowers act, written by the Law Commission and under examination by the government, which would empower the CVC to issue directives to government departments.[1] Instead the resolution merely allows the CVC to issue advice to the departments concerned once whistleblowers' complaints have been investigated. The draft act would also stipulate that once criminality is established the designated agency can directly ask for prosecution of errant government officials, while under the current resolution sanction for prosecution is needed from higher authorities.

The role of the courts and civil society in stemming political corruption

State parliamentary elections of November 2003 saw the first extensive test of an important initiative to improve electoral transparency. Following a directive of the supreme court in May 2003, the election commission issued guidelines requiring all candidates contesting elections to declare their education, criminal record, assets and financial liabilities. Despite a shaky start in local elections in K. R. Puram, a township on the eastern outskirts of Bangalore (where 30 out of 170 candidates failed to fully declare their assets), all of the candidates in the parliamentary elections made declarations, and the information was published extensively in the media.

The supreme court also took the lead in deciding the outcome of state elections in Bihar. In April 2004 the Patna High Court ordered a recall of votes in constituencies where the candidates were in prison facing serious charges including murder, extortion and kidnapping. The supreme court stayed the order of the Patna High Court on the grounds that the election (of 26 April) had taken place before the order of the High Court (announced on 30 April).[2] The case remains open, however, awaiting a final ruling of the supreme court. Nevertheless, the Patna High Court decision may lead to new measures to prevent those convicted of serious offences from contesting elections.

Another effort to increase accountability and political transparency came in the form of a lawsuit initiated by an NGO, Krishak Bharat, seeking to recover money owed for electricity, water and telephone charges by 656 current and former members of parliament. The money was owed to the New Delhi Municipal Corporation and the Mahanagar Telephone Nigam. In March 2004, the Delhi High Court directed the election commission to make this information public. Later, the High Court asked the secretariats of both houses of parliament to ensure recovery of dues from parliamentarians.[3]

The civil society group Lok Sevak Sangh filed a petition to the supreme court in July 2003 seeking the scrapping of the Member of Parliament Local Area Development Scheme. The programme, which entitles a member of parliament to spend 20 million rupees (US $440,000) every year on welfare schemes in their constituency, has been plagued by misuse, according to a report by the comptroller and auditor-general submitted to the president in 2001. The group contends that the scheme gives incumbent members of parliament an unfair advantage against their opponents at election time.

A coalition of 22 NGOs formed an 'election watch' for state elections in Delhi, Chhatisgarh and Gujarat in 2003–04. During the general election of April–May 2004, an election watch was mounted in 12 states across the country. The task of the election watchdogs was to raise awareness among voters about their right to vote, collect data on the criminal records and financial liabilities of the candidates, and keep the public informed about their candidates. Observers also monitored the corrupt practices of political parties during the campaign and on election day.

The election watch NGO coalition called on all the parties to declare their policy on corruption, particularly their positions on establishing an ombudsman's office at national and state levels, a code of ethics for ministers and parliamentarians, a regular audit of the accounts of political parties and a bill on whistleblowing.

There have been positive steps towards electoral transparency in India. The electoral commission's requirements were by and large respected and civil society initiatives have achieved significant results. On the negative side, while the parties made statements about the need to fight corruption they did not commit to specifics. Furthermore, despite the declaration of candidates' assets and criminal records, several candidates with criminal backgrounds were still elected. This can be explained in part by the popularity of particular candidates, but also many voters continue to base their decisions on a system of patronage, whereby politicians are known to buy votes through offering improved access to public services.

P. S. Bawa (TI India)

Further reading

Centre for Media Studies, *Corruption in Urban Public Services* (New Delhi: 2003), www.cmsindia.org

S. K. Das, *Public Office, Private Interest: Bureaucracy and Corruption in India* (New Delhi: Oxford University Press, 2001)

Garry Jeffrey Jacobsohn, *The Wheel of Law* (Princeton and Oxford: Princeton University Press, 2003)

Bhure Lal, *Corruption: Financial Anarchy in Governance* (New Delhi: Siddharath Publications, 2002)

TI India: www.ti-bangladesh.org/ti-india/

Notes

1. *Indian Express* (India), 7 May 2004.
2. *The Hindu* (India), 2 May 2004.
3. *Indian Express* (India), 2 May 2004.

Indonesia

Corruption Perceptions Index 2004 score: 2.0 (133rd out of 146 countries)

Conventions:
UN Convention against Corruption (signed December 2003; not yet ratified)
UN Convention against Transnational Organized Crime (signed December 2000; not yet ratified)

Legal and institutional changes

- The long-awaited **anti-corruption commission** was set up in December 2003. The commission has powers to try corruption cases over IDR 1 billion (US $106,300) to coordinate corruption prevention, to oversee the investigation and trial of corruption cases by prosecutors and police, to order a high-ranking public official under investigation to be released from his or her post, and to order banks to disclose suspicious transactions and freeze accounts. The commission can also take over corruption investigations from police and prosecutors that drag out – a common symptom of corruption in Indonesia. At the time of writing the commission had received 800 corruption cases from the public. Its first case involved alleged corruption by the governor of Aceh province. The limited size of the commission and the protracted process of creating it, however, gave rise to concerns about the degree of political commitment to this institution.

- A **presidential decree on public procurement** was issued in December 2003 to replace regulations existing from 2000. The decree prescribes the establishment of a national procurement office as an oversight body for all public procurement. New rules require full disclosure of all bidding information. Bidding procedures are to be announced in the press at least one month before a deadline for submitting bids. The decree allows civil society to monitor the procurement process. Pre-qualification of bidders is restricted. However, the decree still allows for direct appointment of contractors in emergency situations. As the definition of what constitutes an emergency is not specified, this opens loopholes for government officials to delay procurement until it is too late to conduct a proper bidding process. At the time of writing, the national procurement office was yet to be established.

- In October 2003 parliament passed a **law on money laundering** to amend existing legislation from 2002. This followed criticism of the 2002 law from the OECD's Financial

Action Task Force on Money Laundering (FATF) that put Indonesia on the FATF's list of Non Cooperative Countries and Territories. The new law makes modifications to several controversial articles in the old law, including: eliminating the minimum amount of laundered money required to be considered under the law, shortening the time limit for reporting suspicious transactions from 14 days to three days, adding the post office to the list of financial institutions and including terrorism and human trafficking related transactions. The law's amendment also allows the Centre for Reporting and Analysis of Financial Transactions (PPATK) to report its findings to the public. But at the time of writing, Indonesia's status on the FATF list remained unchanged. PPATK, had recorded 807 suspicious transactions since May 2002, of which 132 were reported to police but only one of these cases was prosecuted.[1]

Anti-corruption movement takes root

Whereas in the past the fight against corruption was primarily addressed by NGOs, 2003–04 saw a broadening of the anti-corruption movement in Indonesia as business and religious organisations joined the campaign for more transparency and accountability. The Indonesian Chambers of Commerce and Industry (KADIN) announced a written pledge to curb bribery in October 2003. Two weeks later, Nahdhatul Ulama and Muhammadyah, the two largest Islamic organisations in Indonesia, also made a declaration against corruption.

Public perceptions of the two newcomers to the anti-corruption struggle vary considerably. The widespread belief that a number of the signatories to the KADIN declaration have been involved in collusion and corruption with Indonesian public officials has led to a perception that the declaration is window dressing. In contrast, Indonesians have welcomed the declaration by the two Islamic organisations and look to it with high expectations. According to the 2001 Governance and Anti-Corruption Survey of the Partnership for Governance Reform, religious organisations are by far the most trusted in Indonesia.

The declarations have brought about a heightened awareness of corruption among the public. Nahdhatul Ulama passed a *fatwa* (holy decree) that someone found guilty of corruption should not be given a proper Muslim ceremony when they die. Their efforts, together with those of the country's anti-corruption NGOs, succeeded in influencing the election agenda. Corruption was one of the key issues during the 2004 legislative and presidential elections, with all parties and presidential candidates pledging to fight corruption if elected.

While the religious parties clearly have the confidence of the public, there is still work to be done in moving from statements to real action. The biggest challenge faced by Nahdhatul Ulama and Muhammadyah is how to actually integrate transparency and accountability into Islamic schools, the distribution of charitable donations and the management and administration of mosques. The issuing of a *fatwa* or Islamic teaching on corruption is no guarantee of effectiveness and there is little evidence thus far that behaviour has changed.

Money politics reign during the 2004 elections

The 2004 Indonesian elections were riddled with 'money politics' – the purchase of public support by political parties. In the Indonesian context money politics takes various forms: donations to religious bodies, providing public facilities, offering door prizes at rallies, promising to donate part of a candidate's salary if elected, distributing basic goods (such as rice and other food), throwing money at the audience at rallies and outright vote-buying.

The General Election Supervisory Committee reported 57 such cases to the police, while Transparency International Indonesia reported 93 such cases and

Indonesia Corruption Watch reported 48. Only 21 cases were taken to court. Of these, only nine resulted in prosecutions by the time of writing – with fines imposed of IDR 1–1.5 million (US $110–160) and up to two months' imprisonment.

The failure to comply with campaign finance rules and regulations can be traced to the weakness of the election law of 2003. The law includes little in terms of sanctions. The maximum penalty for breech of the law is 12 months in prison and a fine of IDR 10 million (US $1,060). There is no sanction for failing to submit a list of donors or campaign accounts, which tied the hands of the election commission when 14 of the 20 parties failed to submit their lists of donors by the deadline in 2004.

Other irregularities were also present during the elections. It was widely held that campaign expenditure was greater than was reported to the election commission. Hidden campaign accounts were common during the 2004 elections.

Although Indonesia's electoral law is in urgent need of reform, there has been clear progress towards democracy. For the first time, political candidates were known to their electorate and direct elections forced candidates to articulate their policies, including public commitments to combat corruption, for which they can be held accountable.

Legislators on the take

Since the end of the Suharto era, a new form of corruption has emerged. Prior to 1998, large-scale corruption centred around the former president, along with his family and cronies. With the long awaited decentralisation that defines the 'reform era' in Indonesia, however, has come a fear that corruption has been exported to the local and national legislature. Evidence that these fears are justified is now emerging.

In May 2004 a court in Padang, West Sumatra, sentenced 43 of the province's 55 councillors to two-year prison terms and fines of IDR 100–127 million (US $11,000–14,000) for embezzlement of IDR 4.6 billion (US $500,000) of state funds. The trial was the result of a two-year advocacy campaign by the Forum of Concerned Citizens of West Sumatra and a group of law professors from Andalas University.[2]

The ruling is not final and all 43 defendants have appealed. Nevertheless many Indonesians have widely welcomed the West Sumatra verdict and the cases in Pedang have had a snowball effect on civil society's efforts to make parliamentarians more accountable. Since the verdict was announced, 12 other corruption cases involving legislatures have been investigated.

Unlike during the Suharto era, legislatures now have the power to determine government budgets, to make decisions about procurement and development funds and to investigate complaints from the public. These powers are vital to control the executive branch, but is also clear that many Indonesian legislators are willing to abuse their authority for private gain. There are increasing reports in the media of irregularities over allowances, travel, health insurance and pension funds.

Emmy Hafild (TI Indonesia)

Further reading

Merly Omar Khouw, *The Private Sector Response to Public Sector Corruption, Business in Indonesia: New Challenges, Old Problems* (Singapore: Institute of Southeast Asian Studies, 2004)
Pranowo U. Tantowi, *Membasmi Kanker Korupsi* (Eradicating the Cancer of Corruption) (Jakarta: Pusat Studi Agama dan Peradaban Muhammadiyah, 2004)
W. Zakiyah, D. Widyoko, I. Kusuma and R. A. Edi, *Menyingkap Tabir Mafia Peradilan* (Uncovering court mafia) (Jakarta: Indonesian Corruption Watch, 2002)

TI Indonesia: www.ti.or.id

Notes

1. Information from PPATK's public relations office.
2. See www.laksamana.net/vnews.cfm?ncat=35&news_id=7069.

Ireland

Corruption Perceptions Index 2004 score: 7.5 (17th out of 146 countries)

Conventions:
Council of Europe Civil Law Convention on Corruption (signed November 1999; not yet ratified)
Council of Europe Criminal Law Convention on Corruption (ratified October 2003)
OECD Anti-Bribery Convention (ratified September 2003)
UN Convention against Corruption (signed December 2003; not yet ratified)
UN Convention against Transnational Organized Crime (signed December 2000; not yet ratified)

Legal and institutional changes

- In October 2003 Ireland ratified the Council of Europe's Criminal Law Convention on Corruption, which applies to money laundering as well as bribery in both the private and public sectors. The previous month it ratified the OECD Anti-Bribery Convention, making it a crime to bribe foreign public officials.

Tribunals of inquiry

Allegations of wrongdoing involving political and business interests prompted the establishment of a number of tribunals of inquiry in the 1990s.[1] The origins of the Moriarty tribunal into payments to politicians and the Flood tribunal into planning corruption in Dublin lay, respectively, in a dispute about control of the Dunnes Stores supermarket group in the mid-1990s, and allegations made to a firm of solicitors in Northern Ireland following a request for information on planning malpractice. The material that came to light created the momentum for investigations to which the political system was compelled to respond. The government and political parties viewed tribunals as the best means possible of establishing the facts and commanding public confidence. Some had hoped that such an approach would also serve to take corruption off the immediate political agenda. This latter hope has not prevailed since the tribunals have heightened perceptions of systemic corruption at all levels of Irish government.

The Flood and Moriarty tribunals have been in existence since late 1997 and show no sign of ending. Both have enjoyed spectacular success in uncovering complex networks of covert financial payments to politicians and public officials. If they have not yet proved that money definitively bought political favours, they have increasingly posed the question of why some businessmen contribute so lavishly to individuals in a position of power.

The 1997 McCracken investigation into payments to the former taoiseach (prime minister), Charles Haughey, reported that he received more than £8 million (US $14.7 million) in the course of a long political career, but failed to substantiate he was guilty of corruption. The McCracken tribunal also identified payments to the Fine Gael politician Michael Lowry, but again it found there was no political impropriety.[2] At the time of writing the Moriarty tribunal was still investigating the payments to Lowry.

Only one politician was found to have received a corrupt payment as a result of evidence from the various tribunals. The second interim report of the Flood tribunal in 2002 found there had been a number of corrupt payments to the former minister of foreign affairs and communications, Ray Burke.[3] Burke rejected the tribunal's findings. In September 2004 his application for costs was refused by the tribunal on the grounds that he had obstructed its work.

The planning tribunal, now chaired by Mr Justice Alan Mahon, has spent much of its time investigating claims by property developer Tom Gilmartin that, after a meeting in February 1989 with senior government ministers, including the present taoiseach, Bertie Ahern, a party representative asked him to 'donate' £5 million (US $9.2 million) to clear the way for building a shopping complex in west Dublin. Most observers estimate that at current rates of progress the planning tribunal will only end in 2020, 23 years after it was established. Politicians bear some responsibility for the delay, given the initial failure to augment the number of judges in the face of repeated pleas from Justice Flood that he had insufficient resources to pursue his terms of reference.

The allegedly corrupt dealings of George Redmond, the most important planning official in Dublin for over a quarter of a century, were first drawn to public attention by the Flood tribunal in 1999. When threatened with up to two years in jail for misleading the tribunal, he admitted he had received large sums of money from a variety of builders and landowners. When he retired as the assistant county manager of Dublin city and county in 1988, he was receiving a salary of €24,000 (US $29,200). However, his investments were then in the region of €830,000 (US $1 million) and he banked €217,000 in that year alone.[4]

Subsequently convicted of failing to make tax returns, Redmond was investigated by the Criminal Assets Bureau.[5] He was found guilty on two charges of corruption in November 2003 and was sentenced to 12 months' imprisonment. This was the first high-profile conviction of a senior public figure on corruption charges arising from the planning tribunal. Redmond appealed his conviction and it was quashed in July 2004 when new evidence he produced made the earlier evidence of the person who made the payment unsafe. No retrial was ordered since Redmond had already served most of his sentence. Notwithstanding his acquittal, there can be no doubt that the decision to send him to trial in the first place demonstrated that the director of public prosecutions was treating accusations of white collar crime with a new seriousness.

The planning tribunal's third report, issued in January 2004, stated that Redmond had received corrupt payments from a property developer and a builder, relating to land developments in the late 1980s. The report dealt with four allegedly corrupt payments to Redmond and stated that he had received regular kickbacks from planners and developers since the 1960s.[6] These claims followed the tribunal's second report, issued in September 2002, which accused the former minister of foreign affairs, Ray Burke, of also receiving corrupt payments from various builders. The report was sent to the director of public prosecutions, the police commissioner, the Criminal Assets Bureau, the Revenue Commissioners and the office of the Director of Corporate Enforcement. One reason for the length of time the report has been with these authorities lies in the nature of the law on tribunals of inquiry, which stipulates that no admission made by a person before a tribunal can be admitted as evidence against that person in a criminal proceeding.

The Morris inquiry into the police

Another ongoing tribunal of inquiry, the Morris tribunal, is investigating complaints concerning police officers in Donegal. In July 2004 it issued its first interim report, in which it stated that two police officers, including a superintendent, orchestrated the planting of ammunition and hoax explosive devices to boost their careers. In addition senior officers were criticised as negligent because they failed to uncover the plot organised by the two.

The report, said Mr Justice Morris, must lead to significant reforms, including more hands-on control by police headquarters, tougher discipline within the force, a new promotions structure and improved record keeping. The minister for justice, equality and law reform, Michael McDowell, noted that the systemic problems in Garda management were not confined to Donegal.[7]

As a result of the report, there are likely to be substantial changes to forthcoming legislation on the police. At the time of writing the government was also expected to move to establish a new audit unit that would have the power to conduct random spot-checks in police stations. What might be even more effective would be the establishment of a police ombudsman, similar to that which exists in Northern Ireland, to provide an independent, impartial police complaints system. The establishment of such a body in the Republic of Ireland would go some way towards rebuilding public confidence in the police.

Raising standards in public life

Assessing the extent of political corruption in Ireland has proved contentious. In July 2003 Mr Justice Matthew Smith, chairman of the Standards in Public Office Commission (SIPO), which polices ethics legislation and the funding of political parties, rejected claims (made in a study by the British-based Joseph Rowntree Charitable Trust) that corruption was a 'central theme' of Irish politics. While warning of potential damage to Ireland's reputation, he acknowledged that there was a pressing need to monitor and raise standards in the public interest. The judge wrote that it was a cause for regret that the examination of past difficulties in such a public manner had led to criticism of the system of governance: 'This criticism is not, in the main, supported by the facts, which, in my view, would show that the integrity of the decision-making process has not been impugned.'[8]

But as the planning tribunal has so far only dealt with allegations of corruption in Dublin, leaving unexamined questions about malfeasance in other regions, it is impossible to state with certainty just how accountable decision-making processes really are. What is certain is that the tribunals running since 1997 have done the state much service, through providing crucial insights into the way Ireland has governed itself in the very recent past.

Partly because of the tribunals, the government has initiated a comprehensive ethics programme and all the main political parties have introduced codes of conduct for members and have comprehensive policy positions on standards in public life. SIPO itself has played an important role in ensuring that the concepts of openness, accountability and transparency are embedded in Ireland's ethics legislation.

Some critics have argued that the tribunals are expensive and futile, but shutting them down would send out the wrong signal about attitudes to corruption. The tribunals should be allowed to continue their work, making the Irish body politic face up to its past and creating pressure for higher standards in public life in the future.

Gary Murphy (Dublin City University, Ireland)

Further reading

Neil Collins and Mary O'Shea, 'Political Corruption in Ireland', in M. J. Bull and J. L. Newell, *Corruption in Contemporary Politics* (Basingstoke: Palgrave Macmillan, 2003)

Council of Europe, 'GRECO, First Evaluation Round, Compliance Report on Ireland' (2003), www.greco.coe.int/evaluations/cycle1/GrecoRC-I(2003)14E-Ireland.pdf

Paul Cullen, *With a Little Help from my Friends: Planning Corruption in Ireland* (Dublin: Gill and Macmillan, 2003)

Colm McCarthy, 'Corruption in Public Office in Ireland: Policy Design as a Countermeasure', in Economic and Social Research Institute, *Quarterly Economic Commentary* (2003), www.esri.ie/pdf/QEC1003SA_McCarthy.pdf

Gary Murphy, 'A Culture of Sleaze: Political Corruption and the Irish Body Politic 1997–2000', *Irish Political Studies* 15 (2000)

Notes

1. The tribunal of inquiry is a device set up by the Irish parliament to investigate matters of urgent public importance.
2. See www.irelandsown.net/tribunal.htm
3. See www.ireland.com/newspaper/special/2002/flood/index.html
4. *Irish Times* (Ireland), 20 December 2003.
5. The Criminal Assets Bureau was established in 1996 to identify assets of persons deriving, or suspected of deriving from criminal activity.
6. See www.planningtribunal.ie/images/SITECONTENT_219.pdf
7. *Irish Times* (Ireland), 16 July 2004.
8. See www.sipo.gov.ie/281e_246.htm

Japan

Corruption Perceptions Index 2004 score: 6.9 (24th out of 146 countries)

Conventions:
OECD Anti-Bribery Convention (ratified October 1998)
UN Convention against Corruption (signed December 2003; not yet ratified)
UN Convention against Transnational Organized Crime (signed December 2000; not yet ratified)

Legal and institutional changes

- **Whistleblower protection** was approved in June 2004 and will come into force within two years. The fact that many recent corporate misdeeds were revealed by insiders' communication to the relevant authorities made the public and the government aware of the need for better whistleblower protection. The law will protect employees who reveal illegal corporate behaviour that runs counter to the public interest. A public servant who blows the whistle on such behaviour will also be protected under the law.

- **Nationality jurisdiction** was introduced in June 2004 to Japan's legislative measures to implement the OECD Anti-Bribery Convention and the Japanese Unfair Competition

Prevention Law (UCPL). This amendment enables law enforcement authorities to investigate and prosecute cases of bribery committed outside the territory of Japan. The reform was made in line with a recent amendment to the penal code, under which public servants receiving bribes outside the country and private persons paying bribes outside the country are punishable.

- A draft amendment to the law for the Punishment of Organized Crimes, Control of Crime Proceeds and other Matters was submitted to parliament, which would extend **confiscation of proceeds to bribe payers.** The existing legislation only provides powers for freezing the assets of those receiving bribes. At the time of writing the amendment had not been approved. The procedure would apply to the offence of bribe payment provided for by the penal code, as well as to the offence of bribery of foreign public officials under the UCPL, which is not mandatory under the OECD Convention.

- The government established in May 2004 a new unit in the cabinet office charged with promoting deregulatory reforms. The move is part of a three-year plan that includes measures to strengthen the anti-monopoly law, empower the Fair Trade Commission and **improve the quality of government procurement**, all of which are expected to have a positive impact on the prevention of corruption.

- **Cronyism in hiring** practice by local governments has long been an issue that needs to be addressed. In February 2004 the ministry of internal affairs and communications announced plans to amend the Local Officials Law with the view of expanding the powers of its disciplinary committee – whose function was previously limited to reviewing complaints over penalties given to employees – so that it will be able to monitor and control employment procedures. Prefecture governments and designated cities have independent personnel committees supervising employment practices, but no counterparts are installed in local governments, where heads of the administration are deeply involved in hiring. The expansion of the disciplinary committee, which is independent of the administrative offices, is an improvement if not a total solution to the problem.

Discretionary police funds under the spotlight

Police slush funds have been a subject of concern for at least a decade. Citizens' groups resorted to information disclosure procedures in a bid to make local police departments accountable for such money. Critical information, however, remained undisclosed in most cases. Several lawsuits filed by citizens' groups were successful in court, leading to rulings that facilitated further disclosure of police information. In April 1998, the Sendai High Court partially overruled a district court's rejection of a citizens' group's demands that the Miyagi prefectural government disclose information on travel expenditures by the prefecture's police and assembly. This was the first ruling

on disclosure of information concerning police expenses, but, as with subsequent cases, it had only limited impact on police transparency.

Insider revelations of such funds have helped speed up progress in this area. A senior official in the Hokkaido police department confessed in February 2004 that officials routinely made efforts to secure discretionally funded money from the national police budget. In the same month a senior official of the Fukuoka police department told a television show how he and his colleagues earmarked such money, and how it was spent. According to him, a division of the department secured ¥10–20 million (US $90,000–180,000) each year that was secretly spent boosting police officials' wages, or on entertainment and gifts. It has long been a tradition that on a top official's transfer to another posting, he is given all the money still left in the safe as a parting gift.

Amid rising public doubts about police honesty, the National Police Agency (NPA) issued instructions in March 2004 to police departments urging them that if a local office is involved in mismanagement, it should apologise and return the amount misspent from its own accounts where possible. The NPA is also reportedly considering changing the receipts system, allegedly another hot bed of corruption in which those on the receiving end of funds use false names.

The steps taken to prevent or reduce police corruption deserve credit, but surveillance of police by citizens' groups must continue. Further steps to be taken include reforming the auditing system so that external auditors are used, but the police authorities have so far refused.

Laws aimed at curbing electoral corruption are seen to be implemented

For the past few years there has been visible improvement in the enforcement of the Political Funds Control Law (PFCL), which obliges political parties and organisations to submit an annual financial report to the designated authorities. Three members of the Diet have been arrested and indicted in the past four years under the terms of the law.

One of last year's most widely reported scandals involved the daughter of Governor Yoshihiko Tsuchiya of Saitama prefecture, who has held the posts of speaker for the upper house of parliament and head of the environment agency. She was arrested and indicted for false reporting in her father's political fund organisation, in violation of the PFCL. In April 2004 she was sentenced to 18 months' imprisonment, which was commuted to a four-year suspended sentence after she showed remorse. Governor Tsuchiya stepped down from office after

the allegations surrounding his daughter surfaced in July 2003.

Another scandal involved the chairman and executives of the Japan Dental Association (JDA), a long-time supporter of the ruling Liberal Democratic Party (LDP). Unaccounted funding contributions by the JDA reportedly amounted to ¥100 billion (US $910 million) in the years 2000–02, and many people believe that much of it went directly into politicians' pockets. In April 2004 authorities arrested the executives of the JDA for bribing public officials.

Police also cracked down on vote buying in elections for the lower house of parliament in November 2003. Arrests included two incumbent LDP parliamentarians on charges they had delivered cash to voters in violation of the Public Offices Election Law. Such arrests were previously rare in Japan. In a parallel development, the police announced it had decided to rigorously apply a five-year exclusion rule preventing a candidate whose campaigners are convicted of vote buying from running in a future election, even if the candidate was not directly involved in the offence. Allegations have been reported that Hiroshi Kumagai, a former head of the Conservative Party who announced his retirement from politics after being defeated in Shizuoka prefecture, may have gone for this reason.

Corruption shakes the medical world

A wave of medical malfeasance was exposed in 2003–04. A professor in the faculty of medicine at Tokyo University was found to have misused subsidies from a private foundation, and was given disciplinary punishment in October 2003. The misappropriation of subsidies by a professor of medicine at Jikei Medical College came to light in March 2004, and he was dismissed.

In April 2004 an investigation revealed that as many as 1,500 doctors from over

50 universities had lent their names to medical institutions to which they were not officially attached. That number is likely to increase as the investigation continues. The public was largely unaware of the practice, whereby hospital officials 'trade' the names of respected doctors at university hospitals either to gain reputation or to meet the requirements in receiving government grants.

A separate scandal involving the Japanese Dental Association (JDA) was revealed in the same month. Executives from several medically related organisations, including the Social Insurance Agency, the Japanese Trade Union Confederation (RENGO) and the Central Social Insurance Medical Council operated by the ministry of health, labour and welfare, were arrested on suspicion of accepting bribes from the chairman of the JDA. In a related development, the Japanese Dentist Federation, the political wing of JDA, was at the time of writing under investigation on suspicion of having made unlawful political donations (see above). This investigation might ultimately incriminate senior political figures affiliated with the ruling Liberal Democratic Party.

Being a medical doctor in Japan gives one considerable advantages, in addition to a job for life. Unlike lawyers or accountants, medical doctors do not need clients; they can thrive inside established institutions such as social and health insurance schemes, which utilise their influence to engage in political lobbying. These institutions help to keep medical treatment in Japan costly and spending of medical research high. Their sense of privilege can lead to the concealment of malpractice by fellow institutions at the expense of their patients.

There are welcoming signs that the integrity of medical society in Japan is about to improve, however. The number of cases in which medical institutions or doctors have been held accountable for malpractice increased by 35 per cent to 248 in 2003. The public is demanding more transparency and disclosure, and a number of whistleblowers have revealed the misdeeds of doctors and institutions. Mechanisms to evaluate medical institutions have been introduced. The Japanese Council for Quality Health Care, a foundation established in 1995, has undertaken independent evaluations on medical institutions for the purpose of accreditation since 1997, and a number of private organisations, including rating agencies, began evaluating medical institutions in 2003. These developments are expected to lead to greater competition and improved quality of medical services.

TI Japan

Further reading

Youichi Ishii, *Sekai-no-oshoku, Nihon-no-oshoku* (Corruption in the World, Corruption in Japan) (Iwanami: 2003)

Kazuo Kawakami, *Oshoku-Zoushuuwai: Sono Sousa-no-jittai* (Corruption in the Light of Police Investigations) (Kodansha: 2003)

Kazuko Miyamoto, *Naibu-kokuhatsu-no-jidai* (The Age of Whistleblowing) (Kaden-sha: 2002)

Hajime Mizuno, *Daremo-kakanakatta Nihon-ishikai* (Untold Stories of the Japan Medical Association) (Soushi-sha: 2003)

TI Japan: www.ti-j.org

Kenya

Corruption Perceptions Index 2004 score: 2.1 (129th out of 146 countries)

Conventions:
AU Convention on the Prevention and Combating of Corruption (signed December 2003; not yet ratified)
UN Convention against Corruption (ratified December 2003)
UN Convention against Transnational Organized Crime (acceded June 2004)

Legal and institutional changes

- The **Public Officer Ethics Act**, passed in May 2003, lays down a code of conduct for public officers. Its main thrust is wealth declaration: public officials are legally obligated to declare their assets. Critics say that while it is laudable to require public officials to declare their wealth, doing so in secret as stipulated in the act – an October 2003 deadline was silently observed – surely defeats the purpose. No government official has been prosecuted in connection with the legislation, and it has been difficult for the media or any other independent agency to access information.

- Several bodies established under the **Anti-Corruption and Economic Crimes Act** passed by parliament in May 2003 became operational in 2003–04. The main investigating body for economic crime, the **Kenya Anti-Corruption Commission**, has powers to investigate corruption but not to prosecute. The **Public Complaints Office**, established under the same legislation, functions as an Ombudsman's office. The **Public Service Integrity Programme** aims to establish an anti-corruption prevention plan within every public institution. It creates the position of an integrity assurance officer in each public body to act as an in-house watchdog.

- In May 2004 the government launched a **National Anti-Corruption Steering Committee** to run a country-wide anti-corruption awareness-raising campaign. The committee is composed of representatives from government, civil society and the private sector.

- The ministry of justice and constitutional affairs has established several **tribunals and commissions** to hear allegations into past economic crimes. The two most significant examples are the Goldenberg Commission and the judicial tribunals (see below).

Fresh scandals show that corrupt networks persist

In May 2004 a Kenyan daily newspaper ran an article with the headline: 'Five cabinet ministers face corruption probe'. The article, quoting the chairman of parliament's public accounts committee, alleged that one cabinet minister 'irregularly acquired a staggering Ksh 800 million [US $10 million] which he has stashed in banks both in the country and abroad'. A day earlier, the same paper printed a large photograph of another cabinet minister alongside an article entitled 'Overnight millionaire?' This story alleged that the minister used his cabinet position to acquire government contracts for an insurance company in which he is a director.

While the minister denied the allegations, the story demonstrated that Kenya is in a state of flux. As a new order struggles to establish itself, the old order fights to retain its old constituencies – patronage networks that continue to exist both within and outside mainstream politics and the bureaucracy. Credibilities are being questioned, and it is difficult to determine where the truth lies. The articles cited above, for example, were published in the *East African Standard*, a newspaper controlled by former president Daniel arap Moi. Similarly, the most popular television and radio stations are owned by individuals allegedly connected to the old regime. Rumours abound, and they are fuelled by a flourishing and increasingly influential yellow press that established itself as a force in the latter years of Moi's rule. Many of these informal publications are said to have been sponsored by politicians connected to Moi, although it has been difficult to ascertain ownership. The new regime has been slow to communicate its agenda in what is turning out to be a propaganda war.

At this writing, the National Rainbow Coalition (NARC) government, had been in power for 18 months. In December 2002 this grouping of key opposition figures and disgruntled elements of the Moi regime won a historic general election by a two-thirds majority. They defeated the KANU (Kenya African National Union) regime, which had held on to power by virtue of an intricate patronage system financed by the proceeds of official corruption. NARC's platform was anti-corruption and for constitutional reform. Today, the question on the minds of many Kenyans is whether the country is returning to the bad old days of KANU.

Anti-corruption investigations: smokescreen or resurrection?

To the new government's credit, moribund watchdog institutions have been revived, not least the parliament's Public Accounts Committee (PAC) and the office of the auditor and controller general. Whereas under the KANU government the two bodies would routinely submit reports years late – with recommendations that were often ignored – in the first few months of 2004 both the PAC and the auditor general's office acted swiftly on new cases of corruption. At the same time, the permanent secretary of governance and ethics, the president's special adviser on corruption, on a number of occasions moved quickly to prevent emerging cases of corruption.

The PAC played a particularly prominent role investigating the so-called Anglo-Leasing scandal that broke in April 2004. According to the press, this passport-procurement scandal cost the state almost Ksh 2.7 billion (US $34 million). The storm broke when it emerged that a routine upgrade of Kenyan passports that should have cost about US $10 million had ballooned to three times that amount. Opposition legislator Maoka Maore named in parliament several prominent individuals in connection with the scandal, including the vice-president, the minister of finance, two permanent secretaries and senior civil servants, in addition to a Swiss company. The president acted swiftly, suspending both of the permanent secretaries involved. A PAC investigation was launched, and it is likely that heads will roll as the PAC investigation proceeds. None of the public officials initially named had been exonerated at the time of writing.

A possibly worrying aspect of the scandal is that, while the president was quick to suspend senior government officials, he did not punish the sitting cabinet ministers implicated. This may suggest that, like the KANU regime before him, the president is content with sacrificing the small fry but is reluctant to give up the big fish. Whether or not this is the case, the damage done to the new regime's credibility by these and other highly-publicised scandals has been considerable. Public confidence in the NARC government has fallen as a result of the return of official corruption, internal wrangles between the two main coalition partners and, most importantly, the government's foot-dragging on constitutional reform.

The government's ambivalence regarding constitutional reform has meant that the powers of the presidency – by far the biggest sticking point during the constitutional review debate – remain largely intact. While the president has remained largely above direct criticism on this matter, his circle of supporters has been criticised for perpetuating the KANU legacy of arbitrary and partisan appointments of individuals to public institutions. In Kenya, this has always been a sure route to accessing state largesse and personal capital accumulation. It is the president's so-called 'kitchen cabinet' that is rumoured to be at the centre of many of the corruption scandals currently besieging the government.

Progress on the judiciary and repatriation of stolen assets

Nevertheless, there is little doubt that many within the government are committed to the fight against corruption. There is no shortage of anti-corruption rhetoric, and the rhetoric has been backed by real action. Two cases in particular demonstrate this: the clean-up of the judiciary and the appointment of a permanent secretary for governance and ethics.

One of the new government's first popular victories came on the judicial front with the dismissal in February 2003 of the chief justice, Bernard Chunga. Chunga was viewed by many as one of the most cynical appointments made by former President Moi. During Chunga's tenure, there was a huge backlog of cases and justice was up for sale as judges, magistrates and judicial officers were routinely bribed.

Chunga's replacement, Chief Justice Evans Gicheru, immediately ordered an inquiry into corruption in the judiciary. Released in September 2003, the report named 23 judges and 82 magistrates, all of whom were accused of participating in various acts of corruption and incompetence. All were given the option of either resigning or responding to the charges through a judicial tribunal. Most opted to resign, although, significantly, a number of judges have recently sued

the judiciary for wrongful termination of employment. Two judges opted to face tribunals, and the cases are ongoing.

Public expectations of the new government's commitment to fighting corruption were raised a notch higher by the appointment in January 2003 of John Githongo as the president's special adviser on corruption. John Githongo, a prominent anti-corruption activist, was one of a number of civil society leaders from the pre-NARC era appointed to a senior position in government. His efforts since taking office have brought largely positive results. In 2003–04 his biggest achievement was to identify the location of US $1 billion stashed away in foreign accounts by individuals close to the Moi regime, though there had been no news of progress in recovering the funds at the time of writing. In addition, he stopped at least two irregular procurement deals before they went ahead.

Mixed results from the Goldenberg Commission

While the new government has been unable to shake off criticisms that it is not doing enough to fight corruption within its ranks, it has taken major steps to deal with economic crimes of the past. In addition to the shake-up of the judiciary, another significant example has been the government's handling of the Goldenberg case, the biggest financial scandal in Kenya's history.

Ten years ago, a young gold trader somehow convinced the government that there was enough gold in Kenya for export. As a result, parliament passed an export-compensation bill (in a single afternoon) exclusively for this purpose. It soon emerged that Kamlesh Pattni, the gold trader, was falsifying gold exports – actually not exporting gold at all – but still claiming export compensation. The Goldenberg scandal cost the country an estimated US $1 billion.

One of the first actions of the new government was to set up a public tribunal to investigate the allegations. The Goldenberg tribunal has no prosecutory powers but is widely expected to recommend the arrest and prosecutions of many of those implicated. More than 1,000 individuals have been informed by the chairman of the Goldenberg Commission, Justice Samuel Bosire, that they will be adversely mentioned at the commission. Among the most prominent are former president Daniel arap Moi, former vice-president and Minister of Education George Saitoti, former finance minister Musalia Mudavadi, two governors of Kenya's central bank and numerous senior civil servants.

However, at the time of writing there had been little sign of real progress. After sitting for close to one year, the legitimacy and impartiality of the Goldenberg Commission had been repeatedly questioned. Indeed, in mid-2004 cross-examination of Kamlesh Pattni pointed to the possibility of improper actions within the commission itself. Questions were asked about the veracity of his testimony, with allegations that he may have cut a deal to keep prominent members of the NARC government out of his testimony.

Playing to the donors

While the government has appeared to be fighting corruption – both past and present – the public's diminishing confidence has dented its credibility. Where the government has institutionalised the fight against corruption, it has been accused of doing so principally for the benefit of donors. In February 2003 the president recalled parliament early, primarily to pass two bills: the Anti-Corruption and Economic Crimes Act and the Public Officer Ethics Act (see above). The intent of both is to institutionalise the fight against corruption, in the former, mainly by establishing a constitutionally protected independent anti-corruption body and, in the latter, by making it a statutory requirement for public officers to declare their wealth. Both bills were passed in record time. The passing of anti-corruption legislation was a key factor in securing large donor-aid commitments in December 2003, which had been suspended since 1991.

By mid-2004, however, it was clear that the government–donor relationship had begun to unravel, precisely on the issue of corruption. Many observers, for example, questioned the effectiveness of the Public Officer Ethics Act. In July 2004, the British High Commissioner, Edward Clay, who had carved himself a niche as a negotiator between the warring factions in the government coalition, launched a scathing attack on corruption in the government. While the government reacted angrily, his remarks were met with widespread public support.

Parselelo Kantai (TI Kenya)

Further reading

TI Kenya: www.tikenya.org

Latvia

Corruption Perceptions Index 2004 score: 4.0 (57th out of 146 countries)

Conventions:
Council of Europe Civil Law Convention on Corruption (signed February 2004; not yet ratified)

Council of Europe Criminal Law Convention on Corruption (ratified February 2001)
UN Convention against Corruption (not yet signed)
UN Convention against Transnational Organized Crime (ratified December 2001)

Legal and institutional changes

- Adopted by the government in March 2004, the **National Anti-Corruption Strategy** is Latvia's first ever umbrella strategy on corruption. The strategy is complemented by the **updated National Corruption Prevention Programme**, first created in 1998. More than 100 operations and institutions are included in the programme for 2004–08. The strategy is intended to strengthen financial control over political parties, improve criminal investigations and anti-money-laundering procedures, provide transparent public budgeting and protect whistleblowers. Many of the initiatives are concerned with raising awareness of legal responsibilities among public officials and the wider public.

- Amendments to the **law governing the financing of political parties** were adopted in February 2004 (see below). This reform sets limits on the overall campaign expenditure of political parties, prohibits corporate donations, and provides for comprehensive reporting requirements and control mechanisms. The law is one of the most progressive in the region.

- Amendments to the **public procurement law** came into force in April 2004 in accordance with conditions set by the European Commission (EC) for Latvian entry into the European Union (EU). However, the new provisions actually reduce transparency and accountability. Prior to this legislation, pressure from civil society had led the then prime minister, Einars Repše, to implement measures making all public tender information available to the public, including the final agreement with the winner. The EC, however, required that public access to tender agreements be denied. They also required the withdrawal of a clause allowing a public institution to request information concerning the real owners of a company, which could be used, for example, if an offshore company was applying to tender. The EC argued that the changes would prevent violation of general EU regulations on free competition and protection of commercial secrets.

- Parliament appointed a **new head of the Anti-Corruption Bureau** in May 2004. The bureau, which during its two years in operation had already seen one fully appointed and three acting heads, had been undermined by lack of permanent leadership. A civil society consultation council for the bureau was created which includes public interest NGOs, business associations, a council of foreign investors and organisations representing doctors and patients, construction workers and bankers.

- A supervisory body at the Data Protection Inspectorate was set up in January 2004 to oversee the implementation of the 1998 **Law on Freedom of Information**. Despite long-term criticism from research and civil society bodies, the supervisory mechanism for this crucial law remains severely under-resourced.

Amendments to party finance law trigger change of government

Following the 2002 parliamentary elections there was increasing public disquiet about the fierce competition between political parties to collect ever greater donations to finance media campaigns with little political content.[1] Since 1995, when the law requiring regular reporting by political parties was first introduced, election costs have quadrupled.[2]

In consequence, amendments to the law governing the financing of political parties were adopted in February 2004 allowing each party to spend no more than 0.20 lats (US $0.35) per voter – around US $550,000 in total. The new law also places tighter controls on the income side, a proposal of the new Anti-Corruption Bureau. Following from their work on disclosure forms in 2003, the bureau estimated that false, or so-called third-party donations (in which a 'false' donor serves as a proxy for another donor who has used up his/her donation limit), comprised more than half of all declared donors during the 2002 elections. However, according to its then acting head, Juta Strīķe,[3] the bureau lacked the means to prove such donors had lied.

Under the new legislation individuals are entitled to donate US $17,000 (reduced from US $46,000), but will only be allowed to donate money from their legally declared and taxable income of the previous three years. These changes will improve the chances of proving that funds from one donor are not being spread over several, technically unconnected, entities. The amended law also bans corporate donations.[4]

Even given the difficulty in establishing third party donations, the Anti-Corruption Bureau was able to prove that the 13 biggest parties had received illegal funds of roughly US $230,000.[5] Faced with the first ever external examination of their party accounts, the Greens and Farmers Union (the party of the prime minister since March 2004, Indulis Emsis, and the parliamentary speaker, Ingrīda Ūdre) have initiated legal action to establish whether administrative penalties are applicable. The case is still pending.[6]

Prior to the 2004 elections, changing the political party finance law was a priority for both the newly established Anti-Corruption Bureau and the then prime minister and leader of the New Era party, Einars Repše. He also had the backing of three other government coalition parties. At the last reading of the amendment, however, the First party suddenly opposed the change, protesting against setting the same limits to party membership and admission fees as for other donations.

The conflict between the prime minister and First Party leader (and deputy prime minister), Ainars Šlesers, led to a major rupture between the two leading parties and was the official reason for the government's resignation in February 2004. The New Era party, however, gained political momentum because it was expected to form the new government, and managed to put pressure on parliament to pass the party finance bill.

Up to the 2002 elections, Latvian political policies were largely dictated by behind the scenes donations. This has led to favourable privatisation deals, laws favouring certain businesses, the writing-off of debts, employment patronage and the dubious awards of public contracts. While the amended law seems well placed to address these issues, the real test for the new legislation will be its ability to control the income and expenditure limits for the local elections in March 2005.

Finding a head for the Anti-Corruption Bureau

The Anti-Corruption Bureau has comprehensive reach and powers, but too much of its independence and efficiency can be determined by the individual at its head. Manoeuvrings within the Latvian political system have led to leadership battles at the bureau which have thrown serious doubt on the ability of the office to remain clear of political influence.

In the summer of 2003, Prime Minister Repše launched an open competition to find a leader for the Anti-Corruption Bureau, attracting 58 candidates for the job. A special selection commission led by the prime minister and composed of the prosecutor general, the auditor general, representatives of the state chancellery and several ministers, and monitored by civil society, unanimously voted for a 33-year-old security police officer, Juta Strīķe.

However, opposition groups within parliament, widely believed to be associated with the Greens and Farmers Union, twice blocked Strīķe's appointment.[7] Repše responded by using his powers under the Civil Service Act to appoint Strīķe as the deputy head of the bureau and then to appoint her as acting head of the bureau. Despite heavy criticism for this action from coalition partners, opposition parties and civil society organisations, Strīķe continued working for 10 months without the approval of parliament and gathered widespread popular support.

Following the change in administration in early 2004, and in just his second week as prime minister, Indulis Emsis (Greens and Farmers Union) unilaterally announced a new candidate as head of the Anti-Corruption Bureau, despite Strīķe's popularity and his own verbal support for her. However, the candidate refused to run after receiving heavy criticism from the media and civil society. Only after this did the prime minister open another public competition for the post.

A similar selection commission to the previous one voted in favour of Strīķe by three out of six votes. The prime minister, however, refused to put forward her name alone to the cabinet of ministers, and instead nominated three candidates. During the open cabinet meeting, but without proper explanation, ministers voted unanimously for Aleksejs Loskutovs.

When Aleksejs Loskutovs' appointment was confirmed by parliament for a term of five years in May 2004, the reaction from anti-corruption experts was generally positive. Widely considered to be of the 'new generation', he was a lecturer in criminology and criminal law. Loskutovs told the media: 'I do not owe anything to politicians for this vote',[8] and promised to run the bureau in an independent and professional manner.

However, the independence of the bureau has yet to be proved. Sections of the media have suggested that the cabinet selected Loskutovs because he was opposed to Strīķe, a useful thing for the cabinet's own political interests.[9] Indeed, one of Loskutovs' first steps in the job has been to launch an internal investigation into the work of Strīķe. A high level of media and civil society attention may prevent Loskutovs from firing Strīķe this time, but it is alleged that political players behind the scenes are hoping that he will.[10]

Inese Voika (TI Latvia)

Further reading

GRECO, *Evaluation Report on Latvia* (Council of Europe, 2004), www.greco.coe.int

Valts Kalnins and Lolita Cigane, *On the Road Toward a More Honest Society: The Latest Trends in Anti-Corruption Policy in Latvia* (Riga: Latvian Institute of International Affairs, 2003), www.policy.lv

TI Latvia: www.delna.lv

Notes

1. Public Survey Opinion, SKDS company, February 2003.
2. *Analysis of Campaign Finance of the 2002 Parliamentary Elections* (TI Latvia, Delna and the Soros Foundation, 2003).
3. Presentation by the bureau head, Juta Strīķe, at the round table 'Party Financing – What are We Going to Change?' (2003), www.politika.lv/index.php?id=107578&lang=lv
4. *Diena* (Latvia), 2 February 2004.

5. *Diena* (Latvia), 22 November 2003.
6. *Diena* (Latvia), 2 July 2004.
7. NRA, *Deputāti dievojas: balsojuši par. Strīķi neapstiprina* (2004).
8. LETA news service (Latvia), 27 May 2004.
9. *Diena* (Latvia), 26 May 2004.
10. *Diena* (Latvia), 29 July 2004.

Nicaragua

Corruption Perceptions Index 2004 score: 2.7 (97th out of 146 countries)

Conventions:
OAS Inter-American Convention against Corruption (ratified March 1999)
UN Convention against Corruption (signed December 2003; not yet ratified)
UN Convention against Transnational Organized Crime (ratified September 2002)

Legal and institutional changes

- Since late 2002, but more markedly in the first six months of 2004, the ruling Partido Liberal Constitucionalista (PLC) presented a series of bills whose sole aim was to free former president **Arnoldo Alemán**, who was jailed for 20 years in 2003 for money laundering, fraud and embezzlement. The PLC's efforts, which had all failed at the time of writing, led to a political crisis that effectively paralysed the national assembly; not a single law was adopted in the first five months of the year.[1] Among the proposed PLC-led bills were: an amnesty covering all acts of administrative corruption by public officials from 1997 to 2001; an attempt in January 2004 to put forward a new interpretation of the law on money laundering (under which Alemán was principally condemned) that would have limited its application to crimes connected to drug trafficking; an attempt in March 2004 to modify the penal code so that ex-presidents serve out their prison sentences under house arrest; a law that safeguards state property, which the executive is promoting in the context of a conflict between the opposition Sandinistas and the state-owned national insurance and reinsurance institute, Instituto Nicaragüense de Seguros y Reaseguros (INISER); and a bill to reform the judiciary (see below for a fuller discussion).

- In June 2004 the government signed a 'Compact to Promote Transparency and Combat Corruption' with the G8 countries, which pledged to **provide technical assistance** in the areas of public budgets and financial management, including revenues, expenditures, government procurement and the letting of public concessions.

- The ministry of finance and public credit and the Integrated Financial Management System (SIGFA) have increased **budget transparency** by posting national budget allocations and spending on the Internet.[2] The NGO Coordinadora Civil, which has been analysing the budget since it was presented in October 2003, found hidden government spending allocations in the budget amounting to almost US $80 million.

- In July 2003 the national assembly elected five new **supreme court judges** out of a total of 16, in a move that some analysts say has increased the body's already high level of political polarisation. For more than six months, the court failed to choose its president or make the appointments for which it has responsibility. In this period, the judges openly considered the benefits of an agreement to alternate the presidency of the supreme court between the main political parties on an annual basis.

Challenges in establishing a judicial career law

The Consultative Group for Nicaragua, made up of 12 governments, bilateral donors, the World Bank and the Inter-American Development Bank, met in September 2003 in Managua to reiterate what national and international organisations had long been saying: institutional reform, particularly in the judiciary, is crucial to the country's development. The current judicial system is criticised for its sluggishness and excessive politicisation. The supreme court submitted a draft judicial career law to the national assembly at the end of 2003.[3] In its June evaluation of corruption in Nicaragua, the G8 cited the bill as an important component of the administration's anti-corruption agenda, but described its chances of passing in the current political climate as 'moderate'.

Several versions of the bill were discussed by the national assembly, but no law had been approved at the time of writing. The reasons for this failure reflect the lack of political will from parties with an interest in blocking the bill's two main reforms: the 'professionalisation' of the judiciary through transparent and competitive appointments; and the fostering of its external and internal independence, which would require the supreme court to relinquish its current responsibility for administering appointments and salaries.

The supreme court's proposal addressed the lack of merit-based mechanisms for hiring and promotion, but continued to give itself control over the administration of judicial careers. Experts criticised it for failing to separate the administrative and judicial functions of the judiciary and, therefore, not addressing the issue of internal independence.

There are three main views of the proposed legislation in the national assembly. The PLC – which does not have a sufficiently large majority to pass laws on its own – argues that the judiciary sympathises with the Frente Sandinista, Nicaragua's second largest party, since the majority of its members were appointed in the Sandinista revolutionary period. Because of this, and the fact that the current judiciary imprisoned former president Alemán on corruption charges, the PLC wants to use the new law to replace judicial officials.

The Frente Sandinista rejects the bill, citing the constitution which grants the supreme court authority over the 'administration of justice'. They argue that this guarantee cannot be altered by any law adopted under normal procedures, but would need a qualified majority of parliamentarians to amend the constitution. In the past few years they have found allies in a number of judges, nervous about the loss of power and political relevance that the proposed judicial career law might entail.

A third faction is headed by President Enrique Bolaños, whose aim is to depoliticise the judicial system. This was a campaign promise and it is widely seen as key to Nicaragua's economic development.

Given that the majority required for constitutional reform is impossible without the support of the Frente Sandinista, it will be difficult to win approval for the proposed law. This political logjam highlights the barriers confronting any attempt to instigate institutional reform in Nicaragua.

Accusations of corruption against the president highlight the need for electoral reform

When President Bolaños announced in 2002 that charges had been filed against Alemán for corruption that had cost the state at least US $100 million, he could scarcely have imagined his action would lead to further charges related to his own use of funds, allegedly embezzled by Alemán.

The money embezzled and laundered by Alemán allegedly ended up in three different places: the pockets of the officials involved; monthly 'under-the-table' payments to 500 officials from the executive, legislative and judicial branches of government; and the coffers of the PLC election effort, including Enrique Bolaños' campaign.

It appears that no legal consequences will follow the use of these funds to pay PLC officials, including Bolaños, who has not denied that as vice-president at the time he received US $500,000 of the total. There is also concern that the president and his circle allegedly failed to register the payments and evaded taxes.

Nevertheless, in condemning Alemán to 20 years in prison, Judge Juana Méndez left open the possibility that charges for electoral crimes might one day be brought against President Bolaños and his closest campaign advisers. Nicaragua's electoral law forbids the misuse of state funds (whether direct or indirect) in electoral campaigns.

Nicaragua's current legislation is far from being a model of political finance regulation. The law does, however, dictate that the misuse of state funds is a clear violation of the law, and implicates both the party involved and all who knew about the origins of the funds.

Initially President Bolaños publicly renounced his immunity to face the charges, though he signally failed to keep the promise to cooperate with the prosecution, the general comptroller's office and even the presiding judge. Meanwhile, the evidence of unreported funds entering his election campaign accounts continues to grow, though there is no proof that he was personally aware of their possibly illicit origins.

There is concern that rather than being handled transparently, the case will continue to be used as a bargaining chip by the Frente Sandinista and the PLC, since the two parties between them have enough votes to strip the president of his immunity and force him into

court. The courts themselves have shown no sign of being either willing or able to prosecute him without political approval.

The crisis serves to underscore the need for reform of the electoral law. Since the last reform took place in 2000, Nicaragua's electoral system has proved to be one of the most expensive in the world in per capita terms. Another defect is the excessive politicisation of the authority responsible for overseeing elections. National and international election observers have called for root-and-branch reforms.

Following a study by the NGO Grupo Cívico Etica y Transparencia (TI's chapter in Nicaragua), a group that includes electoral observers, human rights groups and small political parties tried in 2003–04 to come up with a draft bill to reform the electoral process in the hope that it would receive the endorsement of President Bolaños, who campaigned for electoral reform. The bill aims to reduce the cost of elections, regulate party financing, improve the internal democratic processes of political parties and reduce the influence of individual political parties over the bodies responsible for overseeing the elections. The proponents of the bill want to present it to the national assembly, where the two leading political parties are well aware of the deficiencies in the electoral law, but are torn between the loss of political credibility if they ignore them and a potential loss of power if they back reform. This last point will be critical and might water down any genuine attempt at reform.

Grupo Cívico Etica y Transparencia has separately called for private financing to be eliminated or at least monitored as international observers recommend, to limit escalating costs and make elections more equitable. Private and public financing need to be transparent and subject to proper controls if elections are to be fair, and sanctions need to be imposed for infractions and applied fairly by a legitimate authority.

Roberto Courtney (Grupo Cívico Etica y Transparencia, Nicaragua)

Further reading

Grupo Cívico Etica y Transparencia (TI Nicaragua): www.eyt.org.ni

Notes

1. Other bills that would have had a positive impact on corruption were presented in the reporting period but either not discussed or not approved. They include a bill on the judicial career structure and a bill protecting state property.
2. Although making budget information available on the Internet is a positive step, a related and unresolved problem is that the budget does not include full information on tax revenue. The NGO network Coordinadora Civil has complained about this failure for two consecutive years.
3. The supreme court is able to submit draft laws to the legislature about judicial matters.

Norway

Corruption Perceptions Index 2004 score: 8.9 (8th out of 146 countries)

Conventions:
Council of Europe Civil Law Convention on Corruption (signed November 1999; not yet ratified)
Council of Europe Criminal Law Convention on Corruption (ratified March 2004)
OECD Anti-Bribery Convention (ratified December 1998)
UN Convention against Corruption (signed December 2003; not yet ratified)
UN Convention against Transnational Organized Crime (ratified September 2003)

Legal and institutional changes

- Parliament enacted three new sections of the civil penal code in July 2003. The provisions are stricter than the ones they replace and comply with the Council of Europe Criminal Law Convention on Corruption, but in some respects they go further than required. They introduce the concept of 'improper advantage', a standard whose scope will eventually be determined by case law. The jurisdiction of the rules is universal, applying within Norway, as well as to Norwegian nationals acting abroad. Section 276(a) stipulates that any person actively supplying, or passively accepting, an offer of improper advantage in connection with a post, office or commission will be punishable by fines or imprisonment up to three years. Section 276(b) criminalises gross corruption with sentences of up to 10 years. Police investigative powers will increase when gross corruption is suspected, with courts empowered to sanction the surveillance of communications. Section 276(c) criminalises trading in influence.

- Some of the recommendations made in 2002 by the Council of Europe's evaluation body, GRECO, have yet to be implemented, including legal clarification of the right or duty of public servants to report unlawful, improper or unethical behaviour, or behaviour involving maladministration. This lack of clarity means not all allegations of impropriety in the public sector are reported to the police or prosecutor's office. In June 2004 the government announced it would review the issue. It also announced new 'quarantine regulations' for public servants, such as a prohibition of re-employment in the private sector for a period of time, to prevent conflicts of interest.

• The government announced in June 2004 that it would ensure greater transparency in corporate payments to foreign states. It plans to make it mandatory for companies to publish in their accounts to which states they have transferred payments.

• A new law on the Office of the Auditor General (OAG) entered into force in July 2004, following a much-needed review of the regulatory framework for cooperation between the OAG, the police, the National Authority for Investigation and Prosecution of Economic and Environmental Crime (Økokrim) and other law enforcement bodies. The OAG is now allowed to report any suspicions to the police/Økokrim immediately and confidentially upon discovery while a public audit is ongoing. The audited office does not have to be informed of the suspicion. When police initiate a criminal investigation, the OAG may disclose to them documentation from its audit, irrespective of any obligations of confidentiality regarding information of a personal nature or concerning trade secrets. This reform came in response to a specific GRECO recommendation in 2002.

• In May 2004 the government published a White Paper, *Fighting Poverty Together*, in response to the challenges posed by the UN Millennium Development Goals. The document acknowledged that development assistance may contribute to corruption when donors close their eyes to its illegitimate use. The document outlined the government's anti-corruption policy in development assistance. The government intends to focus on anti-corruption in its bilateral dialogue with countries receiving aid, and to encourage other states to ratify the UN Convention against Corruption. The government also stated that it will pursue a dialogue with the Norwegian private sector 'to increase the awareness of how to counter corruption', support the Extractive Industries Transparency Initiative, and support asset recovery initiatives. The government has not yet specified the resources available for implementation nor outlined benchmarks for monitoring progress, making it difficult to hold the government accountable for the proposals.

Norwegian corruption comes home

Allegations of corporate corruption received substantial media attention in 2003–04, but it was the Statoil–Horton affair that made the biggest headlines. State-owned Statoil is Norway's largest company. In June 2002 Statoil signed a 10-year, US $15 million consulting agreement with Horton Investments to exploit Iran's oil and natural gas. Horton Investments, a company owned by exiled Iranian Abbas Yazdi, was also allegedly a financial intermediary for Mehdi Hashemi Rafsanjani, son of Iran's former president, director of the National Iranian Oil Company (NIOC) and an influential figure in the country's energy sector.

In autumn 2002 Statoil was awarded operational control of South Pars, the world's largest offshore gas field, in partnership with a NIOC subsidiary. Statoil committed to spending US $300 million to construct three production platforms and a pipeline. After completion, control of South Pars reverts to NIOC and Statoil will recover its project costs and a share of NIOC sales.

In September 2003 Statoil's internal auditors reportedly questioned a US $5.2 million payment to Horton Investments' account in the Turks and Caicos Islands, leading to an investigation by Økokrim, Norway's economic crime unit. Statoil's chairman Leif Terje Løddesøl and CEO Olav Fjell both resigned. Økokrim concluded that the payment was an offer of improper advantages in return for influence in securing the Iran deal. In June 2004 Økokrim issued penalty notices against Statoil and the former director of its international department, Richard Hubbard. A NOK 20 million (US $2.9 million) fine was imposed on Statoil.

Statoil was also under investigation by the US Security and Exchange Commission for breaching the US Foreign Corrupt Practices Act, which is applicable because of the company's listing on the New York Stock Exchange. The Iranian parliament looked into the allegations against Statoil, while Swiss authorities investigated Abbas Yazdi for alleged money laundering. A major delaying factor in the inquiry was Rafsanjani's refusal to submit to interrogation, thereby underlining the procedural obstacles facing investigators who seek to enforce anti-corruption legislation beyond their domestic jurisdiction.

Another high-profile case involved the construction concern Veidekke, the lead company in the consortium contracted to build the Bujagali hydropower plant in Uganda. In 2002 it was alleged that the company had made a payment to Uganda's energy minister, Richard Kaijuka, less than a year before the contract was awarded to the Veidekke consortium without competitive bidding. Veidekke's British subsidiary, Nor-icil Ltd, allegedly transferred US $10,000 to a London bank account held by Kaijuka. After the World Bank Group halted financing for the scheme, Økokrim launched an investigation, but the case was dismissed in 2003 due to lack of evidence.

These and other cases involving questionable practices abroad raised the profile of corruption issues in Norway. One key question was whether Norwegian companies applied different standards in their dealings at home and abroad. Another debate was when and how to apply 'zero-tolerance' policies. But recent surveys suggest that corruption by Norwegian companies is still higher than they admit. While a majority of Norwegian business leaders think that some bribery is necessary to win contracts in developing countries, most do not acknowledge that their companies encounter corruption in international business transactions.

Norway's annus horribilis

A survey by Norway's largest insurance company, Gjensidige NOR, showed 25 per cent of business leaders now believe that corruption exists in their own industry sector, though only 10 per cent admitted it affected their company.[1] Perhaps the survey's most important message, however, was that Norwegians no longer consider corruption an exclusively foreign, or developing-country issue. More business leaders recognise the domestic dimension of the problem. Gjensidige NOR's survey followed press coverage of a string of cases involving alleged private sector corruption and conflicts of interest.

At the time of writing four large construction companies were under investigation for price fixing, collusive tendering and market sharing in both public and private works contracts. A cartel that included Veidekke, Selmer Skanska, NCC Construction and Reinertsen Anlegg was taken to court in February 2003 by the Norwegian Competition Authority for alleged illegalities encompassing the construction of industrial developments, power plants, bridges, docks and Oslo airport. NCC Construction admitted to 'illegal cooperation' with its competitors, issuing false invoices and compensating competitors who lost the tender. Veidekke, Selmer Skanska and NCC Construction were also under investigation for cartel activity in the concrete market.

Finance Credit, a financial services company, was under criminal investigation at the time of writing, accused of siphoning off funds it borrowed from six Norwegian banks to offshore tax havens. The charges involved fraud worth US $200 million and false and misleading accounting. Finance Credit's public relations company, Madland & Wara, allegedly attempted to 'buy' an investigative journalist to silence him.[2]

An external consultant hired by the international classification and certification company, Det Norske Veritas, to assess the need for a new IT system was convicted in May 2004 of soliciting bribes by demanding a 10 per cent kickback from UNISYS in return for recommending procurement.[3] In a case that was ongoing at the time of writing, a former finance director of the Norwegian Red Cross and his two brothers were on trial for allegedly embezzling US $1 million during the rehabilitation of the Red Cross headquarters and bribing an independent building inspector to approve false invoices.[4] The trial was postponed until September 2004.

Cases like these have been characterised in the Norwegian media as symptoms of a business community that has lost its virtue. This is a new phenomenon in Norway and the public debate has been as lively as it has been mixed. Most have welcomed the new focus on corruption, the media revelations and the enhanced debate about ethics and corporate responsibility. But shallow and rosy declarations about zero tolerance, and a lack of public recognition of corruption in everyday practice do not make for a convincing anti-corruption strategy or promote genuine corporate progress. While companies recognise the need to strengthen protective measures and internal controls, they have yet to acquire the knowledge and tools to implement effective anti-corruption policies.

Fiduciary duties in the health sector

Norway's public administration purchases one quarter of all mainland investment and employs one third of the labour force. It is currently undergoing deep structural change. Public responsibilities are being outsourced, privatised and exposed to market forces, reorganisation and demands for efficiency improvements. An increasing number of private businesses now depend wholly or partially on public budgets, tenders, loans, regulations, relocations and privatisation projects. The sums involved in public procurement pose challenges to the integrity of the individuals responsible for administering them. Current safeguards in procurement practice do not constitute a sufficient deterrent against illegality and corruption, especially in districts and municipalities.

Particular relationships in the management of public funds foster grounds for potential conflicts of interests. A case in point concerned the Research Council of Norway (RCN), a national funding agency for research and innovation. In 2003–04 the media exposed allegations of external advisers hired by RCN who reportedly, after submitting and accepting their own funding applications, rejected applications from other researchers. Following an independent inquiry into its procedures, the RCN issued new guidelines in 2004 that compel its external advisers to absent themselves from proceedings where they have a conflict of interests.

Another example concerned the nexus between government funding of public medication and pharmaceutical companies' efforts to convince doctors and hospitals to procure and prescribe their products. Pharmaceutical companies finance medical congresses and courses, and commission medical research, bringing undeniable benefits to the participants. But the fact that the government covers most medication costs through a rights-based approach to each patient could constitute an incentive for doctors to disregard both the patient's and the government's interests.

Sending costs to the government creates a situation in which the controlling and funding entity is distant from the decision-making process, resulting in the possible prescription of prejudiced, unnecessary or costly medications. To counter increased corruption, 250 doctors signed a petition in 2004 that called for greater transparency and more control measures in the profession, as well as regulations to govern relations between the pharmaceutical industry and medical personnel. They proposed a duty to inform on doctors who participate in testing and approval procedures for new drugs.

Jan Borgen, Henrik Makoto Inadomi and Gro Skaaren-Fystro (TI Norway)

Further reading

TI Norway: www.transparency.no

Notes

1. *Dagens Næringsliv* (Norway), 14 April 2004.
2. odin.dep.no/odin/engelsk/nytt/nyheter/032091-210355/index-dok000-n-n-a.html
3. www.okokrim.no
4. Ibid.

Palestinian Authority

Corruption Perceptions Index 2004 score: 2.5 (108th out of 146 countries)

Legal and institutional changes

- A draft **law dealing with unlawful gains** passed its second reading in the Palestinian Legislative Council (PLC) and was referred to the Council of Ministers in April 2004. If enacted, this law will require government officials to account for property and funds acquired during their term of office.

- A draft law dealing with the functioning of the **administrative and financial monitoring office** passed its second reading in the PLC and was referred to the Council of Ministers in April 2004. The office is currently accountable only to the president of the Palestinian Authority (PA), who has power to appoint the director. Under the proposed provisions, the appointment of the director will be subject to the approval of the PLC which, along with the head of the executive, will also receive reports from the office. If enacted the law will have far-reaching consequences for the public monitoring of all government activities.

- **Private sector monopolies** have been a huge source of corruption in the PA, giving rise to widespread allegations of bribery of government officials to secure control of lucrative markets. A draft law giving incentives to competition and prohibiting monopolies passed its first reading in the PLC in April 2004.

- A draft law concerning **the powers of the constitutional court** passed through the stage of general discussion in the PLC in December 2003. If enacted, it will weaken the far-reaching powers of the executive. A clear separation of powers can make corrupt ministers or high officials accountable in a court of law, without being able to rely on the protection of the head of the executive (the president), as has happened in the past.

The reform agenda

Reform has dominated the public discourse of Palestinian civil society and business sectors since the mid-1990s, with allegations of corruption forming a common thread. The eruption of the second intifada in September 2000, however, raised questions about reform priorities, particularly whether reform should retain priority over resistance to the Israeli occupation. This issue has become increasingly urgent as the economic and security situation has deteriorated and as the PA has become unable to provide basic services amid spiralling unemployment.

Although the reforms contained in the so-called Road Map (for example, the appointment of an 'empowered' prime minister, the drafting of a constitution and holding elections), which were adopted by the 'Quartet plus Four',[1] reflected the concerns of many Palestinians, the fact that the reform agenda was presented by external parties raised questions for many about the real motives behind the reforms. Nevertheless, popular support for reform and for the fight against corruption remained strong. Following the resignation of the government of Mahmoud Abbas in September 2003, Prime Minister Ahmed Qurei's government sought much-needed popular legitimacy through the formation of a civil society coordinating committee for reform,[2] and its representation in the National Reform Committee (NRC).

By the time of writing, the NRC had met three times since the formation of Qurei's government and a number of reform measures had already been taken. The prime minister and the council of ministers presented quarterly reports of their activities – in accordance with the amended Basic Law – to the president of the PA, and to the PLC (it should be noted, however, that the power to pass and amend key legislation remains in the hands of the president).

Increasing financial transparency is seen as particularly important. Measures have been taken to unify and integrate all the PA's financial operations and to establish the Palestinian Investment Fund as an independent legal entity. The PLC and civil society institutions view the government's punctual presentation of the draft budget to the PLC for the last two financial years as a positive development.

The ministry of finance has been able to make an inventory of all the PA's investments, to apply the principle of a unified budget, and to unify the treasury of the West Bank with that of the Gaza Strip. In April 2004 the ministry was finally able to enforce the payment of salaries to the security and police services through the banking system, which significantly reduces opportunities for the misappropriation of public funds when payments are made in cash.

Acknowledging the significant steps towards reform that have been taken in respect of the PA's finances, the World Bank announced its intention of establishing a fund to support the PA's budget, which has accumulated a deficit of US $650 million for the year 2004. On the negative side, a law regulating the salaries, promotion and pensions of civil servants has not been implemented (ostensibly because of the PA's difficult financial situation), permitting the continued abuse of public office in respect to appointments – in terms of public perception one of the most common forms of 'low-level' corruption in the PA.[3] The chairman of the PLC's budget and financial affairs committee announced that he expected the amended law to be implemented in July 2004, affecting those employed in the civil administration from that date, and those employed in the police and security services by the end of the year. Regretfully, this legislation would still fall short of being applicable to all those employed by the PA.

Elections as mechanisms to combat corruption

A key reform to increase accountability and enhance the fight against corruption would be the immediate organisation of elections – be they internal political party, legislative, presidential or local. The suspension of nearly all electoral activity within the Palestinian Authority has strengthened the power of individuals whose interests are well served by the stasis caused by the political and military deadlock between the PA and Israel.

Elections are widely seen as a mechanism for the renewal of the PA, and for the creation of a new dynamic in the Palestinian political system through encouraging the participation of opposition political parties in the process of legislation (through the PLC) and policy-making (through participation in government). General elections could provide Palestinians with a chance to elect representatives who are more able, have more integrity, and are more ready to fight corruption.

General elections have been due since May 1999, but the political and military conflict with Israel, particularly since September 2000, created objective obstacles to the holding of such elections, such as an extensive system of road blocks and checkpoints and sections of the separation wall that intrude into PA territory. The PA leadership (that is, the Fateh leadership) has been unwilling to call for elections even within their own party. Municipal elections have been due since 1997. Although the frequent incursions in the Gaza Strip and West Bank and the armed confrontations have made any serious progress towards presidential and legislative elections unrealistic, the holding of local elections is widely seen as both plausible and crucial for fighting corruption and reducing the inefficiency of centrally appointed municipal and village councils.

Calls by political and civil society groups for local elections have been insistent and regular. Nearly two-thirds (64 per cent) of Palestinian adults surveyed in March 2004 said there is discrimination in the provision of services by local government councils, and 70 per cent said that family and kinship connections play a part in appointments in local government. Some 69 per cent of the public believe corruption exists in local government councils.[4]

The holding of general and local elections is an essential part of the reform agenda, and a certain degree of change may now be inevitable. The prime minister announced that the council of ministers had decided in a joint meeting with the National Security Council under the chairmanship of President Arafat (held in May 2004) to start holding local elections in August 2004, after making the necessary amendments to local government election law. The meeting also decided to ask the PLC to approve a general election law, and to ask the Quartet Committee to work with the PA to create suitable conditions to hold general elections, and to set a date for them.

Jamil Hilal (TI Palestine)

Further reading

Aman – The Coalition for Accountability and Integrity, *Apparatuses for Overseeing, and Systems of Accountability in the Palestinian Public Sector* (Ramallah: Miftah publications, 2003) (in Arabic)

Civic Forum Institute and Friedrich Naumann Foundation, *Reform: A Palestinian Perspective – Between Reality and Aspirations* (Ramallah, 2003)

Jamil Hilal et al., *The Criminal Justice System in Palestine* (Beirzeit: Institute of Law, 2003)

Palestine Economic Policy Research Institute (MAS), *Social Monitor*, issue No. 6, (Ramallah, 2004)

TI Palestine: www.aman-palestine.org

Notes

1. The 'Quartet' of Middle East mediators comprises the European Union, the Russian Federation, the United Nations and the United States; four other bodies involved in negotiations are Japan, Norway, the World Bank and the IMF.

2. The committee is composed of representatives of various civil society bodies, including Aman – The Coalition for Accountability and Integrity (TI Palestine), private sector companies, Palestinian professional associations and the General Union of Palestinian Women.
3. A majority of Palestinians in the West Bank and Gaza Strip believe that corruption exists in the PA, and 77 per cent believe that jobs in the PA are, to a large extent, obtainable through informal connections (Palestinian Centre for Policy and Survey Research, Ramallah, poll number 11, 14–17 March 2004).
4. Poll No. 3 (25–27 March 2004) conducted by PANORAMA (Palestinian Center for the Dissemination of Democracy and Community Development, Ramallah, 2004).

Panama

Corruption Perceptions Index 2004 score: 3.7 (62nd out of 146 countries)

Conventions:
OAS Inter-American Convention against Corruption (ratified July 1998)
UN Convention against Corruption (signed December 2003; not yet ratified)
UN Convention against Transnational Organized Crime (ratified August 2004)

Legal and institutional changes

- A draft **code of parliamentary ethics and honour** was submitted to the legislative assembly in September 2003, setting out the behaviour expected of parliamentarians and their substitutes when faced with a conflict of interest situation, nepotism, attempted bribery and the abuse of office for personal gain.[1] Several allegations of corruption involving legislators emerged in the period under review, but the bill had not been passed at the time of writing.

- A draft law to reform the 1998 **regulations governing the legislative assembly** was submitted in September 2003. The bill aimed to improve the legislature's public image at a time when the credibility of its members had been damaged by media reports about high levels of absenteeism and allegations that parliamentarians were abusing a right to import cars for personal use by selling them on to third parties. The proposed reforms include the introduction of salary cuts for failure to attend plenary and commission sessions, and the reduction of the right to import cars from three to one car per legislator, and two to one car per substitute. At this writing the bill had not been passed.

- A draft law modifying secondary legislation that enforces a constitutional provision against **administrative corruption** was also introduced in September 2003. If passed, the law will compel high-ranking officials to declare the value of their assets before taking up office and upon leaving it. The reform would give the auditor general powers to ensure that a full asset declaration is made. It would also lower the burden of proof for complainants to file allegations of illegal enrichment; circumstantial evidence would be sufficient to convict, rather than summary evidence as at present. Civil society organisations are calling for asset declarations to be made public, for an annual audit of them to be kept by the auditor general, and for public notaries to facilitate investigations in case of a complaint. At this writing the bill had not been passed.

- A draft law was submitted in September 2003 to modify a 2002 law on **transparency in public administration**. The reform would eliminate the requirement that anybody requesting information must first prove that he or she has a direct link to the information requested. The condition was added to the original law by executive decree in May 2002 and is considered the main obstacle to implementation of the transparency law. After the May 2004 elections the supreme court ruled that the section of the decree relating to access to public information was illegal. At this writing the reform of the law had not been passed.

• A draft law submitted in December 2003 aims to expand a law on the **transparency of public procurement** processes by disclosing the owners or shareholders of companies that do business with the state. Under the bill shareholders of companies that win state contracts would have to certify ownership of their shares and pass this information to the public prosecutor's office or to the auditor general. At this writing the reform of the law had not been passed.

Corruption takes centre stage in the third general elections

Martín Torrijos was elected president in May 2004 on a platform of zero tolerance for corruption, in an election that was widely praised for its transparency and fairness. As in the elections in 1994 and 1999, voter turnout was high at 77 per cent and both Panamanians and the international community generally regarded them as honest. This was in sharp contrast to the 1989 elections, which were annulled because of electoral fraud. The winning candidate was announced four hours after voting centres closed and his three rivals acknowledged defeat a few moments later.

President Torrijos ran for Patria Nueva, a coalition of the Partido Revolucionario Democrático and the Partido Popular. His election platform featured 16 anti-corruption promises, including pledges to create a National Council of Transparency and the Fight against Corruption; to implement a professional civil service career structure; and to submit a salary bill to the legislative assembly. The pledges read well in principle, but the experience of his predecessor in office, Mireya Moscoso, contains a cautionary tale. Her plan of action also included measures to fight corruption and the fact that they were never carried to fruition generated disappointment among the public.

All four candidates in the 2004 presidential election placed corruption high on their agendas. In December 2003, TI Panama sent them a 'minimum agenda to fight corruption' and each responded by adopting around half of the 13 proposed actions. President Torrijos now has a majority in the legislative assembly and therefore little excuse not to push through the legislative changes called for under his anti-corruption agenda.

Other actions may require more than political will, however. Anti-corruption institutions need to be strengthened and consideration should be given to the creation of a body charged with the prevention of corruption, such as a public ethics office, an anti-corruption office or a prosecutor general specialised in corruption. Whistleblower protection also needs to be introduced – at present the Panama Canal Authority is the only public institution in Panama that provides full protection for whistleblowers, making investigations easier to carry out. Another challenge is to strengthen the widely discredited supreme court and attorney general's office. In order to do so, a proper career structure needs to be created, with nominations based on merit so that judges do not act in the interests of the government that selected them.

A deep reform of electoral law is also required. The electoral court is expected to set up a commission in 2005 to evaluate changes to the electoral code. One proposal is to call for a second round of voting if the leading candidate fails to win 50 per cent of the vote. President Torrijos only obtained 47.3 per cent; Moscoso won in 1999 with 44.8 per cent; and Ernesto Pérez Balladares won in 1994 with 33 per cent. Another set of proposals, already being discussed in the legislature as part of a constitutional reform package, is to limit the campaign period and reduce the period of transition from four to two months. A third issue, and one that has received a lot of public attention, is establishing ceilings on campaign donations and requiring disclosure of campaign funding sources. A previous electoral reform commission discussed the issue, but only one party supported a proposal to require parties to disclose the size and sources of donations. The text that the legislature eventually approved only requires parties to present accounts to the electoral court in 'a confidential manner'.

The number of electoral irregularities denounced to the prosecutor responsible underscored the need for reform. There are currently 1,186 cases under investigation and, while the majority are related to voter fraud (chiefly, falsely registered addresses), a number are related to campaign finance. Several legislators have been accused of misusing public or private funds in their re-election bids, for instance by handing out scholarships, supermarket vouchers and cheques in exchange for votes. One of the biggest scandals involved legislator Haydée Milanés in the province of Darién who was found guilty of channelling US $370,000 of government funds through 28 bank accounts into her re-election campaign. The case was widely publicised and Milanés eventually went on hunger strike in protest at the accusations.

Monitoring the Inter-American Convention against Corruption

Within the framework of the monitoring mechanism provided by the Organization of American States (OAS) to oversee the implementation of the Inter-American Convention against Corruption (IACAC), civil society organisations identified shortcomings in Panama's compliance with the provisions of the convention. These failings were echoed by the OAS committee of experts.

In February 2004 civil society organisations presented an alternative report to the government on the state of compliance with the convention at a hearing with the OAS panel of experts. Civil society organisations acknowledged the advances made by the current government, spoke of difficulties in implementing the IACAC and issued recommendations. Among the positive developments mentioned was the adoption in July 2001 of reforms to the penal and judicial code and new norms to prevent corruption.

There was also agreement between civil society and the experts about obstacles to fighting corruption. First, in terms of access to information, the committee of experts strongly recommended that Panama revise and modify the decree regulating the law on transparency (see above). Second, there are problems with the national anti-corruption directorate, which was created by executive decree in 1999 but has never been regulated through secondary legislation. The directorate is coordinated by an interim director and does not have national reach. Third, concerns were expressed about the regulations for financial disclosure by public officials, since there is little evidence that they are being implemented efficiently.

Both civil society organisations and the panel of experts agreed in recommending a number of actions, including: strengthening the implementation of laws and enforcement systems with regards to conflicts of interest in order to underpin a practical and effective system of public ethics; creating and establishing mechanisms for publicising asset declarations (of income, debt and assets); and carrying out a full evaluation of the powers currently in the hands of the national anti-corruption directorate, with a view to creating a new national office of governmental ethics.

The OAS experience of civil society inclusion in anti-corruption work highlights the importance of listening to non-governmental voices that are able to penetrate official rhetoric in assessing the state of corruption. The UNDP has also taken some steps in engaging civil society organisations in the effort to promote public integrity and transparency, though its Foro Panama 2020, a forum for the government, political parties and civil society to debate public policies until 2020.

Angélica Maytín Justiniani (TI Panama)

Further reading

Marianela Armijo, 'Investigación diagnóstica de la administración pública panameña y lineamientos de acción' (Diagnostic investigation of Panama's public administration and lines of action) (Procuraduría de la administración del Ministerio Público de Panamá, 2004), www.procuraduria-admon.gob.pa/

Linette Landau, 'Revisión de legislación anticorrupción, Panamá' (Review of Panama's anti-corruption legislation) www.respondanet.com/spanish/anti_corrupcion/legislacion/revision_legislacion_el_panama.pdf

Rafael Pérez Jaramillo, *Índice de impunidad* (Impunity Index) (Panama: Editorial Libertad Ciudadana, 2003)

La Prensa (Panama), *Las caras de la corrupción* (The faces of corruption) special reports 14, 2004, www.prensa.com/especial/2004/corrupcion/corrupcion.htm

TI Panama: www.libertadciudadana.org

Note

1. Each legislator has two substitutes.

Peru

Corruption Perceptions Index 2004 score: 3.5 (67th out of 146 countries)

Conventions:
OAS Inter-American Convention against Corruption (ratified June 1997)
UN Convention against Corruption (signed December 2003; not yet ratified)
UN Convention against Transnational Organized Crime (ratified January 2002)

Legal and institutional changes

- A framework law for a participatory budget, adopted in August 2003, is aimed at increasing **transparency and citizens' participation in budgetary decision-making** in the municipalities and the newly created regions. Civil society groups had pushed for the law which, while a positive step, is stated in very general terms and lacks clarity about how civil society organisations are to be identified and encouraged to participate.

Secondary legislation adopted by the finance and economy ministry in November 2003 failed to clarify these points (see below).

- Peru's first ever law regulating political parties was adopted in November 2003. One of the aims was to improve the transparency of **political party financing**, which had previously been poorly regulated. The new law bans funding from certain clearly stated sources; sets a ceiling on private donations; establishes auditing procedures; regulates campaign advertising; and establishes some sanctions. There are still flaws in the legislation, however: it does not call for disclosure of sources of financing and does not establish sanctions for all infractions.

- A law adopted in October 2003 created the Special Commission for the Integrated **Reform of the Justice Administration** (CERIAJUS), as called for by a wider commission for restructuring the judicial system. Reform proposals under consideration include public ethics training for judges, steps to make it easier for people to file complaints, and the introduction of asset-declaration mechanisms for judges. The civil society recommendation that external controls on the judicial system be introduced was not adopted, however.[1]

- A series of scandals involving serving government officials prompted the cabinet chief in February 2004 to announce **new anti-corruption measures**, though these were not widely discussed and have not been fully implemented. They included the re-launch of the National Anti-Corruption Commission (CNA) with new functions and a new president (the first president stepped down in February 2003 to take up a diplomatic post). Four months after the announcement, the justice minister designated a group made up almost entirely of civil society representatives to review and revive the wide-ranging anti-corruption proposals made by the National Anti-Corruption Initiative (INA), the working group set up by the transition government that recommended the creation of a robust and independent CNA.

Lack of political will to root out corruption

The transition to democracy in Peru had a strong anti-corruption element from the outset, but its focus was always on the past. Specialised anti-corruption courts, prosecutors and police divisions were set up to investigate and prosecute the grand corruption that took place during the regime of former president Alberto Fujimori. There were important successes: the main heads of Fujimori's corruption racket have been charged and many have been convicted. But fewer successes can be claimed against corruption that unfolded under the transitional administration or under the new democratically elected government.

There is a clear need for a national anti-corruption strategy to tackle not just past corruption cases, but current and future cases. This involves looking at prevention as well as enforcement and requires an anti-corruption policy that is interdepartmental and has short-term, as well as long-term, objectives.

This does not mean that such a blueprint for change does not exist – the INA working group set up under the transitional government drew up a comprehensive set of recommendations which the government has so far failed to implement. Nor does it mean that there are no departmental or institutional initiatives to fight corruption in Peru. The clearest example is the project to restructure the judiciary, as outlined above. Other important areas of reform are the police and armed forces, previously the pillars of Fujimori's corrupt network, and the development of online procurement systems. But these efforts have not been sufficient to curb corruption, as demonstrated by the number of scandals exposed by the press in recent years.[2]

President Alejandro Toledo selected a new cabinet in February 2004 and the cabinet chief took responsibility for drawing up an 'exit strategy' for overcoming the political crisis amid plummeting approval ratings. The cabinet chief's proposals included a series of disparate anti-corruption measures that are individually positive (for example, actions against contraband, new extradition mechanisms and a commitment to formulate a coherent anti-corruption plan), but once again fail to add up to a strategy that goes to the structural roots of corruption.

President Toledo has always spoken of his will to fight corruption, but he has failed to translate this into effective initiatives, arguably because of the restraining factor of allegations of corruption against people and interest groups who are close to him. Media sources have reported a number of corruption allegations involving family members, legislators affiliated to the president's party, close friends, ministers, ex-ministers and the first lady.[3] The fact that there are legislators aligned with the ruling party who were closely tied to the Fujimori regime adds to suspicions that the president lacks the necessary distance from groups or individuals who might be compromised by an effective fight against corruption.[4]

The chances of a national anti-corruption policy being drawn up are inevitably linked to the evolution of the political crisis, which at present threatens to fell the president and produce an early election. The creation of a working group to revive proposals made by the aforementioned INA is positive, but comes at a difficult time. If the elections are brought forward and the new government also lacks the political will to address the roots of corruption, the recommendations could once again be shelved.

Decentralising corruption

Various sectors of Peruvian society, especially the poorest and most marginalised, have long been calling for the devolution of power to the regions. In the second half of the 1980s the Aprista government initiated a process of decentralisation that was dismantled by Fujimori after 1992. During the 2001 election campaign after Fujimori's escape to Japan, the question of decentralisation was again raised as an election promise. When Alejandro Toledo won, expectations were high that he would fulfil his campaign pledge.

Public demands for an immediate start to the process of decentralisation led to an announcement in 2002 that elections would be held for presidents of regions that had yet to be fully constituted. The organic law on regional governments was not promulgated until November 2002, four days after the elections took place.

The speed with which the operation was implemented meant there was no time to put in place the necessary control mechanisms to supervise the new local government institutions, let alone work out a timetable for when programmes would be transferred. The only control mechanisms in place were those that already existed, namely the auditing bodies created under Fujimori, ostensibly to oversee the Transitory Regional Administration Councils but in practice to ensure that social programmes were allocated along political lines to benefit the former president's election campaign in 2000. The fact that the same mechanisms had failed to prevent Fujimori from spinning a web of corruption begged the question whether they would exercise real control over the new regional governments.

The question was answered in 2003 and the first half of 2004: corruption was decentralised along with political and administrative powers, as a number of experts had predicted. By the time of writing, eight of the 25 regional presidents had already been subjected to investigation on suspicion of corruption, and one had been deposed for bribery and embezzlement.

The 'decentralisation' of corruption may be explained by the limited access to information and civil society monitoring in Peru.

Access to public information was enshrined in law in August 2002, but many institutions seem not to understand the contents of the law or lack the resources necessary to implement it.[5] Implementation is also hindered by 'attitudes of mistrust and reticence to provide information when it is requested ... attitudes [that] were associated in many cases with the disinformation of public officials with regard to norms and procedures', the civil society monitoring network Vigila Perú found.[6]

According to Vigila Perú's survey of 12 regional governments, the barriers to accessing information related to the budget have lessened since 2003. The same is true for political and normative information produced by the Regional Council, the highest regional government body, and the Council for Regional Coordination. Transparency of information about purchases and acquisitions has also improved. While these improvements are important, it is equally important to note that regional governments are moving towards minimal compliance with the law, and not beyond. At the level of municipal government the problems are much worse: they are notorious for disorganised information systems and for having 'difficulty' locating relevant documents, particularly from the past.

The lack of civil society participation is also critical. In almost all sub-national arenas there is a political component that strains relations between the government and civil society, as the political opposition can abuse monitoring functions by using audits as a weapon against the authorities. Hence officials tend to reject attempts by civil society to monitor government, even when they are provided for in legislation. By law, the Council for Regional Coordination must include provincial mayors and representatives of civil society elected by member organisations, but in practice, according to ongoing research by TI's chapter in Peru, Proética, sub-national governments have found ways to keep institutions that do not support them out of the council. In addition, two public hearings must be held each year to monitor the budget. In past hearings, however, only those institutions that support the administration were invited, or invitations were poorly distributed. In other cases, public hearings were not carried out at all.

This situation provides the backdrop to the high level of corruption in decentralised administrative bodies in Peru, where authorities have very low approval ratings among the population.[7] As a result, the process of decentralisation has been called into question. A tragic indictment of this state of affairs occurred in April 2004 when part of the population in Ilave, Puno, outraged by allegations of corruption made by the political opposition, lynched their mayor.

Samuel Rotta Castilla (Proética, Peru)

Further reading

Apoyo Opinión y Mercado, Proética, *II encuesta nacional sobre corrupción* (Second national survey on corruption) (Lima: Proética, 2004), www.proetica.org.pe

Ciudadanos al Día, *Transparencia en las municipalidades: El caso de las licencias de funcionamiento* (Transparency in municipalities: the case of operating licences) (Lima: CAD, 2004), www.ciudadanosaldia.org

Lorena Alcázar, José López-Calix and Eric Wachtenheim, *Las pérdidas en el camino. Fugas en el gasto público: Transferencias municipales, vaso de leche y educación* (Losses on the way. Public spending links: municipal transfers, state milk programme and education) (Lima: Instituto Apoyo, 2003)

Vigila Perú, *Reportes nacionales 1, 2 y 3* (National reports 1, 2 and 3) (Lima: Grupo Propuesta Ciudadana, 2003), www.participaperu.org.pe

Proética (TI Peru): www.proetica.org.pe

Notes

1. CERIAJUS supported the proposal, but the commission for restructuring the judicial system – which looks at all aspects of judicial reform, not just judicial administration – argued in favour of the existing system of self-regulation.
2. Some of the most notorious cases involve the national intelligence council (which is currently being reorganised), and political interference in the media and the judiciary.
3. For the most part these allegations have not been confirmed by official investigations, with the exception of the case of César Almeyda, a friend of the president's and former chief of the national intelligence council who has been in prison since February 2004 for business dealings with the Fujimori corruption racket.
4. *Global Corruption Report 2004.*
5. See, for example, a study by Proética on the health and education departments of the Lambayeque regional government, César Guzmán Valle, *Diagnóstico de la organización de la documentación en el gobierno regional de Lambayeque*, available at www.proetica.org.pe
6. Vigila Perú, *Reportes nacionales* (National reports) (Lima: Grupo Propuesta Ciudadana, 2003), www.participaperu.org.pe
7. *II encuesta nacional sobre corrupción* (Second national corruption survey) (Lima: Apoyo Opinión y Mercado, 2004).

Poland

Corruption Perceptions Index 2004 score: 3.5 (67th out of 146 countries)

Conventions:
Council of Europe Civil Law Convention on Corruption (ratified September 2002)
Council of Europe Criminal Law Convention on Corruption (ratified December 2002)
OECD Anti-Bribery Convention (ratified September 2000)
UN Convention against Corruption (signed December 2003; not yet ratified)
UN Convention against Transnational Organized Crime (ratified November 2001)

Legal and institutional changes

- In September 2003 a **law creating Voivodship tax administrative bodies** and amending other laws entered into force. The law on tax control was amended by specifying groups of persons obliged to submit annual property and income declarations. The specified groups include tax inspectors, employees of tax offices and customs officials. Monitoring is the responsibility of an office within the finance ministry. By increasing the transparency of the personal finances of administrative officers, the law should reduce the incentive for tax and customs officers to abuse their position by demanding bribes.

- Also in September 2003 the lower house of parliament adopted **legislation on military service** (which entered into force in July 2004), which prohibits professional soldiers from holding positions in companies or foundations, and from earning money for advisory roles. The law requires military commanders, deputy commanders and chief accountants to submit property declarations. The introduction of the law followed several recent corruption scandals in which officials with influence in military procurement decisions were shown to have positions in private companies bidding for the contracts.

- In January 2004 a new law on **public procurement** was passed, following amendments to the previous law in August 2003. The changes were intended to tighten controls, increase transparency and improve appeals procedures (see below).

Buying laws in parliament

In April 2004 investigations into 'Rywingate', Poland's most notorious corruption scandal of recent years, drew to a close, prompting widespread questions about the extent to which legislation in Poland can be bought by business interests. The case involved an attempt in 2002 by film producer Lew Rywin to intervene on behalf of the Agora media consortium during the passage of legislation that would have prevented Agora from purchasing the Polsat television station. Rywin allegedly represented senior members of the government, including then prime minister Leszek Miller, and demanded a US $17.5 million bribe.[1]

In its decision of April 2004 the district court in Warsaw sentenced Rywin to two and a half years' imprisonment and a fine of 100,000 zloty (US $27,000). When issuing the sentence, the court modified the charge from paid protection to fraud. One legal effect of this modification was to prevent the implication in the crime of a 'power-holding group', an informal set of persons with influence in the administration of the state. The sentence was condemned by many who argued that the trial should have implicated other influential figures. Adam Michnik (chief editor of *Gazeta Wyborcza*, and the man who first disclosed the scandal), described the court's decision as 'a big gift for the "power-holding group"'.[2]

Subsequently, in May 2004, the lower house of parliament voted to accept one of the six reports prepared by different members of a specially appointed parliamentary commission of inquiry. The adopted report, perceived to be the most

critical of the six, specified that the 'power-holding group' in the case were Leszek Miller (prime minister at the time), the head of the prime minister's office, one of the prime minister's advisers, the former chairman of public television and the secretary of the National Council for Radio and Television. The report recommended that members of the group should bear legal responsibility, and also recommended that Miller, the president (Aleksander Kwaśniewski) and the former justice minister should be taken to the Tribunal of State and bear constitutional responsibility.[3]

Rywingate was a breakthrough in uncovering political corruption in Poland. For a long time there had been allegations of corrupt, informal connections in public policy-making, but no proof until Michnik recorded a conversation with Rywin on tape. Rywingate has already motivated investigations into other cases. Allegations were made that laws affecting pharmaceuticals, bio-fuels and mobile telephones have also been affected by the 'dirty lobbying' of politicians. A media investigation that began in August 2003 resulted in allegations of inappropriate lobbying and links to organised crime in the passage of a bill that would benefit the owners of slot machines.[4]

Another effect of Rywingate was to make clear that the existing legislation on political party financing was not sufficient to prevent businesses influencing the legislative process. The buying of legislation in Poland is eased by the centralised nature of the political party system. Members of parliament vote strictly along party lines, as the penalty for breaching party discipline is often exclusion from the list of candidates in elections. Polish electoral law makes it impossible to participate in elections without being on a party list. As a result, a lobbyist need only have contact with one senior party figure to win an entire party's votes in parliament.

In order to prevent the buying of laws, two bills on lobbying have been prepared, one by the ministry of the interior and the second by non-governmental organisations, including the Institute of Public Affairs. There was also increasing pressure to modify the electoral law. In May 2004 more than 400 prominent figures published an 'appeal of those concerned about the destiny of the country', addressed to the president. It included an appeal for urgent modification of the electoral law to a majoritarian system based on single-member constituencies. Among those who signed the appeal were Władysław Bartoszewski (the former foreign minister), Stefan Bratkowski (honorary chairman of the Polish Journalists Association) and the professors and rectors of leading universities.

Public procurement

A series of measures were introduced in 2003–04 to tighten controls on public procurement, and to increase transparency and improve appeals procedures. First, in August 2003 the lower house of parliament adopted amendments to the public procurement law. The amendments granted power to the chairman of the Office of Public Procurement (UZP) to designate the arbitrators considering appeals against public procurement decisions. Previously the UZP had only selected one arbitrator, with the involved parties selecting the others, with no controls against the risk of corruption in the choice of arbitrators. Subsequently, in November 2003, the UZP chairman issued regulations introducing more transparent methods of arbitrator selection. In addition, the legal amendments gave public access to a wide range of documentation including bids, declarations and certificates submitted in the course of public procurement proceedings (except for confidential business information), with documents to be made available before the end of the tender award process.

In January 2004 parliament adopted a new law on public procurement, which entered into force in March 2004. The law strengthened the powers of the chairman of the UZP and tightened monitoring procedures, with mandatory control of the proceedings before the conclusion of high-value tenders. The law introduced the institution of independent observer, to monitor public procurements worth more than €5 million (US $6 million) in supplies and services and €10 million (US $12 million) in construction works. The law provides for control at two stages: ex ante, preventive measures before the conclusion of tenders; and ex post, allowing procurement proceedings to be examined up to three years after the awarding of a contract. An independent observer is designated by the chairman of the UZP from a list of arbitrators. The law also allows for the possibility of awarding public contracts through an electronic auction system. The regulations on the selection of arbitrators were further tightened, and the chairman of UZP was granted the right to impose cash penalties for breaches of the law.

Julia Pitera (TI Poland)

Further reading

Maria Jarosz, *Władza, Przywileje, Korupcja* (Power, Privilege and Corruption) (Warsaw: Wydawnictwo Naukowe PWN, 2004)

Janusz Kowalski and Rafał Zgorzelski, eds, *O Nową Polskę* (For a New Poland) (Opole: Stop Korupcji, 2004)

Anna Kubiak, *Łapownictwo w świadomości i Doświadczeniu Potocznym Polaków* (Bribery in Perception and Everyday Experience in Poland) (Wydawnictwo Uniwersytetu Łódzkiego, 2003)

Julia Pitera, ed., *Mapa Korupcji w Polsce* (A Map of Corruption in Poland) (Warsaw: TI Poland, 2003)

TI Poland: www.transparency.pl

Notes

1. See *Global Corruption Report 2004*.
2. *Warsaw Voice Online* (Poland), 5 May 2004, www.warsawvoice.pl
3. *Polish News Bulletin* (Poland), 27 September 2004.
4. *Gazeta Wyborcza* (Poland), 29 November 2003.

Romania

Corruption Perceptions Index 2004 score: 2.9 (87th out of 146 countries)

Conventions:
Council of Europe Civil Law Convention on Corruption (ratified April 2002)
Council of Europe Criminal Law Convention on Corruption (ratified July 2002)
UN Convention against Corruption (signed December 2003; not yet ratified)
UN Convention against Transnational Organized Crime (ratified December 2002)

Legal and institutional changes

- In October 2003 the Romanian parliament passed a set of constitutional amendments designed to combat corruption in Romania. The **immunity of MPs** was restricted to political opinions, and the power of the ministry of justice over administrative and disciplinary matters relating to magistrates was entrusted to the council of the magistracy, substantially improving the **political autonomy of magistrates**.

- February 2004 saw the passage of the first **code of conduct** for civil servants, which set out the fundamental principles of modern administration: rule of law, priority of public interest, equality of treatment, professionalism, impartiality, independence, moral integrity, good faith and transparency. Improving on previous law, the code clarifies conflicts of interest legislation by defining public interest, personal interest and situations in which conflicts of interest can arise. Other provisions prevent civil servants from carrying out political activities, or using their official status for the promotion of commercial activities. Civil servants are prohibited from accepting gifts, services or any other advantage for themselves or their family, parents, friends or business and political associates. However, the effective range of the code applies only to civil servants, leaving elected and appointed officials out of reach.

- Emergency ordinance 24, passed in April 2004, amended earlier provisions on **asset disclosure** for politicians and clarified the sanctions. The law imposes the same obligations on all candidates for elective positions (presidency, parliament, local and county councils, mayors), and declarations must be published on the Internet. The political opposition criticised the timing of the measure in the run-up to the June elections, claiming there was insufficient time to fill out the forms while candidates for the party in power had known of the requirement in good time. Despite the wide coverage, no investigations have been triggered by suspicious declarations, suggesting ineffective implementation or a lack of political will. Additional concerns are that whistleblowers are left open to charges of libel, that the disclosure requirements exclude art, 'patrimony' and precious metals, and that there is no cross checking with annual income tax declarations.

- A government decision in July 2003 established the structure and function of the Government Control Office (CCG). The CCG exerts internal administrative control on central and local government, investigates complaints on **conflict of interest legislation**, coordinates anti-fraud activities and protects the financial interests of the EU in Romania (see below). However, since the CCG itself is subordinate to the cabinet, it may have its own problem with conflicts of interest.

- In April 2004 the **National Anti-Corruption Prosecution Office** (PNA) was awarded a substantial increase in resources (23 per cent) and increased financial autonomy from the ministry of justice. On the other hand, the range of PNA's activities was broadened to include smaller acts of corruption greatly increasing its workload. The PNA has, in the past, come in for criticism for dodging the 'big sharks' and NGOs have questioned its independence. Despite the above amendments, the PNA remains directly subordinate to the ministry of justice and the ministry appoints and disciplines prosecutors.[1] The PNA's head recently declared that the PNA would not submit its annual report to parliament, restricting reporting to the ministry of justice. Shortly before the June 2004 elections the PNA reopened a case against the opposition leader Traian Basescu (though the investigation was later suspended until after the election) even though the same administration had investigated the case in 1997 and been forced to drop it for lack of evidence.

- The controversial **Independent Service for Anti-Corruption and Protection** (SIPA) within the ministry of justice changed its name to the General Office for Anti-Corruption and Protection (DGPA). Notwithstanding the new body's formal accountability to parliament and its declared duties to prevent and identify criminal acts in prisons, corruption and acts that undermine national security or the security of magistrates, the need for a 'secret service' in the judiciary remains questionable.

Judicial independence: to be or not to be

Romanian justice has been widely criticised both locally and internationally for corruption, delays in resolving cases and lack of independence.[2] According to a survey carried out in early 2004, 63 per cent of Romanians do not believe that justice can be obtained through the courts, compared to just 21 per cent who feel the opposite.[3] Reports from the European Commission have repeatedly warned of the acute need for judicial reform, particularly 'the improvement of judicial independence and the reduction of the influence of the executive on judicial decisions'.[4]

At a regulatory level, judicial independence has been compromised since 1992, when Romania's first law on the organisation of the judiciary came into force. This legislation established a judicial structure whereby career path, disciplinary responsibility and salaries for magistrates are all at the discretion of the ministry of justice.

In late 2003 the ministry of justice introduced a package of draft laws to allow the cabinet to finalise EU accession negotiations on the judicial chapter, a critical benchmark of Romania's readiness to join the EU in 2007. The ministry initiated two laws on the organisation of the judiciary and the status of magistrates but crucially maintained many of the same levers of control (career path, disciplinary responsibility, management of courts, and so on).

In early 2004 several Romanian NGOs held a press conference to raise awareness of the faults in the reform package.[5] They successfully demanded that the juridical commission in the lower house of parliament prevent the two laws from being adopted until a third draft law on the Superior Council of the Magistracy (CSM) had been finalised. It was later discovered that the latter law was in the ministry pipeline, but had been deferred until late 2004.

Debates between civil society, the ministry of justice and the CSM have continued but a draft guaranteeing the independence of the judiciary has still not been achieved. During negotiations during early 2004, drafts thought agreed among the various parties have appeared on the ministry's website substantially modified for the worse. The final draft addresses the main reform issues (disciplinary responsibility, career path and administrative autonomy) but crucially the financial autonomy for the judiciary was denied. Furthermore, effective oversight of the legislation has been severely hampered by the denial of full-time status to the members of the CSM.

Conflicts of interest at work

Romania has been given the largest portion of EU funding for accession countries and, used wisely, EU structural funds have the power to redress the social, economic and educational imbalances between Romania and the other accession states. The large sums involved, however, have also tempted the corrupt, and the means by which some of the structural funds have been distributed has revealed gaping legal and administrative flaws in the Romanian public integrity system.

A major scandal erupted in February 2004 when the media revealed that several EU Sapard projects in Suceava county had been marred by conflicts of interest because of links between the civil servants awarding the contracts and the boards of the winning companies.[6] Out of a total of 37 signed contracts, 16 were found to have broken some aspect of conflict of interest legislation. The European Commission demanded a full inquiry into the Suceava contracts.[7]

The responsible agency subsequently launched a nationwide verification of all contracts under the national programme. It found that of approximately 150 active contracts, more than one third had been in breach of conflict of interest legislation.[8] Romania has registered the highest number of irregularities reported to the EU's European Anti Fraud Office (OLAF), according to the auditing agency's report for 2002–03.

Because of such cases, there has been a notable increase in state sensitivity to the issue of conflicts of interest. In July 2003 the head of the European integration portfolio, Hildegard Carola Puwak, secured €150,000 from an EU-funded educational programme for companies owned by her husband and son. Two contracts had been approved before Puwak took over the ministry, but others were endorsed after she entered office. OLAF and the PNA both opened inquiries which concluded that there had been no breach of contract-awarding procedures since she had not taken part directly in the decision-making process. Even so, the minister was forced to resign in October 2003.[9]

Adrian Savin (TI Romania)

Further reading

Evaluation of the Integrity and Resistance to Corruption of the Judiciary (Bucharest: Romanian Ministry of Justice, 2004), www.just.ro/bin/anticoruptie/EN%20FULL.htm

GRECO, *Evaluation Report on Romania* (Strasbourg: GRECO, 2002), www.just.ro/bin/anticoruptie/GrecoEval1Rep(2001)13E-Romania.pdf

Government of Romania, *Combating Corruption in Romania: Measures to Expedite the Implementation of the National Strategy* (Bucharest: Government of Romania, 2002), www.gov.ro/obiective/pganticoruptie/anticoruptie-2002–2.pdf

TI Romania: www.transparency.org.ro

Notes

1. At the time of writing a draft law is being processed on the Superior Council of the Magistracy that aims to make prosecutors independent of the ministry of justice.
2. According to TI's Global Corruption Barometer 2003, Romanians perceive the justice system as second only to political parties in terms of corruption.
3. Centre for Urban and Regional Sociology, *Sondaj la Nivel National in Mediul Urban* (National Urban Survey) (2004).
4. Report on Romania's application for membership of the European Union and the state of the negotiations, see www.europarl.eu.int/meetdocs/committees/afet/20000710/406856_en.doc
5. *Justiție, Reformă, Integrare Europeană, O Ecuație Pentru Societatea Românească* (Justice, Reform, European Integration, An Equation for the Romanian Society) (Bucharest: Citybank, 2004).
6. *Evenimentul Zilei* (Romania), 25 February 2004.
7. *Gardianul* (Romania), 28 February 2004.
8. BBC News, 28 March 2004.
9. Radio Free Europe/Radio Liberty, 2004.

Russia

Corruption Perceptions Index 2004 score: 2.8 (90th out of 146 countries)

Conventions:
Council of Europe Civil Law Convention on Corruption (not yet signed)
Council of Europe Criminal Law Convention on Corruption (signed January 1999; not yet ratified)
UN Convention against Corruption (signed December 2003; not yet ratified)
UN Convention against Transnational Organized Crime (ratified May 2004)

New legislation and institutional developments

- President Vladimir Putin signed a decree in November 2003 creating the **Council for the Struggle against Corruption**. The council, a consultative body, consists of the prime minister, the speakers of both chambers of parliament, the heads of the constitutional, supreme, and higher arbitration courts. According to the decree, the main goal of the council is to identify the reasons for the spread of corruption and to help the president determine policies for fighting it.

- In April 2004 a **Special Commission for the Struggle against Corruption** was founded by the new parliament, elected in December 2003. Its tasks consist of analysing laws and draft bills to detect flaws that might provide opportunities for corruption. It also serves as an agency to take citizens' complaints, receiving roughly 100 in its first two and a half months of existence.

- In March 2004 the **Federal Financial Monitoring Service** (FFMS) was reorganised. This 'finance intelligence' service monitors all property contracts and transactions exceeding a value of 3 million rubles (US $100,000). When organisations carry out such transactions, they are obliged to inform the FFMS immediately. Obligations to inform the FFMS also apply for certain cash operations, transactions with accounts held anonymously, operations by legal entities registered within the past three months, financial leasing operations, and also interest-free loans that exceed 600,000 rubles (US $20,000).

Putin's anti-corruption policy

Curbing corruption has become one of the catchwords for legitimising Vladimir Putin's 'strong presidency' and rebuilding the so-called 'power vertical' – Putin's main project to modernise and strengthen the Russian state. In line with this project, the struggle against corruption is characterised by top-down, campaign-style measures, and the creation of new agencies. As the anti-corruption campaign has built up momentum in Russia, however, it has also become evident that, as in some other countries in the Commonwealth of Independent States (for example, Ukraine and Belarus), the struggle against corruption is becoming a powerful tool in the hands of the president who may turn it selectively against unhelpful officials or political opponents.

The 'Yukos affair' is a case in point. In October 2003 Mikhail Khodorkovsky, chief executive of the Russian oil giant Yukos, regarded as the richest man in Russia, and a major financier of the reformist Yabloko Party, was arrested on charges of fraud, forgery, embezzlement and tax evasion. Many observers believe the affair was triggered not only by Khodorkovsky's rising political ambitions, but also by an incident during a meeting between Putin and the so-called oligarchs in early 2003, when Khodorkovsky supposedly criticised the pervasiveness of corruption in the executive.

As early as April 2002 Putin had criticised the state administration as being badly run and corrupt, and called for institutional reforms in his annual state of the nation address, since then no measures were taken. Two days after Khodorkovsky's arrest, however, Putin declared corruption a threat to national security and called for a 'systemic anti-corruption policy'. In November 2003 he instigated the Presidential Council for the Struggle against Corruption, which consists of two commissions – one to fight corruption, and the other to uncover conflicts of interest which may arise when government officials accept gifts from, or spend vacations with, company executives.

The formation of a presidential council is a long-established method within Russia of dealing with difficult issues. The council is directly subordinate to Putin and is limited to an advisory role. Its design is interpreted by many analysts as signalling a victory for liberals over hard-liners within the Kremlin who had stipulated the establishment of a special agency commanding an armed force, either independent or as part of the interior ministry. While the latter approach would have been unnecessarily heavy handed (and particularly opposed by Russia's business elite),[1] critics of the winning, 'soft' solution question the council's effectiveness in the absence of law enforcement. In any case, at the time of writing the council has been inactive.[2]

Another element of Putin's anti-corruption activities is civil service reform. The first visible step in this regard was the creation by presidential decree of a commission on administrative reform in July 2003. The call for administrative reform rests on two assumptions. Firstly, sweeping bureaucratic discretionary power, responsibilities that cut across multiple agencies and excessive arbitrariness in the application of state regulations all cause corruption. Secondly, civil servants' low salaries give rise to bribery. While the first problem has received little attention so far, the second was addressed when in April 2004 salaries were substantially raised by presidential decree. For some, the decree represents a real breakthrough, while others point out that increased salaries has to be accompanied by other measures.[3] Public opinion, too, remains sceptical that this measure will be effective.[4]

Curbing corruption: civil society activities

Civil society in Russia is weak. Grassroots organisations face difficult hurdles because access to politics is limited to the ruling elite and media restrictions also serve to stifle the growth of civil society.[5] That said, anti-corruption initiatives from business and civil groups that have access to independent resources have begun to surface.

One initiative was started by the Russian Union of Industrialists and Entrepreneurs (RUIE), the most influential business association in Russia. In August 2003 RUIE founded a joint arbitration system in cooperation with two minor business associations. The new arbitration courts can bypass the regular, often corrupt, courts in cases of dispute settlement among business partners. Although appealing to the arbitration court is voluntary, and presupposes the consent of both partners, its decisions are binding. Non-compliance will be punished by entry onto a 'blacklist'. The arbitration system is so far the most important step undertaken by RUIE to

improve the business climate in Russia. As one commentator ironically stated, the main beneficiaries of the new system are the small and medium-sized entrepreneurs since 'big business has already established long-term relations with the courts'.[6]

A second noteworthy initiative is 'Antikorruptsiya', founded in February 2004 by representatives of the Association of Small Businesses and human rights organisations. It aims to 'consolidate the resources of the civil society' and to help and urge the government to curb corruption. Antikorruptsiya seeks to carry out investigations by questioning officials and politicians and to publish the results in the mass media and online. It monitors compliance with the law by public officials, and will take cases to court if necessary. The first lists of questions relating to allegedly corrupt activities were presented in May 2004 to the general prosecutor, the ministers of transport and communications, and the chief of the Moscow city court, amongst others.[7]

A third source of non-state anti-corruption initiatives draws heavily on the support of the United States Agency for International Development, which started a 'Partnership against Corruption' (PAC) programme designed to build government integrity, accountability and transparency in Russia's regions. Local 'partnerships' have been established, non-profit organisations that arrange anti-corruption measures, bringing together regional and local state agencies, businesspeople and civil society activists.[8]

In a different approach, the National Anti-Corruption Committee (NAC), a 'club' of 55 politicians and political analysts and the regional PACs cooperated closely with government agencies to try to strengthen honest politicians at the top. The NAC believes that the pervasiveness of corruption in Russia is led by the Russian bureaucracy and that Putin is the only person able to rid the system of corruption. The NAC recommends that Putin use his broad popular support as a 'presidential resource' in the battles ahead.

Although there is an anti-corruption network of non-state actors in the making which builds around a small core of activists, assessing the real importance of these initiatives is no easy task. The general weakness of civil society encourages a 'top-down' approach, as does the structure of some anti-corruption groups who are connected to elite interest groups rather than being broad-based popular movements. The current appeal of an 'iron hand', however, is problematic in an environment where anti-corruption campaigns may also serve as a political weapon against opponents.

Marina Savintseva (TI Russia) and Petra Stykow (Ludwig-Maximilians-University, Germany)

Further reading

Bogdanov and Kalinin, *Corruption in Russia: Socio-Economic and Legal Aspects* (Moscow: Russian Science Academy, Institute of the Socio-Political Researches, 2001) (in Russian)

Vladimir Shlapentokh, 'Russia's Acquiescence to Corruption Makes the State Machine Inept', *Communist and Post-Communist Studies* 36(2) (2003)

Fond Indem, 'Diagnostika Rossiiskoi Korruptsii: Sotsiologicheskii Analiz' (2001), www.anti-corr.ru/awbreport/index.htm

Timothy Frye, 'Capture or Exchange? Business Lobbying in Russia', *Europe-Asia Studies* 54(7) (2002)

Richard Sakwa, 'Russia: From a Corrupt System to a System with Corruption?', in Robert Williams, ed., *Party Finance and Political Corruption* (Basingstoke: Macmillan, 2000)

TI Russia: www.transparency.org.ru

Notes

1. *Moscow Times* (Russia), 26 November 2003.
2. Interview with Georgy Satarov, *Gazeta* (Russia), 9 April 2004.
3. See www.grani.ru/Politics/Russia/Cabinet/p.67340.html and www.chuvashia.com/cap_xp/main.asp?prev=9151&pos=153
4. Public Opinion Foundation, http://bd.fom.ru/report/map/projects/finfo/of0416/of041603
5. Briefing Report: 'Corruption, Biased Media Turn Russian Election Into "Farce"'. JRL 8108, 9 March 2004, www.cdi.org/russia
6. *Financial Times* (Britain), 6 August 2003.
7. www.iamik.ru/15674.html
8. See: www.stopcor.ru, www.nakhodka.info, http://coalition.tomsk.ru, http://a-corruption.irkutsk.ru/index.htm

Serbia

NB: This report does not cover developments in Montenegro or Kosovo

Corruption Perceptions Index 2004 score:[1] 2.7 (97th out of 146 countries)

Conventions:
Council of Europe Civil Law Convention on Corruption (not yet signed)
Council of Europe Criminal Law Convention on Corruption (acceded December 2002)

UN Convention against Corruption (signed December 2003; not yet ratified)
UN Convention against Transnational Organized Crime (ratified September 2001)

Legal and institutional changes

- A **law on political party financing** was adopted in July 2003 and implemented from January 2004. The law provides state funding both for general party finances (e.g. running costs) and to fund candidates in electoral campaigns, 0.15 per cent of the national budget, and 0.1 per cent of national budget respectively. The maximum amount of private contributions allowed is US $800,000 per party or candidate in parliamentary or presidential elections. Violations of the law attract steep fines by national standards. However, the law was passed with little public discussion and its implementation was poorly prepared. Loopholes in the text led to a number of misinterpretations by parties, state bodies and even electoral experts in the run-up to the presidential election in June 2004 (see below).

- The newly elected parliament adopted a **law on prevention of conflict of interest in public office** in April 2004 after a long period of lobbying by TI Serbia, among others. The law did not meet civil society expectations, but does provide for the creation of a control body for resolving conflicts in favour of the public interest. Implementation got off to a shaky start, with uncertainties surrounding the enforcement mechanisms. Some have criticised the law for failing to make conflicts of interest a criminal offence and its lack of positive incentives (see below).

- The **law on public procurement** was amended in May 2004 to facilitate tender procedures and enhance bidders' rights through an improved complaints mechanism. Unsuccessful bidders can take their suspicions of unfair tendering first to the client itself and then to a commission for the protection of bidders' rights, which has powers to confirm or override all or part of the tender procedure before contracts are signed. The amendment falls short of best practice, which would require the appeal body to be independent of the executive and to report directly to parliament.

- A **draft law on access to information** was submitted to parliament in July 2003, but withdrawn after too many discrepancies were found to make amendment possible. After the change of government, work resumed on the draft in April 2004. If passed, the new version would provide access to information possessed by the executive, legislature and judiciary, local government, public enterprises and any other entities performing public functions. A special commissioner would be created with appeals and advisory functions. Access can be denied when the relevant information represents a threat to national security, or violates confidentiality or the legal protection of personal data. The media would enjoy enhanced rights of access. Concerns have been raised over the vague definitions for exempted categories. The draft also fails to make provisions for protecting whistleblowers from criminal prosecution or other disciplinary action.

Party financing descends into chaos

There are clear shortfalls in the provisions of the latest legislation governing party financing in Serbia, which came into effect in January 2004. In particular, the control mechanisms have been heavily criticised on the grounds that the submission of reports is made to the electoral commission – a body created for other purposes and with little capacity for checking reports. The most pressing problem however, is the state's attempts to renege on one of the fundamental pillars of the legislation – the provision on state financing for political campaigns.

The core of the new legislation is a multi-pillared approach in which stricter restrictions on party funding are supplemented with state support for running costs and election campaigns. The specific aim of state funding is to strike a balance between public and private sources, and so to decrease the dependence of political parties on private donors.

To finance campaigns the January 2004 law provides 0.1 per cent of the national budget for political parties or 'citizens groups'. Based on figures for Serbia's national budget of 2004, the total figure available for election expenses would be 227 million dinars (US $4 million).[2] One-fifth of the amount is to be disbursed to all candidates equally, and four-fifths to the party that proposed the winning candidate. The maximum amount of private contributions allowed is set at one-fifth of the overall national budget, 45.3 million dinars (US $800,000). Funds not spent on campaign expenditures should be reimbursed to the state.

However, at the first test for the legislation, the June 2004 presidential elections, the provision of state funding collapsed in disarray. Apparently by mistake, in March 2004, the ministry of finance calculated a much lower sum for state support for election campaigns based on presidential election laws which had been superseded by the January 2004 legislation. Claiming national budget constraints, the state subsequently attempted to enshrine the lower figure in law by passing an amendment to the January 2004 legislation.[3]

On the basis of the prior law governing the provision of presidential electoral expenses, total state commitments amounted to 12 million dinars, compared to the 227 million dinars discussed above (making a difference between US $200,000 and US $3.8 million). Following the rejection of the amendment enshrining the lower budget allocation (0.01 per cent of the state budget),[4] the government eventually offered 45 million dinars (US $740,000). Representatives of 11 of the 15 first-round candidates announced their willingness to challenge the decision of the ministry of finance to disperse them 607,000 dinars (US $10,000), claiming entitlement to five times this amount.[5]

With the legal confusion created by state donations, private contributions also became mired in uncertainty. As noted above, levels of private financing are tied to levels of state financing. In the context of uncertainty over the levels of state funding it is unclear what sum is available for candidates and parties from private sources or what legal consequences arise from using the higher figure.

It is still uncertain whether it is the state's intention to abandon the central concept of the law (balanced financing from public and private sources) or merely to make short-term savings for budgetary purposes. What is certain is that if the law is to work all the political parties must achieve a common interpretation of the law's provisions before September 2004 local elections. Legal amendments must also be made to remove any ambiguities. Implementation controls must be improved, and a proxy should be appointed by the election commission to engage certified auditors in a process of verification.

A long way to conflict of interest legislation

Public awareness of the issue of conflicts of interest reached its peak due to a series of conflict of interest scandals throughout the summer of 2003. Allegations were made against the minister for transport and communications and one of the prime minister's advisers.[6] These cases were bought to public attention through opposition political parties, and in the run up to the elections in December 2003, opposition groups sought maximum political capital from the scandals, and in the process closely aligned themselves with the commitment to legislative reform. In consequence, the law on the prevention of conflict of interest in the discharge of public functions was one of the first that the new administration enacted on assuming power.

While the legislation covers many important aspects of conflicts of interest and imposes tight restrictions on state officials at central, provincial and local levels, it also shows the hallmarks of hasty drafting and a shortfall in expert input. The law covers only a small part of the area that should be regulated.

There are also concerns over the legislation's implementation mechanisms. The central control body of the law is the Republic Board for Resolving Conflict of Interest. This body consists of nine members nominated by the supreme court, the academy of science and arts and the bar association. There are concerns that this body will be able to deal with the workload, particularly given that a provision to create regional oversight boards was dropped in the law's adoption process. Cooperation with other government agencies is not guaranteed, and despite the complexities of the task before them, salaries for the board members are low.

A further problem with the legislation is that it does little to provide positive incentives to engage state officials. The law imposes many restrictions governing their behaviour – restrictions on sources of income, obligations to declare personal and family assets and interests – but offers little in return, such as an explicit reference to future salary increases. One rather weak incentive is offered in terms of a new, safe mechanism for resolving potential conflicts of interest cases by seeking advice from a control body on potential infringements of the law prior to engaging in a particular business venture or accepting a gift.

The expectations of some that conflicts of interest would be made a criminal offence were not realised. That said, there are indications that in the Serbian context, this shortfall may not be as far reaching as it would at first appear. Opinion polls in Serbia show that despite a general preference for severe penalties there is a relatively high degree of public confidence that political sanctions could be effective.[7] This may be due to the level of public sensitivity about conflict of interest and an apparent readiness not to vote for implicated politicians. It is also not clear that more legislation is helpful given that legislation covering abuse of power by politicians is already extensive.

Nemanja Nenadic (TI Serbia)

Further reading

World Bank, 'Serbia and Montenegro – Recent Progress on Structural Reforms' (2003), http://siteresources.worldbank.org/INTSERBIA/Resources/SaM_Recent_Progress_on_Structural_Reforms.pdf

Nemanja Nenadic, *Conflict of Public and Private Interest and Free Access to Information* (Belgrade: Transparency International-Serbia, 2003), www.transparentnost.org.yu/publications/conflict.pdf

Boris Begovic and Bosko Mijatovic, *Corruption in Serbia* (Belgrade: Centre for Liberal-Democratic Studies, 2001), www.clds.org.yu/pdf-e/e-korupcija.pdf

Centre for Policy Studies, *Korupcija u Novim Uslovima* (Corruption in a New Environment) (Belgrade: 2002), www.cpa-cps.org.yu/cpa-cps/cpa/projekti/zavrseni/Sadrzaj/ent_2002-10-06-16-26-02

TI Serbia: www.transparentnost.org.yu

Notes

1. The CPI score applies to Serbia and Montenegro.
2. Amounts are calculated according to 2004 budget figures.
3. *Glas javnosti* (Serbia), 20 April 2004.
4. *Glas javnosti* (Serbia), 15 April 2004.
5. BETA News Agency (Serbia), 19 June 2004.
6. Ibid.
7. See www.transparentnost.org.yu/publications/conflict.pdf

Slovakia

Corruption Perceptions Index 2004 score: 4.0 (57th out of 146 countries)

Conventions:
Council of Europe Civil Law Convention on Corruption (ratified May 2003)
Council of Europe Criminal Law Convention on Corruption (ratified June 2000)
OECD Anti-Bribery Convention (ratified September 1999)
UN Convention against Corruption (signed December 2003; not yet ratified)
UN Convention against Transnational Organized Crime (ratified December 2003)

Legal and institutional changes

- An **amendment to the code of criminal procedure and the criminal code** came into effect in December 2003. The powers of the office of 'agent provocateur' were expanded to permit initiating corrupt actions. Procedures were introduced for reducing sentences for offenders who turn state's evidence. The amendment also introduces punitive measures for conspiring to commit a corrupt act. A person who could plausibly inform on another person committing, or conspiring to commit, corruption was also made liable for imprisonment of up to three years.

- The **law on a special court and prosecutor to fight corruption and organised crime** was passed in October 2003. The law establishes a centralised anti-corruption institution with considerable autonomy. Its particular structure is designed to prevent tampering of courts, prosecutors and politicians, and to overcome the unwillingness of judges to prosecute corruption cases (see below).

- A **new law on protection of the public interest** in performing the functions of public officials was adopted by parliament in May 2004 (due to come into force in October 2004). The law sets out conditions for protecting the public interest, and for incompatibility of public functions with other activities. It also addresses the accountability of officials for breach of the law (see below).

A conflict of interest

Before May 2004, conflict of interest legislation in Slovakia was anchored in the 1995 constitutional law relating to senior officials and state officers in the discharge of their public functions. While the earlier act looked promising on paper, it suffered from weak implementation and the exclusion of great numbers of state officials from its scope. The Association of Towns and Villages, a professional organisation of mayors of

Slovakia, successfully lobbied to eliminate municipal bodies and local administrations from coming under the purview of the act. Information, such as property declarations, was rarely verified and was not made public. The oversight body, the Committee of the Parliament of the Slovak Republic (CPSR), had no mandate to refer any matter to other state bodies such as the tax authority.

The inadequacies of the old law were highlighted by several high profile cases involving well-known public officials. Most notably, in 2003–04, the former Slovak premier, Vladimír Mečiar, become the focus of media scrutiny and intense public speculation about the amount of property he owned, and the means with which he acquired it. Despite the public furore, Mečiar refused to disclose his assets within the deadline set, bringing to widespread public attention the lack of force behind conflicts of interest legislation in Slovakia.[1]

A steady stream of such scandals provided a great impetus for change, and a number of civil society coalitions have developed to campaign on the issue. After several failed attempts by the government to pass stronger conflicts of interest legislation, TI Slovakia initiated the formation of the Alliance – Stop Conflict of Interest, an informal association of more than 240 NGOs who worked with Minister of Justice Daniel Lipsic to present a draft bill to parliament. Amendments to the draft bill by parliamentary committees led Lipsic to withdraw the bill in early 2004, but the initiative had generated the impetus for legal reform. Unsurprisingly, the bill eventually adopted by the Slovakia parliament in May 2004 was much weaker than that presented by Lipsic and replicated many of the failings of the existing legislation both in terms of scope and implementation.

In terms of scope, the law does not apply to state representatives of the national property fund, nor does it apply to state representatives in commercial companies in which the state has a property stake lower than 100 per cent. Some sections of municipal councils are also excluded.

In terms of implementation, the decision-making processes are complex and heavily weighted against making a decision to impose sanctions. The threshold level for deciding to pursue a corrupt official is very high. To initiate proceedings, at least three-fifths of the respective parliamentary committee members are required to agree that the case before them constitutes a conflict of interest; a minimum of 90 members of parliament are required to decide on sanctions. On past experience, such rigorous demands render the act without effective sanction.

The law has other shortcomings too. The public disclosure of the source of loans for public officials is not required, nor does the law require the public disclosure of property declarations submitted by family members of parliamentarians. The law has weak post-employment restrictions, focusing only on post-public sector employment which provides earnings that are more than 10 times the minimum wage.

While the act clearly introduces some positive elements, for example, the need for members of parliament to make property declarations for family members (though not publicly) and the inclusion of more public authorities and officers under its remit (deputies of some municipal councils are still not included), its weaknesses cast some doubt on its ability to deal with the problems of conflicts of interest in Slovakia. That said, some remain optimistic and the law, and the will to implement it, is yet to be fully tested.

Detecting and prosecuting corruption

The law on establishment of a special court and the office of a special prosecutor became effective in May 2004. It aims to create a centralised unit of legal experts focusing on organised crime and corruption. The central office is to be run under a special regime to isolate it from relations which often facilitate corruption.

The unit is to provide enhanced security measures for personnel and enhanced remuneration for staff. Staff are required to undergo a rigorous screening process conducted by the national security office, and will include members of parliament, government members, chairmen of state administration central bodies, chairman and vice-chairman of the Supreme Audit Office, judges of the constitutional court, judges and prosecutors. A special court shall decide on criminal acts of corruption, while the most serious financial cases are to be verified by a special investigator and tax and financial experts.

On the positive side, the state has allocated a relatively large amount of money for its operations, and the first special prosecutor was appointed at a meeting of the Slovak parliament in May 2004 and is widely held in high esteem. On the other hand, there is great concern that the power of the office was substantially weakened as a result of political manoeuvring within the coalition government.

As with the new conflicts of interest law, discussed above, one way in which the initiative was weakened was by interest groups within the legislature limiting which public officials are to come under the scope of the institution. The wording of the law was also weakened so that the law only applies to acts directly related to execution of a public official's job. In practice, this means that criminal acts committed by a public official before or after his period in office remain under the purview of the general prosecutor.

There was significant resistance to the passing of this law from political opposition groups, particularly SMER who rejected the bill wholesale on the grounds of its potential for abuse against those not participating in the coalition government. Concerns had been raised over the office of the general prosecutor and its relation to the office of the special prosecutor. The law provides that the special prosecutor was to be chosen by the National Council of the Slovak Republic from a selection of candidates forwarded by the general prosecutor. The office of general prosecutor was also strengthened by the provision that the prosecution of a member of parliament by the special prosecutor requires the consent of the general prosecutor and the national parliament.

In sum, the establishment of the office of special prosecutor and the special court is a positive but not sufficient condition for successfully combating corruption in Slovakia. There seems to be some commitment from the state to create and finance the institutions at this time, but the law has also been weakened by self-interest in the legislature.

Emília Sičáková-Beblavá and Daniela Zemanovičová (TI Slovakia)

Further reading

E. Sičáková-Beblavá and D. Zemanovičová, *Corruption and Anti-Corruption Policy in Slovakia (evaluation report)* (Bratislava: Transparency International Slovakia, 2003)

D. Zemanovičová and E. Beblavá, *The Country of Equal and More Equal – Slovakia and Corruption* (Bratislava: Kalligram, 2003)

V. Pirošík, E. Sičáková-Beblavá and B. Pavlovič, *Decentralization and Corruption* (Bratislava: Transparency International Slovakia, 2004)

TI Slovakia: www.transparency.sk

Note

1. *Daily Pravda* (Slovakia), 10 December 2002.

Sri Lanka

Corruption Perceptions Index 2004 score: 3.5 (67th out of 146 countries)

Conventions:
UN Convention against Corruption (ratified March 2004)
UN Convention against Transnational Organized Crime (signed December 2000; not yet ratified)

Legal and institutional changes

- The Sri Lankan government enacted the **Fiscal Management (Responsibility) Act No. 3** in 2003. The law aims to enhance transparency and financial accountability and ensure that the government's fiscal strategy is based on responsible fiscal management. Under the law, the finance minister is required to publicly disclose the government's fiscal policy and performance. The law's effectiveness will depend on vigilant public scrutiny of the finance minister's reports, and state commitment to enforcement and oversight mechanisms.

- Drafting of the **Audit Act** was completed at the end of 2003. The bill will widen the mandate and strengthen the powers and independence of the office of the auditor general. Under the law, the auditor general's report must be presented to parliament within five months of closure of the financial year (reduced from the current requirement of 10 months). The law widens the auditor general's authority to audit all income and expenditure of parliament.

- The need for a **freedom of information law** was recognised by the cabinet in December 2003 and was scheduled to go before parliament in late 2004. If passed the bill should overcome a severe deficit in public access to government documents such as the audit report, recruitment and promotion schemes for public sector staff, and public contracting transactions. The inability to access such information has resulted in widespread cronyism and misappropriation of public funds. The proposed legislation is flawed in that it is unclear in its scope, and various provisions within the legislation provide ample opportunity for restrictions.

An ailing judiciary

According to a Transparency International survey, the judiciary is perceived to be the second most corrupt public institution in Sri Lanka after the police.[1] A further study carried out by Marga Institute also revealed the extent of the problem in the Sri Lankan judicial system. Of the 50 judges (including retired judges) who responded to a questionnaire, 41 reported 226 incidents of bribery within the judiciary. Among the respondents, the prevalent view (84 per cent) was that Sri Lanka's judicial system was corrupt.[2]

Even the highest authority in the Sri Lankan judiciary has been tainted with allegations of corruption. There have been two attempts to impeach the chief justice, Sarath Nanda Silva, on charges including obstruction of justice, violation of the constitution, abuse of power and inappropriate personal behaviour relating to the status of a supreme court justice.[3] The second impeachment was presented to the speaker of parliament in November 2003.

Neither attempt has led to a parliamentary inquiry because the president dissolved parliament, on both occasions, before proceedings could be completed.

Faced with a malfunctioning judiciary, urgent reforms are needed. First, any proceedings or inquiries involving judges should be resolved by appropriate and timely judicial action. Impeachment proceedings against the chief justice should be dealt with rapidly and according to due process of the law. Bar associations and judges should address the issue of integrity while maintaining high standards themselves. Support for the judiciary from the executive and the legislature must be ensured while guarding against bias, and the perception of bias, in court proceedings and in the selection of judges. Strict discipline of the lower judiciary must be ensured through an independent judicial service commission.

Election abuses spark reforms

The Sri Lankan constitution provides for an election commission whose powers are limited to issuing written orders. Following a constitutional amendment in 2001, designed to distance the commission from executive influence, the power to select appointees was taken away from the president and given to a constitutional council whose selections, nevertheless, have to be endorsed by the president. The failure of the president to endorse such nominees created a lacuna in combating electoral corruption and the responsibility to oversee the elections fell to the election commissioner – an office ill-equipped to deal with the widespread electoral abuse in Sri Lanka.

A civil society initiative, the Programme for the Protection of Public Resources (PPPR),[4] sought to monitor the abuse of public resources in the 2004 elections through gathering information from the political parties, media scrutiny and the use of investigative teams. The PPPR published weekly reports containing the names of abusers and details of their abuses.

The findings of the PPPR highlighted the election commissioner's inability to address electoral abuse over a wide range of areas, but particularly his failure to prevent the abuse of the state's electronic media by the incumbent party, the United People's Freedom Alliance (UPFA).

In their survey of the state electronic media, PPPR found that a large number of special programmes were broadcast to promote the election of the UPFA. These programmes criticised the main opposition party and did not feature opposing opinions. News bulletins also predominantly supported the UPFA. Sri Lanka Rupavahini Corporation (SLRC), the main state television channel, carried 101 news items favouring the UPFA, while presenting only one unfavourable news item. In contrast, there were only 22 positive news items about the main opposition party, the United National Front (UNF), and 46 negative ones. Air time granted to political parties free of charge was also abused. For example, the president, who was leading the election campaign for the UPFA, made a 28-minute speech billed as an 'address to the nation' which contained criticism of the other parties and their policies. Discussion programmes were also found to be highly biased in favour of the UPFA, though the boycott of such programmes by the UNF should be taken as a contributing factor here.

Prior to the election campaign, the election commissioner had introduced guidelines[5] to ensure balanced reporting in the media and to give equal air time to all political parties. Once it became clear that the state electronic media had violated these guidelines, the election commissioner utilised his powers under the law to appoint a competent authority to oversee these media organisations. Not only did the state media challenge the powers of the competent authority, but they also ignored its directives not to air certain programmes.

Beyond abuse of the state media, the PPPR received reports of 555 state vehicles utilised for election work, mainly by the UNF, and found evidence substantiating 129 of these cases. Public facilities and buildings, including the presidential residence, were used free-of-charge for publicity work of the UPFA. A number of government employees were released from certain state duties to enable them to support certain candidates in their political activities. There were also reports of emergency aid received by the state being distributed by politicians to win favour with voters.

Anushika Amarasinghe (TI Sri Lanka)

Further reading

Institute of Human Rights and Transparency International Sri Lanka, *Final Report on Misuse of Public Resources* (Colombo: Vishvalekha Printers, 2004)

Marga Institute, *A System under Siege: An Inquiry into the Judicial System of Sri Lanka* (Colombo: Rasanjala, 2002)

Victor Ivan, *An Unfinished Struggle – An Investigative Exposure of Sri Lankan Judiciary and the Chief Justice* (Colombo: Ravaya Publication, 2003)

TI Sri Lanka: www.tisrilanka.org

Notes

1. Transparency International, *Corruption in South Asia* (2002).
2. Marga Institute, *A System under Siege: An Inquiry into the Judicial System of Sri Lanka* (Colombo: Rasanjala, 2002).
3. See www.thesundayleader.lk/20031109/spotlight-2.htm
4. PPPR is a joint project of Transparency International Sri Lanka, the Institute of Human Rights, and the Centre for Monitoring Election Violence.
5. *Daily Mirror* (Sri Lanka), 10 March 2004.

Turkey

Corruption Perceptions Index 2004 score: 3.2 (77th out of 146 countries)

Conventions:
Council of Europe Civil Law Convention on Corruption (ratified September 2003)
Council of Europe Criminal Law Convention on Corruption (ratified March 2004)
OECD Anti-Bribery Convention (ratified July 2000)
UN Convention against Corruption (signed December 2003; not yet ratified)
UN Convention against Transnational Organized Crime (ratified March 2003)

Legal and institutional changes

- At the time of writing a draft **anti-corruption law** was being reviewed in parliamentary committees. It was prepared by the ministry of justice and, if passed, would alter existing laws regarding the prosecution of corruption offences. The draft law lists all those activities that are to be considered corruption offences and the procedures to be followed in their prosecution. It also extends the statute of limitations and revises a host of other related legislation such as the criminal code, the tax code and drug enforcement laws. It also contains provisions covering paying reparations and damages, whistleblower protection and the training of civil servants. The draft legislation features a temporary clause allowing bank owners who have illegally siphoned deposited funds for personal use to avoid incarceration by repaying their depositors directly, rather than the burden being placed on the state. Unlike anti-corruption laws in other countries, it would not establish an independent entity dedicated to fighting corruption.

- A new law that came into force in August 2003 criminalises **false reporting by banks**, including misreporting deposit amounts. This piece of legislation is known as the Uzan Law, named after the family that owns the Imar Bank. Under the new law, the state assumed control of the bank, which was involved in Turkey's largest ever banking scandal (see below).

- Moving towards greater public transparency, a new **access to information law** was approved by parliament in October 2003. The law is designed to increase transparency in public management and allows citizens access to information about public activities. The law came into force with the passing of regulations in April 2004. Definitions of state and commercial secrets are noticeably absent from the new law.

- Public pressure led to the introduction of a **public procurement law** in January 2002. However, the current administration used its majority in parliament to reverse many of the provisions of the reform with an amendment law passed in July 2003. Powerful interest groups, including government entities, continue to lobby for exclusion from its provisions.

- A **law establishing a public servants ethics commission** was passed by parliament in May 2004. The law fails to set out any aims, definitions or guiding principles. In addition, the law states that the president, members of parliament and the cabinet of ministers are not subject to the articles of the law.

Banks siphon funds from public accounts

A recurring focus of scandal since the late 1990s has been the illicit use by bank owners and high-level managers of public accounts, with money being transferred to external companies or their personal accounts – sometimes out of the country – or used unethically to obtain credit.

The largest and most organised of these skimming operations was exposed in July 2003. It involved the Uzan family, who in addition to the Imar Bank owned a national daily newspaper and two national television stations and who operated electrical companies which they leased from the state. The family used their media outlets to support political candidates and to undercut their business rivals. One of the family's sons

won a significant share of the vote in the November 2002 election, but did not break the 10 per cent threshold that would have admitted him to parliament.

In mid-2003, following an investigation by the Banking Supervisory and Regulation Agency (BDDK), the government took over the management of Imar Bank. The BDDK inspectors found a huge discrepancy between registered deposits and money actually deposited by the public. The hidden deposits in the Imar Bank case amounted to US $5.7 billion, 90 per cent of the deposits collected.[1]

The consequent public outrage led to the rapid drafting of the so-called 'Uzan Law' in August 2003. This law amended the banking code so that misreporting deposits would be classified as a crime. Banking regulations were further tightened with parliament's enacting in December 2003 a law to improve the supervision of banks. The law ostensibly forces banking groups to reach remuneration settlements with the government in the case of banks siphoning money, though the difficulty of recovering funds transferred out of the country leaves a big question mark over the efficacy of this legislation.

In the past seven years the state has been obliged to take over 22 banks whose owners and senior officials are on trial for embezzlement, involving a cost to the Turkish taxpayers of US $42 billion.[2]

Claims of corruption and bribery in the judiciary

In January 2004 events surrounding financial irregularities in Turkish medical services and judicial corruption dating back more than a year finally came to light. In early 2003 a legal investigation into medical procurement programmes in which pharmaceutical companies had allegedly been bribing doctors and hospital managers to use and prescribe specific brands resulted in numerous arrests. The owners of the pharmaceutical companies were arrested first, followed several months later by a raft of medical professionals and hospital administrators.

Allegations of judicial corruption subsequently arose over the release of a number of the accused pharmaceutical company owners after a brief time in custody. A very low bail was set, and their release was processed even though it was a weekend and the court was not in session.

Following widespread public criticism, investigations were launched that revealed that the Edin family, one of whom who had owned a pharmaceutical company implicated in the procurement affair, had allegedly used a group of lawyers to bribe high-level justice officials to obtain the release of family members that had been arrested.[3] These allegations were substantiated by taped telephone conversations which allegedly confirmed the payment of bribes. Consequently, lawyers and others were arrested along with members of the Edin family – all of whom were later released on bail.[4]

Despite such high-profile cases indicating the depth of corruption within the judiciary in Turkey, there is little indication that reform will be forthcoming. The chief prosecutor of the high court opined that if there were bad apples, they should remove themselves. The impact of such statements was, unsurprisingly, limited and at the time of writing there had been no new developments in the Edin case or sanctions against other corrupt judges.

Ercis Kurtulus (TI Turkey)

Further reading

Selçuk Cingi, Umur Tosun and Cahit Güran, *Yolsuzluk ve Etkin Devlet* (Corruption and Effective Government) (Ankara: Ankara Chambers of Commerce Publication, 2002)

Fikret Adaman, Ali Çarkoğlu and Burhan Şenatalar, *Survey: Causes and Recommendations for the Prevention of Corruption from a Business Perspective* (Istanbul: TESEV Publications, 2003)

Kemal Özsemerci, *Türk Kamu Yönetiminde Yolsuzluklar: Nedenleri, Zararları ve çözüm önerileri* (Corruption in Turkey's Public Administration: Causes, Effects and Recommended Solutions) (High Audit Court Publications, 2003)

Tuncay Özkan, 'Yeniden Yapılandırırken Yolsuzluk Mücadelesi' (Anti-corruption and restructuring) (Aksam: 2003)

TI Turkey: www.saydamlik.org

Notes

1. *Financial Times* (Britain), 6 October 2003.
2. Ibid.
3. *Hurriyet* (Turkey), 12 July 2003.
4. *Vatan* (Turkey), 17 January 2004.

Vanuatu

Corruption Perceptions Index 2004 score: not surveyed

Conventions:
UN Convention against Corruption (not yet signed)
UN Convention against Transnational Organized Crime (not yet signed)

Legal and institutional changes

- The Public Prosecutor Act was passed in August 2003, establishing the **Office of the Public Prosecutor** and its functions. Previously, the public prosecutor functioned under constitutional powers only, and there was no legislatively established office. The new law should help ensure that staff are appointed on merit and that the office remains independent. The law also requires the public prosecutor to develop a procedural manual and a code of ethics.

- One legislative trend was the passage of laws aimed at ensuring that **managers of statutory authorities are correctly appointed**. Revisions to the Broadcasting and Television Act, which came into effect in September 2003, now require the general manager of the Vanuatu Broadcasting and Television Corporation to have primary competence and experience in management, with secondary competence if possible, in broadcasting, finance, law or journalism. The Chamber of Commerce and Industry of Vanuatu Act was amended in January 2004 to state explicitly that the general manager must be appointed on merit. On the same day, the Vanuatu National Provident Fund Act was amended to the same effect.

- In December 2003 an amendment to the Vanuatu Commodities Marketing Board (VCMB) Act **increased the powers** of the VCMB. Previously, only the VCMB and its agents were permitted to export prescribed commodities. The amendment means that the VCMB now also controls the purchase of prescribed commodities within Vanuatu. In the past, the VCMB has been the subject of several Ombudsman's reports, and there have been allegations of political interference and mismanagement. Any increase in its powers could, therefore, increase the potential for corruption, although the amendment also increased its reporting requirements.

The re-election of Barak Sope

In mid-2002 Barak Sope was sentenced to three years' imprisonment for forging government guarantees while holding the office of prime minister.[1] Sope had provided government guarantees to two private companies – one for US $5 million and the other for US $18 million – to enable them to procure loans, but he did not follow proper procedures, thus rendering them worthless. The supreme court ruled that

Sope had been fully aware he was creating false documents. Since Sope was a member of parliament at the time, he was stripped of his seat. Later that year, after President John Bani pardoned Sope on the grounds of poor health, he appealed against the loss of his constituency. In early 2003 the supreme court rejected Sope's challenge, but ruled that the pardon allowed Sope to run in a by-election.[2] The election was held in November 2003 with Sope standing for the party he leads, the Melanesian Progressive Party. His main rival was Foster Rakom of Vanua'aku Pati, a party generally perceived as free of corruption. Voter turnout was low at 46 per cent, but Sope was re-elected by a comfortable margin.

The result highlighted the nature of voter choices in Vanuatu and the apparent lack of opposition to crimes of corruption. The issue has been raised in the past when voters re-elected politicians who were the subject of ombudsman's reports on corrupt practices. There are a number of explanations as to why voters re-elected Sope. One is that voters did not really understand why Sope was wrong in his actions. Some voters considered his actions to be related to him not 'following the rules' within a 'white man's system'.[3] Media reports that indicated that 'jailing has increased [Sope's] popularity among local ni-Vanuatu, who regard him as strong on land issues and Vanuatu nationalism' support this explanation.[4]

But another explanation is that voters do not perceive the relevance of the political system to their lives and are indifferent to parliamentarians' behaviour. The most they expect is a little money in exchange for their votes, rather than any improvement in services. Related to this is the cultural expectation that 'big men' are not questioned in public, which acts as a further check on criticism.[5] While these explanations are only hypotheses, there are clearly fundamental problems in public attitudes to corruption and the relationship between the electorate and the political system in Vanuatu.

Presidential election

In March 2004 President John Bani's term expired and Alfred Maseng Nalo was elected in his place. It soon came to light that Nalo was a convicted criminal and, at the time of his election, was serving a two-year suspended sentence for aiding and abetting, misappropriation and receiving property dishonestly after money went missing following sales of cocoa. Nalo was acting as an agent for the VCMB at the time. The conviction would automatically have disqualified Nalo as a candidate, but the electoral commission, which is responsible for conducting background checks, did not detect it because the certificate of previous offences, issued by the police, had allegedly been filled out incorrectly.[6]

Nalo refused to step down, forcing the government to take the issue to court. In May the supreme court ordered Nalo's removal from the presidency, a decision later confirmed by the court of appeal. Until a new president can be appointed, the speaker of parliament has taken on the role of acting president, in accordance with the constitution.

While a number of chiefs, NGOs and political leaders called on Nalo to resign, he appeared not to accept blame for making a false declaration. Indeed, the blame tended to fall on the police, the electoral commission and the prime minister who, according to some critics, bore ultimate responsibility for ensuring that only suitable candidates stand for election.[7] What is certain, however, is that the public does not appear to decry Nalo for any wrongdoing. There was even a public perception that, as president, Nalo could legally use his powers to pardon himself.

Changes of government

Vanuatu experienced two major changes of government in 2003–04. In November 2003 there was a change of coalition. Then, in the May 2004 parliamentary session, it appeared that a no-confidence motion would succeed in removing Prime Minister Edward Natapei and the Vanua'aku Pati from government. To avoid this Natapei persuaded the acting president to dissolve parliament. Critics considered the dissolution a misuse of power and a ploy to remain in office, though the government claimed it was done in the interests of stability. New elections were due to be held on 6 July.

Instability is a long-term feature of politics in Vanuatu, and is perceived to arise because of the abuse of power for personal advantage by individual members of parliament. It is common for members to cross the floor of parliament because a new party can offer more personal benefits than their old one. Legitimate reasons for crossing the floor, such as fundamental disagreements about policy, are rarely the motive for such defections.

The lack of continuous government also contributes to corruption. A recent review of the national integrity system indicated that frequent changes of government in Vanuatu perpetuate institutional weaknesses, creating an environment in which corruption flourishes. Parliament's public accounts committee, which is responsible for examining audit documents, is particularly vulnerable to disruption after frequent changes in government.

The main weakness of the civil service is that it is not clearly separate from the executive. Changes in the executive lead to changes in the civil service, with appointments often based on family, business or political connections rather than merit. Similarly, appointments to the boards of statutory bodies are usually made at the discretion of a particular minister and, as ministers change, so do the boards. Appointments are often seen as patronage for political supporters. One notable example of mismanagement due to politicisation was the VCMB's decision in 2001 to pay higher crop prices to farmers than they could actually sell it for. The decision was widely seen as a ploy to ensure popularity for the UMP government in an upcoming election.

Frequent changes of government are indicative of, and contribute to, wider systemic issues relating to public understanding of the role and operation of the political system. There is a growing perception that political leaders take as much as they can because they think that they will only be in power for a short time. It is possible that further regulation could be developed to inject more stability into Vanuatu's system of government but, given the wider systemic issues, such measures are unlikely to be entirely successful. Instead education to develop public expectations of parliament, and to train parliamentarians and party members on their roles within a functioning democracy, is necessary. These issues cut to the core of corruption, since they involve the development of both political will to act within the bounds of power, and public will to ensure that leaders do so.

Vanuatu Maritime Authority

The Vanuatu Maritime Authority (VMA) was established in 1998 with the primary aim of regulating and promoting the maritime industry. There have been rumours of political interference and mismanagement for some time, but their potential increased when the composition of the VMA was altered in 2002. Initially the VMA consisted of one ministerial appointee, and a number of senior civil servants, including the attorney general, the financial services commissioner, the commissioner for maritime affairs and several director generals. The Vanuatu Maritime Authority (Amendment) Act 2002 altered this so that the VMA is now entirely appointed by the incumbent minister.

This change in composition led to a number of changes in VMA's management. The commissioner for maritime affairs, John Roosen, left in April 2003, followed two months later by Marie Noelle Patterson, the former Vanuatu ombudsman and current president of TI Vanuatu, whose position as corporate director was terminated. Both had been critical of changes to the composition of the VMA including the appointment as chair of Christopher Emelee, who as manager of the Tuna Fishing Agency faced a conflict of interest. In August 2003 Timbaci Bani, the VMA's acting commissioner and Roosen's former counterpart, was suspended reportedly for resisting efforts by the new board members to prevent their rivals from sailing and favouring their friends and allies.[8] Bani was initially replaced by Donald Hosea, who admitted misappropriating VMA money in early 2002, and was removed from the post.

As a result of continued reporting of the VMA story in the *Vanuatu Daily Post*, publisher Marc Neil-Jones was assaulted outside its office in September 2003. The following day Emelee's lawyer filed for an injunction in the magistrate's court to prevent the *Vanuatu Daily Post* from publishing anything about the VMA or Emelee and his family. A court initially granted this injunction, but the supreme court overturned the decision several days later.

The VMA saga appears to demonstrate numerous aspects of political interference, although prior to the dissolution of parliament it appeared that the government might be taking steps to rectify problems. Emelee was removed as chair, and the post of commissioner was advertised to allow for a politically neutral appointment. However, the future of the VMA appears to depend on the outcome of the next election, and whether the next minister responsible for the body resists political interference.

Anita Jowitt (University of the South Pacific)

Further reading

Anita Jowitt and Tess Newton Cain, *National Integrity Systems, TI International Country Study Report: Vanuatu* (Transparency International, 2004), www.transparency.org.au/nispac/vanuatu.pdf

Notes

1. *Public Prosecutor* v. *Sope Maautamate* [2002] VUSC 46. www.paclii.org
2. Details of the supreme court and court of appeal decisions can be found in *Sope Maautamate* v. *Speaker of Parliament* [2003] VUCA 5. www.paclii.org
3. Immediately after Sope's imprisonment there were calls for him to be pardoned – and threats of protests if he were not – on the grounds that the trial had been an example of 'neo-colonialism', and that Sope had been victimised by Australia and New Zealand. See Pacific Islands Report, 24, 25 and 30 July 2004. A recent TI study on Vanuatu's National Integrity System indicates that one of the major contributors to a lack of public outrage in response to corruption by leaders is the lack of personal connection to events within the political system. (Anita Jowitt and Tess Newton Cain, *National Integrity Systems, TI International Country Study Report: Vanuatu*, TI, 2004).
4. *Vanuatu Trading Post*, 14 January 2003.
5. Jowitt and Cain, *Country Study Report: Vanuatu*.
6. Port Vila Presse Online, 28 April 2004, www.news.vu/en/news/national/nalo-election.shtml
7. *Vanuatu Daily Post*, 23 April 2004.
8. *Vanuatu Daily Post*, 19 August 2003.

Vietnam

Corruption Perceptions Index 2004 score: 2.6 (102nd out of 146 countries)

Conventions:
UN Convention against Corruption (signed December 2003; not yet ratified)
UN Convention against Transnational Organized Crime (signed December 2000; not yet ratified)

Legal and institutional changes

- In March 2004 the standing committee of the national assembly issued a resolution calling on candidates in the April 2004 elections to **declare their assets**. Candidates were asked to declare their land and property. They were also required to declare their business activities, including fixed and liquid assets, and any items worth more than VND 50 million (US $3,250).

- In a major step towards improving corporate governance, the government issued a decree in March 2004 that strengthens regulations pertaining to the provision of independent auditing services. There were few regulations governing the **standards and activities of auditors** prior to the issuance of this decree.

- In April 2004 the State Bank of Vietnam (SBV) submitted to the government a draft decree aimed at combating **money laundering** and the financing of terrorism. According to the SBV's inspection department, the decree will provide guidance for setting up systems for the detection and reporting of suspicious transactions. The draft decree also stipulates possible sanctions against money laundering.[1]

- The national assembly has passed a new **inspection law** designed to increase the effectiveness of the official investigative agencies in their efforts to prevent and detect corruption. The law, which passed in May 2004, includes regulations on the function, rights and powers of inspectors.

The Nam Cam affair

The Communist Party of Vietnam has long been aware that the erosion of its probity is the most serious threat to its maintenance of popular support and legitimacy. General Secretary Nong Duc Manh, who came to office in April 2001, has repeatedly affirmed the determination of the party and state to tackle corruption. His predecessor, Le Kha Phieu, staked his reputation on a similar campaign, but failed to maintain the momentum. Manh has adopted much tougher anti-corruption rhetoric and is adamant that harsh penalties will be handed down to make examples of wrongdoers.

An opportunity to prove the seriousness of the anti-corruption drive arose in a high-profile case that centred on the activities of the Ho Chi Minh City gang leader, Truong Van Cam, also known as Nam Cam. After a highly publicised three-month trial, which involved 155 defendants in three courtrooms, Nam Cam was found guilty in June 2003 of bribery and ordering a rival's murder. He was executed in June 2004. Although it was notable that a figure as well connected as Nam Cam was convicted, it was also significant that a number of prominent government figures were also found guilty, either for turning a blind eye to organised crime or helping Nam Cam to avoid prison on previous occasions. (A special police force from neighbouring Tien Giang provinces was brought in to arrest Nam Cam, because the Ho Chi Minh City police had been so corrupted by his network.) Tran Mai Hanh, a former central committee member and director of state radio, was sentenced to 10 years in prison; Pham Sy Chien, a former deputy state prosecutor, received a six-year sentence; and Bui Quoc Huy, a former deputy minister for public security and central committee member, was sentenced to four years. The outcome of the trial was hardly surprising. Vietnamese lawyers commented that the trial was closely monitored and guidance provided to the court by the relevant party committee. The appeals of three senior officials found guilty of accepting bribes and failing to perform their duties were refused in October 2003.

The outcome of the trial sent a warning to other senior officials that they were not beyond the reach of the law. In a widely reported speech to the national assembly in mid-2003, Deputy Prime Minister Nguyen Tan Dung said the government would 'severely punish every corrupt official, without exception'.[2] This determination presents the leadership with a double-edged dilemma: the more evidence the party produces that it is rooting out corruption from its own ranks, the more it undermines its legitimacy. Failing to act, however, would similarly reinforce the perception that corruption is rampant. The authorities are likely therefore to continue to make an example of prominent figures who are found guilty, promoting such cases as evidence that the party is making headway in the fight against corruption. To avoid any major damage to the party's image, however, investigations will probably remain selective, rather than extensive.

With tight state control over the media, there is little independent investigation into the wrongdoing of senior officials. Indeed, in spite of the high number of officials implicated in the Nam Cam scandal and the unusual degree of media coverage allowed, there are still doubts as to the thoroughness of the investigation. Soon after the trial ended, Nguyen Khoa Diem, head of the party's ideology and culture commission, announced that the media could no longer report freely on the scandal. He also stated that the media must not 'reveal secrets, create internal division or obstruct the key role of propaganda'.[3]

Ministers are being held to account for wrongdoing

The national assembly has been gradually shedding its reputation as a rubber stamp for the party by displaying a greater determination to hold senior officials accountable for their actions.

In June 2004 deputies voted to oust minister of agriculture and rural development Le Huy Ngo for failing to prevent the corruption scandal surrounding the operations of a state-run investment and marketing company affiliated with the ministry. (The company's former director, La Thi Kim Oanh, was sentenced to death in December 2003 for misappropriating US $4.7 million. Two former deputy ministers, Nguyen Thien Luan and Nguyen Quang Ha, were given suspended sentences of three years for their part in the scandal.[4]) Ngo offered to resign, but Prime Minister Phan Van Khai proposed that the minister be relieved of his responsibilities by the legislature.

The tenure of post and telecommunications minister Do Trung Ta may also end prematurely after allegations of wrongdoing in the management of the state-owned conglomerate, Vietnam Posts and Telecommunications Corporation (VNPT). Following an investigation that started in late 2003, the state inspectorate accused VNPT officials in May 2004 of widespread violations in the methods used to award contracts over the previous five years. The inspectorate called for the dismissal of four senior executives: VNPT's deputy general director; the head of its marketing and pricing department; and the director and deputy director of VNPT's cell phone network.

Also under the spotlight is the decision to renegotiate the profit-sharing arrangements in a contract with VNPT's mobile phone partner, Sweden's Comvik International Vietnam. According to local media reports, the new arrangement may have deprived the government of around US $45 million in revenue. The telecommunications minister was chairman of VNPT's board when the contract with Comvik was agreed, and may suffer the same fate as Le Huy Ngo should he be implicated in wrongdoing. Prime Minister Khai set up an interministerial group to investigate the matter further, but by the time of writing the group had not reported its findings.

Administrative reforms curtail opportunities for graft

Much of the focus of the crackdown on corruption has been on punishing prominent offenders, but efforts are also being made to reduce the opportunities for more junior officials to abuse their positions in order to boost their income. The government is near the middle of the 2001–10 Public Administration Reform Master Programme, which aims to improve the delivery of administrative services at provincial, district and commune levels. The most notable initiative in terms of limiting the opportunities for graft is the expansion of the 'One-Stop Shop' (OSS) network. OSSs are central to the government's efforts to improve service delivery through the creation of single agencies that deal with applications for a range of activities, including construction permits, land-use rights certificates, business registrations, and approvals for local and foreign investment projects.[5]

In September 2003 the government announced that it intended OSSs to be established at provincial and district levels in all of Vietnam's 64 cities and provinces by the end of 2004, and to be developed at the commune level from January 2005. Despite teething problems, the expansion of the OSS network reflects a genuine attempt to improve the state's administrative capabilities. The transparency of administrative procedures has also improved since OSS publish details of their services and fees, thereby limiting the opportunities for officials to demand additional payments.

There are concerns, however, that the pace of legal reform has not kept up with administrative reforms. Recent amendments to the Law on Citizens' Complaints and Denunciations focused on increasing the roles and responsibilities of officials in the administrative courts overseeing cases, but did not expand the review and enforcement powers given to the courts. As it stands, courts are only permitted to consider decisions that violate or exceed legal regulations, but they lack the jurisdiction to consider administrative bias or enforce decisions against recalcitrant officials.

Local and foreign investors are also still discouraged by the burdensome red tape and the overlapping of government approvals that provide officials with opportunities to line their own pockets. The results of a survey of business sentiment were revealed at the Vietnam Business Forum in December 2003. Of the 143 foreign and local firms that responded, 54 per cent complained that bureaucracy and corruption were their biggest hindrances.[6] Similar findings emerged from a 2004 survey by Hong Kong's Political and Economic Risk Consultancy of expatriate businessmen and women, and their perceptions of corruption in 12 Asian countries. Vietnam was ranked behind Indonesia and India (Bangladesh was not included) as the third most corrupt nation in the region, with a score of 8.67 (on a scale of 0 to 10, with 10 reflecting the worst case).[7]

Further initiatives aimed at improving investor confidence and tackling corruption are in the pipeline. Deputy Prime Minister Nguyen Tan Dung has stated his commitment to implementing a range of measures including: developing a legal framework that includes policies on public finance management; setting up an independent judicial system; reforming public sector salaries; and opening forums for the media and the public to offer opinions on the management of public investment projects.[8]

The implementation of such measures is long overdue. Given the Communist Party's determination to retain control, however, it is unlikely that the pace of change will match up to the expectations of foreign investors and donors.

Danny Richards (Economist Intelligence Unit, Britain)

Further reading

World Bank, 'Vietnam – Combating Corruption' (2000), www.worldbank.org.vn/publication/pub_pdf/anticorup_e.pdf

Tim Lindsey and Howard Dick, eds, *Corruption in Asia – Part III, Vietnam* (New South Wales: Federation Press, 2002)

Notes

1. Agence France-Presse (France), 26 April 2004.
2. Reuters (Britain), 2 June 2003.
3. Reporters Sans Frontières, Vietnam – 2003 Annual Report, www.rsf.org/article.php3?id_article=6491
4. VietnamNet online, 2 January 2004.
5. For an evaluation of the One-Stop Shop mechanism see 'One-Stop Shops in Vietnam', Swiss Agency for Development and Cooperation, July 2003, www.deza.ch/ressources/product_7_en_625.pdf
6. Reuters (Britain), 1 December 2003.
7. See www.asiarisk.com
8. Vietnam News Agency (Vietnam), 1 April 2004.

Zimbabwe

Corruption Perceptions Index 2004 score: 2.3 (114th out of 146 countries)

Conventions:
AU Convention on the Prevention and Combating of Corruption (signed November 2003; not yet ratified)
UN Convention against Corruption (signed February 2004; not yet ratified)
UN Convention against Transnational Organized Crime (signed December 2000; not yet ratified)

Legal and institutional changes

- In January 2004 the legislature enacted the Bank Use Promotion and **Suppression of Money Laundering** Act which came into operation a month later. The legislation is intended to promote the use of the banking system; to limit its abuse for the purpose of money laundering; and to aid the identification and confiscation of the proceeds of serious crime. The act, drafted in reaction to the crisis caused by a shortage of bank notes in 2003, provides for the creation of a unit in the Reserve Bank whose mandate is the detection and investigation of money laundering in the financial system. The inspectors will have general investigating powers and may seize property and enter premises in connection with their enquiries, but they must refer their findings to the relevant law-enforcement authorities.

- The **Criminal Procedure and Evidence Amendment Act**, passed in June 2004, gave police the power to detain suspects for 21 days without charge. Ostensibly part of a package of anti-corruption measures, the act targets the unlawful possession of precious metals or stones, money laundering, the contravention of exchange control regulations, and unlawful dealing in grain. The presumption of innocence is eliminated by the new law and judicial officers have been divested of their discretion to grant bail to those covered by the law. The provisions seem calculated to augment the provisions of the much-criticised Public Order and Security Act, and the potential for abuse by police, political officials, judges and others is enormous. When the bill first came before parliament on 22 June, a number of legislators from the ruling ZANU (PF) party walked out.[1] At the time of writing the legislation was awaiting presidential assent.

- The **Anti-Corruption Commission Bill** was introduced to parliament in April 2004 and passed in June. At the time of writing it was awaiting presidential approval. The bill provides for the establishment of an anti-corruption commission and confers upon it powers to investigate suspected cases of economic crime. Legislation on an independent anti-corruption commission has long been a priority advocacy issue for civil society and the private and public sectors in Zimbabwe. The constitution was amended as early as 1999 to provide for the creation of such a commission.

- A new ministry of special affairs in the president's office responsible for anti-corruption and anti-monopolies was created in February 2004 with a mandate to deal with issues of corruption and **abuses of power**. However, the creation of the new ministry was considered a non-event since adequate entities to fight corruption already existed within the executive. What was always missing was the political will to enforce the existing laws and provisions against corruption and other improprieties.

- A Zimbabwean chapter of the **African Parliamentarians' Network Against Corruption** was launched in November 2003. The chapter has already been instrumental in presenting anti-corruption strategies to parliament on behalf of civil society.

Anti-corruption drive?

Zimbabwe's economy has been persistently stripped of its assets by corruption in the private and public sectors. Over the past year this has been driven in large part by the chaotic land reform process that led to the virtual collapse of the agricultural economy. This in turn precipitated a chain reaction as Zimbabwe ran out of basic commodities such as fuel, foreign currency and foodstuffs. With an inadequate legal infrastructure to contain the problem within formal structures, the result has been a parallel, informal market that is a haven of corrupt practices. Substantial amounts of local and foreign currency have been externalised illegally. Observations on the ground suggest that corruption has drastically increased over the past year and it is being held officially responsible for the socio-economic conditions that have bedevilled Zimbabwe since the late 1990s. Hyperinflationary pressures, foreign exchange shortages, the proliferation of black markets for basic items and rising poverty levels are in part the symptoms of corrupt business practices, though both they and the corruption are largely the result of financial and political mismanagement.

The unveiling of a new monetary policy by the new governor of the Reserve Bank of Zimbabwe in December 2003 may be a turning point. The governor made a number of recommendations to address irregularities in the banking system. Over the following months, a number of business executives were arrested or placed on the wanted list for crimes ranging from theft and fraud to corruption and the flouting of exchange regulations. Among those detained were James Makamba of the ruling party's central committee and Chris Kuruneri, the then finance minister. At the time of writing, both cases were still being heard in the courts. President Robert Mugabe has declared that anyone involved in corrupt activity will be dealt with severely, though critics say his anti-corruption drive is selective and forms part of his political campaign in the run-up to the 2005 general elections.

The Bank Use and Suppression of Money Laundering Act seeks to promote the use of banking and simultaneously to introduce measures to suppress its abuse by money launderers. Unlike money launderers themselves, the measures are limited to the banking sector. Nevertheless, the new law is a fundamentally positive step since no other piece of legislation explicitly deals with money laundering in Zimbabwe and there have been widespread complaints from law enforcement agencies, legal practitioners, judicial officers and the private and public sectors. The law creates a financial intelligence unit and provides it with an opportunity to acquire the relevant level of specialisation regarding the detection and investigation of money laundering cases. It also has a mandate to train other institutions on how to identify and prevent money laundering. The Reserve Bank is in a better position to attract qualified personnel than the government where one of the major causes of high staff turnover is poor remuneration.

However, the nomination process for the unit's inspectors, who may be recruited from the Reserve Bank, the ministry of finance and the revenue authority, is likely to cause conflict of interest. The officers will come from different departments with different interests and operational methods. One clear problem is that the minister responsible is a political appointee, while both the governor of the Reserve Bank and the commissioner general of the revenue authority are more independent. Another shortcoming is the investigators' lack of extensive powers to investigate or arrest suspects. To carry out their mandate effectively, inspectors will need powers at least equal to the police, rather than the current situation in which they must refer their findings to them, with all the bureaucracy that inevitably entails. Lengthy reporting procedures can only work against the tracking of funds that can be transferred elsewhere at the click of a mouse.

The passing of the Anti-corruption Commission Bill in June 2004 was a response to the SADC Protocol against Corruption of 2001 to which Zimbabwe is a signatory. The preamble specifically refers to the protocol as a basis for enacting the new legislation and it is hoped that the commission will draw on the experiences of other countries in the region where similar institutions already exist. However, the bill requires strengthening in several respects.

First, the independence of the commission is crucial to discharging its mandate. The commission must not be controlled by the executive. The appointment of commissioners and other key officers should not be the prerogative of the government alone, and should involve a more prominent role for parliament.

The commission also requires that extensive powers of investigation, arrest, search and seizure should be conferred on its officers. It should be borne in mind that the commission was created to ensure the existence of a specialised unit to deal with corruption because of the failure of other law enforcement agencies to tackle such issues effectively. To give those same agencies the power to make crucial decisions on the commission's anti-corruption enquiries is both retrogressive and counterproductive.

Further shortcomings include the lack of provision for penalising persons who obstruct officers in the execution of their duties, or those who provide false information; the recruitment of Zimbabwean citizens only; and restricting officers to men or women who are over 40 years old. Senior officers in the new commission, such as the chairperson, his or her deputy, commissioners and officers also remain vulnerable to legal action under the wording of the legislation, which also fails to make provision for the protection of informants and whistleblowers.

Rampant disregard of ethics

Zimbabwe witnessed an unprecedented onslaught on its national integrity systems during 2003–04. Critical shortages of basic commodities, such as fuel, basic food stuffs, foreign currency and bank notes, added significantly to the 'culture of corruption'. The worsening economic crisis played a fundamental role, but there was no serious consultation between the government and other stakeholders to resolve the crisis.

The most regrettable development is that almost everyone from every section of society was involved, voluntarily or involuntarily, actively or passively, in some form of corrupt activity. Most people had little choice but to obtain basic commodities on the illegal parallel market. The same scenario applied to the availability of foreign currency, as reflected by the large number of cases that came before the courts in 2003–04. Most businesses and banks traded foreign currency on the black market, and even state institutions did so.

New types of business flourished while the rest of the economy went down. Banks declared 'super' profits and the profession of asset management became suddenly attractive. It was only after December 2003 that it came to light, following the announcement of the new monetary policy by the Reserve Bank, that most banks and asset management firms were not as sound as they had conveyed to the public. Most asset management firms were revealed to be shams calculated to defraud unsuspecting members of the public.[2]

There is now a crucial need for the country to begin rebuilding confidence by sending a clear message that corruption will be dealt with severely. What has always been lacking is the political will. The reason for the apparent change of attitude by the government is, however, subject to conjecture. One view is that the current anti-corruption drive is genuine, as demonstrated by the number of cases in the courts, but many observers believe it is merely cosmetic and intended to sway public opinion ahead of the 2005 general elections.

A further dimension to the argument is that the recent revelations by the new governor of the central bank presented the government with an opportunity to blame the current economic turmoil on corruption, rather than on the failure of its own policies. Regardless of the motive, however, most Zimbabweans hope the initiative will go beyond the general elections and any possible change of political leadership.

The regulation of asset management firms, banks and money transfer agencies is now the domain of the Reserve Bank, and requirements have been made much more stringent to ensure that only persons of good business repute, and entities with adequate resources and buffer funds to provide client security, are registered.[3]

There have been positive signs at last that there is political will to fight the endemic problem of corruption in Zimbabwe and that the government may be yielding to recommendations from civil society and the private sector on appropriate anti-corruption strategies. Demand for anti-corruption information is also on the rise across Zimbabwe as citizens become more questioning about the shortages of basic commodities, foreign currency and bank notes experienced during the last 12 months.

Idaishe Chengu and Webster Madera (TI Zimbabwe)

Further reading

Constance Kunaka and Noria Mashumba, *Strategies Against Corruption in Southern Africa* (Human Rights Trust of Southern Africa, 2002)

Tulani Sithole and Goodhope Ruswa, *Zimbabwe's Land Reform Programme: An Audit of the Public Perception* (Konrad Adenauer Foundation, 2003)

www.kubatana.net

TI Zimbabwe: www.transparency.org.zw

Notes

1. *Financial Gazette* (Zimbabwe), 24–30 June 2004.
2. Court records show that hundreds of thousands of US dollars were lost to asset managers who took deposits on the pretext of investing money in return for profits. The money was usually converted for personal enrichment.
3. Previously registration was the prerogative of the ministry of finance and economic development. The Reserve Bank only regulated banking.

Part four

Research on corruption

8 Introduction

Robin Hodess[1]

While the 23 research contributions in this year's *Global Corruption Report* represent only a small selection of ongoing work, they demonstrate nevertheless the tremendous progress being made by corruption researchers. It is crucial that these innovative research efforts be made known, both to the anti-corruption stakeholders who can put the findings into practice and to other researchers. What kinds of patterns are emerging from the empirical study of corruption?

Corruption and the poor

Research in the *Global Corruption Report 2005* confirms that corruption adversely affects the poorest within societies, exerting the highest costs on those who can least afford them. Transparency International's own Global Corruption Barometer 2004 (page 239) shows that the poorest perceive the greatest negative impact of corruption on their lives and are most pessimistic about future levels of corruption. The Mexican National Survey on Corruption and Good Governance (page 248) reports that the cost of bribes for the poor is particularly high, while the Kenya Bribery Index (page 245) finds that public services are frequently denied to those who cannot afford to pay bribes. In short, corruption exerts a regressive tax on the poor, particularly when it features in common activities for citizens, from dealing with traffic violations to turning on household utilities.

Corruption and good governance

In debates on policies for good governance, the fight against corruption is seen as central. Sarah Repucci (page 255) reports on a new Freedom House tool – 'Countries at the Crossroads' – that assessed aspects of government performance in 30 countries that were low performers in other Freedom House surveys. A striking finding was that of all the indicators related to governance, governments' transparency and anti-corruption efforts were weakest. This finding underlines the urgent need to assist weaker states in developing integrity systems, a point that drives Transparency International's work.

Much of the research featured in the *Global Corruption Report* focuses on public sector institutions. In Kenya, for instance (page 246), the police rank very poorly, while in the Pacific island states ombudsmen are viewed as ineffective (page 243). In a study on crime victimisation based on surveys in nine Latin American countries, Seligson (page 283) reports that corruption victimisation in the public sector is most prevalent in the education system and in interactions with local government. Budget transparency is a particular focus of recent research, one with a growing research base. Fundar, the Mexican think tank, assessed budget transparency in 10 Latin American countries (page 278), building an index based on their results.

Corruption, crime and trust

A new area of research relevant to policy-making involves the linkage of corruption to other crimes. Azfar (page 285) finds that the higher the rate of corruption, the higher the level of both homicides and theft. Soares (page 289) finds that corruption is also related to the rate of crime reporting – the greater the perceived level of corruption, the less likely it is that crimes will be reported. This has crucial policy implications, since public trust in institutions, especially the police, is central to an effective anti-corruption system. Indeed, Uslaner shows that levels of trust in a society have a substantial impact on corruption (page 262). But the corruption–crime link may prove significant in other ways: those working against corruption may be able to garner further public support for their efforts by making it clear that reducing corruption also reduces crime.

Corruption and the business environment

Several studies assess the link between bribery and the business climate, looking at trade and investment, as well as the likelihood that a firm will pay bribes (Chavis, page 308; Gray and Anderson, page 271). Much of this work points to the high costs of corruption, both for businesses and for the economy as a whole. Uhlenbruck et al. (page 302) examined telecommunications infrastructure projects in developing countries. They found that the more pervasive the corruption, the more likely foreign investment is to be short term in nature. Habib and Zurawicki (page 305) also found that corruption inhibits foreign direct investment, and that businesses seeking to invest abroad find it particularly difficult to win the confidence of potential business partners if they come from countries with a high level of corruption.

Corruption, gender and the environment

Research in this year's report adds to research presented in previous *Global Corruption Reports* on the links between corruption and gender, and corruption and the environment. Sung's research on gender (page 296) confirms other findings (see Mukherjee and Gokcekus in the *Global Corruption Report 2004*) that increasing the proportion of women in government does not reduce corruption. Welsch (page 299) provides results from a study on the relationship between corruption and the environment, concluding that corruption increases pollution, and that the damage is particularly great in low-income countries.

Can we stop corruption?

Given these many harmful effects of corruption, the good news from the research presented here is that the level of corruption can be reduced. A number of research projects seem to indicate – with important exceptions – that the level of corruption has fallen (Kenya Bribery Index 2004, page 245; Mexican National Survey on Corruption and Good Governance, page 248). Gray and Anderson's comparison (page 271) of two major surveys of businesses shows a recent fall in corruption in many transition countries that had been particularly affected by corruption in the 1990s. While these time series are still in their early stages, they are important in providing benchmarks to assess progress.

Several of the research projects focus on specific methods for reducing corruption. Sandholtz and Gray (page 268), for example, show that a country's integration into the international system, via membership of international organisations and an advanced degree of economic integration, is reflected in a lower rate of corruption. Experimental research (reviewed in Andvig, page 265) is a new field for testing anti-corruption policies. Experiments suggest that both 'positive' incentives such as high wages and 'negative' incentives such as harsh punishment may limit corruption and that loyalty to an organisation may be even more important than incentives.

The role of surveys in understanding corruption

Many of the findings presented in the *Global Corruption Report* are based on survey results: either household surveys (for example, in Kenya, page 245) or expert assessments (for example, Hofbauer, page 278). In Transparency International's own research, surveys were specially commissioned to evaluate some aspect of (anti-)corruption. Other surveys have broader purposes (such as polls that look at crime victimisation or at the business environment) but include corruption-related questions. An output of one study was a comparison of household surveys and expert assessments (Razafindrakoto and Roubaud, page 292), which suggests there may be a systematic difference between the two. While expert surveys will remain an important source of understanding perceptions of corruption, this finding points to the importance of household-level, experience-based research instruments.

Qualitative research – reaching new levels of analysis

While most contributions to this report are quantitative, Larmour (page 242) demonstrates the value of qualitative assessments in a project that evaluated anti-corruption systems ('national integrity systems') in 12 Pacific island states. The project showed that while many of the states have proper regulatory provisions against bribery and conflicts of interest, corrupt acts remain difficult to define and prosecute, with lines between official and familiar roles often blurred. This type of finding can only emerge from the depth of a country study that involves expert assessments, local stakeholders (via interviews and focus groups), and a clear methodological framework to allow comparisons between countries.

The Public Integrity Index (page 252) also involved qualitative country studies of integrity systems, but then transformed the qualitative findings into scores and rankings. Experts scored 80 indicators, which were peer reviewed and then aggregated to form an overall index, with countries ranked from very weak to strong (no country was very strong) in terms of their public integrity. The UN system has provided a rich catalogue of country studies, most recently in its assessment of transparency and accountability in the Arab region (page 275).

Taking stock

The *Global Corruption Report 2005* offers summaries of some of the latest research on corruption, reflecting the growing expertise and interest in the issue. While these studies show the necessity of maintaining and enhancing international datasets (such as the Business Environment and Enterprise Performance Survey – BEEPS – and the International Crime Victimisation Surveys – ICVS – as well as Transparency International's own Corruption Perceptions Index, page 233; and Global Corruption Barometer, page 239), they also demonstrate the richness of national and even sub-national analysis, particularly for diagnostic work and policy development. After 10 years spearheading the fight against corruption, Transparency International and our partners have increasing evidence of how corruption degrades public institutions and both the economic and physical environment. But we also have some indication that the many forces at work in the battle against corruption may be making an impact.

Note

1. Director of Policy and Research, Transparency International.

9 Corruption Perceptions Index 2004

Johann Graf Lambsdorff[1]

The year 2004 marks the tenth publication of Transparency International's Corruption Perceptions Index (CPI). The index assembles expert perceptions vis-à-vis corruption. In an area where objective data is not available, such an approach helps our understanding of real levels of corruption. That is why many economists, political scientists and sociologists use the CPI as a starting point for investigating the causes and consequences of corruption in a cross-section of countries. Since the first publication of the CPI in 1995, there has been a wave of research publications based on the CPI and our knowledge is still expanding rapidly.

The CPI aggregates the perceptions of well-informed people with regard to the extent of corruption, defined as the misuse of public power for private benefit. The extent of corruption reflects the frequency of corrupt payments and the resulting obstacles imposed on businesses. While methodological innovations are introduced continuously, the results from different years show a high level of consistency. A remarkable improvement this year is the expansion of the index from 133 to 146 countries.

This year's CPI used data collected between 2002 and 2004. The CPI is a composite index. Altogether 18 data sources were used in the 2004 CPI, from 12 different institutions: (1) the World Economic Forum; (2) the Institute of Management Development (in Lausanne); (3) the Economist Intelligence Unit; (4) Information International from Beirut (Lebanon); (5) the World Markets Research Centre (in London); (6) Gallup International, on behalf of Transparency International; (7) Freedom House's *Nations in Transit*; (8) the Merchant International Group Limited (in London); (9) the Political and Economic Risk Consultancy (in Hong Kong); (10) Columbia University; (11) a multilateral development bank; and (12) the Business Environment and Enterprise Performance Survey of the EBRD and the World Bank.

One precondition for the inclusion of a source is that it must provide a ranking of nations. Another is that it must measure the overall level of corruption. Ensuring these conditions is essential to guaranteeing that we are not mixing apples with oranges. Inappropriate sources exist that merge the level of corruption with other variables, such as xenophobia, nationalism, political instability or expected risks due to changes in corruption. Including such sources would distort the measurement of perceived levels of corruption, rendering a resulting composite index defective for wide areas of academic research and public awareness. We take a conservative approach, only including sources that strictly compare levels of corruption.

The strength of the CPI lies in the combination of multiple data sources in a single index, which increases the reliability of each individual score. The benefit of combining data in this manner is that erratic findings from one source can be balanced by the inclusion of at least two other sources, lowering the probability of misrepresenting a country's level of corruption.

The high correlation of the different sources used in the CPI indicates its overall reliability. The reliability is also depicted in Figure 9.1, which shows the confidence intervals for each country included in the 2004 CPI. This range indicates how a country's score may vary, depending on measurement precision. Nominally it depicts a range within which the true score lies with 90 per cent probability. However, when few observations are available this level of certainty cannot be met. For example, when only five observations are available, an unbiased estimate of the mean coverage probability is 80 per cent. As the figure indicates, most countries are measured with sufficient precision to allow a ranking of nations.

The index provides an annual snapshot of the views of decision-makers. Comparisons with the results from previous years should be based on a country's score, not its rank. A country's rank can change simply because new countries enter the index. However, year-to-year comparisons of a country's score result not only from a changing perception of

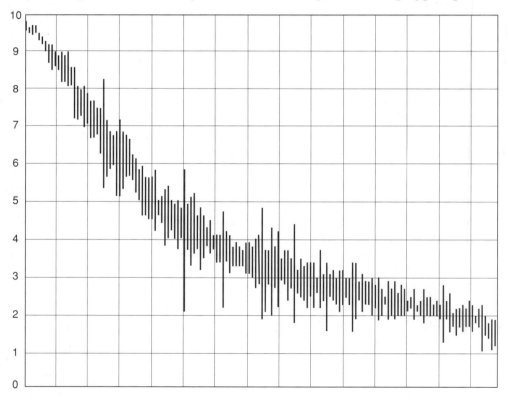

Figure 9.1: 2004 CPI and confidence intervals

a country's performance, but also from a changing sample and methodology – each year different viewpoints are collected and somewhat different questions asked. Research on long-term trends is currently being carried out and findings are expected in 2005–06.

The CPI gathers perceptions that are invariant to cultural preconditions and represent a global perspective. The robustness of the CPI findings is enhanced by the fact that surveys containing residents' viewpoints were found to correlate well with surveys that polled expatriates. In the past, the viewpoint of less-developed countries seemed under-represented. Since 2003, however, Gallup International on behalf of Transparency International has surveyed respondents from less-developed countries, asking them to assess the performance of public servants in industrial countries. A similar approach was applied by Beirut-based Information International and a multilateral development bank. The results correlate well with the other sources used in the 2004 CPI, corroborating the robustness of the CPI.

A more detailed description of the methodology is available at www.transparency. org/surveys/index.html#cpi or at www.icgg.org

Table 9.1: Corruption Perceptions Index 2004

Country rank	Country	CPI 2004 score[a]	Surveys used[b]	Standard deviation[c]	High–low range[d]	Confidence range[e]
1	Finland	9.7	9	0.3	9.2 – 10.0	9.5 – 9.8
2	New Zealand	9.6	9	0.2	9.2 – 9.7	9.4 – 9.6
3	Denmark	9.5	10	0.3	8.7 – 9.8	9.3 – 9.7
	Iceland	9.5	8	0.2	9.2 – 9.8	9.4 – 9.7
5	Singapore	9.3	13	0.3	8.5 – 9.5	9.2 – 9.4
6	Sweden	9.2	11	0.2	8.7 – 9.5	9.1 – 9.3
7	Switzerland	9.1	10	0.3	8.6 – 9.4	8.9 – 9.2
8	Norway	8.9	9	0.5	8.0 – 9.5	8.6 – 9.1
9	Australia	8.8	15	0.8	6.7 – 9.5	8.4 – 9.1
10	Netherlands	8.7	10	0.4	8.3 – 9.4	8.5 – 8.9
11	United Kingdom	8.6	12	0.5	7.8 – 9.2	8.4 – 8.8
12	Canada	8.5	12	0.9	6.5 – 9.4	8.1 – 8.9
13	Austria	8.4	10	0.7	7.3 – 9.3	8.1 – 8.8
	Luxembourg	8.4	7	0.8	7.3 – 9.6	8.0 – 8.9
15	Germany	8.2	11	0.6	7.5 – 9.2	8.0 – 8.5
16	Hong Kong	8.0	13	1.5	3.5 – 9.4	7.1 – 8.5
17	Belgium	7.5	10	0.8	6.6 – 9.1	7.1 – 8.0
	Ireland	7.5	10	0.7	6.5 – 8.7	7.2 – 7.9
	USA	7.5	14	1.1	5.0 – 8.7	6.9 – 8.0
20	Chile	7.4	11	0.7	6.3 – 8.7	7.0 – 7.8
21	Barbados	7.3	3	0.7	6.6 – 8.0	6.6 – 7.6
22	France	7.1	12	1.1	5.0 – 9.0	6.6 – 7.6
	Spain	7.1	11	0.6	5.6 – 8.0	6.7 – 7.4
24	Japan	6.9	15	1.4	3.5 – 9.0	6.2 – 7.4
25	Malta	6.8	4	1.9	5.3 – 9.1	5.3 – 8.2
26	Israel	6.4	10	1.4	3.5 – 8.1	5.6 – 7.1
27	Portugal	6.3	9	0.9	5.0 – 7.3	5.8 – 6.8
28	Uruguay	6.2	6	0.6	5.6 – 7.3	5.9 – 6.7

Table 9.1: *continued*

Country rank	Country	CPI 2004 score[a]	Surveys used[b]	Standard deviation[c]	High–low range[d]	Confidence range[e]
29	Oman	6.1	5	1.2	4.2 – 7.3	5.1 – 6.8
	United Arab Emirates	6.1	5	1.5	4.7 – 8.0	5.1 – 7.1
31	Botswana	6.0	7	1.3	4.4 – 8.0	5.3 – 6.8
	Estonia	6.0	12	1.2	5.0 – 9.1	5.6 – 6.7
	Slovenia	6.0	12	1.0	5.3 – 8.7	5.6 – 6.6
34	Bahrain	5.8	5	0.5	5.3 – 6.6	5.5 – 6.2
35	Taiwan	5.6	15	1.0	3.7 – 7.8	5.2 – 6.1
36	Cyprus	5.4	4	0.5	4.7 – 6.0	5.0 – 5.8
37	Jordan	5.3	9	1.2	3.7 – 6.8	4.6 – 5.9
38	Qatar	5.2	4	0.6	4.3 – 5.8	4.6 – 5.6
39	Malaysia	5.0	15	1.3	2.6 – 8.0	4.5 – 5.6
	Tunisia	5.0	7	0.9	3.7 – 6.6	4.5 – 5.6
41	Costa Rica	4.9	8	1.3	3.6 – 7.8	4.2 – 5.8
42	Hungary	4.8	12	0.5	4.1 – 5.6	4.6 – 5.0
	Italy	4.8	10	0.7	3.4 – 5.6	4.4 – 5.1
44	Kuwait	4.6	5	1.0	3.4 – 5.6	3.8 – 5.3
	Lithuania	4.6	9	1.3	3.1 – 7.7	4.0 – 5.4
	South Africa	4.6	11	0.7	3.4 – 5.8	4.2 – 5.0
47	South Korea	4.5	14	1.0	2.2 – 5.8	4.0 – 4.9
48	Seychelles	4.4	3	0.8	3.7 – 5.3	3.7 – 5.0
49	Greece	4.3	9	0.7	3.8 – 5.6	4.0 – 4.8
	Suriname	4.3	3	2.2	2.1 – 6.6	2.1 – 5.8
51	Czech Republic	4.2	11	1.2	3.4 – 7.3	3.7 – 4.9
	El Salvador	4.2	7	1.5	2.1 – 6.3	3.3 – 5.1
	Trinidad and Tobago	4.2	6	1.2	3.3 – 6.6	3.6 – 5.2
54	Bulgaria	4.1	10	0.9	2.9 – 5.7	3.7 – 4.6
	Mauritius	4.1	5	1.1	2.5 – 5.6	3.2 – 4.8
	Namibia	4.1	7	0.9	2.6 – 5.3	3.5 – 4.6
57	Latvia	4.0	8	0.4	3.5 – 4.8	3.8 – 4.3
	Slovakia	4.0	11	0.9	3.0 – 5.6	3.6 – 4.5
59	Brazil	3.9	11	0.4	3.5 – 4.8	3.7 – 4.1
60	Belize	3.8	3	0.5	3.4 – 4.3	3.4 – 4.1
	Colombia	3.8	10	0.7	2.5 – 4.5	3.4 – 4.1
62	Cuba	3.7	4	1.7	1.6 – 5.6	2.2 – 4.7
	Panama	3.7	7	0.7	3.0 – 5.1	3.4 – 4.2
64	Ghana	3.6	7	0.9	2.5 – 5.1	3.1 – 4.1
	Mexico	3.6	11	0.5	2.6 – 4.5	3.3 – 3.8
	Thailand	3.6	14	0.7	2.5 – 4.5	3.3 – 3.9
67	Croatia	3.5	9	0.4	2.7 – 4.2	3.3 – 3.8
	Peru	3.5	8	0.4	2.6 – 4.0	3.3 – 3.7
	Poland	3.5	13	0.9	2.4 – 5.3	3.1 – 3.9
	Sri Lanka	3.5	8	0.8	2.5 – 4.5	3.1 – 3.9
71	China	3.4	16	1.0	2.1 – 5.6	3.0 – 3.8
	Saudi Arabia	3.4	5	1.0	2.0 – 4.5	2.7 – 4.0
	Syria	3.4	5	1.1	2.1 – 5.1	2.8 – 4.1
74	Belarus	3.3	5	1.9	1.6 – 5.8	1.9 – 4.8
	Gabon	3.3	3	1.1	2.1 – 4.3	2.1 – 3.7
	Jamaica	3.3	6	0.7	2.1 – 4.2	2.8 – 3.7

Table 9.1: *continued*

Country rank	Country	CPI 2004 score[a]	Surveys used[b]	Standard deviation[c]	High–low range[d]	Confidence range[e]
77	Benin	3.2	3	1.6	2.0 – 5.1	2.0 – 4.3
	Egypt	3.2	8	1.0	2.1 – 5.1	2.7 – 3.8
	Mali	3.2	5	1.5	1.5 – 5.1	2.2 – 4.2
	Morocco	3.2	7	0.5	2.5 – 3.9	2.9 – 3.5
	Turkey	3.2	13	0.9	1.9 – 5.4	2.8 – 3.7
82	Armenia	3.1	5	0.9	2.3 – 4.3	2.4 – 3.7
	Bosnia and Herzegovina	3.1	7	0.6	2.3 – 4.0	2.7 – 3.5
	Madagascar	3.1	4	1.7	1.7 – 5.3	1.8 – 4.4
85	Mongolia	3.0	3	0.4	2.6 – 3.4	2.6 – 3.2
	Senegal	3.0	6	0.8	2.0 – 4.2	2.5 – 3.5
87	Dominican Republic	2.9	6	0.7	2.0 – 3.6	2.4 – 3.3
	Iran	2.9	5	0.8	1.6 – 3.7	2.2 – 3.4
	Romania	2.9	12	0.9	1.7 – 5.1	2.5 – 3.4
90	Gambia	2.8	5	0.9	1.6 – 3.8	2.2 – 3.4
	India	2.8	15	0.5	2.2 – 3.7	2.6 – 3.0
	Malawi	2.8	5	1.0	2.0 – 4.5	2.2 – 3.7
	Mozambique	2.8	7	0.6	2.1 – 3.7	2.4 – 3.1
	Nepal	2.8	3	1.0	1.6 – 3.5	1.6 – 3.4
	Russia	2.8	15	0.8	2.0 – 5.0	2.5 – 3.1
	Tanzania	2.8	7	0.6	2.0 – 3.7	2.4 – 3.2
97	Algeria	2.7	6	0.5	2.0 – 3.4	2.3 – 3.0
	Lebanon	2.7	5	0.9	1.6 – 3.7	2.1 – 3.2
	Macedonia	2.7	7	0.8	2.1 – 4.3	2.3 – 3.2
	Nicaragua	2.7	7	0.4	2.1 – 3.5	2.5 – 3.0
	Serbia and Montenegro	2.7	7	0.6	2.1 – 3.5	2.3 – 3.0
102	Eritrea	2.6	3	1.4	1.6 – 4.2	1.6 – 3.4
	Papua New Guinea	2.6	4	1.2	1.6 – 4.3	1.9 – 3.4
	Philippines	2.6	14	0.6	1.4 – 3.7	2.4 – 2.9
	Uganda	2.6	7	0.8	2.0 – 3.7	2.1 – 3.1
	Vietnam	2.6	11	0.6	1.6 – 3.7	2.3 – 2.9
	Zambia	2.6	6	0.5	2.0 – 3.4	2.3 – 2.9
108	Albania	2.5	4	0.6	2.0 – 3.3	2.0 – 3.0
	Argentina	2.5	11	0.6	1.7 – 3.7	2.2 – 2.8
	Libya	2.5	4	0.7	1.8 – 3.5	1.9 – 3.0
	Palestine	2.5	3	0.5	2.0 – 2.9	2.0 – 2.7
112	Ecuador	2.4	7	0.2	2.1 – 2.6	2.3 – 2.5
	Yemen	2.4	5	0.7	1.6 – 3.5	1.9 – 2.9
114	Congo, Republic	2.3	4	0.4	2.0 – 2.9	2.0 – 2.7
	Ethiopia	2.3	6	0.8	1.6 – 3.7	1.9 – 2.9
	Honduras	2.3	7	0.4	1.5 – 2.9	2.0 – 2.6
	Moldova	2.3	5	0.6	1.8 – 3.4	2.0 – 2.8
	Sierra Leone	2.3	3	0.5	2.0 – 2.9	2.0 – 2.7
	Uzbekistan	2.3	6	0.2	2.0 – 2.5	2.1 – 2.4
	Venezuela	2.3	11	0.3	2.0 – 3.0	2.2 – 2.5
	Zimbabwe	2.3	7	0.7	1.2 – 3.3	1.9 – 2.7
122	Bolivia	2.2	6	0.2	2.0 – 2.5	2.1 – 2.3
	Guatemala	2.2	7	0.3	1.6 – 2.5	2.0 – 2.4

Table 9.1: *continued*

Country rank	Country	CPI 2004 score[a]	Surveys used[b]	Standard deviation[c]	High–low range[d]	Confidence range[e]
	Kazakhstan	2.2	7	0.7	1.6 – 3.7	1.8 – 2.7
	Kyrgyzstan	2.2	5	0.3	1.8 – 2.6	2.0 – 2.5
	Niger	2.2	3	0.4	2.0 – 2.6	2.0 – 2.5
	Sudan	2.2	5	0.2	2.0 – 2.5	2.0 – 2.3
	Ukraine	2.2	10	0.4	1.6 – 2.9	2.0 – 2.4
129	Cameroon	2.1	5	0.3	1.7 – 2.6	1.9 – 2.3
	Iraq	2.1	4	1.0	1.2 – 3.5	1.3 – 2.8
	Kenya	2.1	7	0.5	1.6 – 3.1	1.9 – 2.4
	Pakistan	2.1	7	0.8	1.2 – 3.3	1.6 – 2.6
133	Angola	2.0	5	0.3	1.5 – 2.1	1.7 – 2.1
	Congo, Democratic Republic	2.0	3	0.5	1.5 – 2.5	1.5 – 2.2
	Côte d'Ivoire	2.0	5	0.4	1.6 – 2.5	1.7 – 2.2
	Georgia	2.0	7	0.6	1.0 – 2.6	1.6 – 2.3
	Indonesia	2.0	14	0.6	0.8 – 3.2	1.7 – 2.2
	Tajikistan	2.0	4	0.4	1.6 – 2.6	1.7 – 2.4
	Turkmenistan	2.0	3	0.5	1.6 – 2.5	1.6 – 2.3
140	Azerbaijan	1.9	7	0.2	1.6 – 2.1	1.8 – 2.0
	Paraguay	1.9	7	0.5	1.2 – 2.6	1.7 – 2.2
142	Chad	1.7	4	0.7	1.0 – 2.6	1.1 – 2.3
	Myanmar	1.7	4	0.3	1.5 – 2.1	1.5 – 2.0
144	Nigeria	1.6	9	0.4	0.9 – 2.1	1.4 – 1.8
145	Bangladesh	1.5	8	0.8	0.3 – 2.4	1.1 – 1.9
	Haiti	1.5	5	0.6	0.8 – 2.4	1.2 – 1.9

a. 'CPI 2004 score' relates to perceptions of the degree of corruption as seen by business people, academics and risk analysts, and ranges between 10 (highly clean) and 0 (highly corrupt).

b. 'Surveys used' refers to the number of surveys that assessed a country's performance. A total of 18 surveys were used from 12 independent institutions, and at least three surveys were required for a country to be included in the CPI.

c. 'Standard deviation' indicates differences in the values given by the sources: the greater the standard deviation, the greater the differences in perceptions of a country among the sources.

d. 'High–low range' provides the highest and lowest values given by the different sources.

e. 'Confidence range' provides a range of possible values of the CPI score. This reflects how a country's score may vary, depending on measurement precision. Nominally, with 5 per cent probability the score is above this range and with another 5 per cent it is below. However, particularly when only few sources are available an unbiased estimate of the mean coverage probability is lower than the nominal value of 90 per cent. It is 65.3 per cent for 3 sources; 73.6 per cent for 4 sources; 78.4 per cent for 5 sources; 80.2 per cent for 6 sources and 81.8 per cent for 7 sources.

Note

1. Johann Graf Lambsdorff is professor of economics at the University of Passau, Germany, and director of statistical work on the CPI for TI. Contact: jlambsd@uni-passau.de

10 Global Corruption Barometer 2004

Marie Wolkers[1]

The Global Corruption Barometer, first launched by Transparency International (TI) in 2003, is a public opinion survey of perceptions, experiences and attitudes towards corruption. The barometer is carried out for TI by Gallup International, as part of their Voice of the People survey. Complementing TI's Corruption Perceptions Index (see page 233), which captures perceptions among business people and country analysts, the Global Corruption Barometer surveys the general public. This year's edition is based on interviews conducted between June and September 2004 with 50,000 people in 60 countries.[2]

One of the most striking findings in 2004 was that globally, just as in 2003, the public perceived political parties as the sector most affected by corruption, followed by parliament/legislature, the police and the legal system/judiciary (see Figure 10.1). On a scale from 1 ('not at all corrupt') to 5 ('extremely corrupt'), political parties received a global score of 4 and obtained the worst assessment in 30 out of 54 countries, most notably in Ecuador (4.9), Argentina and Peru (both 4.6). Similarly, when asked to compare the impact of corruption on different spheres of life, 7 out of 10 respondents worldwide judged political life to be affected by corruption, which was more than the number who said that corruption affected the business environment (6 out of 10) or personal and family life (4 out of 10).

Across the world, people view corruption as one of the biggest problems their country faces. Grand/political corruption was one of four issues identified as a very or fairly big problem by 85–90 per cent of respondents (the other three issues being unemployment, poverty and insecurity/crimes/violence/terrorism). Petty/administrative corruption was mentioned by 78 per cent of respondents.

Petty/administrative corruption was not considered to be an issue in most industrialised countries, but there were important differences regarding grand/political corruption. Although grand corruption was considered to be a very or fairly big problem by only 25 per cent of Danes and 27 per cent of Norwegians, it was seen as a matter of concern by between 86 and 95 per cent of respondents in Italy, France, Greece and Portugal, whose level of concern surpassed that of the public in some less developed countries such as Afghanistan and Malaysia, where the figure stood at 74 and 77 per cent.

In the developing world, both grand/political corruption and petty/administrative corruption were of high concern, especially in Latin America and Africa. Brazil saw the most striking results, with 99 per cent of respondents regarding both petty and grand corruption as very or fairly big problems.

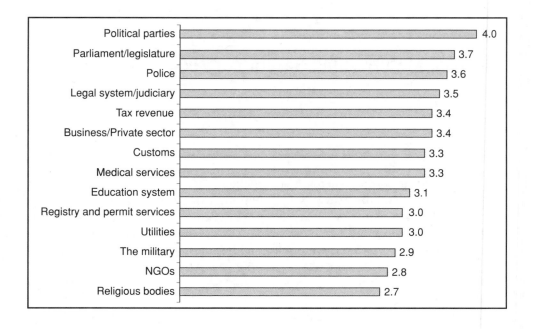

Political parties	4.0
Parliament/legislature	3.7
Police	3.6
Legal system/judiciary	3.5
Tax revenue	3.4
Business/Private sector	3.4
Customs	3.3
Medical services	3.3
Education system	3.1
Registry and permit services	3.0
Utilities	3.0
The military	2.9
NGOs	2.8
Religious bodies	2.7

Figure 10.1: Sectors affected by corruption[a]

a. Respondents were asked: '*To what extent do you perceive the following sectors in this country to be affected by corruption?*' Answers on a scale from 1 to 5 (1 = not at all corrupt, 5 = extremely corrupt).

Differences between developed and developing countries were similarly seen when respondents were asked about the impact of corruption on personal and family life. Corruption's impact was seen to be very low in most developed countries, with the exceptions of Canada, Greece and the United States, where 43 per cent said that corruption affected their personal life to a moderate or large extent. A negative personal impact was reported by three out of four respondents in Brazil, Ecuador, Korea, Mexico, the Philippines and Turkey.

Worldwide, one in 10 respondents said that they or other members of their household had paid a bribe in the previous 12 months. The most frequent direct experience of corruption was in Cameroon, where more than half the respondents reported experiences of bribery during the year, followed by Kenya, Lithuania, Moldova and Nigeria (see Table 10.1). At the other extreme, in 18 countries only 2 per cent of respondents or fewer stated that they had paid a bribe in the previous 12 months.

Turning to expectations of the future, 43 per cent of respondents expected the level of corruption to increase in the next three years. The most pessimistic country was Ecuador, with 75 per cent anticipating a rise. Indonesia was the most optimistic country, with 66 per cent forecasting a reduction in corruption in the coming years, followed by Georgia (with 59 per cent) and Kosovo (52 per cent).

For more information on the Global Corruption Barometer, see www.transparency.org/surveys/index#gcb

Table 10.1: Experience of bribery – the 10 countries reporting the highest levels[a]

	Yes (%)	No (%)	Don't know/NA (%)
Cameroon	52	34	14
Kenya	36	60	4
Lithuania	32	64	5
Moldova	32	62	6
Nigeria	32	60	9
Albania	30	67	3
Bolivia	29	68	3
Ecuador	27	71	2
Romania	25	61	14
Ukraine	25	64	10

a. Respondents were asked: *'In the past 12 months, have you or anyone living in your household paid a bribe in any form?'*

Notes

1. Marie Wolkers is responsible for corruption measurement issues in Transparency International's research department (contact: mwolkers@transparency.org).
2. The results of the Global Corruption Barometer 2004 included 54 countries at the time of writing: Albania, Argentina, Austria, Bolivia, Bosnia and Herzegovina, Brazil, Britain, Bulgaria, Cameroon, Canada, Croatia, Denmark, Ecuador, Egypt, Estonia, France, Georgia, Germany, Greece, Guatemala, Hong Kong, Iceland, Indonesia, Israel, Italy, Japan, Kenya, Korea, Kosovo, Lithuania, Luxembourg, Macedonia, Malaysia, Mexico, Moldova, Netherlands, Nigeria, Norway, Pakistan, Peru, Philippines, Poland, Portugal, Romania, Russia, South Africa, Spain, Switzerland, Taiwan, Turkey, Ukraine, Uruguay, the United States and Vietnam. More countries (including Afghanistan, Costa Rica, Czech Republic, Finland, Ghana, India, Ireland, Latvia and Singapore) may be added before the expected publication date in December 2004.

11 National Integrity Systems in the Pacific island states

Peter Larmour[1]

TI Australia carried out a survey of National Integrity Systems (NIS) in 12 small states in the South Pacific. The NIS is imagined as a series of pillars, upholding integrity in government. The surveys used a standard questionnaire, derived from ideas in TI's Source Book,[2] and already used in surveys of more than 60 other countries (including the larger Pacific countries: Australia, Fiji, New Zealand and Papua New Guinea (PNG)). Additional questions were added about traditional institutions which remain influential in the South Pacific region, and about corruption in the private sector and NGOs. The median population of the states surveyed is about 50,000 people, ranging from about 2,000 (Niue) to about 500,000 (Solomon Islands).

The research was coordinated by Peter Larmour and Manu Barcham at the Australian National University (ANU). Each country study was prepared by an expert or small team of experts on the country in question. The experts tended to be academic political scientists or anthropologists or former senior officials who were no longer closely associated with the government. Seven of the 12 studies were conducted by citizens of the country. In almost every case the researcher held a public forum in which the results were discussed – and the seeds were sown for follow-up once the report was completed. The researchers were also brought together for a workshop in Fiji in March 2004, hosted by the University of the South Pacific. There they discussed their findings and an overview prepared by ANU, and agreed a set of recommendations.

The reports found that almost every country had legal provisions against bribery, and most had public service regulations that prohibited conflicts of interest. Several had or were devising 'leadership codes' that specified appropriate behaviour for senior officials and ministers. However, the reports found confusion in the general public as well as disagreement about what counted as corruption and – particularly in Vanuatu – whether it really mattered. The small size of these countries made popular supervision of government easier as everyone knew what was going on, but it also made it difficult to keep family matters separate from official roles.

Every country studied (except Tonga) is a democracy, but there was strong concern about political manoeuvring to win elections and stay in government. Political parties are weak or absent in every country. Politicians are elected on personal promises to constituents, while governments have to assemble majorities from among independent members of legislatures. Leaders offer government jobs in exchange for support.

Government ministers are most often suspected of corruption through abuse of their powers to regulate and license, through funding projects in their own constituencies, and through interfering with public service promotions and training opportunities.

The NIS pillars include the executive, the legislature and independent bodies such as an auditor, ombudsman or public service commission. The reports found that ombudsmen were generally ineffective, and audit reports rarely read or acted upon. Ironically, the country with the most elaborate legal provision for independent oversight – the Solomon Islands – has a chronic corruption problem, which grew particularly out of the logging industry in the 1990s.[3]

Traditional institutions and practices remain strong in most parts of the Pacific, and the surveys asked about their role in preventing or encouraging corruption. They found that courts, particularly in Kiribati, successfully distinguished traditional gifts from bribes. Nobles in Tonga did not feel particularly accountable to the people, and it was hard to draw a line between the public and private faces of the monarchy there. People generally had different expectations of the behaviour of chiefs and government officials, with elected politicians in an ambiguous position between them: the report on the Federated States of Micronesia criticised politicians for 'behaving like chiefs'. Cultural factors such as deference to leadership and reluctance to 'rock the boat' inhibited people from reporting corruption.

The surveys found civil society and the private sector to be unevenly developed throughout the region. There are TI groups in two of the countries (Solomon Islands and Vanuatu), and interest was shown at public meetings about the survey reports in Samoa and Tonga. In some states (for example, Cook Islands, Vanuatu and Solomon Islands) there is a lively civil society, while in others, such as Kiribati, it is less developed. The private sector is also often very small and dependent on government. The surveys found concern about corruption in NGOs, particularly in churches that dealt with large sums of money and property. Most found the media important in raising corruption issues, particularly in Palau, but they also found that pressure from government, and from advertisers, put limits on reporting.

The reports came up with a common set of recommendations about what should be done. Governments should display more political will, and a stronger civil society could press them to do so. Stronger political parties might inhibit political manoeuvring, though the Samoa report raised the danger of political parties being so strong that they inhibit criticism. Independent commissions against corruption could provide a focus for anti-corruption activity, though the research also cast doubt on the value of independent commissions, which create new positions to be filled by patronage and are typically starved of resources. Codes of practice would help define appropriate behaviour, where the reports had found there was disagreement and uncertainty.

In June 2004 representatives of TI Australia and TI PNG presented an overview of the studies to the annual meeting of the economic ministers of the Pacific Islands Forum (the regional economic and political organisation of which the island states, Australia and New Zealand are members). In the final 'Action Plan' ministers noted the study's findings, and committed themselves to increasing efforts to strengthen institutions and laws to prevent corruption, including its causes, and to improve public sector governance at national levels.

Notes

1. Peter Larmour is a senior lecturer in policy and governance at the Australian National University.
2. Transparency International, *The TI Source Book 2000, Confronting Corruption: The Elements of a National Integrity System* (Berlin: Transparency International, 2000), www.transparency.org/sourcebook/index.html
3. The Solomon Islands government requested foreign intervention after a police-led *coup d'état* and a subsequent breakdown in law and order. The Australian-led intervention has strengthened the capacity of the government to investigate and prosecute corruption, and many members of the police force have been prosecuted (though the outcomes of the cases are not yet known).

12 Kenya Bribery Index 2004

Mwalimu Mati and Osendo Con Omore[1]

The Kenya Bribery Index 2004 reports the findings of TI Kenya's third national survey on bribery. The index ranks 38 public and private sector organisations according to ordinary citizens' experience of bribery in their daily interactions with them. It measures (so-called) petty bribery – it does not capture grand corruption, such as the bribery involved in major public procurement projects.

A structured questionnaire was administered nationwide by personal interview in households. In December 2003 a total of 2,407 individuals were interviewed in all eight provinces of Kenya; 1,160 in urban and 1,247 in rural residences. Respondents provided information on their experience with bribery over the last 12 months: in which organisations they encountered bribery, where they paid bribes, how much, for what, and whether they reported the episode.

Table 12.1 presents the findings on the 10 organisations most prone to bribery in Kenya. For each organisation, six indicators capture different dimensions of the magnitude and impact of the problem:

1. **Incidence** measures the likelihood that a person visiting an organisation will be asked to, or feels it is necessary to, offer a bribe.
2. **Prevalence** indicates the percentage of the population affected by bribery in the organisation.
3. **Severity** captures the level of impunity – whether service is denied for declining to bribe.
4. **Frequency** measures the average number of bribes paid per year per person having contact with the organisation.
5. **Cost** indicates the estimated proceeds from bribes, and can be interpreted as the 'bribery tax' per adult citizen (for those having contact with the organisation).
6. **Size** refers to the average size of bribes paid by those having contact with the organisation.

In addition, an aggregate index was then constructed as an unweighted average of the six indicators. The index has a value range from 0 to 100, where the higher the value the worse the performance. The frequency indicators (incidence, prevalence, severity) were computed as a percentage of observations. The value data (frequency, cost, size) were scaled by the highest value to obtain a normalised score with a value between 0 and 100 (whereas the actual values are reported in Table 12.1).

Table 12.1: Index scores for the 10 most bribe-prone organisations, 2003

Rank	Organisation	Aggreg. index	INDICATORS					
			Incidence[a]	Prevalence	Severity[b]	Frequency	Cost[c]	Size[c]
1	Kenya Police	57.3	82.1	28.4	31.7	12.5	251.59	635
2	Department of Defence	37.7	75.0	0.3	40.0	2.1	39.63	27,917
3	State corporations	30.1	37.6	2.1	9.7	3.3	191.89	10,188
4	Immigration Department	30.1	89.6	2.2	25.4	4.2	43.46	4,467
5	Kenya Revenue Authority	28.8	63.8	1.5	18.8	9.0	31.90	1,486
6	Provincial administration	26.7	53.4	20.3	16.2	4.1	90.61	636
7	Nairobi City Council	26.2	74.1	4.1	19.1	5.8	28.06	863
8	Central government	25.5	60.8	2.3	23.5	5.8	37.42	1,816
9	Ministry of Public Works	24.7	71.4	0.5	38.1	3.8	5.57	2,035
10	Ministry of Lands	24.5	73.2	3.2	21.4	2.9	40.23	3,620

a. Percentage of encounters.
b. Percentage of refusals that resulted denial of service.
c. Cost and size are in Kenya shillings.

Sadly, bribery remains a significant burden on already poverty-stricken Kenyans, though it appears to be decreasing. In 2002, two out of three encounters with ranked organisations involved bribery. By 2003, the proportion had fallen to two out of five. In addition, the number of bribes per person fell from 2.4 per month in 2002 to less than 1 per month in 2003. Police officers retain the top position for extracting the most money from the public through bribery. However, this sum fell sharply from 1,270 shillings (US $16.90) per person per month in 2002 to 250 shillings (US $3.30) in 2003. When asked about their perception of the level of corruption, more Kenyans were of the view in 2003 that the problem of bribery was decreasing than was the case in 2002 (32 per cent, up from 14 per cent the year before), but the majority (55 per cent) still felt there was no change in the level of corruption.

However, though the average expenditure on bribery per month (the 'bribery tax') fell from 3,905 shillings (US $52) in 2002 to 1,261 shillings (US $16) in 2003, the average bribe size increased from 2,318 shillings (US $30.90) in 2002 to 3,958 shillings (US $52.70) in 2003. This may reflect a risk premium consequent to the zero-tolerance policy adopted by the Kibaki government after it took power in December 2002.

Unfortunately, many Kenyans do not report bribery to the authorities. We asked respondents what action they took, if any, on encountering bribery. In the majority of instances (58 per cent), the respondents paid bribes and kept quiet about it. Only 5 per cent of respondents said that they had declined to pay a bribe and reported the incident to the authorities. The low level of reporting indicates a lack of trust in official law enforcement channels, principally the police.

The consequences of declining a bribe demand are still severe – there is a substantial likelihood of service denial in many organisations. In the Department of Defence, 40 per cent of refusals to pay a bribe result in denial (generally in recruitment exercises), while in the Immigration Department there is a 25 per cent chance of denial of service if one fails to bribe.

Note

1. Mwalimu Mati is deputy executive director, TI Kenya (email: mmati@tikenya.org). Osendo Con Omore is deputy programme officer, TI Kenya (email: comore@tikenya.org).

13 Measuring corruption in public service delivery: the experience of Mexico

Transparencia Mexicana[1]

The National Survey on Corruption and Good Governance (NSCGG) is a tool for monitoring corruption in public service delivery. As it compares both states and specific public services, it may foster competition in efforts to curb corruption and enhance quality. The survey was conducted twice, in 2001 and 2003. It measured the experience of Mexican households as regards corruption in the 32 federal regions of Mexico (including the Federal District), and for 38 public services. In total the survey covered 14,019 homes, with between 383 and 514 households surveyed in each federal region.[2]

The data gathered by the survey generated a national Index of Corruption and Good Governance (ICGG). The index consists of two components, one ranking public servants and the other ranking federal regions. For specific public services, the index is the number of times respondents claimed to have obtained the service by paying a bribe, as a proportion of the total number of times that all respondents used the service during the same year. For the federal regions, the index is the number of times respondents obtained any of the 38 specified services in that region by paying a bribe, as a proportion of the total number of times all respondents in the region used any of the 38 services. The ICGG uses a scale of 0 to 100: the lower the index, the lower the corruption level.

Changes in an index between 2001 and 2003 provide a reference value for assessing public policies aimed at fighting corruption. In 2003, 11 federal regions saw an increase in corruption (as measured by the ICGG) relative to 2001, while 21 saw a reduction. Having had the highest corruption score of all regions in 2001, the Federal District (Mexico's capital city) saw the biggest fall in the ICGG by 2003. However, this achievement was not reflected in comparative terms, as the Federal District only moved up one position in the rank ordering (see Table 13.1). San Luis Potosí was the region that saw the largest increase in corruption, deteriorating from 7th position in 2001 to 27th in 2003.

Significantly, Chiapas, which has the lowest Human Development Index in Mexico, is among the 21 regions that succeeded in improving their ICGG score. After learning of the results of the 2001 NSCGG, the Chiapas local administration implemented an e-government programme for public service delivery. By 2003, Chiapas had risen 10 places in the ranking, from 16th to 6th, suggesting that concrete, well-focused actions can reduce corruption even in the short term.

Table 13.1: Results by federal region in 2001 and 2003

Federal regions with the lowest corruption level, according to the ICGG 2003

| Place | | Region | ICGG | |
2001	2003		2001	2003
2	1	Baja California Sur	3.9	2.3
10	2	Quintana Roo	6.1	3.7
1	3	Colima	3.0	3.8
15	4	Hidalgo	6.7	3.9
3	4	Aguascalientes	4.5	3.9
16	6	Chiapas	6.8	4.0
4	7	Coahuila	5.0	4.4
5	8	Sonora	5.5	4.5

Federal regions with the highest corruption level, according to the ICGG 2003

| Place | | Region | Score | |
2001	2003		2001	2003
9	25	Guanajuanto	6.0	8.9
18	26	Nuevo León	7.1	9.9
7	27	San Luis Potosí	5.7	10.2
30	28	Guerrero	13.4	12.0
26	29	Durango	8.9	12.6
31	30	Mexico	17.0	12.7
32	31	Federal District	22.6	13.2
29	32	Puebla	12.1	18.0

Procedures for phone connections, provided by a private firm in Mexico, was the sole service to post a worse index score in 2003 than in 2001. All the other services saw an improved score. The service that most frequently involved a bribe was recovering a car from a detention centre to which it had been taken, or preventing it from being sent there by a traffic warden (see Table 13.2). The lowest frequency of bribery was found for procedures relating to real estate (for example, paying property taxes).

The services for which the largest total value of bribes was given included garbage collection by local government, payments to recover stolen cars, and payments to traffic wardens to avoid detention. On average, the highest bribe of all was required to obtain loans from private institutions, for which individual payments reached US $700, followed by bribes to speed up gas reconnections and to obtain loans from state-run entities.

Extrapolated to the whole population, the results imply almost 101 million acts of corruption in the 38 services during the year. The survey found that each *mordida* (act of bribery) involved on average 107 pesos (US $9). Taken together these figures suggest that nearly US $1 billion were paid in bribes in 2003 to obtain public services in Mexico. Households that claimed to have paid bribes devoted on average 7 per cent of their income to bribes. For the poorest households that claimed to have paid bribes

– those with income at the level of the minimum wage – this regressive tax accounted for 29.5 per cent of their income.

Services with the lowest corruption level, according to the ICGG 2003

Place		Kind of act	Score	
2001	2003		2001	2003
1	1	Procedure concerning real estate	1.6	1.4
2	2	Procedure filed to get authorisation for incapacity or health problems	2.8	1.5
6	3	Fiscal procedure in the treasury: RFC, return, quarterly or annual affidavit	3.2	1.7
4	4	Phone-related procedures	2.9	2.3
11	5	Getting urgent care for a patient, or skipping queues in hospitals to get assistance	4.3	2.5
3	6	Procedure filed to obtain residential gas connections or re-connections	2.9	2.8
14	7	Procedure to get support, or to access government programmes such as PROGRESA, PROCAMPO, milk, etc.	5.9	2.8
8	8	Procedure to get draft registration documents/deferment for military service	3.9	3.0
10	9	Correspondence received	3.8	3.2
13	10	Procedure to get loans in cash for a house, business or car, in private institutions	5.0	3.2

Services with the highest corruption level, according to the ICGG 2003

Place		Kind of act	Score	
2001	2003		2001	2003
29	29	Procedure to get a demolition, building, alignment, or official number licence or permit	16.8	13.2
30	30	Procedure to work or sell in street stalls	18.7	16.0
31	31	Procedure for sewage cleaning	25.8	16.5
33	32	Procedure to avoid detention in the public ministry/file a report, accusation or claim/get follow-up for cases	28.3	21.3
32	33	Request a garbage truck from the local government to remove waste	27.0	24.4
34	34	Procedure to get through customs points, booths or border posts	28.5	25.8
35	35	Procedure to recover stolen vehicles	30.3	26.0
37	36	Parking in places controlled by people who take hold of them	56.0	45.9
36	37	Avoiding fines or detention by traffic wardens	54.5	50.3
38	38	Preventing traffic wardens from taking vehicles to the detention centre/taking the car out of the said centre	57.2	53.3

Notes

1. Transparencia Mexicana is the Mexican national chapter of TI. Transparencia Mexicana formed a Technical Advisory Council (TAC) responsible for designing the study. The TAC members included more than 20 specialists in surveys and public opinion polls, among them political analysts and academics. The composition of the TAC was modified for the design, execution and dissemination phases, according to the technical requirements of each stage.
2. In 73 per cent of households, questionnaires were answered by the head of the household. Only after several failed attempts to interview the household head were interviewers allowed to interview other household members. Error margins for national results are less than 1 per cent. At the regional level, error margins increase because of smaller sample sizes, and can be as large as +/–4 to 7 per cent.

14 The Public Integrity Index: assessing anti-corruption architecture

Marianne Camerer and Jonathan Werve[1]

The Public Integrity Index is the centrepiece of the Global Integrity Report, a 25-country study on anti-corruption mechanisms released in April 2004 by the Center for Public Integrity. Providing a quantitative scorecard of governance practices in each country, the Public Integrity Index does not measure corruption itself, but rather the opposite of corruption: the institutions and practices that citizens can use to hold their governments accountable to the public interest. A government with weak public integrity systems may not necessarily be corrupt – but it is far more difficult and rare to maintain a clean government where public integrity mechanisms are weak.

The 25 countries were chosen to generate a global sample with geographic, economic and political diversity. The selection of countries includes six from Africa and seven from Latin America, as well as the most populous democracy on each continent. The index assesses the national governance framework. In many cases, particularly in federal states, the experience at the local level diverges from national experiences, and these local situations are not reflected in the index.

The Public Integrity Index measures three things:

1. the **existence** of public integrity mechanisms, including laws and institutions that promote public accountability and limit corruption
2. the **effectiveness** of these mechanisms
3. the **access** that citizens have to public information to hold public officials accountable.

The index is composed of 80 main indicators and 212 sub-indicators (292 in total). These are grouped into 6 main categories and 21 sub-categories (see Table 14.1). The categories and the indicators were chosen on the basis of a comprehensive survey of the academic literature on anti-corruption safeguards. For example, Category 3 – 'branches of government' – has three sub-categories that focus on (1) the *executive* branch of government, including accountability mechanisms, immunity from prosecution, conflict-of-interest regulations and citizen access to financial disclosure records of the head of government; (2) the *legislature*, including accountability mechanisms, immunity from prosecution, conflict-of-interest regulations, as well as legislative control over the national budgetary process; (3) the *judiciary*, including issues of independence and accountability, as well as the safety of judges and witnesses in corruption-related cases.

Table 14.1: Index categories and sub-categories

1. Civil society, public information and media	Civil society organisations; access to information law; freedom of the media
2. Electoral and political processes	National elections; election monitoring agency; political party finances
3. Branches of government	Executive; legislature; judiciary
4. Administration and civil service	Civil service regulations; whistleblowing measures; procurement; privatisation
5. Oversight and regulatory mechanisms	National ombudsman; supreme audit institution; taxes and customs; financial sector regulation
6. Anti-corruption mechanisms and rule of law	Anti-corruption law; anti-corruption agency; rule of law and access to justice; law enforcement

The index is based on peer-reviewed expert assessments. The lead social scientist in each country assigned an initial score to each indicator. To derive the final score the indicators, comments and references generated by the lead social scientist were critically reviewed by a panel of experts familiar with the country, and then consolidated by the central scoring team in Washington. Each indicator score was averaged within its parent subcategory, to produce a subcategory score. The subcategory score was in turn averaged with the other subcategory scores in a parent category. Category scores were finally averaged to produce a country score.

Country scores are presented in Figure 14.1. Countries are grouped into 5 broad scoring tiers that reflect an assessment of the strength or weakness of a country's public integrity system: very strong (90–100), strong (80–90), moderate (70–80), weak (60–70) and very weak (less than 60). No country was rated 'very strong'.

There are two major advantages to this research model. First, the index is transparent in its scoring and methodology. Readers can learn not only how a country scored, but also see exactly why it scored that way, down to the existence of an individual law, or the performance evaluation of a specific institution.

Second, the indicators themselves serve as a checklist of incremental steps that governments can use to enhance anti-corruption reforms. As a tool for dialogue and reform, the index is also useful for civil society groups that do advocacy work to confer with governments and define achievable and measurable goals for improving public integrity. The index is not a tool to shame poor performers. Instead the scores are diagnostic, highlighting weak areas in a country's anti-corruption architecture.

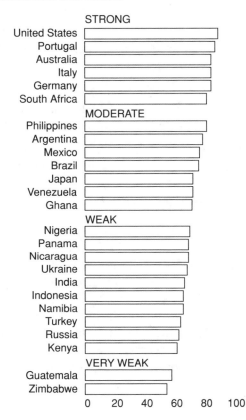

Public Integrity Index

The Index measures the existence, effectiveness and accessability of the institutions that hold a government accountable to its citizens.

Figure 14.1: Public Integrity Index

For the full 25 country reports including country facts, corruption timelines, corruption notebooks, integrity assessments, integrity scorecards and integrity indicators, please see www.publicintegrity.org/ga. In 2005 we plan to update the 25 country reports and expand the study.

Note

1. Marianne Camerer is director of Global Access, and Jonathan Werve is associate director, Global Access, at the Center for Public Integrity, United States, www.publicintegrity. org/ga

15 A survey of governance in 30 underperforming states

Sarah Repucci[1]

The international community has focused increasing attention on governance in recent years. The US government's Millennium Challenge Account (MCA) exemplifies this trend – it is a pool of foreign aid that will be given only to countries whose leaders 'rule justly, invest in their people, and encourage economic freedom'. In May 2004 the Millennium Challenge Corporation announced the first 16 countries eligible to apply for funds.

Currently, Freedom House's *Freedom in the World* survey provides some of the criteria utilised by the US government to determine whether a country is 'ruling justly'. In order to examine in more detail some of the issues pertinent to the MCA, Freedom House designed a survey to focus on government performance in 30 countries. These countries represent a range of geographic areas and polities – monarchies, dictatorships, struggling nascent electoral democracies, and those suffering insurgencies – but all are low performers in *Freedom in the World*. Carried out with support from the US State Department's Bureau of Democracy, Human Rights and Labor, the new *Countries at the Crossroads* survey is not yet an official indicator for the MCA. However, its methodology was designed to track the MCA criteria and to help inform the MCA process. Of the 63 MCA candidate countries in 2004, 18 were covered in the first edition of *Countries at the Crossroads*. The other countries were chosen for their geopolitical or strategic importance.

The survey combined four core components in narrative and numerical form: civil liberties, rule of law, anti-corruption and transparency, and accountability and public voice. It included 83 questions that were divided into the four topical areas and grouped into 16 subsections. Freedom House hired one expert per country to write narratives answering the questions. The experts came from a variety of backgrounds, both academic and professional (including journalists and policy analysts), both domestic and international. In addition to the narratives, the experts rated their countries on a scale of 0 (weakest performance) to 7 (strongest) for each of the questions. By averaging the scores in each subsection and then averaging the averages within the topical areas, Freedom House came up with four scores for each of the countries covered (see Table 15.1). The reports covered events in the year from October 2002 to September 2003.

The corruption section was an especially important feature of the report, since this is the only MCA criterion that can eliminate an otherwise eligible country. *Countries at the Crossroads* used a distinctive corruption indicator: rather than measuring corruption in each country, it focused on the governmental environment and how it might encourage or suppress corruption. In keeping with the focus of the survey, non-governmental corruption was not addressed. The four subsections of anti-corruption and transparency were:

- the environment to protect against corruption (addressing levels of bureaucracy and the degree of official control over and involvement in the economy)
- the existence of laws, ethical standards and boundaries between private and public sectors (addressing regulations to prevent corruption and ensure state financial accountability)
- the enforcement of anti-corruption laws (addressing the effectiveness of investigation and prosecution of corruption)
- governmental transparency (addressing disclosure of government practices).

Table 15.1: Country scores for *Countries at the Crossroads* (scale 0 weak to 7 strong)

	Civil liberties	Rule of law	Anti-corruption and transparency	Accountability and public voice
Afghanistan	2.48	1.67	1.56	2.21
Armenia	3.96	3.26	2.75	2.98
Azerbaijan	3.74	2.92	1.57	2.63
Bahrain	3.67	3.33	2.83	3.32
Cambodia	3.21	2.04	2.11	3.04
East Timor	4.77	4.76	2.42	4.77
Georgia	3.90	3.89	2.30	3.68
Guatemala	3.70	2.66	2.47	3.84
Haiti	3.19	2.34	2.81	3.09
Indonesia	3.38	2.95	2.46	4.03
Jordan	3.46	2.75	2.92	2.94
Kazakhstan	3.53	1.90	1.58	1.94
Kenya	4.74	3.97	3.80	4.22
Kyrgyzstan	3.17	2.62	2.34	1.84
Malaysia	3.64	3.52	2.31	3.11
Morocco	2.84	2.42	1.54	2.42
Nepal	3.91	3.96	3.81	3.84
Nicaragua	4.56	3.95	2.69	4.56
Nigeria	4.49	3.60	3.00	4.02
Pakistan	2.61	2.03	2.12	1.89
Qatar	3.69	3.74	2.58	3.27
Sierra Leone	3.81	3.76	3.01	4.13
Sri Lanka	4.59	4.49	3.97	4.45
Uganda	4.33	4.08	3.77	3.82
Ukraine	3.85	3.32	2.82	3.48
Uzbekistan	2.31	1.93	1.31	1.35
Venezuela	4.32	3.21	2.89	3.64
Vietnam	2.80	2.36	2.45	1.30
Yemen	3.63	3.45	1.85	3.23
Zimbabwe	2.97	2.48	1.86	2.19

One of the most striking findings was that the anti-corruption and transparency scores were significantly lower than those of each of the other topical areas.[2] Thus, among these already poor performers, the state of corruption appears to be worse than other aspects of their governance.

Freedom House also found anti-corruption and transparency to be less highly correlated with the other three topical areas than the latter were with one another. The civil liberties, rule of law, and accountability and public voice sections had correlations with each other of around 0.85, whereas the correlation of anti-corruption and transparency with each of these three was closer to 0.67. This finding further suggests that corruption was the exception among the areas we looked at, with conditions for corruption being somewhat independent of the wider political environment.

In general, the survey found that most of the countries under consideration had passed legislation to address international standards but were failing to implement it. However, in the case of anti-corruption and transparency measures, laws were not consistently in place. This further suggests that corruption is a greater problem than other areas of governance, and that special attention needs to be given to the drafting of appropriate laws.

Beyond the scores, each country narrative provided recommendations that highlighted the most urgent priorities for government action. The most common recommendations on corruption were for improved protection for whistleblowers, increased transparency in the awarding of government contracts, publication of financial statements of government officials, and freedom of information legislation.

The full report is available at www.freedomhouse.org/research/crossroads/cac.htm. The survey will be carried out again in 2004–05 with 30 new countries.

Notes

1. Sarah Repucci is a Researcher at Freedom House, United States.
   Contact: repucci@freedomhouse.org
2. Some caution should be exercised when comparing areas in the survey, although Freedom House did make every attempt to use the same scale across areas.

16 Global Index of Bribery for News Coverage

Dean Kruckeberg, Katerina Tsetsura and Frank Ovaitt[1]

At a time when the accuracy and reliability of the media have come under intense scrutiny around the world, the International Public Relations Association and the Institute for Public Relations in the United States has developed a comprehensive index that ranks 66 nations according to the likelihood that print journalists will seek or accept cash for news coverage from government officials, businesses or other news sources.

While bribery is also known to occur with broadcast and other types of media, the researchers confined their focus to print media to ensure a common frame of reference. The researchers suspect that each country's numerical score and ranking for daily consumer newspapers is very similar for other news media, but this was not measured because of the range of possible media programming formats, for example, print magazines, free-circulation 'shopper' newspapers, websites, radio and television.

The index provides a numeric-value score and ranking of 66 countries. The countries were selected primarily for their global economic and political importance and – to some extent – the availability of reliable data for variables in the index.

Because of the virtual impossibility of measuring the phenomenon of cash being paid for news coverage through direct observation, the researchers employed a composite index methodology. They sought a surrogate set of measures that would be predictive and correlated, but not necessarily causative. A critical challenge was how to select these factors.

To solve this problem, an email survey instrument was used to seek the collective expertise of two worldwide groups affected by bribery for news coverage. These were the International Public Relations Association's board and council; and the International Press Institute's board, national committee members and fellows. Representing public relations practitioners and journalists respectively, the worldwide leadership of these two institutions were asked for their expert views on the relevance of potential index factors; they were asked what are the leading factors that they – through their observation and years of experience – believe correlate with the phenomenon of 'cash for news coverage'. This approach is somewhat analogous to a physician who is unable to examine a patient directly, and who instead asks questions about factors that point to the probability of a specific disease by isolating and identifying those variables that are believed to be correlated with the presence of the illness.

The researchers thereby selected eight variables for which objective data were available. The data on each factor was numerically scored on a scale from 0 (linked to a high likelihood of bribery) to 5 (low likelihood), and the eight scores were then averaged in order to generate a rank order of the 66 countries. The variables, and the data source for each, were:

- length of tradition of self-determination by citizens (derived from the *CIA World Factbook 2001*, with scoring according to the number of years)
- perception of comprehensive corruption laws with effective enforcement (as measured by TI's 2001 Corruption Perceptions Index)
- accountability of government to citizens at all levels (involving evaluation of government type, legal system, suffrage and elections, as reported by the *CIA World Factbook 2001*)
- adult literacy (as reported by UNESCO's Institute for Statistics database)
- liberal and professional education of practising journalists (scored according to the reports in the *World Press Encyclopedia: A Survey of Press Systems Worldwide*, 2003)
- the existence of well-established, publicised and enforceable codes of professional ethics for journalists (derived from the International Journalism Network)
- free press, free speech and free flow of information (taken from Freedom House's 'Press Freedom Survey 2002')
- media competition (gathered from *World of Information Business Intelligence Reports 2001* or Walden country reports, and from *Editor & Publisher International Yearbook: The Encyclopedia of the Newspaper Industry 2002*).

The study did not attempt to justify or explain the specific impact of any single variable. It is possible, for instance, that a low score on 'free press, free speech and free flow of information' might in some instances indicate the extent to which journalists are intimidated by governments, rather than the extent to which journalists are bribed. The study simply measured those variables that experts believe to be positively correlated with 'cash for news coverage'.

As shown in Table 16.1, of the 66 countries in the study, bribery of the media is most likely to occur in China, Saudi Arabia, Vietnam, Bangladesh and Pakistan. By contrast, those countries with the best ratings for avoiding such practices are Finland (first place); and Denmark, New Zealand and Switzerland (tied for second place).

The complete study and a detailed description of the methodology is available at www.instituteforpr.com/international.phtml?article_id=bribery_index

Note

1. Dean Kruckeberg is a professor in the Department of Communication Studies at the University of Northern Iowa (contact: kruckeberg@uni.edu). Dr Katerina Tsetsura is an assistant professor in the Gaylord College of Journalism and Mass Communication at the University of Oklahoma (contact: tsetsura@ou.edu). Frank Ovaitt is President and Chief Executive Officer of the Institute for Public Relations (contact: iprceo@jou.ufl.edu).

Table 16.1: Global Index of Bribery for News Coverage[a]

	Self-determination	Perception laws	Accountability	Literacy	Professional education	Ethics codes	Free press	Competition	Mean score
Finland	5	5	5	5	5	5	5	4	4.88
Denmark	5	5	5	5	4	5	5	4	4.75
New Zealand	5	5	5	5	4	4	5	5	4.75
Switzerland	5	4	5	5	4	5	5	5	4.75
Germany	5	3	5	5	5	5	5	4	4.63
Iceland	5	5	5	5	3	4	5	5	4.63
UK	5	4	5	5	5	4	4	5	4.63
Norway	5	4	5	Miss. data	4	4	5	5	4.57
Austria	5	3	5	5	5	4	5	4	4.5
Canada	5	4	5	5	5	4	4	3	4.5
Netherlands	5	4	5	5	5	5	5	2	4.5
Sweden	5	4	5	5	5	3	5	4	4.5
Belgium	5	2	5	5	5	5	5	4	4.5
USA	5	3	5	5	5	5	4	4	4.5
Australia	5	4	5	5	3	5	5	3	4.38
Ireland	5	3	5	5	5	3	4	2	4
Israel	5	3	5	5	3	4	4	4	4
Italy	5	1	5	5	5	5	5	2	4
Spain	4	2	5	5	4	5	4	3	3.88
Cyprus	4	Miss. data	5	5	3	3	4	5	3.86
France	5	2	5	5	4	4	4	1	3.75
Portugal	4	2	5	5	3	4	3	5	3.75
Chile	3	3	5	5	3	4	4	4	3.63
Greece	4	0	5	5	4	3	4	5	3.63
Estonia	3	1	5	5	3	4	4	5	3.5
Japan	4	3	5	5	3	4	4	1	3.5
Bosnia & Herz	3	Miss. data	5	5	2	5	2	Miss. data	3.33
Brazil	4	0	4	4	4	5	3	2	3.25
Hungary	3	1	5	5	3	4	4	3	3.25
Puerto Rico	4	Miss. data	4	4	3	Miss. data	3	1	3.17
Korea, S.	4	0	5	5	4	3	4	1	3.13
Latvia	3	0	5	5	3	4	4	3	3.13

Country									Mean
Russia	3	0	3	5	3	4	2	5	3.13
Slovakia	3	0	3	5	3	4	4	3	3.13
Bulgaria	3	0	3	5	4	4	4	1	3
Czech Rep	3	0	3	5	4	3	4	2	3
Hong Kong	1	3	1	5	3	3	Miss. data	5	3
Lithuania	3	0	3	5	3	4	5	1	3
Singapore	4	5	2	5	3	2	1	2	3
Mauritius	3	0	3	4	3	Miss. data	4	4	3
Slovenia	3	1	3	5	3	3	4	2	3
Poland	3	0	3	5	3	3	4	2	2.88
Argentina	4	0	3	5	4	0	3	3	2.75
Mexico	5	0	4	4	1	5	3	0	2.75
Taiwan	4	1	4	4	3	0	4	2	2.75
Ukraine	3	0	3	5	3	3	2	3	2.75
Croatia	3	0	3	5	3	4	Miss. data	1	2.71
Turkey	4	0	4	4	3	3	2	1	2.63
Venezuela	4	0	2	5	4	0	3	3	2.63
South Africa	4	0	3	2	3	4	4	0	2.5
Thailand	2	0	3	5	4	2	4	0	2.5
UAE	3	Miss. data	1	3	2	3	1	4	2.43
Malaysia	4	0	2	4	3	3	1	2	2.38
India	4	0	3	1	2	5	3	0	2.25
Kenya	3	0	3	3	3	5	1	0	2.25
Kuwait	2	Miss. data	1	3	2	Miss. data	2	3	2.17
Indonesia	4	0	2	4	2	3	2	0	2.13
Nigeria	3	0	3	1	3	5	2	0	2.13
Bahrain	1	Miss. data	1	4	1	Miss. data	1	4	2
Jordan	2	0	2	4	2	3	2	1	2
Egypt	4	0	3	1	1	4	0	0	1.63
Pakistan	2	0	2	0	2	3	2	1	1.5
Bangladesh	3	0	2	1	1	3	1	0	1.38
Vietnam	1	0	1	5	1	1	0	2	1.38
Saudi Arabia	2	Miss. data	1	3	2	0	0	1	1.29
China	1	0	1	2	2	0	0	0	0.75

a. Some data are missing ('Miss. data') because they were not available from the standardised sources. The researchers eliminated the categories for these variables in determining the mean scores for those countries for which such data were not available.

17 Trust and corruption

Eric M. Uslaner[1]

Does corruption stem from institutional structures or from a society's culture? To examine this question, this study looked at generalised trust, a moral value predicated on the notion of a common bond between classes and races and on egalitarian values. Generalised trust reflects a belief that you should treat strangers as if they were trustworthy. In the World Values Surveys (WVS) it is measured by the question, 'Generally speaking, do you believe most people can be trusted or can't you be too careful in dealing with people?' Trust (as measured by the WVS) and (lack of) corruption (as measured by Transparency International's Corruption Perceptions Index) are strongly correlated: the simple correlation across 47 countries is .724.

Does corruption lead to less trust, or does trust lead to less corruption? Simultaneous equation (two-stage least squares) models were estimated to sort out the causal order.[2] These models showed that:

1. trust and corruption have a strong reciprocal relationship. Countries with high levels of trust have low levels of corruption and vice versa
2. trust is far more important than structural indicators such as the level of democracy, property rights, decentralisation or political stability, in explaining corruption. Each of these measures became insignificant in models including trust
3. while there is a strong reciprocal relationship between trust and corruption, changes in corruption do not lead to changes in trust, while increases in trust do lead to lower levels of corruption. Thus trust is the key to corruption more than corruption is the key to trust.

What are the consequences of trust and corruption? Simultaneous equation estimation leads to the tentative results in Table 17.1. Corruption seems to matter more than trust for adherence to the law and for red tape in the bureaucracy. But most of the time it is trust that matters more. Governments in societies with large shares of trusting people – more than honest governments – spend a greater share of their gross domestic product on government, spend more on education and on the public sector generally, and have better functioning judiciaries and greater political stability. Because trust and corruption are highly correlated, however, it is difficult to make firm conclusions about which is more important in shaping each outcome variable, so these conclusions are tentative.

Table 17.1: Effects of trust and corruption on political and economic performance[a]

Indicator	Corruption	Trust	Corruption vs trust	Freedom	Significant variables	N
Theft rate	**				1990 per capita income	14
Tax evasion	***	*	Corrupt**		1990 per cap. income, Knowledge diversity	22
Business regulations	**		Corrupt**		Knowledge diversity	23
Top marginal tax rate				**		23
GDP growth rate			Trust**	**		22
Mean yearly GDP growth 1980–90	**			****	Knowledge diversity	23
Government share of GDP			Trust**	**		
Public sector expenditure	**	***	Trust**			22
Education expenditure	**	**	Trust*			21
Transfer expenditure					1990 per capita income	23
Political stability	*	**				
Judicial efficiency	***	****	Trust**			22
Red tape in bureaucracy	****	**	Corrupt***		Knowledge diversity	22
Govt responds to will of people	*				Knowledge diversity	21

**** $p < .0001$; *** $p < .001$; ** $p < .05$; * $p < .01$

a. Each indicator represents the key dependent variable (outcome) in simultaneous equation estimations, with other significant predictors listed in the penultimate column. The asterisks represent significance levels (one-tailed tests) for trust and corruption. The 'corruption vs trust' column indicates which variable has a higher level of significance. The column for freedom indicates the significance level of democratisation.

In work with Gabriel Badescu of Babes-Bolyai University, Romania, the linkage between trust and corruption was also examined at the individual level.[3] Using data from the Gallup Millennium Survey as well as from our own study of Romania in 2001 as part of the Citizenship, Involvement, Democracy survey throughout Europe, we estimated simultaneous equation models for trust and perceptions of corruption and whether the government is run for the good of the people. We found that perceptions of corruption had a strong effect on perceptions of representativeness in the 'well-ordered' society of Sweden, but no effect on trust in Romania, where people seem to have become inured to corruption.

We found this result puzzling, so we investigated it in greater depth in a 2003 survey of Romanians, in which we distinguished low-level and high-level corruption.[4] Low-level corruption focuses on the extra 'gift' payments people make to doctors, banks, the police and teachers. High-level corruption involves bribery and corruption by politicians, business executives and the courts. We found that low-level corruption did not lead to lower levels of trust. Most people do not see these payments as making others 'rich', and often see such 'gifts' as making a bureaucratic system more efficient. In contrast, we found that high-level corruption affected perceptions of growing inequality, the evaluations of the performance of the government improving the quality of life, and trust both in other people and in government. Having to pay off city officials, and especially officers of the court, together with the beliefs that most politicians and business people were corrupt, led people to believe that the system was stacked against them, that government could not be trusted, and that even ordinary people were not trustworthy. There are different types of corruption, and citizens in post-communist countries clearly distinguish between them.

Notes

1. Eric Uslaner (contact: euslaner@gvpt.umd.edu) is professor of government and politics at the University of Maryland. For the full article, see Eric M. Uslaner, 'Trust and Corruption', in Johann Graf Lambsdorff, Markus Taube and Matthias Schramm, eds, *Corruption and the New Institutional Economics* (London: Routledge, 2004).
2. The corruption measures were taken from TI's 1998 Corruption Perceptions Index and (for changes) the 1980–83 Business International Corruption Index. While these indices are not directly comparable over time because they are based upon different sources, they are highly correlated ($r = .87$, $N = 37$) and thus indicate much stability. The estimated R^2s are .762 for trust and .863 for corruption ($N = 23$), with economic inequality and percentage Catholic also included in the trust equation. In the corruption equation were measures of democracy (Freedom House scores), property rights, openness of the economy, and religiosity (from the World Values Survey). The change equations had R^2 values of about .490 for each equation, with predictors mostly based upon change in economic and trading situations for both equations and change in democratisation in the corruption equation.
3. Eric M. Uslaner and Gabriel Badescu, 'Honesty, Trust, and Legal Norms in the Transition to Democracy: Why Bo Rothstein is Better Able to Explain Sweden than Romania', in Janos Kornai, Susan Rose-Ackerman and Bo Rothstein, eds, *Creating Social Trust: Problems of Post-Socialist Transition* (New York: Palgrave, 2004).
4. Eric M. Uslaner and Gabriel Badescu, 'Making the Grade in Transition: Equality, Transparency, Trust, and Fairness', available at www.bsos.umd.edu/gvpt/uslaner/working.htm

18 Experimental economics and corruption: a survey of budding research

Jens Chr. Andvig[1]

Empirical research on corruption has mostly relied on indirect and 'noisy' observations of corrupt transactions. Noise has been reduced through more detailed and direct questioning and through case studies, but few corrupt actions can be observed in a systematic way. The difficulty of observation makes corruption a natural candidate for experiments, though so far only a few have been carried out. This article summarises the findings of four examples of this new field of research.

Corruption as a game of trust

Abbink et al. start their corruption experiments from established research on so-called sequential trust games, in which one person repeatedly has a chance to influence a second person (for example, through a bribe) to change his behaviour, but, each time he does so, must ultimately trust the second person to act accordingly.[2] In the Abbink et al. experiment, the first person was interpreted as a businessman and the second as a public official, and each pair performed 30 transactions with each other.

Abbink et al. found that the 'businessmen' on average gave bribes worth more than 10 per cent of the gains they stood to make, and the 'public officials' changed their behaviour in favour of the 'businessmen' 65 per cent of the time.

Abbink et al. then amended the game in a number of ways. In one extension, a given pair would be severely punished when a bribe in one of the 30 rounds was 'discovered', though the rate of discovery was set low. The negative effect on the rate of bribing was found to be considerable – the 'public officials' only changed their behaviour 43 per cent of the time. When, in addition, partners were reshuffled at each of the 30 rounds – intended to simulate a rotation of officials – there was a strong preventive effect, with the frequency of behaviour change falling to 14 per cent. When the 'salaries' of the public officials were increased, however, the effects were negligible.

The experiment suggests that harsh, low-probability punishment of corruption may be more preventive than most economists believe. Furthermore, rotation of officials may also be effective and should be introduced in high-risk areas. However, the question of the validity of such results for real economies remains.

Corruption – a monitoring paradox

In the experiments reported by Frank and Schulze, punishment had no clear preventive effects and even increased the frequency of corrupt transactions.[3] Members of a student film club were asked to act on behalf of their club in awarding a contract that would result in funds being raised for the club. Acting as the procurement agent for their club, each student had to choose from 10 competing bids from different companies. The bids varied in how much the film club would have to pay the company for its service, and also in the size of bribe offered to the student by the company. The more the bidding company was paid, and the greater the bribe, the smaller the amount of funds raised for the club. To add realism, some of the students were then randomly selected to receive both a fixed amount and the bribe they accepted.

In one part of the experiment no punishments were meted out. In the second, the probability of being caught increased with the size of the bribe accepted. Strikingly, Frank and Schulze found that 9.4 per cent refused a bribe in the absence of punishment, whereas when they risked punishment only 0.9 per cent refused a bribe and the average bribe was also higher. How could an anti-corruption measure increase corruption in this way? Frank and Schulze argue that in their experiment an extrinsic incentive not to be corrupt (punishment) reduced an intrinsic motivation not to be corrupt (the students' loyalty to their club), and that the net effect was an increase in corruption.

The result should interest policy-makers. If an organisation starts to monitor its members in an effort to fight corruption, it may signal distrust and thereby cause corruption to increase. Again, however, the results may be tied to the specifics of the experiment; in this case to the positive attributes of the organisation in question: the film club was considered poor and was highly regarded by its student members.

An experiment highlighting political corruption

The most ambitious experiment on corruption was reported by Azfar and Nelson in the *Global Corruption Report 2004*.[4] In their experiment there were decision-makers – 'politicians' – who could embezzle, 'attorney generals' who controlled them and voters who elected the politicians. In some cases the attorney generals were elected by the voters and in some cases they were appointed by the politicians. The probability of being caught for embezzlement varied systematically.

Azfar and Nelson found that an increased probability of being caught reduced the frequency of embezzlement. When caught, politicians were unlikely to be re-elected, so higher wages for the politicians also reduced embezzlement. Interestingly, elected attorney generals were more vigilant than appointed ones and made the politicians less corrupt. The experiment has been replicated with a few modifications among nursing students in Ethiopia, with roughly the same results.[5] The finding that elected attorney generals reduce corruption may well contrast with real-world observations. The explanation may lie in the design of the experiment, which prevented the attorney generals and politicians from colluding.

Corruption and bureaucratic speed

González et al. conducted an experiment to study the effects of corruption on bureaucratic speed.[6] In the experiment a 'businessman' proposes a project that needs to be accepted by two different officials in order to go through. The officials have fixed salaries, but if the project is accepted, it generates a pie to be shared by all concerned. Both officials have veto power, but only one has delaying power. The size of the pie shrinks as time goes by. As expected, González et al. found that the larger the bribe to the official with delaying power, the faster the project was accepted.

While the experiment may not be the best one for the study of either bureaucratic delays or corruption, it does indicate that corruption in relation to queues and other forms of time-consuming bureaucratic behaviour is well suited to laboratory studies. Further experiments in this field may be particularly important given the extensive use of queues in public administration.

Conclusion

The study of corruption by experimental methods is still in its infancy and has clear limitations. The results are not immediately valid for real-world situations. Nevertheless, by allowing systematic variation of potential explanatory variables, such as the probability of being discovered or the control of collusion, the laboratory may generate more precise and better grounded hypotheses about the causes and effects of corruption than we would otherwise be able to formulate. Moreover, the many ways the institutional setup can be controlled in the laboratory may give rise to new ideas about anti-corruption policy. Anti-corruption practitioners may in future have to watch the results from the laboratory.

Notes

1. Jens Chr. Andvig is senior researcher at the Norwegian Institute of International Affairs. Contact: jensc.andvig@nupi.no
2. K. Abbink, B. Ihrenbusch and E. Renner, 'An Experimental Bribery Game', *Journal of Law, Economics and Organization* (2002).
3. B. Frank and G. Schulze, 'Deterrence versus Intrinsic Motivation: Experimental Evidence on the Determinants of Corruptibility', *Economics of Governance* 2 (2003).
4. O. Azfar and W. R. Nelson, 'Transparency, Wages and the Separation of Powers: An Experimental Analysis of the Causes of Corruption', in Transparency International, *Global Corruption Report 2004* (London: Pluto Press, 2004).
5. A. Barr, M. Lindelöw and P. Serneels, *To Serve the Community or Oneself – The Public Servant's Dilemma*, World Bank Policy Research Working Paper No. 3187 (Washington, DC, 2004).
6. L. González, W. Güth and M.V. Levati, *Speeding Up Bureaucrats by Greasing Them – An Experimental Study*, Max Planck Institute for Research into Economic Systems, Papers on Strategic Interaction No. 5 (Jena, 2002).

19 International determinants of national corruption levels

Wayne Sandholtz and Mark Gray[1]

Anti-corruption norms and ideas have gained increasing international prominence over the past decade. The efforts of transnational networks (such as Transparency International) and international organisations (such as the IMF, OECD, UN and World Bank) have substantially strengthened and diffused international anti-corruption values and norms. Do these developments on the international plane have measurable effects on the level of corruption within countries?

We suggest that international factors affect a country's level of corruption through two principal channels. One channel is economic incentives, altering for various actors the costs and benefits of engaging in corrupt acts. The second is social integration and the transmission of values and norms; norms in international society delegitimate and stigmatise corruption.

On the economic side, cross-national trade and investment ties can constrain corruption by increasing its costs. Numerous previous studies have found that the more open a country is to international trade, the lower its corruption level tends to be. Corrupt practices can perpetuate themselves more easily in closed economies, cut off from competitive pressures. Our empirical analysis included a set of variables measuring economic integration: trade openness (total trade/GDP), gross foreign direct investment per capita, international air freight and air passengers per capita, and international telecommunications traffic per capita.

In addition, the interactions associated with trade and cross-border investment may also be mechanisms for the communication of ideas, values, and norms. Other loci for the transmission of international norms and values are international organisations (IOs). To measure a country's degree of international social integration, we focused on memberships in international organisations. This set of indicators included: the total number of memberships in international organisations; years of membership in the IMF; years of membership in the UN; and years of membership in the General Agreement on Tariffs and Trade and the WTO.

Our first step was to conduct a factor analysis of the independent variables. The factor analysis produced two important results. First, the variables clustered into three independent factors, which we labelled 'international economic integration', 'IO memberships', and 'development'.[2] This clustering strongly confirmed our expectation that the three sets of variables captured distinct and independent phenomena. Second, we could use the factor scores as independent variables in the multiple regression, thus avoiding the problem that the variables in each cluster correlated strongly with each other.

In order to demonstrate the robustness of our results, we used two measures of the dependent variable (level of perceived corruption): the Transparency International Corruption Perceptions Index (CPI) and the Graft-CPIA data produced by researchers at the World Bank Institute.[3] For the CPI model, we averaged the independent variables for the period 1995–98 and the dependent variables for 1999–2002. The Graft-CPIA was only available for 1997–98, so we used data for the independent variables from 1996, again avoiding temporal overlap.[4]

The results of the regression analysis strongly supported our initial hypothesis.[5] Table 19.1 presents the principal findings.

Table 19.1: Regression analysis of corruption scores[a]

	CPI scores, 1999–2002		Graft-CPIA scores, 1997–98	
	B (S.E.)	Beta	B (S.E.)	Beta
Development (factor)	−.730*** (.188)	−.310	−.590*** (.120)	−.325
International economic integration (factor)	−.848*** (.134)	−.360	−.398*** (.106)	−.218
IO memberships (factor)	−.407** (.165)	−.173	−.411*** (.118)	−.219
Democracy score (Freedom House)	−.305*** (.108)	−.220	−.155*** (.032)	−.336
Adjusted R^2	.847		.796	
Number of cases	97		153	

**p < .05, ***p < .01.

a. Dependent variable is the corruption score, inverted so that higher scores represent higher levels of perceived corruption. The Graft-CPIA scores have been converted to a 1–10 range. Ordinary least squares regression with pairwise deletion. B reports unstandardised coefficients, with standard errors below, in parentheses. Beta reports standardised coefficients.

Our most notable finding is that both of our international level variables – international economic integration and IO memberships – show a strongly significant negative relationship with corruption. In other words, countries that are more open to the international economy and participate more broadly in international organisations tend to have lower levels of perceived corruption. In order to make sure that our results were not being driven by the wealthy democracies, we ran the models again, omitting the OECD countries. The results did not change, increasing our confidence in the findings.

The policy implications of our study are clear. Support for democratisation, including competitive elections and a free press, may produce the ancillary benefit of constraining corruption.[6] Countries where corruption problems are intense would probably also benefit from increasing international integration, in both the economic and the socio-political dimensions. International trade and investment tend to increase the costs of corruption. Encouraging greater participation in international organisations and in private sector networks might help speed the transmission of anti-corruption norms and ideas. Though our results must be taken with some caution, it does appear that the ongoing efforts of both official institutions and non-governmental networks do play a useful role in reducing corruption.

Notes

1. Wayne Sandholtz is in the Department of Political Science at the University of California, Irvine, United States (contact: wsandhol@uci.edu). Mark M. Gray is at the Center for Applied Research in the Apostolate, Georgetown University, United States (contact: mmg34@georgetown.edu). This research was originally reported in Wayne Sandholtz and Mark Gray, 'International Integration and National Corruption', *International Organisation* 57 (2003).
2. We included two measures of development: gross domestic product per capita, and literacy.
3. Using the CPI allows for comparisons with previous research that employed that index; utilising the Graft-CPIA data permits a much larger set of countries (153 rather than 97), thus avoiding errors due to sample bias (as small, less-developed countries are underrepresented in the CPI).
4. It is possible that in the expert surveys underlying both the CPI and the CPIA scores, experts rate more severely those countries that do not participate widely in international organisations. But because low corruption has never been a condition of membership in any international organisation (including the EU), we are confident that any effects of this potential bias are minimal.
5. Our independent variables were the three factor scores (international economic integration, IO memberships and development) plus a number of variables to control for other factors that have a possible relationship with corruption levels, including: British heritage; religious affiliation (percentage Protestant, Catholic, Muslim); democracy (Freedom House scores); and government economic intervention (Heritage Foundation scores).
6. The possibility of reverse causation (from higher levels of corruption to lower income levels, lower levels of participation in international economic exchange and lower levels of participation in international organisations) warrants some caution. However, previous research provides evidence that causation does run from low GDP per capita to corruption and from trade openness to corruption. With respect to memberships in IOs, none of those used in our measure has used low corruption as a condition of membership.

20 Corruption in transition economies

Cheryl Gray and James Anderson[1]

Anticorruption in Transition – A Contribution to the Policy Debate, prepared in advance of the World Bank-IMF Annual Meetings in Prague in 2000, broke new ground in the quest to understand corruption and why it is so persistent in transition countries. A new report by Cheryl Gray, Joel Hellman and Randi Ryterman, *Anticorruption in Transition 2* (ACT-2), continues the tradition of bringing empirical evidence to bear on this question.[2]

Based on two rounds of the EBRD-World Bank *Business Environment and Enterprise Performance Survey* (BEEPS), the report delves into the complexities of corruption in relations between business enterprises and the state. The two rounds of the BEEPS, covering altogether more than 10,000 firms in 27 countries,[3] provide an opportunity to examine not only the current state of corruption, but changes over time, the factors that influence levels and patterns of corruption, the areas of corruption on the wane and those posing new challenges. These surveys have provided information on how much and how often firms pay bribes and broader views of managers on how much of an obstacle corruption creates for business.

ACT-2 provides rigorous evidence that the prevalence and costs of some types of corruption are becoming more moderate in many countries in the region (see Figure 20.1). Managers' responses in almost half of the transition countries suggest a decline between 1999 and 2002 in the overall frequency of bribery and the impact of corruption on their business, a finding that is particularly important for this region. Nowhere has corruption been a bigger social and political issue than in the transition economies of Central and Eastern Europe and the former Soviet Union, where essential steps to privatise the economy and rewrite the rules of commerce after the demise of socialism were often accompanied by widespread corruption.

The report underscores, however, that there is no cause for complacency. Levels of corruption are still high in many countries and in many sectors of the economy. While bribes appear less prevalent for public services, for example, they appear more common than in 1999 for taxes and procurement. Nor is the news universally positive at the country level, as some indicators suggest a worsening of corruption in some countries, for example in South Eastern Europe. What is more, firms in most transition countries still view corruption as a formidable obstacle, among the most severe they face.

Encouragingly, the report finds that better policies and institutions can help to reduce corruption over the medium term. Many transition countries have undertaken policy and institutional reforms in recent years that have led to significant changes in the

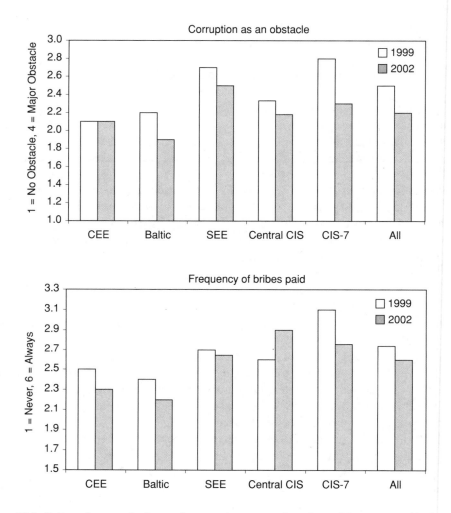

Figure 20.1: Ratings by sample firms of corruption as an obstacle and frequency of bribes paid, by sub-regional groupings 1999–2002

Sources: ACT-2 and BEEPS 1999 and 2002.

'rules of the game', helping to fill voids left with the abandonment of communism. These changes and the resulting declines in certain forms of corruption should in many cases prove sustainable, underscoring the critical importance of an active, credible and well-implemented reform process.

Alas, better policies cannot take all of the credit for the observed improvements. The report finds that firm-specific factors play a significant role, with smaller private firms typically paying more bribes and foreign firms fewer bribes than average. In addition, managerial 'optimism' plays an important role in influencing managers' views on corruption, as much of the perceived reduction in corruption can be explained by more general perceptions of improvements in the business environment. However, while managerial attitudes should be taken into account in analysing survey data, their influence on perceptions of corruption does not undermine the usefulness of corruption surveys. After all, attitudes and perceptions do affect important business decisions. Furthermore, the evidence described in ACT-2 shows real changes in levels of corruption even after controlling for managerial attitudes in the analysis.

ACT-1 argued that one of the most pernicious forms of corruption is 'state capture' – corruption influencing the formation of laws, rules and regulations. While relatively fewer firms complained of being affected by state capture in 2002 than three years earlier, relatively more firms said that they were engaged in such activities (see Figure 20.2). It appears that state capture is changing in some settings from a strategy of political influence practised by a small share of firms to a more widespread practice.

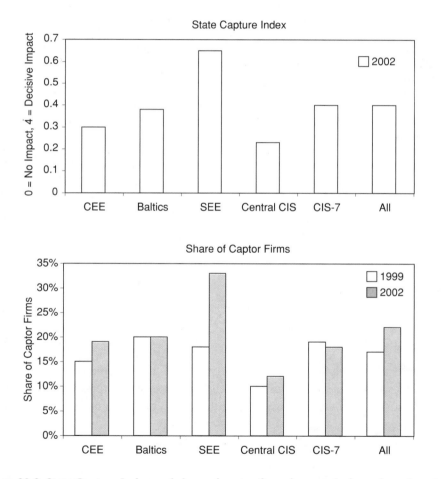

Figure 20.2: State Capture Index and share of captor firms for sample firms, by sub-regional groupings 2002

Sources: ACT-2 and BEEPS 1999 and 2002.

The best news from ACT-2 is that progress is possible. Countries can effectively fight corruption through reforms in public institutions and aggressive pursuit of anti-corruption policies, and detailed survey data can help to pinpoint priorities for action in individual countries. Most promising of all, there is now solid evidence that the reforms in the past few years in many transition countries have begun to show results. A third round of the BEEPS, tentatively planned for 2005, will help to verify if progress is continuing.

Notes

1. Cheryl Gray is Sector Director, and James Anderson is Senior Economist, in the World Bank's Europe and Central Asia region, Poverty Reduction and Economic Management department.
2. Cheryl Gray, Joel Hellman and Randi Ryterman, *Anticorruption in Transition 2 – Corruption in Enterprise–State Interactions in Europe and Central Asia 1999–2002* (Washington, DC: World Bank, 2004). This and related publications are available at www.worldbank.org/eca/governance. An earlier version of this summary appeared in *World Finance Review*, Spring 2004.
3. The countries and their regional groupings are as follows: Central and Eastern Europe (CEE) includes the Czech Republic, Hungary, Poland, Slovenia and the Slovak Republic; the Baltic states include Estonia, Latvia and Lithuania; South Eastern Europe (SEE) includes Albania, Bosnia and Herzegovina, Bulgaria, Croatia, the former Yugoslav Republic of Macedonia, Romania, and Serbia and Montenegro; Central Commonwealth of Independent States (CIS) includes Belarus, Kazakhstan, Russia and Ukraine; and the CIS-7 countries include Armenia, Azerbaijan, Georgia, the Kyrgyz Republic, Moldova, Tajikistan and Uzbekistan.

21 Transparency and accountability in the public sector in the Arab region

UN Department of Economic and Social Affairs[1]

In 2002–03, the UN Department of Economic and Social Affairs (DESA) conducted a comparative study on public sector transparency and accountability in the Arab region. The study covered six countries: Jordan, Lebanon, Morocco, Sudan, Tunisia and Yemen.

The project aimed to assist participating countries to improve transparency and accountability in the public sector through comparing existing practices in financial, human resources and information management. The project was intended to identify good practices and gaps in them, as well as to assist in policy and programme choices and funding decisions. The participating countries were chosen to represent the diversity of the Arab region, based on consultations between the UN and governments, so that other countries in the region could also benefit from the study.

The analytical framework was a checklist of institutions, rules and practices, which were assessed through a combination of document analysis and expert interviews. Knowledgeable national consultants prepared country case studies, analysed documents and carried out over 400 expert interviews,[2] using DESA questionnaires requesting statistical data, administrative information and expert perceptions of daily practices. DESA then constructed a database and wrote the final report.

In order to ensure reliability, as well as the participation of regional and national stakeholders in the research process, the project was assisted by a Project Advisory Group. This group was composed of representatives of the Arab Organization of Supreme Audit Institutions, the Arab Administrative Development Organization, the Arab Council for Economic Unity, the Federation of Arab Journalists, the Arab Social Science Research Network, the League of Arab States and the Union of Arab Banks.

Selected findings are presented in Table 21.1. The main findings were:

- Access to data on the structure and employment of the public sector is highly limited in many countries.
- Among the public sector areas examined, financial management is the most developed. Good practices in human resources management and the relatively newly-introduced information management (both in and outside the public sector) are less well implemented.

- Although all three areas examined (financial management, human resources management and information management) are interrelated and important to transparency and accountability, to make quick gains the countries should target information management reforms and encourage freer information flows within and outside the public sector.

Table 21.1: Breakdown of main findings

Financial management:	Human resources management:	Information management:
• Although the legislative and administrative framework for financial transactions is in place, general financial controls are not highly visible. • Many improvements have been made in revenue collection practices, but the recourse to effective appeals procedures is less satisfactory. • Independent verifications of public payroll amounts and reconciliations take place consistently, but not the physical identification of personnel. • Public competitive bidding for large contracts consistently does not lead to the best bids winning the contracts. Making the evaluation of bids more transparent by consistently stating criteria and keeping *all* records may help. • Regarding payments, verifications of goods and services and computations are made, but payments can be delayed and overspending occurs frequently, without being adequately addressed. • The role of internal and external audit needs to be reinforced through greater independence of operations and better-trained staff.	• Officially stated core values (most frequently defined as neutrality, legality, fairness or equality) are enshrined in pertinent laws, but are not well communicated or demonstrated by the leadership. • Standards of conduct are not systematically enforced. • Recruitment and promotions are not based primarily on merit or sufficiently protected from political interference. • Only three countries reported conflict-of-interest disclosure requirements, and no country reported mandatory reporting of wrongdoing or protection for whistleblowers. • Investigations, apart from criminal investigations carried out by the police, are not seen to be independent. • Disciplinary procedures are clearly set out, but are not consistently applied.	• The legislative and administrative framework for managing information is in its early stages, despite the recent introduction or updating of laws. • There are few independent and alternative sources of reporting on public information, apart from government-sponsored sources. • Public consultations have been limited and confined to traditional forms (for example, advisory council). • Record keeping in the public sector is not of high quality. • Investigative journalism is underdeveloped. • Although civil society organisations generally have freedom of association in the participating countries in the study, they have only a limited role in civic education and in monitoring public sector performance.

These findings are consistent with other recent research carried out in the Arab region. In its *Arab Human Development Reports 2003–04* the UNDP identifies a knowledge deficit among the development challenges, and advocates building a knowledge society. In its regional report, the World Bank notes striking weaknesses in external accountability, leading to a governance gap between this and other regions.[3]

Project documents (including a comprehensive regional overview and individual country case studies) and a database of survey data are available at: www.unpan.org/technical_highlights-Transparency-Arabstates.asp

Notes

1. Contact Guido Bertucci, Director (bertucci@un.org) or Elia Yi Armstrong, Public Administration Officer (armstronge@un.org) in the Division for Public Administration and Development Management, Department of Economic and Social Affairs, UN.
2. The figure includes some multiple interviews with individual experts.
3. World Bank, 'Better Governance for Development in the Middle East and North Africa: Enhancing Inclusiveness and Accountability', *MENA Development Report* (Washington, DC: World Bank, 2003).

22 Latin American Index of Budget Transparency

Helena Hofbauer[1]

Several indexes have recently emerged which attempt to measure government transparency. Transparency requires the reasons for all governmental and administrative decisions, as well as the costs and resources committed in applying these decisions, to be accessible, clear and communicated to the public. Transparency in public spending is particularly important given the centrality of the budget in government policy. Budget analysis allows evaluation of who truly wins and loses in the distribution of public resources. In addition, it reveals the degree of efficiency and effectiveness of public spending, by revealing potential cases of corruption. Analysis of the degree of transparency of the budget process contributes to strengthening democratic institutions and consolidating the rule of law.

In 2001 eight organisations from five Latin American countries developed the first edition of the Latin American Index of Budget Transparency. This measurement and evaluation tool was replicated in 2003 in 10 countries: Argentina, Brazil, Chile, Colombia, Costa Rica, Ecuador, El Salvador, Mexico, Nicaragua and Peru. The study was composed of an analysis of the legal framework regulating the budget process, a fact-based questionnaire, and a perception survey answered by experts. Experts were selected using comparable criteria in all countries and included: members of the legislature's budget committee, academics who have published on budgetary issues, NGOs working on the topic, and journalists covering the issue. A total of 996 people were identified (nearly 100 per country), of whom 63 per cent answered the survey.[2]

Experts were asked to rate the degree of budget transparency both at the beginning of the survey and at the end. In each case their perceptions were averaged on a scale from 1 to 100, with 100 being highly transparent. As Figure 22.1 illustrates, most of the countries received overall ratings of between 40 and 50 points. Chile had the highest rating, 61.7 points, while Ecuador had the lowest, 30.6 points.

Respondents were also asked to evaluate a series of particular aspects of the budget process in their countries, and their responses were combined into 14 categories. Each of these categories offers a perspective on access to budget information, the willingness of officials to seek input from citizens on budgeting decisions, and the credibility of institutions such as internal and external auditors, among others. The figures below record the proportion of respondents who gave a positive response ('agree' or 'totally agree') to a number of statements for which agreement implies high transparency.

As reported in Table 22.1, citizen participation in the budget process received extremely low ratings across the region. Brazil, the highest-rated country in this category, was

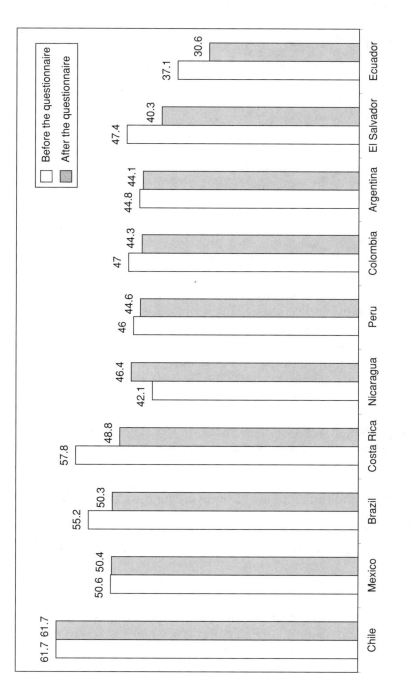

Figure 22.1: General Index of Budget Transparency

rated positively by only 20 per cent of respondents. Ecuador, El Salvador, Peru, and Costa Rica received positive ratings below 10 per cent.

Table 22.1: Evaluation of selected aspects of budget transparency (percentage of positive responses)

	Citizen participation in the budget	Evaluation of internal comptroller	Information on macroeconomic budget criteria
Argentina	11	27	49
Brazil	20	33	53
Chile	14	33	76
Colombia	15	4	43
Costa Rica	8	46	47
Ecuador	3	0	36
El Salvador	5	n/a	33
Mexico	16	18	64
Nicaragua	12	11	24
Peru	7	6	58

The credibility of internal auditors also received markedly few positive ratings. Not a single respondent in Ecuador believed internal auditing to be credible, while positive ratings for Colombia and Peru were only 4 and 6 per cent, respectively. Even Costa Rica's 46 per cent rating, the region's highest, does not suggest an overwhelming level of confidence in internal auditors.

The category with the most positive responses was the availability and quality of macroeconomic information. Leaders in this category were Chile (76 per cent), Mexico (64 per cent) and Peru (58 per cent).

On the basis of the categories identified in the perception survey, general recommendations for each country were drawn from the study of the legal framework and the fact-based questionnaire. Enhancing budget transparency in the ten countries will involve such steps as:

- creating opportunities for public input during the legislature's consideration of the budget
- enhancing the authority and capacity of the internal auditor
- disseminating budgetary information more quickly, more frequently and in greater detail.

Reactions to the study in each of the participating countries varied: in Argentina, Congress revised the study and included it in its formal agenda; in Chile, President Ricardo Lagos reacted to the positive ranking of the country; several official institutions commented and enquired about the study in Costa Rica, while the internal comptroller analysed its results in Mexico. In all the countries, the index has helped to shed light on a hidden topic, to evaluate the extent to which access to information laws are working, and to strengthen the arguments of independent groups assessing the budget.

Notes

1. Helena Hofbauer is the executive director of Fundar, Mexico.
2. The study is available in English and Spanish at www.internationalbudget.org/themes/ BudTrans/LA03.htm. It was coordinated by Fundar, a Mexican think tank, which is also responsible for integrating the third edition of the study, to be carried out in 2005. For more information, contact Helena Hofbauer or Briseida Lavielle at fundar@fundar.org. mx

23 The Latin American Public Opinion Project: corruption victimisation, 2004

Mitchell A. Seligson[1]

The *Global Corruption Report 2004* contained a chapter reporting on surveys measuring corruption victimisation in several Latin American countries. In 2004 those surveys were repeated in nine countries in the region and were carried out by the Latin American Public Opinion Project, formerly of the University of Pittsburgh and now of Vanderbilt University, with funding from the United States Agency for International Development. In this report on the surveys, the focus is on corruption victimisation in the workplace and among users of four popular services: health, the courts, schools and local government. The studies were all conducted using face-to-face interviews, with nationally representative samples of about 1,500 respondents in each country except Ecuador, where 3,000 people were interviewed.[2]

For this group of 15,000 Latin Americans, it was disappointing to see that corruption victimisation was greatest in the school system, among respondents who had children in school during the year covered by the survey (see Figure 23.1).[3] One likes to think of school systems as largely immune from the more sordid aspects of life that adults

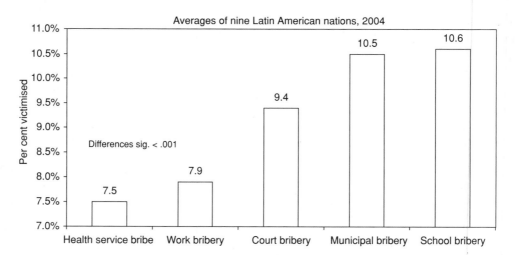

Figure 23.1: Reported bribery victimisation at work and among service users

Source: Latin American Public Opinion Project, Vanderbilt University.

must face, but in Latin America this is clearly not the case. In fact, since schools are a major transmission mechanism of cultural values, the youth of these countries are being socialised into systems in which corruption is endemic.

These overall results hide sharp differences among the countries in the sample. Table 23.1 shows that whereas in Colombia 'only' one in 20 parents who had children in school reported paying bribes in the year prior to the study, nearly one in four parents in Ecuador faced this problem in their schools. School-related corruption is also a serious problem for parents in other countries in the region, especially Mexico and Honduras.

Table 23.1: Percentage of corruption victims among users of services, by country[a]

	School system	Local government	Courts
Colombia	5.5	5.3	5.1
Costa Rica	8.6	5.6	2.7
Ecuador	23.8	15.0	20.5
El Salvador	7.3	5.3	4.0
Guatemala	8.7	8.2	5.0
Honduras	11.3	10.2	6.6
Mexico	12.8	20.8	13.5
Nicaragua	9.5	12.9	15.5
Panama	6.7	9.3	6.5

a. Differences sig. < .001.

Corruption victimisation among those who carried out some transaction with local municipal governments (for example, asking for a permit) was commonplace, as shown in Table 23.1. In Mexico, 20.8 per cent of users of local government services reported having to pay a bribe, compared to Colombia, Guatemala and Costa Rica where the victimisation rate was only one-quarter as high.

Although the court system is frequently discussed as an important venue of corrupt practices, our data show that, on average, corruption is less frequent there than among other public services. In Costa Rica, for example, such corruption is rather uncommon (only 2.7 per cent of court users). In contrast, in its neighbour to the north, Nicaragua, court-based corruption is over five times more common.

What stands out in this analysis is not only the frequency of corruption victimisation among users of public services, but the wide variation among the countries studied and the variation among distinct venues for corrupt practices. Mexico and Ecuador stand apart from the other countries as being far more subject to corruption than the others, while overall the school system and local government are especially vulnerable to the penetration of corrupt practices. These results should help target public policy anti-corruption efforts in these countries, demonstrating where the problems are more serious and where the problem is more under control.

Notes

1. Mitchell A. Seligson is the centennial professor of political science, Vanderbilt University, United States. Contact: m.seligson@vanderbilt.edu
2. Since the Ecuador sample is twice as large as the others, the responses for this country are weighted by .5 in order not to distort the overall means for the nine-country sample.
3. While the overall results are statistically significant for the combined sample, the differences among the forms of corruption measured are between health service bribes and work bribery on the one hand, and the remaining three categories on the other. Approximately half of the respondents in each of the countries had experience with corruption in the health services, work and schools, whereas about one-third had such experiences with municipal governments and an average of about 15 per cent in the courts. The lower frequency of corruption victimisation in these last two categories widens the confidence interval of the estimates compared to the other categories.

24   Corruption and crime

Omar Azfar[1]

One of the fundamental roles of government is to protect the lives and property of citizens from criminals. We would expect corruption to lower the effectiveness of law enforcement, leading to higher crime rates. Criminals may bribe the police and avoid punishment, while corruption in the hiring process may undermine the quality of the judiciary and the police force. Anecdotal accounts suggest that corruption does indeed affect the police force and both the willingness and ability to commit crimes. However, previous studies have found only a weak relationship between corruption and crime.[2] In ongoing work at the IRIS Center of the University of Maryland, we examined the links between corruption and two kinds of crime: theft and homicides. In each case we found a significant relationship, with higher levels of corruption associated with more crime.

Theft

There are two possible sources of data on theft: Interpol, for a large number of countries; and the International Crime Victimisation Surveys (ICVS), for a smaller number. However, the Interpol data comes from police sources and is unreliable, because crimes may not be reported to the police, and crimes may not be reported by the police to international agencies. This under-reporting is large in magnitude, and the rate of under-reporting itself is highly correlated with corruption (see Soares in this report, page 289). Average crime rates calculated from the ICVS are measured with some noise but there is likely to be less bias. Hence, we used data on crime incidence from the ICVS.

The ICVS collects data from approximately 1,000 respondents in 67 countries. Data is collected on both crime rates and crime reporting rates for a variety of crimes including burglary, robbery, bribery, fraud and assault. Of these crimes theft is by far the most prevalent, and hence measured with the greatest accuracy. Across the sample of 67 countries, 16.2 per cent of respondents had been the victim of a theft of personal property (other than car-related crimes) in the past two years.

We found the rate of theft to be highly correlated with the World Bank Institute measure of corruption.[3] This relationship remained statistically strong after controlling for various factors like inequality, urbanisation, literacy, contract enforcement and legal origin.[4] Figure 24.1 depicts the relationship.

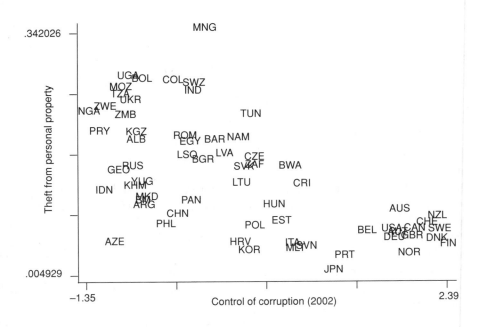

Figure 24.1: Corruption and theft

The relationship between corruption and theft was also found to be significant in an instrumental variables regression, which suggests that the link is a causal one.[5] If it is correctly interpreted as causal, then reducing corruption by one standard deviation – from the level of India to that of South Korea – would reduce theft by approximately 4.4 thefts per 100 people every two years. In global terms this would represent a reduction of hundreds of millions of thefts a year.

Homicides

There are two possible sources of data on homicides: the World Health Organisation (WHO), which publishes statistics on mortality for various causes including homicide; and Interpol, which publishes police-reported statistics on homicides. Again, there are questions about the accuracy of the Interpol data. Besides possible misreporting, there are also some definitional problems: the Interpol definition of homicides includes attempted homicides, but the data provided by police forces often excludes attempted homicides. In addition, we found the difference between the WHO and Interpol numbers to be correlated with the level of corruption – one possible explanation is that homicides are less likely to be reported to or by the police in poorly governed countries. We therefore used the WHO data.

We found a very strong correlation between homicide rates and the level of corruption.[6] This relationship remained large and significant after controlling for income, inequality, schooling and ethnic fractionalisation.[7] The relationship remained significant in an instrumental variable regression that tested for causality.

Figure 24.2 shows the relationship between homicides and corruption. Improving a country's corruption score by one standard deviation – from the level of Ukraine to Slovakia, or from the level of Brazil to Cost Rica – would reduce the homicide rate by 50 per cent. For Brazil alone, this would imply a reduction in homicides of more than 10,000 per year. Globally a reduction in homicides of this magnitude would reduce homicides by hundreds of thousands of deaths a year.

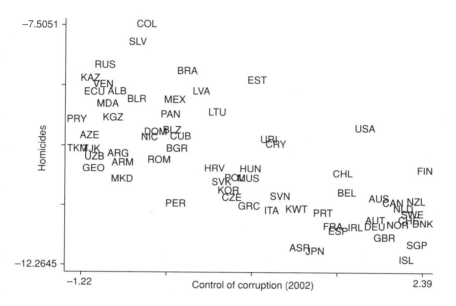

Figure 24.2: Corruption and homicides

The relationships we found are evident even with the highly imperfect data on crime. We hope that the quantity and quality of the data will improve in future and that more sophisticated analyses will become possible. In addition, there needs to be an examination of the mechanics by which corruption facilitates crime. Once these links become clearer, it may become possible to use the evidence on corruption and crime as a way to mobilise public opinion against corruption more effectively.

Notes

1. Omar Azfar is a research associate at the Center for Institutional Reform and the Informal Sector at the University of Maryland, United States. Contact: omar@iris.econ.umd.edu
2. Daniel Lederman, Norman Loayza and Rodrigo Soares, *Accountability and Corruption: Political Institutions Matter*, mimeo (Washington, DC: World Bank, 2004).
3. The correlation coefficient was 0.65. See Omar Azfar and Tugrul Gurgur, *Crime, Crime Reporting and Governance*, mimeo (IRIS, University of Maryland, 2004).
4. T-stat = 3.00, easily significant at the 1 per cent level.
5. The relationship was significant at the 5 per cent level. The instruments were whether a country was democratic in 1946, whether it was ever colonised, whether there was malaria

in 1946 (as a proxy for settler mortality), and the interaction terms of 'ever-colonised' multiplied with 'malaria in 1946' (as settler mortality should have a larger impact in colonies). The first stage regression explained 80 per cent of the variation in governance and easily passed the Over-Identifying Restrictions Test.

6. The correlation coefficient was 0.73. See Omar Azfar, *The Rule of Law, Corruption and Homicides*, mimeo (IRIS, University of Maryland, 2004).

7. T-stat = 3.86, easily significant at the 1 per cent level.

25 Measuring corruption: validating subjective surveys of perceptions

Rodrigo R. Soares[1]

Objective data on corruption and institutional quality are rare, even though recent initiatives have shown that household surveys can be quite effective as a source of information on individuals' experiences with corruption. Due to data availability, virtually all the empirical work in the area has focused on subjective surveys of perceived levels of corruption and public sector efficiency, and there is no objective evidence of the adequacy of such indicators. It is therefore essential to search for alternative data sources, in order to substitute, or at least validate, subjective surveys. One option is to look for data generated by individuals' actual behaviour in situations where it should be affected by corruption, such as the rate of crime reporting.

The rate of crime reporting is the proportion of crimes committed that is reported to the police, and can be estimated by dividing the official crime rate by the crime rate obtained in victimisation surveys.[2] In principle, the rate of crime reporting should be correlated with several dimensions of institutional development that researchers are interested in, such as confidence of citizens in the system, efficiency of public services, sense of civic duty and, particularly, corruption. Corruption can reduce the gains from reporting a crime through something like a tax on the recovered good. In addition, it reduces the efficiency of the police force, since it increases the probability that the force is actually working together with the criminals.

The credibility of existing corruption indices would be reinforced if they were strongly correlated with the rate of crime reporting. To test this possibility, the rate of crime reporting was constructed using two international data sources: the International Crime Victimisation Surveys (ICVS) and the United Nations Survey of Crime Trends and Operations of Criminal Justice Systems (UNCS). The behaviour of this reporting rate was compared to the International Country Risk Guide (ICRG) corruption index. The data used were averages for the first half of the 1990s. Data for both reporting rates and the corruption index exist for roughly 40 countries, including several Western and Eastern European countries, North America, and some Asian, African and Latin American countries.

The fraction of the total number of crimes reported to the police varies widely across countries and across different types of crimes, from virtually zero (as for thefts in Egypt or India) to almost one (as for burglaries in Austria and Finland). The relationship between these rates and the ICRG corruption index is illustrated in Figure 25.1, with the reporting rates of burglaries. Countries classified as having low corruption report, on average 37 per cent of the burglaries committed, while countries classified as having high corruption report only 3 per cent. The same pattern is present when we look at other crimes, such as thefts or violent crimes, though the differences are not so large. The simple correlation between the corruption index and the reporting rate is 0.41 for burglaries, 0.65 for thefts, and 0.62 for violent crimes (in the ICRG index, higher values correspond to lower corruption).

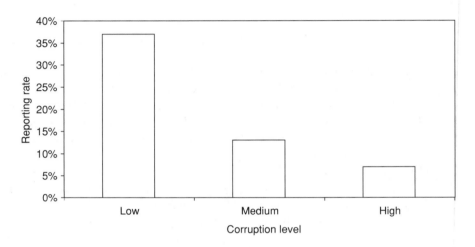

Figure 25.1: Reporting rate of burglaries according to corruption levels, country averages, 1990s

This correlation does not seem to be spurious, or generated by the indirect relation of some other variable to corruption and reporting rates. Data from several international sources show that crime reporting is strongly related to institutional stability, police presence and perceived corruption. This is true even when the analysis controls independently for the number of years under an uninterrupted democratic regime, a variable widely known to capture the degree of political stability in the system.[3]

The statistical analysis implies that if Russia reduced its perceived level of corruption to that of the United States, reporting rates of burglaries would increase from 1.8 to 5.7 per cent, reporting rates of thefts would increase from 3.1 to 6.1 per cent, and reporting rates of violent crimes would increase from 1 to 1.84 per cent. Perhaps more importantly, the evidence supports the use of subjective surveys of perceived corruption as a measure of actual corruption.

Notes

1. Rodrigo R. Soares is an assistant professor of economics at the University of Maryland (contact: soares@econ.umd.edu).
2. Victimisation surveys are less subject to underreporting than official crime statistics. This phenomenon is truer of 'economic crimes' such as thefts and burglaries than of crimes

associated with social stigma, such as domestic violence and sexual crimes, for which even victimisation surveys give an underestimate.

3. This analysis also controlled for the other dimension of the ICRG corruption index – the 'political risk' involved in corruption – that might be thought to bias the results. For full results, see Rodrigo R. Soares, 'Crime Reporting as a Measure of Institutional Development', *Economic Development and Cultural Change* 52 (2004).

26 How far can we trust expert opinions on corruption? An experiment based on surveys in francophone Africa

Mireille Razafindrakoto and François Roubaud[1]

Traditionally we have relied on expert opinions for our understanding of the incidence of corruption – and more widely of bad governance. An alternative approach, based on public opinion polling – tracking both the perceptions and the experiences of the public – is emerging, albeit not so frequently employed because of the substantial financial and human resources needed for a representative sample to be surveyed and statistics to be updated on a regular basis.

Although initially heavily criticised, expert panels have acquired a degree of legitimacy, for several reasons. First, there is sufficient correlation between indicators based on different, independent expert panels. Second, a growing number of studies have established the link between these indicators and economic growth, investment, international trade and poverty. Nevertheless, there is no proven link between these expert perception indicators and the actual level of corruption, which is the subject of this chapter. Our survey compares expert opinion on the subject with the perceptions and actual experiences of corruption by the general population.

Some questions on corruption were included in the General Household Survey on Governance and Democracy conducted between 2001 and 2003 in eight African capitals.[2] In a parallel 'mirror survey', the same questions on corruption were asked to a panel of experts in the North and South (including researchers, development experts, decision-makers, senior civil servants and politicians).[3] The experts were asked two types of questions: (1) their personal opinion on a given issue; and (2) what they believed the public would reply.

Comparing the two surveys clearly shows that experts overestimate the extent to which the general population experiences corruption (see Table 26.1). On average, 13 per cent of the population experienced acts of corruption in the past year, whereas experts expected a figure of 54 per cent. Moreover, only 5 per cent of the public believed bribery to be an acceptable practice, while experts expected a figure of 32 per cent. Overall, experts hold a far more negative view of reality than the general public.

This overestimation of real levels of corruption would not be so bad if it were consistent, but it is not, as there are significant differences between the two surveys concerning the relative positions of the eight countries. The relatively good reputation of Burkina Faso in the eyes of experts – as seen in the low incidence of small-scale corruption in expert opinions and the lowest percentage of experts believing it to be

Table 26.1: Comparing the General Household Survey with the 'mirror survey'

Percentage	Benin	Burkina Faso	Ivory Coast	Madagascar	Mali	Niger	Senegal	Togo	Average
Incidence of corruption									
General population[a]	8.7	15.2	16.5	16.3	10.1	8.2	10.8	9.6	**13.1**
Expert panel (what they believe public would reply)	54.1	35.2	60.7	57.1	52.0	56.1	51.1	62.5	**54.0**
Beliefs that making a bribe is acceptable behaviour									
General population[a]	3.6	8.2	5.2	10.5	5.0	3.1	2.2	3.8	**5.2**
Expert panel (what they believe public would reply)	31.3	28.7	29.2	32.9	33.3	33.8	35.5	21.8	**31.5**
Corruption is a major problem									
General population[a]	94.2	87.4	91.0	96.9	88.4	91.6	87.9	82.8	**90.3**
Expert panel (what they believe public would reply)	84.8	67.4	72.3	76.4	67.2	62.3	69.4	84.0	**72.9**
Expert panel (personal opinion)	96.3	65.0	94.1	88.9	78.1	72.7	80.5	92.3	**85.3**

a. In Madagascar, results were drawn from the 2003 survey. In all other countries, small variations between the incidence of corruption and the published results in the *Global Corruption Report 2004* are due to differences in the harmonisation of weighting procedure.

Sources: General Household Survey (35,594 persons interviewed; 4,500 for each country on average); expert panel survey (246 persons surveyed; 30 experts for each country on average).

a major problem – is not sustained in the household survey. Conversely Togo, which according to the household survey suffers from far lower levels of everyday corruption than the regional average, is rated worst by the experts.

There is in fact no correlation between the rates of corruption measured by the household surveys and by the *mirror survey*: the correlation coefficient, although not significant, is actually negative (–0.19). On the other hand, the expert opinion results drawn from the *mirror survey* are similar to corruption indicators found in international databases. The correlation between the expert panel results and the 'control of corruption' indicator built by Kaufmann, Kraay and Zoido-Lobaton (KKZ) in 2002 is –0.52, which is a positive association, since the measure decreases the higher the corruption.[4]

In order to dig a little deeper, we tried to find out the factors that explain the expert opinions on corruption. The models indicated that expert opinions are not linked to the level of corruption observed in the country but to the country's reputation for good economic governance and strength of democracy in the eyes of the outside world (see Table 26.2). The five governance indicators from the KKZ database were tested as explanatory variables of the expert estimation of the incidence of corruption (columns 3 and 4). We found significant associations with the *voice and accountability* indicator (respectively –1.1 and –2.5), the *regulatory quality* indicator (respectively –8 and –17), the

Table 26.2: Explaining the expert opinions stated in the expert panel

Dependent variables:
Incidence of corruption (according to expert panel)[a]

Independent variables:	With incidence of corruption in household survey	With 'control of corruption' indicator from KKZ	With 5 governance indicators from KKZ	With both KKZ indicators and household survey incidence
Incidence of corruption (according to public opinion survey)	0.2			–6.1*
Indicators from the KKZ database				
Control of corruption		–0.5**	2.6**	9.7**
Voice & accountability			–1.1**	–2.5**
Regulatory quality			–8.0**	17.0**
Government effectiveness			3.9**	9.9**
Rule of law			–2.6*	–10.1**
Individual expert's characteristics				
Expert from African country	0.0	0.0	–0.1	–0.1
Claims good knowledge of the country	0.2	0.3	0.1	0.2
Claims good knowledge of the subject	–0.4**	–0.4**	–0.4**	–0.4**
Constant/intercept	0.6	0.1	–0.9*	–13.8*
R^2	0.03	0.05	0.09	0.11
R^2 adjusted	0.01	0.03	0.06	0.07
Number of observations	233	233	233	233

** Coefficient is statistically significant at 5 per cent. * Statistically significant at 10 per cent.

a. The indicators showing incidence of corruption have been normalised (to a tolerance of –2.5 to 2.5 as for other indicators) in order to work with comparable coefficients.

Sources: Expert panel, General Household Survey, and Kaufmann, Kraay and Zoido-Lobaton database, 2002.

rule of the law indicator (–2.6 and –10.1), with the expected negative signs. The experts' profile (their gender, nationality or institution) did not influence their perceptions of corruption. Reassuringly, however, good knowledge of the subject did reduce the extent to which experts overestimated corruption.

The results do not invalidate the relevance of expert opinions since they do capture common perceptions of corruption. Nevertheless, the study suggests that expert opinions should be combined with a new set of indicators based on objective measures and not only on perceptions if we are to understand the full complexity of corruption.

Notes

1. Mireille Razafindrakoto is an economist at DIAL (Développement et insertion internationale), France. Contact: razafindrakoto@dial.prd.fr. François Roubaud is also an economist at DIAL and director of the research unit CIPRE at the Institut de recherche pour le développement, France. Contact: roubaud@dial.prd.fr
2. See Mireille Razafindrakoto and François Roubaud in *Global Corruption Report 2004*.
3. The experts were chosen from among a panel of both international and national specialists in corruption/governance issues and/or among experts on at least one of the eight countries under review. For this purpose we mobilised DIAL's international network as well as its institutional partners from the North (GovNet of the OECD, the METAGORA project, the French Ministry of Foreign Affairs, Transparency International, and so on) and the South (social scientists, policy-makers in ministries of finance, high-ranking civil servants, and so on).
4. The 'Spearman coefficient' produces similar results: 0.02 between the expert panel data and the general population poll; –0.50 between the expert panel and data from KKZ.

27 Gender and corruption: in search of better evidence

Hung-En Sung[1]

Corruption levels are often found to be lower in countries where there are more women in government. But does female political participation *reduce* political corruption because women are more scrupulous than men? Should raising female representation in government be recommended as corruption control measures? These causal assumptions and policy prescriptions are being challenged by new hypotheses and data. A recent study argues, and demonstrates, that the link between gender and corruption is spurious and mainly determined by the presence of a liberal democracy that promotes both gender equality and good governance.[2]

In 2001 two research studies using different data and samples reported the same observations: female respondents expressed stronger rejection of government corruption than men in attitudinal surveys, and female political participation and political corruption were consistently negatively correlated in cross-national comparisons.[3] Since female citizens were less tolerant of corruption and their representation in government was associated with less corruption, researchers urged governments to increase the number of female officials in government. Yet several methodological weaknesses underlie this early research, and among them one limitation stands out as the most critical: the 'fairer sex' argument had not been tested against a competing theory.

More data on gender and corruption have since become available. Contrary to the gender–corruption link previously reported among ordinary citizens, surveys of state officials have revealed no significant differences in perceptions of and attitudes toward corruption between male and female government officials.[4] What occurred among ordinary civilians did not necessarily hold for state agents, and what existed across individuals did not automatically take place across organisations. Different explanations are needed at different levels of analysis. What then about national levels of corruption?

Alexis de Tocqueville observed in the nineteenth century that expanded opportunities for women went along with a social structure that was generally more participatory, and hence more receptive to democracy. Could it be possible that both female participation in government and lower levels of corruption are dependent on a liberal democratic polity? In a liberal democracy, ideological emphases on equality and egalitarianism facilitate women's entry into governmental positions, while institutional checks and balances minimise opportunities for systemic corruption. To test the linkages, indicators of the 'fair sex' hypothesis (for example, women in parliament, women in ministerial positions, and women in sub-ministerial positions) were pitted against measures of liberal democracy (for example, rule of law, press freedom and elections) in a study based on the 99 countries that were included in Transparency International's 1999 Corruption Perceptions Index.[5]

Overall, the gender–corruption link was refuted as a largely spurious relationship, and the liberal democracy hypothesis received strong support. Levels of women both in government and in liberal democracy were found to be significantly related to lower corruption when they were isolated from each other. But when forced into the same model, the effects of gender on corruption became statistically insignificant, whereas liberal democracy remained a very powerful predictor (see Table 27.1).

Table 27.1: Regression analysis relating women in cabinet (ministerial positions) with corruption

Variables	Step 1			Step 2		
	B	SE	Beta	B	SE	Beta
Control variables						
GNP	−.000	.000	−.737***	−.000	.000	−.514***
Poverty	.025	.012	.157*	.022	.011	.138*
Illiteracy	−.010	.011	−.072	−.009	.010	−.059
Female participation						
Women in cabinet	−.042	.020	−.147*	−.030	.019	−.105
Liberal democracy						
Rule of law	–	–	–	−.174	.071	−.184**
Freedom of press	–	–	–	−.025	.010	−.235**
Electoral democracy	–	–	–	.467	.404	.87
R^2		.770***			.818***	
Incremental R^2		–			.47***	

* $p < .05$; ** $p < .01$; *** $p < .001$ (one-tail test)

Freedom of the press showed the most powerful influence on corruption, followed by the rule of law indicator. Vibrant investigative journalism that scrutinises officials' behaviours enhances government transparency, while the subordination of the use of state power by officials to predefined laws and the punishment of public misconduct foster government accountability. Democratic elections exerted a positive effect on corruption but failed to attain the significance level, which suggests that competitive elections by themselves are not an automatic cure to political corruption and could be vulnerable to dishonest manipulations.

To increase female participation in public life is a noble and just end in itself, but would not be an effective means to engineer a clean government.

Notes

1. Hung-En Sung is a research associate at the National Center on Addiction and Substance Abuse at Columbia University, United States. Contact: hsung@casacolumbia.org

2. See H.-E. Sung, 'Fairer Sex or Fairer System? Gender and Corruption Revisited', *Social Forces* 82 (2003).
3. D. Dollar, S. Fisman and R. Gatti, 'Are Women Really the "Fairer" Sex? Corruption and Women in Government', *Journal of Economic Behavior & Organization* 46 (2001); A. Swamy, S. Knack, Y. Lee and O. Azfar, 'Gender and Corruption', *Journal of Development Economics* 64 (2001), summarised in the *Global Corruption Report 2003*.
4. For syntheses of this more recent research, see both R. Mukherjee and O. Gokcekus, and V. Vijayalakshmi, in the *Global Corruption Report 2004*.
5. Data on female participation in government were gathered from the United Nations and the Inter-Parliamentary Union. The rule of law measure was compiled by researchers at the Fraser Institute, who based their estimation on the judicial independence index published by the World Economic Forum. The press freedom rating was performed by Freedom House's analysts who examined and rated each country's laws and regulations governing media content, incidents and patterns of political control and intimidation of the press, and the presence of economic pressures that influence media content. The electoral democracy variable, also a Freedom House construct, simply identified countries that elected heads of state through universal and fair suffrage.

28 Corruption, pollution and economic development

Heinz Welsch[1]

Case studies have suggested that corruption is an important source of environmental degradation, especially in developing countries, but systematic quantitative assessments of the environmental effects of corruption are only just starting to be undertaken.

There are two distinct ways in which corruption may affect environmental quality, and the two effects differ. On the one hand, corruption may reduce the stringency of environmental regulation or the effectiveness with which environmental regulation is enforced, thus leading to higher pollution. On the other hand, corruption has been found to reduce prosperity. As prosperity (per capita income) is in turn an important determinant of cross-country differences in pollution levels, corruption may indirectly lead to a lower level of pollution. Putting the two effects together, the combined effect of corruption on the environment is uncertain.

Recent research has examined these links between corruption, pollution and economic development.[2] First, it investigated how corruption affects pollution at given levels of income, through corruption's effect on the formation and enforcement of environmental laws (direct effect). Second, it examined the influence of corruption on pollution via corruption's impact on income (indirect effect). It then added the two effects together.

The analysis used cross-sectional data for 106 countries, referring to the mid-1990s. The data set included indicators of ambient air pollution (sulphur dioxide, nitrogen oxides, total suspended particles) and water pollution (dissolved oxygen demand, phosphorus, suspended solids), jointly with data on per capita income and corruption. The latter were subjective indices on corruption, taken from the World Bank Institute.

The methodological approach to disentangling the indirect from the direct effect was to estimate an equation system comprising equations for the six types of pollution mentioned above, and an income equation. The pollution equations included per capita income and corruption as explanatory variables, whereas the explanatory variables for income (per capita) were physical and human capital, and corruption. The direct effect of corruption on pollution was given by the derivative of the six pollution equations with respect to corruption. The indirect effect was given by the derivative of the pollution equations with respect to income, times the derivative of an income equation with respect to corruption. Since, consistent with earlier literature, income affects pollution in a non-linear fashion, both the indirect effect and the total effect may be different at different income levels.[3] The effects of corruption on pollution are presented in Table 28.1.

Table 28.1: Effects on pollution of a one-SD increase in corruption[a]

		Direct effect	Indirect effect	Total effect
Sulphur dioxide	Maximum	0.343	0.071	0.414
	Minimum	0.343	–0.137	0.206
Nitrogen oxide	Maximum	0.358	–0.024	0.334
	Minimum	0.358	–0.063	0.295
Total suspended particles	Maximum	0.209	0.357	0.566
	Minimum	0.209	0.012	0.221
Dissolved oxygen demand	Maximum	0.364	0.185	0.549
	Minimum	0.364	0.005	0.369
Phosphorus	Maximum	0.308	0.316	0.624
	Minimum	0.308	–0.094	0.214
Suspended solids	Maximum	0.404	0.257	0.661
	Minimum	0.404	–0.041	0.363

a. Effects measured in standard deviations.

Putting the direct and indirect effects together, corruption was found overall to increase levels of pollution. This is in spite of the finding on the indirect effects of corruption, that there exist income ranges at which corruption actually reduces some types of pollution by means of lowering the level of income.

In low-income countries, however, both the direct and the indirect effects work in the same direction: both effects result in corruption increasing the level of pollution. A possible explanation is that by reducing the level of income in low-income countries, corruption reduces the resources that are necessary for pollution abatement. In fact, for some specific types of pollution (total suspended particles, dissolved oxygen demand, and suspended solids), the indirect effect strongly reinforces the direct effect. For these types of pollution, the combined harmful effect of corruption on pollution is stronger in poor countries than in both middle-income and rich countries.

As an example of the quantities involved, consider the cases of Burundi and Peru. Burundi is ranked as highly corrupt (1.2 standard deviations (SD) above average) whereas the corruption level of Peru is more moderate (0.2 SD above average). If the corruption level of Burundi were reduced to the level prevailing in Peru, this would be associated with an increase in Burundi's per capita income from less than one-fifth to somewhat more than one-half the level of Peru. Looking at the total effect on pollution, such a reduction in corruption would be associated with a substantial decline in total suspended particles (from 1.65 to 1.1 SD above average), dissolved oxygen demand (from 1.4 to 0.85 SD) and suspended solids (from 1.65 to 1.0 SD).

From a policy point of view, the most important message appears to be that, for most pollutants, the effect of corruption on pollution is particularly strong in low-income countries. Reducing corruption is therefore especially important for the less-developed world. By reducing corruption, low-income countries could considerably improve both their economic and their environmental conditions.

Notes

1. Heinz Welsch is professor of economics at the University of Oldenburg, Germany. Contact: heinz.welsch@uni-oldenburg.de
2. Heinz Welsch, 'Corruption, Growth, and the Environment: A Cross-Country Analysis', *Environment and Development Economics* 9 (2004).
3. The equation system was estimated using the method of 'seemingly unrelated regressions' (assuming that corruption is independent of income and pollution).

29 Firm responses to corruption in foreign markets

Klaus Uhlenbruck, Peter Rodriguez, Jonathan Doh and Lorraine Eden[1]

Government corruption has a widespread but insufficiently studied influence on international business and managerial decision-making. We employed a model that incorporates two fundamental features of corruption – its pervasiveness and arbitrariness – to evaluate how corruption affects international market entry decisions by telecommunications firms.

The experience of corruption can vary widely across countries that rank similarly on one-dimensional indices of corruption. In our two-dimensional measure of corruption, one dimension, 'pervasiveness', reflects the average firm's likelihood of confronting corrupt transactions in a given country. The second dimension, 'arbitrariness', captures the inherent degree of ambiguity surrounding corrupt transactions. Where arbitrariness is high, firms are unsure whether bribes are necessary, whom to pay, what to pay, or whether the payments will have an effect. Taken together, measures of pervasiveness and arbitrariness allow for a richer and more useful depiction of the variance in the nature of government corruption.[2] Research has shown that both the level and the arbitrariness of corruption independently reduce foreign direct investment (FDI).[3]

We derived measures of pervasiveness and arbitrariness from the 1998 World Business Environment Survey (WBES), which was based on the perceptions of company managers. The WBES provided information on both the extent and nature of expectations surrounding corrupt transactions and was drawn from a broad sample of 8,000 firms across 80 emerging countries. The questions used to extract 'pervasiveness' enquired about the frequency of bribery and breadth of government officials and agencies requesting or requiring bribe payments. The questions used to extract 'arbitrariness' enquired about the extent to which the terms of corrupt transactions were predictable and the objects of bribery were usually delivered as agreed once a bribe was paid. Figure 29.1 presents a representative distribution across the two dimensions showing the substantial variation in the nature of corruption.[4]

We combined these data with a database of 400 telecommunications projects started largely between 1996 and 1998 in 96 emerging countries, drawn from the World Bank's Private Participation in Infrastructure (PPI) database. There are several advantages to a focus on infrastructure investments, including the increased likelihood of identifying effects and the fact that the services created cannot subsequently be exported to other countries, thus providing a clear linkage to host country conditions. Because these projects involve more interaction with government agencies, however, there is a higher potential for encountering corruption than for firms in some other industries.

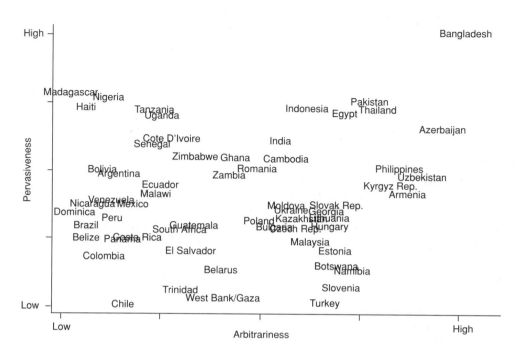

Figure 29.1: Two dimensions of corruption

Our two dependent variables indicate the characteristics of the entry modes of foreign firms. The first indicates whether firms engage in short-term turnkey projects that involve exporting technological know-how, or whether they commit to long-term FDI in the host country by maintaining ownership in the newly created facilities. The second indicates whether a multinational enterprise that pursues FDI engages in a wholly-owned subsidiary or a joint venture with a local partner. The data were analysed with logistic regression.

We found that some firms simply avoid investment in countries plagued by corruption. Other firms adapt their organisation forms and entry strategies in order to buffer their operations from the deleterious effects of corruption. After controlling for restrictions on FDI and country-specific legal and developmental characteristics, we observed that:

- as pervasiveness of corruption increases, entry modes are more likely to take the form of short-term turnkey projects rather than long-term FDI. Firms are more inclined to transfer ownership to local firms or the government, and less willing to remain in countries where pervasiveness is high. Additionally, where both pervasiveness and arbitrariness are high, virtually all projects are sold or transferred after completion

- as arbitrariness of corruption increases, entry modes are more likely to take the form of joint ventures and include local partners. We conclude that investors ally with local partners to navigate environments characterised by ambiguous or highly unpredictable systems of corruption. In addition, the interaction between arbitrariness and pervasiveness increases the likelihood of joint venture entry.

Firms' adaptations to the nature of corruption ultimately generate additional costs to companies, host governments and society. By creating conditions where firms feel forced to divest and exit once projects are completed, or take on local partners solely to protect against corruption, host governments limit the potential benefits of FDI even when they do not completely deter it. However, policy-makers should consider the versatility of multinational firms when formulating investment policies. Rather than forgoing economic opportunities because of highly corrupt environments, firms look for alternative modes to participate in such markets, for instance via short-term engagements such as turnkey projects. While international firms find ways to adapt to difficult conditions, local firms with strong ties to the domestic economy are more constrained and probably suffer the most from government corruption.

Notes

1. Klaus Uhlenbruck is in the Department of Management and Marketing at the University of Montana, United States (contact: klaus.uhlenbruck@business.umt.edu). Peter Rodriguez is at the Darden Graduate School of Business Administration at the University of Virginia, United States (contact: rodriguezp@darden.virginia.edu). Jonathan Doh is in the Department of Management at Villanova University, United States (contact: jonathan.doh@villanova.edu). Lorraine Eden is in the Department of Management at Texas A&M University, United States (contact: leden@tamu.edu).
2. For a detailed discussion of this view of the nature of corruption, see P. Rodriguez, K. Uhlenbruck and L. Eden, 'Government Corruption and Entry Strategies of Multinationals', *Academy of Management Review* (forthcoming, 2005). Also see A. Shleifer and R. Vishny, 'Corruption', *Quarterly Journal of Economics* 108 (1993).
3. See J. E. Campos, D. Lien and S. Pradhan, 'The Impact of Corruption on Investment: Predictability Matters', *World Development* 27 (1999); S.-J. Wei, Why is Corruption So Much More Taxing than Tax? Arbitrariness Kills, NBER Working Paper No. 6255 (1997).
4. The two dimensions are nearly orthogonal. Factor loadings were highly significant and reliabilities (Cronbach's alphas) were all above 0.70.

30 The effect of corruption on trade and FDI

Mohsin Habib and Leon Zurawicki[1]

The impact of corruption on international business has been investigated mainly in the context of foreign direct investment (FDI). Very few empirical studies have examined the adverse impact of corruption on international trade.[2] Also, while corruption (negatively) affects international business, the reverse does not necessarily have to be true.[3] Granted that there are many issues still left for exploration, in this study we focused on differences in the influence of corruption on alternative modes of international business.

Dealing with corruption, whether in the context of foreign trade or investment, raises uncertainties and costs for businesses. Corruption distorts the market and can make competition unfair. Ethically sound companies are not necessarily the most successful ones.

Previous studies have typically focused on corruption in the destination countries for investment and trade. This study considered the impact of corruption in the country of origin as well, using TI's Corruption Perceptions Index (CPI). While the CPI mainly characterises public officials, we infer that it also illustrates the proneness of the private sector to bribe – the supply side of corruption. Accordingly, since a company associated with a corrupt country can behave unethically, its business partners in other countries will have to spend more effort on monitoring and control, thereby diverting valuable resources from other productive areas of business. Assuming all other elements equal, we hypothesised that suppliers of goods, capital and technology from countries deemed less corrupt would tend to be favoured.

The sample of 89 countries for the study was chosen from the International Financial Statistics data published by the International Monetary Fund. Data on country-specific FDI inflows and outflows were collected from the UNCTAD Foreign Direct Investment Online. Data on imports and exports were taken from the International Financial Statistics.

Decisions regarding FDI and trade are usually based on a comprehensive analysis of the business environment. According to the international business literature, there are several determinants of FDI and trade. These factors were incorporated in the analytical model to extract the specific effects of corruption. The independent variables were lagged by one year to measure their effects on the dependent variables. In order to allow meaningful comparisons, identical models assuring the overall best fit were developed to assess the impact of corruption on inward and outward trade and FDI.

Table 30.1: Corruption negatively affects trade and foreign investment

	Log FDI inflow (to a country)	Log export (to a country)	Log import (from a country)	Log FDI outflow (from a country)
CPI coefficients[a]	0.17	0.11	0.11	0.39

a. The CPI coefficients were based on four OLS regressions of log FDI inflow, log export, log import, and log FDI outflow on corruption (CPI), log population, log GDP/capita, distance from USA, distance from France, distance from China, economic ties (part of a regional integration), political risk, and presence of TI chapter. All four models were statistically significant and the adjusted R-squares were 0.65, 0.91, 0.87, and 0.41, respectively. A positive CPI coefficient suggests a negative effect of corruption on the dependent variable, as a higher number on the CPI indicates a 'cleaner' country.

Our results showed negative effects of corruption for the inflow and outflow of FDI as well as imports and exports of a country (see Table 30.1). Further analysis revealed that:[4]

1. In more corrupt markets trade appears to be a safer option. In our opinion this is because FDI as an entry mode is viewed as requiring a greater level of commitment and effort than trade. This increased level of involvement translates into a higher level of risk (and cost) for the companies concerned. Also, corruption can make FDI more vulnerable due to the low redeployability of assets and resources. The proposed relationship between entry modes and a firm's corruption-induced risk and overall flexibility is shown in Figure 30.1.

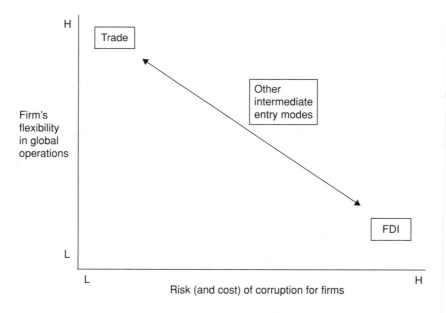

Figure 30.1: Entry modes, flexibility and risk of corruption

2. With respect to FDI, corruption in the country of origin matters more than corruption in the target country, as corroborated by comparing the coefficients for the inflow and outflow of FDI. It seems that choosing a credible business partner is more important when looking at the origin country of FDI than when looking at the destination country. This suggests that future research might benefit from shifting attention from the quantity of the respective flows to the reputation of individual (and overall) firms and the quality of projects.

In policy terms, the findings suggest that decision-makers should pay attention to corruption in the 'country of origin', which precedes the reputation of individual (usually lesser-known) small and medium-sized companies. From a managerial standpoint, other things being equal, a company from a less corrupt country will have an advantage, whether in trade or FDI.

Notes

1. Mohsin Habib is assistant professor in the department of management at the University of Massachusetts, United States (contact: mohsin.habib@umb.edu). Leon Zurawicki is professor in the department of marketing at the University of Massachusetts, United States (contact: leon.zurawicki@umb.edu).
2. J. Lambsdorff, 'An Empirical Investigation of Bribery in International Trade', *European Journal of Development Research* 11 (1998).
3. S. Knack and O. Azfar, 'Trade Intensity, Country Size and Corruption', *Economics of Governance* 4 (2003).
4. General Linear Model multivariate analysis was used to test, for example, whether the slope of FDI inflow (to a country) against corruption (CPI) is significantly different than the slope of exports (to a country) against corruption (CPI).

31 Firms, bureaucrats and organised crime: an empirical examination of illicit interactions

Larry Chavis[1]

The focus of this research was on how the social networks of a firm's owner can affect the bribe payments required of that firm. The aim was to identify networks that empower managers in their negotiations over bribe payments. The research used a 1997 survey of more than 900 firms in Poland, Romania and Slovakia. The survey was carried out in medium-sized cities in each country and was designed to be representative of small to medium-sized firms. The emphasis of the survey was also on entrepreneurship, so more than 90 per cent of the firms in the survey were less than 10 years old. The survey produced data relating to a number of areas such as start-up conditions, supplier and customer characteristics, contract disputes and bribe payments.[2]

The data on bribe payments was obtained by asking firm owners and managers two-part questions relating to bribes to government officials and bribes to organised crime. With regards to government payments, they were asked whether or not the typical firm in their sector would be likely to make 'indirect or direct payments to government officials to obtain permissions, licences and regulations'. A similar question was asked with regard to 'protection payments'. If the managers answered that there were such payments, they were also asked the amount the typical firm in their sector made in such payments. This research assumes that the managers answered these questions with their own experiences in mind.[3] Thus the answers to these questions were taken to indicate the amounts paid in bribes to government officials and organised crime by the firm being surveyed.

A summary of the bribe variables is given in Table 31.1. The mean bribe payment was found to be similar for payments to government officials and to organised crime, although many more firms admitted making payments to government officials. In both cases a substantial proportion of the managers did not report the amount of the bribe payments. For both types of bribes the amount of the payments could be substantial, with more than half the firms that report payments paying more than 2 per cent of their revenues in bribes.

Table 31.2 summarises some of the characteristics of firms that do and do not pay bribes. For example, 28.3 per cent of those firms that do not pay bribes are run by former state-owned enterprise (SOE) managers, while this is true of only 16.6 per cent of those firms that do pay bribes. Similarly the table shows that fewer trade association members pay bribes. On the other hand, firms that are start-ups and thus have fewer connections to the state seem to pay bribes more often. These relationships hold for both payments to government officials and protection payments.

Table 31.1: Summary of bribe variables

	Unofficial government payments	Protection payments
Percentage paying bribes	28	13
Percentage reporting bribe amount	16	9
Mean payment	US $1,379	US $1,428
Note: Standard deviation	*US $2,182*	*US $1,857*
Total payments as percentage of revenues:		
Median	2.0	2.4
Mean	6.4	7.2
Note: Standard deviation	*11*	*11*

Table 31.2: Characteristics of firms that pay/do not pay bribes

	Trade association member	Spin-off	Start-ups	Previously SOE manager
Unofficial government payments (%)				
Firms that pay	30.3[a]	16.1	77.6 [a]	16.6[a]
Firms that do not pay	37.1[a]	20.1	72.4 [a]	28.3[a]
Protection payments (%)				
Firms that pay	26.1[a]	14.3	77.3	16.8[a]
Firms that do not pay	36.5[a]	19.6	3.2	26.1[a]

a. Means are different at 95 per cent level of statistical significance.

To explore the relationship between social networks and bribe payments further, the research regressed the amount of bribe payments on social network variables and other characteristics of the firm.[4] The results of the regressions suggest that social networks are strongly correlated with both the amount of bribe paid and the probability of paying a bribe. What is surprising is that this research suggests the impact of social networks can be much larger than the impact of other, more 'routine' characteristics of the firm like employee size or profits. For a small firm with US $13,000 in yearly profits, it is estimated that having an owner who was a former manager in a state-owned enterprise lowers their yearly government bribe payments by approximately US $3,300. Doubling the same firm's profits to US $26,000 would increase the bribe payment by less than US $20. Thus it may be the case that bribe-takers are more in tune with a firm's social connections than with their profits.[5] We also found that the pattern that emerges for the payment of bribes to government officials is much clearer than for payments to organised crime, and that government officials and organised crime do not seem to coordinate in setting the amounts of bribes to be extracted.

Two of the findings offer hope for policy-makers. One is that trade association membership is associated with a lower likelihood of paying bribes. The other is that firms that have recent positive experiences with the courts make lower bribe payments. Both of these results could be interpreted as the power of 'old boy' networks, whose members enjoy the favour of both the courts and bribe-takers. A more optimistic interpretation is that both trade associations and the courts can empower owners in their interactions with bribe-takers. Thus strengthening courts and trade associations could help lower levels of corruption in these countries. This is a very preliminary conjecture, but one that is worthy of further research to help better understand the mechanisms at work in bribery situations.

Notes

1. Larry Chavis is at the graduate school of business at Stanford University, United States. Contact: chavis_larry@gsb.stanford.edu
2. The survey instrument and resulting data can be found at www2-irps.ucsd.edu/faculty/cwoodruff/data.htm. The data are summarised in the online appendices of S. Johnson, J. McMillan and C. Woodruff, 'Property Rights and Finance', *American Economic Review* 92 (2002).
3. This key assumption is explored further in the working paper version of this research. The assumption is necessary because asking firms directly about their own bribe payments would result in very low response rates. If the assumption does not hold and managers do answer with the 'typical firm' in mind then the results of this research indicate that former managers of state-owned enterprises view bribery as less prevalent than other managers.
4. Since many managers did not report the amount of the bribe payment, there is a serious missing data problem facing regressions using bribe amount as the dependent variable. This issue is dealt with at length in the working paper. The results are found to be robust to this missing data, though the magnitude of the impact of the social network may be slightly overstated in some specifications. However, in all cases, the social network variables remain far more important than variables such as profits or employee size.
5. Profits have played an important role in the theory of bribery because they represent the money that is potentially available for bribe-takers. Thus one normally expects profits to be a key determinant of the amount of a bribe.

Index

Compiled by Sue Carlton

export credit agencies (ECAs) 3, 55–64
    anti-corruption reforms 4, 58–63, 66
    recommended actions for 68

Fiji 242
Finland 140, 259
football 110, 146, 151–2
    2006 World Cup 151
foreign direct investment (FDI) 302, 303,
    304, 305–7
forestry *see* environment
freedom of information *see* access to
    information
Fujimori, Alberto 190, 191

Gagliano, Alfonso 127
gender 230, 296–8
Georgia 95, 147–50, 240
Germany 51–4, 150–3
Global Corruption Barometer 124, 232,
    239–41
Goldenberg Commission 171–2
governance 77–8, 135, 229–30
    Mexican survey (NSCGG) 229, 248–51
    survey of 255–7
governments
    recommended actions for 69–70
        construction 69–70
        public contracting 4–6
GRECO 155
    see also Council of Europe
Greece 154–6, 240
Guatemala 283

Halliburton 85
Haughey, Charles 162–3
health sector 140, 167–8, 182, 213
Honduras 283
Human Rights Watch 149
Hun Sen 121
Hussein, Saddam 84

immunity 108, 196
India 10, 24, 156–9
Indonesia 19–20, 94, 159–62, 240
informal economy 148, 222–4
infrastructure projects
    backed by ECAs or MDBs 55–64
    complexity 37–8, 49
    corruption 2, 12–19, 37–9, 75, 140
        and environmental issues 19–23
        impact on capital investment 13–16, 18

impact on running services 13–14,
    16–17
overcoming 22–3, 49–50, 63
culture of secrecy 38–9
scale of international finance 56–7
see also construction sector
Integrity Pact (IP) 1, 22, 43–4, 66, 67–8
Inter-American Convention against
    Corruption (IACAC) 188–9
International Country Risk Guide (ICRG)
    corruption index 16, 289–90
International Crime Victimization Surveys
    (ICVS) 232, 285, 289
International Federation of Consulting
    Engineers (FIDIC) 4, 40, 41, 67
international financial institutions 3, 4,
    31–2, 35, 50
    aggravating corruption 57–8
    recommended actions for 68
    see also export credit agencies;
        International Monetary Fund;
        multilateral development banks; World
        Bank
International Monetary Fund (IMF) 84, 123,
    148, 268, 305
Interpol 285, 286
Iraq
    managing oil revenues 84–5, 87
    Oil-for-Food (OFF) programme 84
    post-conflict reconstruction 1, 3, 71,
        82–9
Ireland 94, 162–5
Italy
    earthquakes 23, 26–7
    infrastructure investment 14–15, 18

Japan 94, 165–8
Jatigede dam 19–20
Jordan 275
judiciaries 132, 145, 171, 177, 190, 197–8,
    209–10, 213
    failure to prosecute corruption cases 108,
        124
    Latin America 282–4
    reform of 104–5, 140
    selection of judges 94, 119
    special corruption courts 207–8
    stemming political corruption 157–8

Kabila, Joseph 137
Kenya 94, 169–72, 240
    Bribery Index 229, 245–7

Khodorkovsky, Mikhail 200
Kibaki, Mwai 246
Kieffer, Fernando 106, 108
Kirchner, Néstor 97, 99
Korea 240
Kosovo 73
Kozeny, Viktor 101
Kukoc, Yerko 107
Kwaśniewski, Aleksander 194

Lagos, Ricardo 280
Latin America
    budget transparency 230, 278–81
    corruption victimisation 229, 282–4
    education system 229, 282–3
    electricity utility companies 16–17, 18
    public opinion 282–4
Latvia 95, 172–6
Le Kha Phieu 218
Lebanon 86, 275
Lesotho Highlands Water Project (LHWP) 1,
    31–6, 56, 115
Lipsic, Daniel 207
Lithuania 240
lobbying 95, 194–5

mafia
    India 11
    Italy 26–7
Marcos, Ferdinand 20
Martin, Paul 126, 127
Mečiar, Vladimir 207
media 80–1, 87, 105, 154–5, 194, 210, 219
    news coverage and bribery 258–61
medical corruption see health sector;
    pharmaceutical industry
Menem, Carlos 98, 99
Mesa, Carlos 107
Mexico 43–4, 240, 248–51, 278, 280
    governance survey of 229, 248–51
Micronesia 243
Millennium Development Goals 63, 180
Miller, Leszek 194
Moi, Daniel arap 170, 171, 172
Moldova 240
money-laundering 70, 94, 159–60, 173, 176,
    218, 221–2, 223
Morocco 275
Moscoso, Mireya 187, 188
Mozambique 73, 74
Mugabe, Robert 223

multilateral development banks (MDBs) 1,
    3, 55–64
    anti-corruption reforms 58–61
    scale of finance for infrastructure projects
        56–7
    see also international financial institutions

Nalo, Alfred Maseng 215
Natapei, Edward 216
National Integrity Systems (NIS) 114, 224,
    242–4
New Zealand 242, 259
Nicaragua 176–9, 278, 280
Nigeria 14, 240
Nong Duc Manh 218
Norway 179–83

OECD 268
    Action Statement 61, 62
    Anti-Bribery Convention 62, 70, 94
    Best Practices paper 62
    Expert Group on Bribery 113
    1997 Revised Recommendations 62
    Working Party on Export Credits and
        Credit Guarantees (ECG) 61–2
Olympic Games
    Beijing 2008 132
    Greece 2004 155
organised crime 11, 26–7, 111, 112, 113–14,
    133–4
Organization of American States (OAS)
    188–9

Pacific island states 229, 242–4
Pakistan 259
Palau 243
Palestinian Authority 95, 183–6
Panama 186–9
Papua New Guinea (PNG) 242
Paris Club 84
party and campaign financing 74, 78, 98–9,
    109, 125, 173–4, 190, 194, 203–4
Pastrana, Andrés 134
Peru 95, 189–93, 278, 280, 300
Phan Van Khai 219, 220
pharmaceutical industry 139, 182, 213
Philippines 2, 20, 240
plea bargaining 97–8
Poland 193–6, 308
police corruption 128, 155–6, 164, 166–7,
    229, 246
    special police 207–8